# CAGNEY

# CAGNEY

*John McCabe*

*Carroll & Graf Publishers, Inc.*
*New York*

First Carroll & Graf edition 1999

Caroll & Graf Publishers, Inc.
19 West 21st Street
New York, NY 10010-6805

Library of Congress Cataloging-in-Publication Data is available
ISBN: 0-7867-0580-9

Manufactured in the United States of America

For
Linny, Deirdre, and Sean, with many loving
memories of The Senator, Lovie the Princess,
and The Klunk Kid

But I have seen a Proteus that can take
What shape he please, and in an instant make
Himself to anything: be that or this
By voluntary metamorphosis.

Preface to *Jealous Lovers,*
by Thomas Randolph, 1632,
in praise of his actor
friend Thomas Riley

In the very nature of acting . . . there is an
essential gaiety. If it isn't light-hearted, it
becomes absurd. You can achieve every shade
of seriousness by means of ease, and none of
them without it.

Bertolt Brecht,
*Der Messingkauf*
(The Purchase of Brass), 1955

# Contents

*Acknowledgments*   XI

*Introduction*   XIII

1. CARRIE   3

2. THE REARGUARD TOUGH   14

3. HARD KNOCKS, HARD KNUCKLES   23

4. FARMING DEFERRED   31

5. WILLIE   40

6. VAUDEVILLE VARIETY   49

7. BROADWAY   58

8. WARNER BROTHERS   72

9. JACK "THE SHVONTZ"   89

10. THE MIX AS BEFORE   102

11. MORE TROUBLES IN OUR NATIVE LAN'   118

12. EASIER TROUBLE   131

13. OUT OF THE FACTORY   148

14. THE FACTORY GENTRIFIED   159

15. IN FUNCTION   175

16. A DANDY YANKEE DOODLE   199

17. THE WAR   217

18. THE LONE CAGNEYS   227

19. BACK TO THE FACTORY   249

20. OPEN-FIELD RUNNING   268

21. *ANNUS MIRABILIS* 280

22. INDIAN SUMMER 295

23. NOT THE ENDING 309

24. MEMORIES 324

25. *CAGNEY BY CAGNEY* 337

26. MARGE 345

27. ON ACTING 351

28. NEXT TO CLOSING 359

29. LAST BOW 372

*Appendixes:*

*Stage Appearances* 389

*Cagney on Radio* 393

*Feature Films* 397

*Short Films* 421

*Cagney on Television* 423

*Select Bibliography* 425

*Index* 431

# Acknowledgments

My prime obligation is to James Cagney—his informal reminiscences are the heart of this work—but I am also deeply indebted to Frances Willard "Willie" Cagney for insights into her husband's character and life that gave me deeper understanding of his extraordinary personality. For much of my basic understanding of him I owe more than I can ever satisfactorily acknowledge to my old friends Pat O'Brien and Frank McHugh. Over the years of our comradeship at The Lambs Club, they told me Cagney stories that amply confirmed in interesting detail what I had heard and was yet to learn of his tough sweetness, deep kindness, and exemplary gifts of friendship. Pat said, "He was the best man I ever met in the course of my long life—and I've met many and many a man." Frank echoed this.

Marge Zimmermann gave me vivid details of Cagney's last days. She also gave me access to all his personal papers, the most interesting of which was his "composition" book, as he called it—a much-used quarto in which he structured his verse and penned other thoughts.

Special thanks to Selden West, authorized biographer of Spencer Tracy, for urging me to write this book, and to Robert Gottlieb of Alfred A. Knopf, Inc., who gave me the commission to do so, with needed attendant encouragements and incisive editing. Thanks, too, to Ken Schneider, Iris Weinstein, and Abby Weintraub of Knopf. I have a very special obligation to two of the publishing world's bright stars, Ken McCormick and Sam Vaughan, who during their Doubleday years showed their faith in me by asking that I ghostwrite *Cagney by Cagney*, a vital step toward my present work.

Karen Lee Hodgson was a much-valued research assistant, as was Veronica Cullen. I am especially grateful to Ned Comstock, director of the Cinema/TV section of Doheny Library, University of Southern California, and to Stuart Ng, for easeful access to the Warner Brothers Collection there. Thanks also to Sam Gill and his efficient staff at the Library of Motion

Picture Arts and Sciences. And as always through the years I am grateful to Charles Silver and his associate Ron Magliozzi of the Film Study Center of The Museum of Modern Art for their kind help. I am also grateful to Mary Corliss and Terry Geesken of MOMA's Film Still Archive, Bob Cosenia of the Kobal Collection, and Christel Schmidt of the George Eastman House.

For their Cagney memories I am indebted to: Richard Erdman, Harry Flynn, Milos Forman, Shirley Jones, Harris Laskawy, Perry Lafferty, Jimmy Lydon, Virginia Mayo, Don Murray, Brigid O'Brien, Floyd Patterson, Joseph Sargent, James Sherwood, Burt Solomon, Peter Turgeon, Ben Welden, and Roland "Rolie" Winters. I am grateful to Professor Jack Morrison, husband of Jeanne Cagney, for giving me a penetrating look into Cagney family mores. Ray Wemmlenger, librarian of The Players, showed me correspondence between various Players officers and Cagney through the years. Peter Bogdanovich supplied me with a merry account of his wonderful luncheon with Cagney. Special thanks also to the following: Peter Ballante, Steve Cardali, Victoria Cullen, Arnold Karolewski, and John Mainelli for access to their precious Cagney press books purchased at the Doyle Galleries auction, and to Joanne Porino Mounet of Doyle for information about the Cagney memorabilia auction. Robert Costello, lawyer for the Cagney Estate, gave me vital information on the wills of both James and Frances Cagney.

Also thanks to: Peter Boutin, Richard W. Bann, Michael F. Blake for his comments on Lon Chaney and Cagney and for a rare copy of *You, John Jones,* Ron Borst, Paul D. Colford, John Carroll for essential irrelevancies, Frank Carroll, Bill Erwin, Robert Frye (producer of the fine "Biography" treatment of Cagney for A&E Channel), Thom Forbes, Richard Frank for some Hollywood history and a rare photograph of the Cagneys at play, Chuck Gustafson, Madeline Hamermesh, Howard Hays of University of California at Los Angeles for wonderful Cagney newsreel footage, Julio Hernandez-Delgado, Roger B. Hunting, Janis Johnson, Larry Kasha, Lincoln Kirstein for an encouraging phone call, Linny McCabe, Chuck McCann and Betty Fanning-McCann, Pete McGovern, Stephanie McGreevy, Mrs. Frank (Dorothy) McHugh, Lisa Mitchell, Robert Montgomery, old friend Max Morath for insightful comments on *White Heat,* Ruth Neveu, Ann Nunziato and Fr. Tom McSweeney of The Christophers for their help in tracking down *A Link in the Chain,* Donald O'Connor, Elizabeth Plowe, W. T. Rabe, Eulalie Regan, Steffi Sidney for information about her father, Sidney Skolsky; Philip Truex, Peter Turgeon for friendship and two Cagney stories, Whit Vernon, Arthur Weisenseel, M.D., old friends Rube and Liz Weiss for augmenting my Cagney-stimulated knowledge of Yiddish, and Jordan Young.

# Introduction

In 1973 Doubleday and Company asked me to ghostwrite the memoirs of James Cagney. I knew him only through correspondence and tales of him by mutual friends. He had kindly contributed to my book *George M. Cohan: The Man Who Owned Broadway* because of his affection for and admiration of the man he portrayed in so sprightly a manner in *Yankee Doodle Dandy*. The autobiography, *Cagney by Cagney,* duly appeared in 1976 to generally good reviews, the only critical reservation being that Cagney did not tell "all." It was a charge he accepted gladly. "Goddamned right I didn't tell all," he said. "*All* would be boring, boring, boring—and I'm in the business of entertainment. And if I choose to remember only the best parts of my life, I don't know why in hell I should apologize for that." He warmed to the subject. "Some of these film scholars mail me their requests to learn every jot and tittle about a guy's life and work. The average reader—and that's the one I'm interested in—doesn't need or want to know these things." When reminded that he, Cagney, wanted to know jot and tittle about virtually all he was interested in—poetry, conservation, animal husbandry, painting, farming, and more—he smiled and said, "Jot, yes; tittle, no."

These pages will inescapably contain a number of Cagney tittles offered to help us understand better this forthright man who was nothing if not thorough in all his life processes.

*Cagney by Cagney* is indeed all he wanted to tell, and he had to be strongly persuaded by Doubleday to tell even that. The reticence about his professional life flowed directly from his deeply quiet nature, his loner instincts, and his honest belief that there was not a lot to say about what was to him "just a job." It was a phrase he used—indeed, overused—constantly. But he meant it. More, most of his personal life was so joyous—he had married his dream girl at twenty-three, thereby earning long, uneventful decades of happiness—that he could not understand why anyone would really be interested in "just" that. He was a strikingly modest man and truly could not comprehend why people wanted to see the man behind the performances.

But he honored his Doubleday commitment by chatting long hours with me and was not reticent in response to many questions stretching out over two years of interviews. Indeed he was voluble. Twenty years later things were different. Richard Schickel in his excellent overview *James Cagney: A Celebration* (1985) says of his subject: "He was not, and never had been, an easy man to interview. Colleagues who had encountered him the last time he had made himself generally available to the press, when he was presented with the American Film Institute's Life Achievement Award in 1974, had told me that though Cagney was polite, pleasant and obviously trying to be as helpful as he could, his memory was strangely selective. And so it proved to be." Part of that selectivity was not so strange. He was then under contract to Doubleday to tell all he wanted to remember in the pending autobiography. In 1980 Schickel spent several days interviewing Cagney at Shepperton Studios, London, during the making of Milos Forman's *Ragtime*. Schickel found Cagney easily responsive to questions about his early life and the years of adolescence. But, writes Schickel:

> of the texture of his life during the three decades he worked in the movies he had almost nothing to say. That he has a perfect right to guard his personal life closely, no one can dispute. But there are purely professional matters one would like to know more about, something that would give a sense of the quality of his working days. What ambitions did he harbor that were frustrated? Which ones did he exert himself heavily to attain? What projects did he care about passionately? . . . If he didn't want to talk about the directors he came to dislike, could he at least try to recall those he came to trust and admire? . . . What gave him a sleepless night? Or sent him into rage or sulk or rebellion? More than that, since he had another two decades to contemplate in comfortable tranquillity those years of great and greatly loved stardom, it did not seem unreasonable to seek from him some summarizing sense of what the experience meant to him, looking back on it. . . . But no, that was not to be.

Schickel goes on to speculate why it was not meant to be, and his reasoning is accurate. He guesses several things that indeed were fact: that Cagney as an octogenarian suffering a recent stroke, and as one with a parental-imposed sense of modesty, fell inevitably into this reticence. Yet granted all this, Schickel argues, Cagney in most interviews was always content to let his screen persona be generically the tough guy, someone he could portray instinctively given his East Side New York street education. In such interviews he was saying, "You needn't try to pluck out the heart of my mystery because there is no mystery; that street guy, even as G-man, journalist, or pilot, is the man I always basically portray."

Schickel cannot accept this. It leaves him, as an observer, "dissatisfied, edgy. 'Hoodlum.' 'Tough guy.' Implicitly agreed-upon descriptive conventions." No, asserts Schickel, this is not all that Cagney was, despite his saying it was. "The fit of these phrases is too loose." Whereupon he aptly quotes Norman Mailer on Cagney: "Cagney was a gut fighter who was as tough as they come, and yet in nearly all the movies he made you always had the feeling, this is a very decent guy. That's one of the sweetest and most sentimental thoughts there is in all the world, that tough guys are very decent. That's what we all want. There's nothing more depressing than finding a guy as tough as nails and as mean as dirt."

The work in hand will try to verify Schickel's hypothesis that Cagney was more than the tough guy and will offer some answers to his questions about the Cagney career. Some will be tentative answers, some emphatic, but they will come at least mostly from Cagney. In large measure these pages are autobiographical biography. After our work on *Cagney by Cagney* was finished, Cagney and I talked together through the years, particularly in 1980, when we were contemplating a theatrical project based on his life. In those talks, what were background, almost throwaway addenda are now the chief underlay of this book, in which the phrases "Cagney said" or "Jim said" appear *in extenso*. In almost all these phrases the added words "to me" should be understood. These comments are the well-remembered essence of matters discussed during these years. I found James Cagney a rigorously honest man, gentle but firm in his policy of telling me the truth about his life. Like us all, he could be mistaken in his assessments, but they were conscientiously rendered, and his verifiable memories are incisively accurate.

I use the words "Cagney" and "Jim" somewhat interchangeably, but usually the former refers to the performer in action and the latter to the man. "Jim" was the name he always used in personal reference. He did not care for "Jimmy," a Warner Brothers locution.

In preparing *Cagney by Cagney*, we concentrated chiefly on his work. I told him I would seem to be asking questions in excess of need but they would not be irrelevant. For example (I told him), as we discussed a film, I needed to know not only what he thought of it substantively but also his feelings about fellow cast members, director, and script—not (I assured him) that these would become part of the text but that knowing these things would deepen my understanding of the film's creative atmosphere. Since he had total approval of what went into *Cagney by Cagney,* this was a promise easily given. I for my part promised I would never go beyond the limits of confidentiality he occasionally set. I keep that pledge.

He liked most people. The people he did not care for make up a meager list because in his working life Cagney enjoyed his fellow actors (two exceptions, an old actor in *Yankee Doodle Dandy* and a young one in a late film), easily tolerated almost all his directors (some of whom he thought dreadful but efficient hacks), and without exception treasured the technical crews. He saw no difference between him and them. Just people doing a job.

So I shall strive "to give a sense of the quality of his working days" as he thought of them, this mostly from his, the actor's, point of view. (It helps to some degree that I am one.) No earthshaking revelations spring from all this because, as Schickel says, Cagney made a tremendous show of saying it "was just a job," that cliché which he utterly and truly meant. His career, he was fond of saying in similar vein, really existed "to put groceries on the table." Also profoundly true, but it was a job he dearly loved, set in a milieu he found comfortable and with a goal he found heartwarming: the entertainment of millions.

Remembering my conversations with Cagney and rereading my notes have been a deeply moving experience because they confirm all I ever thought about him or learned about him: this was a great artist and an even greater man.

From all this I hope a psychological picture of the "very decent guy" Norman Mailer finds behind the Cagney screen hoodlum will emerge. This guy existed, and was greatly loved by his friends. "A sweet, sweet man," Pat O'Brien called him. "And a faraway fella."

# CAGNEY

# 1 · Carrie

Tiny Jim Cagney sat at the family dining table, transfixed.

His father, James Francis Cagney, his tousled blue-black hair in almost comic contrast with his magenta complexion, his brain half rotted with alcohol, sat facing his son, staring at him. Jim looked at his dad with fear and compassion. The man rocked slowly from side to side.

Then the older Cagney began a low keening, that Irish form of lamentation virtually ceremonial in form, a repetitive wail that begins in the bowels and rises into a near shriek. Whenever little Jim had heard this sad, savage cry before, his mother had always attended to her husband's needs, standing behind him and massaging his neck and forehead. This almost always helped, and the sound would diminish. The family called these episodes "Dad's fits."

This time little Jim was alone in the apartment, his mother having gone shopping. Quickly the boy pulled a chair beside his father, mounted it, and massaged his father's head.

"Christ, what a sound!" Cagney said years later. "It was a cry of agony, and I can still hear it. I used it once in a while in my pictures when I had to portray someone who had fallen into mental disrepair. That was Pa. Sixty shots of rye whiskey a day for years and years had really done their work. He was the most lovable guy who ever lived, but when one of his fits was on him, we learned to stay away and let Mom take over. She usually brought him around."

Jim's father, James Francis Cagney, was born in 1875 in New York City's Lower East Side in that congested and crime-soaked area known as Five Points. He talked little about his parents and ancestry except to say that the original family name was O'Caigne and that they had come from County Leitrim, Ireland. "There was something Pop evidently wanted to hide about his immediate ancestry," said Jim. "He didn't talk about his forebears, immediate or otherwise, if he didn't have to. He was strangely reticent on that subject. I know he didn't like my aunt, his sister, and once in a while a brother of his would show up, and of him we knew even less than Auntie. We all knew the O'Caigne family crest, which contained three sheaves of wheat, maybe an augury of my principal life's interest. Anyway, as the years went by, I never much bothered to find out about my ancestors. I suppose one should be interested, but as I didn't have children of my blood, I figured what the hell. I tend to live in the present anyway."

Cagney's mother, Carolyn Elizabeth Nelson, a woman of full figure with a head of vivid red hair, in contrast with her husband had a heritage of which she was very proud, a living heritage in the person of her lovably eccentric father, Henry Nelson, a river barge captain. Captain Henry (he was the only man aboard the tiny tug) insisted on being called Captain and stoutly maintained the title until he died. He boasted of his Norwegian blood and spoke vaguely of being well known in Norwegian maritime circles. He was married to a bright but self-effacing Irish-American woman. Carolyn loved her parents dearly, and when they came into hard times, she insisted they live with the Cagneys, this at a time when the Cagneys were overcrowded by their own family in a small flat.

Carolyn, or, as her husband always called her, Carrie, had to leave school at twelve to help her folks. She worked six hard years at the Eagle Pencil Company, an experience causing her to say in maturity, "I've had a very real affection for pens ever since."

She was barely eighteen when she married James Francis Cagney, then in his twenty-first year. Young Cagney was at times a telegraphist and bookkeeper. He liked both jobs but preferred the latter because he had an aptitude for mathematics. The definition of geniality, James found what he considered his inevitable occupation when a friend asked him to take over for an absent bartender. Cagney had found his milieu and his downfall. "A lot of people drink to get drunk," he told a friend. "I drink to celebrate, and I like to celebrate all day and into the night. If I can make it that far."

The only things eventually that James loved outside his family were rye whiskey and baseball. When he drank, he always sauced his shots with a gill of beer, and no matter how many he had during the day, he proved to be an excellent pitcher. He had a decisive fastball that earned him his nickname, Jimmy Steam. As the years rolled by, he saw less and less of the playing field and more and more of saloons.

In his first job as substitute bartender, James came across a specific hazard of his trade, a belligerent customer. The man's name was Oppenheimer, a hulking man with massive fists. He had been annoying other patrons of the Lower East Side bar where James worked, causing some people to walk out. Determined to stop this nonsense, James came out from behind the bar, pointed to the swinging doors, and said, "Out!" to the troublemaker. Oppenheimer looked at him incredulously and swung his right fist into James's face. James staggered to the door himself, opened it, sat down on the curb, and carefully spit out twenty-one teeth, counting them one by one as he did so. From then on, when trouble impended at the saloon, James resorted to free drinks to calm dissension.

It has been reported that James Cagney, Jr., was born in an apartment over his father's saloon at the corner of East Eighth Street and Avenue D, New York. This is not so. Cagney was born—on July 17, 1899—in a small apartment on the top floor of a conventional brownstone at 391 East Eighth. His father would acquire the saloon years later, and only then for a brief time. The Cagney birth certificate gives his father's occupation as telegraphist. In this apartment the Cagneys' oldest boys were born: Harry in 1898 and Jim a year later. The bartender job took the Cagneys early in 1901 uptown to Yorkville, where they found a small flat at 429 East Seventy-ninth Street near First Avenue. Here the third Cagney boy, Edward, was born in 1902, followed in 1904 by William, and in 1905 by Gracie, who lived only ten months, dying of pneumonia.

Carrie by disposition was sunny and valiant. She adored her profligate husband, whose daily departure for work was unchanging, dramatic, and deeply relished by his kids. They would go to the front door when he was ready to leave. He would kiss Carrie resoundingly, blow a kiss to each boy, doff a green tweed cap of which he was very proud, tip the cap in comic fashion to the entire family assembled, make the sign of the cross reverently, check his fly to see if it was buttoned, and walk quickly out of the door, frequently singing a current ballad.

Even at his most prodigal moments James Senior could do no wrong in his wife's eyes. Her mother once asked her why she put up with his extended drinking and his absences from home. "I couldn't stand it for a minute, Carrie. Not for a minute."

"Oh, yes, you could, Ma. When you see how much fun he gives the kids. And how much fun he brings *me*."

James Senior was rarely a falling-down drunk. "Only once that I can remember," said Jim. "He came home one night with a bun on, sat down at the piano, and started to play and sing. Then he fell right over, still singing, and didn't know he was not upright. Funniest thing you ever saw. Pop never poured the liquor down. It's what you almost could call a gentle kind of drinking. He'd usually drink just enough to keep him from being sober, but rarely enough to make him truly drunk. Just like Doolittle in *Pygmalion,* he'd drink just enough to make him 'cheerful and lovin' like.' He certainly gave all of us a lot of love—*and* entertainment."

Like most happy turn-of-the-century families, the Cagneys were a great source of diversion to themselves. Almost every evening they sang songs in chorus and solo, recited humorous poems, clog-danced, and told jokes heard on the street corner. Dad—they called him Pop—loved to sing, despite a tendency to off-key tonality, much like Bert Lahr's comic yammering. But Pop's greatest talent, the thing that most delighted his children, was the delivery of conundrums, atrociously contrived ones, in a high, stagy voice. A number of these were old favorites that the kids insisted on hearing night after night, during which the boys would shout out the answers in loud chorus.

Pop would advance to one end of the living room and face the family. "Say, listen: Why did the sausage roll?"

The kids would shout in unison, "We don't know."

"Because it saw the apple turnover." Jeering laughter from the kids, followed by applause.

"What's the best day for making pancakes?"

"We don't know."

"*Fri*day!" Happy groans and applause.

The kids particularly loved the ones where they supplied the gag lines. Pop: "Did you ask Mississippi if she would let Delaware Georgia's New Jersey, which she bought in New York?"

Kids together: "No! But Alaska!"

There was a particular favorite, given every night. Pop: "Does Chicago?"

Kids: "No, but Niagara Falls!"

Carrie was pleased to see that little Jim—he was never Jimmy—was fascinated by newspaper illustrations and would duplicate them endlessly on blank paper he found in the refuse bin of a nearby printer. At the age of five he began to sketch, a habit Cagney pursued all his life:

In the Sunday *Herald* I was fascinated as a kid with that great sketch artist Winsor McCay. He drew a comic strip that meant a lot to me, *Little Sammy Sneeze.* I liked Sammy because he was a little boy just about my size, and whom, I was told, I resembled. Sammy was just like every other boy his age, with one exception. He'd be in some public place, usually at some function or other, and he'd have to sneeze. His sneezes were cataclysmic, and they would sweep everything before him, right off the street. I loved Sammy because like me, he was small, but unlike me, he could let the whole world know who he was.

But little Jim, shy and sensitive, soon found a way to leave his impress on the neighborhood:

We were poor, but didn't know it, I guess, because everybody else around us was poor. Out on the street we soon discovered there was a power hierarchy, however, and that was kind of like being rich— when and *if* you were handy with your dukes, and could hold your own in a fight. I saw that right away, and I used to watch the tough kids, the leaders, the ones who knew how to fight. I didn't *admire* them because mostly they were bullies, but I did admire the way they handled themselves, facing guys way bigger than themselves. Later I could figure out just how they did it. It was in that simple word made out of two other simple words, "foot" and "work." Foot- work. Benny Leonard, Lou Buto, Packy McFarland—fighters I saw and admired, and all the epitome of grace. That is what got me into dancing. I learned how to dance from learning how to fight. It was feint, duck, quick dance around your opponent on your toes mostly, then shoot out the arm like a bullet.

One of the neighborhood tough guys, Moishe, indirectly stimulated Jim to fight—and dance. Moishe had a rhythm to his punches. He never flailed, as so many of the street scrappers did. He held up his fists in defensive arc and rushed in only when he saw an opening. He was adept at seeing the instant when his opponents dropped their guard, and when this occurred, he darted his fist in quickly to the target, then out again just as quickly, standing on tiptoe most of the time. As a seven-year-old Jim began to sense the benefits of standing on his toes either to reach up or to reach in. Dart- ing became second nature to him, and it was to become a key characteristic of his acting. The dance steps of his maturity grow directly from these habits.

As bonus, Jim and the other Cagney boys rejoiced in the greatest fight instructor in their neighborhood: Carrie. This very wise woman, painfully aware that two of her four sons, Harry and Edward, were timid, was deter- mined to give little Jim, the runt of the family, the advantage his small size would not allow. She taught him and the others, despite reluctance on the part of Harry and Edward, the fundamentals of boxing. As a girl she had gone to amateur prizefights with a male cousin keen on the game, and she quickly learned that sluggers always got the bad end of the stick, whereas boxers at least knew how to escape punishment. More, she saw that boxers, those skilled in use of their feet and quick arm thrust, always won.

Carrie got her boys together two afternoons a week and instructed them. She saw that Jim, who had learned the basics of fighting well from Moishe, was her prize pupil. She scheduled regular bouts between her boys in their living room. When they occasionally erupted into anger, she separated them and held the opponents firmly against her sides, a process she called "leaning on yuh." The boys learned to avoid this because the leaning was uncomfortable, Carrie being big of heft and strong of arm.

James Senior loved these sessions and acted as a one-man audience, cheering both fighters and booing whenever he saw unfair advantage taken. He roughhoused lovingly with all his boys and was fond of pretending anger by holding a lad by the neck with one hand, curling the other into a fist, snarling exaggeratedly, "If I thought you meant that—," grazing the chin with the fist. "Simple little thing," said Jim. "Yet so goddamned funny, the way he did it. You'd think—there we were, poor as church mice—you'd think there'd be gloom all over the place. We had our bad moments, sure, when Pop got his fits. But all I mainly remember about the Cagneys in those days was laughter. Songs and laughter."

Despite their mother's expert instruction, Eddie, five years younger than Jim, and Harry, the oldest boy, were gentle souls and soon grew to depend on their brother for protection from neighborhood gangs. Generally one had little to fear from tough guys if one learned to walk quickly from home to destination and back. But Jim, deeply partaking of his mother's indomitable nature, refused that kind of protection. He never sought conflict but never avoided it.

Fighting was simply the neighborhood occupation. Every kid on the block was identified by a nickname. Jim was distinguished in that he had three: Red, his hair color, and two pejoratives that always enraged him when he heard them, Runt and Short Shit. The latter particularly angered him, and the block bullies learned this soon and used it as their prime taunt.

There were two other neighborhood preoccupations, baseball and swimming. The latter was a chancy business, but it became habitual. When they lived on Seventy-ninth Street, Cagney said:

> We were only a short distance from the East River—which incidentally is not a river at all but a tidal estuary—and in good weather we went there to swim. It was, quite simply, a cesspool, and I suspect it's not much better today. I say cesspool because a large sewer close to our street poured its contents right into the river. And we

swam cheerfully right in the midst of all that sewage. Merry *turds* bobbing by. You just ignored them and kept your mouth shut. We must have been pretty tough because we survived those daily immersions. Except one kid. Phil Dooley. The foulness of the river got to him, and he died of typhoid. Where we used to dive in is now a little park with benches, close to the FDR Drive, built right over where we used to do our daily diving. That little park plus some huge apartment buildings are there today where we used to cavort about so happily.

If Harry and Eddie were Jim's gentle siblings, brother Bill, chipper, ever confident, had a far different cut to his jib. He was the businessman incarnate. Although capable of using his fists well, he tended to be too busy for fighting. Nor did he need Jim's protection from neighborhood bullies. From absolutely no one on either side of the family he inherited a fondness for and an ability to find a buck that remained his life's hallmark. How he did it, that he did it at all, was a wonder to his family. Bill very early on figured that the rags–bones–old clothes vendors who came around daily crying for people's discards were on to something. This he translated into his life motto: even the most mundane is sellable to the right person at the right time.

Once a cauliflower vendor stopped his wagon in the Cagney block and motioned Bill and a few children over to offer a proposition: take the vegetables into the various tenements, knock on every door, sell them for six cents apiece, and keep two of the pennies. Bill and two of the kids volunteered, but he was the only one to keep at the task. He went up and down six flights of stairs in as many buildings, carrying a large bag of heavy cauliflower almost his size. He weighed barely fifty pounds. Bill made forty-eight cents, which he gave to his mother, who was not too proud to take them.

Nor was Bill too proud to search through refuse cans and bins up and down the various saloons and shops on nearby First and Second avenues. He found a surprising number of items there that could be repaired or cleaned, then sold for a decent profit: bike wheels, vases, books, crockery, canes. Pawnbrokers in the neighborhood came to know him as the Clean-'Em-Up Kid, the boy who knew how to change dross into something vendible. Bill tended to skip school to ply his wares, but Carrie did not worry about him. She was obsessed with her children's getting an education, but she instinctively knew the difference between kids who needed school for education and those who did not. Bill was preeminently one of the latter.

Brother Jim was one of the former. Initially he was shy of school. He was not afraid of tough guys. School was another matter. It was the great unknown, and when Carrie brought him to the public school nearby, he cried all the way. But when he got to the classroom, his eyes widened at the sight of the teacher, a beautiful young lady who welcomed him with a hug and enchanted him with her scent. As he settled into class, he found excuses to walk up to her desk and smell that ineffable perfume. He longed to ask her what it was, but in school he was the opposite of Jim the street boy: reticent, mild, unobtrusive. Weeks later, after he and Teacher became friends, he asked her what "that pretty smell" was. "Heliotrope," she said, and to the end of his days that scent was Jim Cagney's favorite.

When Eddie's turn for schooling came, he relied on Jim to walk him there as safeguard, but Eddie found his greatest fear in the classroom itself. His teacher, a temperamental opposite of Jim's, was a ferocious disciplinarian. Eddie found this out his second day. A boy next to him leaned over to whisper, "Do you have an extra pencil?" Eddie whispered, "No, I don't," at which point the teacher turned around from writing on the board and rushed down to him. The man pulled Eddie's hair and slapped him brutally three or four times. Eddie wept all the way home, where he sobbed out all the details to Jim and Carrie.

Without a word Carrie walked to school and into the principal's office, where she asked for the teacher. Fortunately for him, he had seen her walk into the building, cue for him to walk out. At home he wrote two notes and sent them on. One was to Carrie saying he had misunderstood Eddie's actions in class; the other, to the principal, said that illness would prevent his teaching the next two days, time enough, he guessed correctly, to soften Carrie's anger. It was known in the neighborhood that Carrie not only owned a thick six-foot-long bullwhip but had actually used it on a night watchman who, after being hazed by neighborhood boys in his shack, had rushed out, collared innocent bystander Harry Cagney, and beaten him up. Carrie thrashed the man with thoroughness and ever after along that block was known as Kill-'Em Carrie.

Her blazing temper derived from her sailor father, Henry Nelson. Nelson talked little about his ancestry, except that he was a native of Drøbak, Norway. Years later Jim discovered from an unimpeachable source that there were no Nelsons in Drøbak, nor had any ever been born there. Jim then recalled that his grandfather's right hand bore a tattoo, "A. S." It was also learned that Drøbak was very full of residents named Samuelson. Cagney family conjecture was that Grandpop Nelson, with the temper of a dozen Furies, had likely committed some malfeasance in his native town forcing him to change his name when he left.

Grandpop Nelson and his wife lived on a coal barge—a modest but well-appointed one—that traversed the Hudson River and nearby waters.

Grandpop bore an amazing resemblance to Popeye in that he too had only one eye, the result of a landlubber job in a lye factory where some of the substance had squirted into his left eye. Moreover, he shared with Popeye fearsome forearms the size of hams. Jim remembered:

Strong, strong, and what a temper! Grandpop wasn't afraid to attack man nor beast nor both. I used to visit him and Grandma for weeks at times, and she was the best doughnut maker in the world, sweet, succulent things, to which I really trace my inordinate love of desserts. Grandpop was a real captain because he was extraordinarily skilled at maneuvering that unwieldy barge right up precisely to the places where they loaded or unloaded. He and Grandma said they loved having me aboard because I loved the water so, just as they did, and because I was always asking such interesting questions. I was perfectly used to Grandpop's temper—my mother had inherited it from him—and I saw plenty of evidence of that whenever some inequity descended on our family. The hen guarding her brood. But Grandpop's temper was triggered by the most unusual and sometimes the slightest things.

I remember, once when I was staying with them, Pop came over with a number of his saloon cronies who were dying to see what life aboard a barge was. They were feeling no pain as usual, and all was high hilarity as my dad showed them proudly all around the craft. He even took them, at Grandpop's invitation, into the cabin to see the wheel as well as the Nelson family album, which contained pictures of my mom as a girl and of Grandpop as a young blade wearing a fancy derby. One of the men made a friendly remark that Grandpop in the picture was "quite a swell." Maybe Grandpop misunderstood that perfectly innocuous remark and thought the man said "smell." Anyway his temper crackled and exploded.

"Get the hell out of here, you sonsabitches," he said, and he grabbed his handy shotgun, and all the men, Pop included, scattered like a cattle stampede and ran up to catch a safe streetcar.

Jim eventually found the barge a lonely place and never stayed more than two or three weeks. He missed his mother, who very much missed him. She did not like Jim staying on the barge all that time, but she saw how the boy's presence pleased her parents—her stubborn, excitable father and her placid Irish mother, who, like Carrie, had to put up with a problem spouse. In later years Carrie delighted her children with descriptions of her dad's hair-trigger temper. Jim remembered one of her descriptions:

He was such a darling, my pa, and so funny, although he never realized he was. Those powerful arms and that heavy squint—that's
where the Popeye resemblance came in. And where it ended. My
dad never won a fight, as far as I know, and he had plenty of them.
Not that that would stop him. Once a waiter didn't thank him adequately, Pa thought, for a good tip, so Pa invited him out on the
sidewalk and the waiter tried to persuade him to forget it, but Pa
went ahead and fought. The waiter knocked Pa down about eight
times, and the eighth time Pa was crawling along the sidewalk,
barely able to lift his head, wiping off the blood, shouting, "Had
enough, you bastard?" The waiter collapsed—from laughter. He
shook his head and walked away. Pa shouted after him, "Well, I sure
trimmed that bastard's lamp, didn't I?"

Jim had a great love of the old man and, when Grandpop was unable to
do barge work, welcomed him into the body of the family. The Cagneys in
1908, already desperately poor, invited the old couple to live with them in
their new, larger, and definitely barer flat at 166 East Ninety-sixth Street.
Even with the added space, it was a tight squeeze. Harry and Ed slept in one
bed of the master bedroom, Jim and his grandma on a floor mattress, Carrie and little Bill in the second bedroom. In the third bedroom Grandpop
slept with James Senior, whose nocturnal habits were highly variable.
Despite the space problem, the old couple felt royally welcomed, but
Grandpop felt restless, uprooted. He hated living on land, and his loneliness
was sharpened when Grandma Nelson died suddenly a few months after
their move. He found some solace in his special affection for Jim but could
not easily express it. His combative personality made any show of love, even
among family members, almost impossible. Young Jim sensed this. He realized how much joy the old man had given him and how strong their bond
was, so waking one morning, he got out of bed, walked over to the old man,
and looked at him. Grandpop was standing alone, looking down, "looking so
goddamned forlorn," Jim said. "So, impulsively, I ran to him, threw my arms
around him and kissed him. He was stunned, and so happy, returning the
kiss. I don't think anyone but my mom and his wife had kissed him in many,
many years. He started to cry, but he was happy, I could tell. He was not the
kind of man who cried. That taught me one thing. Never hide your emotions. Never fail to kiss someone when you know it's right."

Grandpop spent his remaining years with the Cagneys, dying at seventy-
two in 1912. He manfully learned to develop a certain amount of patience
with his errant son-in-law, but it was hard going. James Senior had cultivated

another vice in addition to drink: gambling. He would take off for a variety of racetracks with saloon pals and remain away from home two or three days at a time. Then he would show up, haggard and hungover, early in the morning and fall into bed. On these occasions he would always choose his favorite, his dependable, son for an unvarying chore. "Jim, lad," he'd call out. "Down to Murphy's."

With that, he would hand Jim a quarter. "So, down I'd go to Murphy's saloon," said Jim. "I'd get a quart of that red-eye and bring it back to him to ease the pain. Imagine. Little me, all of nine years old, buying a quart of whiskey in a saloon. In the *morning*. Only the real drunks were in there then, and the sight of me used to delight them, all pals of Pop's. They'd cheer my appearance.

"Life couldn't have gotten much grimmer, we thought, my brothers and I. But it did. A lot grimmer. Yet at the same time, somehow, it seemed to improve because we got closer. Later, out of all this, we Cagney boys devised our own motto: 'We love everybody but don't give a damn about anybody.' We lived those words."

# 2 · The Rearguard Tough

In the late spring of 1907 Carrie took her boys to the then rural area of Flatbush in Brooklyn for a visit with her aunt and uncle Jane and Nick Nicholson.

There is no way to overstress the importance of this fortnight in James Cagney's life. It had the most profound influences on him as a thinker, as a citizen, as a man. He said:

The visit to Flatbush was revelation. This was glory. The obvious thing about those two weeks at Aunt Jane's farm—because small though it was, it was a farm, a real farm, in Brooklyn—was that it somehow or other wakened in me some gene dating back maybe a hundred years to my Irish ancestors on the literal ould sod. I know those genes as inclinations, or whatever you call them, weren't at all in my mom or my dad. They were city folk to their bones. But for me, it was different. I awoke my first morning in Flatbush, and I was in Wonderland. I not only wanted to come back there whenever I could, I wanted to live there, and glory be, I did. [*Jim opened wide his arms to indicate his presence on the 711-acre farm, his last home, in Dutchess County, New York.*] Those few days in Flatbush let me see for the first time live things growing. Well, I *had* seen geraniums in a pot on our fire escape, but at the farm I saw fruit actually growing on trees, instead of in a basket on a First Avenue fruitstand. All kinds of great fruit: fresh red apples, fat purple plums, gorgeous red, red cherries that I could reach up and taste. They had a sweetness I'd never tasted before. I was home.

Another part of the glory at Jane's was the mode of getting there. James Senior, having won a few extra dollars on the ponies, hired a hostler friend to drive them in a splendid rented barouche over the bridge to Brooklyn. The barouche, a four-wheeled carriage with two double seats vis-à-vis, had two ample seats up front for the driver and a footman. Little Jim quickly took the latter and stayed there all the way to Flatbush. He loved the majestic aplomb of the large white horse pulling them, and when they reached Aunt Jane's, Jim got down and memorized the beautiful features of the horse. He had seen many horses in Yorkville streets, but they were all faithful old plugs or dray animals. This was a horse bred not only for strength but for beauty. In his old age he quickly drew a sketch of that horse for a group of friends and said, "That's Mollie. I haven't forgotten her in over seventy years." Mollie became an emblem for him not only of the beauty but of the majesty of nature.

In Flatbush he and his brothers roamed over Aunt Jane's spread, climbing trees, picking flowers for Carrie and their aunt, the latter reminding them that picked flowers quickly died and that these—especially the abundance of morning glories intersticing the white picket fence around the house—were prettier where they were. Thenceforth morning glories became young Jim's favorite flower, and he planted them around every house he ever owned.

The return of the Cagneys to Yorkville after the two weeks of respite from the tensions of street life affected his brothers and mother not at all. For Jim the return was near calamitous, except that he knew, and deeply knew, that in some fashion the farm was an ideograph of his life to come. It was not only what he loved but what he needed.

One of the things he returned to in Yorkville was the fact of neighborhood fighting and the rule of territorial gangs. You joined the gang on your block as a matter of course. There was no choice in the matter except for the rare instance of a boy who was chronically ill. Such a one was given immediate respect, together with a nickname that defined his illness. If tubercular, you were Lungsy or Coughy. A cripple became Gimpy. The name conferred automatic deference. All other boys involuntarily entered the gang; it was simply where you belonged. Jim, as chief battler and skilled boxer, was in a sense entitled to leadership of the gang. But two things prevented this: his loner instinct and his size. "Lucky for me, I *was* small," said Jim. "I wanted no part of running the gang, and size was a prerequisite of power. The biggest kid usually took control simply because he was the biggest. He could have been stupid, as some of the leaders were. But because he was big, he was boss. That was fine with me. I never ran with the gang anyway. But they would call me in to beat up a bully. The gang knew I was available. I became a kind of combination troubleshooter-backup man and never really part of the gang."

He was available for tough jobs, for "cleaning some kid's clock" when a troublemaker in the neighborhood upset the decorum of life along the street. This usually came in the person of a bully who, as usual in such circumstances, pushed the younger, weaker kids into acquiescence on all matters but mostly into supplying him with money or candy. "Send for Red" became a standard cry when this happened, and Jim obliged, unafraid to take on boys far his physical superior.

The classic battle in this mode came when a conflict between Jim and a new bully on the block was consummated. Willie Carney, a gangling youth a head taller and twenty pounds heavier than Jim, moved into the area and quickly took dominion over the younger and weaker boys, among whom was gentle Eddie Cagney. Ed was playing with a golf ball he had found in the street and was bouncing it back and forth on the stoop of the Cagneys' apartment building when Willie darted in and claimed the ball as his own.

Ed protested, tried to reclaim the ball, and was knocked roughly to the sidewalk for his pains, badly bruising his cheek. He rose and was knocked to the ground again by Willie, who, in the sheer exuberance of brutal power, knocked Ed down a third time. Crying, Ed ran upstairs to the Cagney apartment and told Jim what happened. Jim's anger was formidable. Not only was Ed contused and bleeding, but a bad cough that had afflicted him for weeks grew worse. Jim ran down to the street to find Willie had gone. Pals directed him to the street next over, where Willie usually hung out, but Willie wasn't there. Jim went home after telling his friends to scout out Willie's whereabouts. An hour later he was told Willie was "up on First Avenue," fighting yet another local boy. Jim ran there to find another almost defenseless victim of Willie's far-reaching fists. Jim told the boy he would take over but, following street etiquette, said Willie could rest for a minute before resuming battle. Unused to this nicety, Willie said, "Any time, Short Shit," and raised his fists. Jim, stung by the insult, rushed in and crashed a right to Willie's jaw, knocking him down. The boys surrounding the action cheered.

"The surprise in that guy's face was a sight to see," said Jim. "He never expected that from someone my size, and he waded in, giving me blow for blow, but he wasn't used to fighting a boxer, and here I was, dancing in and out, stinging him when he least expected it. He had the advantage of me in reach and height, so I got stung too, but my style of fighting made us equals. By this time, after fifteen minutes of battle, a large crowd had gathered, mostly urging *me* on, I'm proud to say. Then the cops came and broke it up."

Before Willie left, Jim told him to meet him next day, same time, different place. Willie was there at the appointed time, and it all began again, with the same crowd of spectators. It was broken up again by the same cop, who was reluctant to do so. He had heard of Willie's meanness. Yet again a new time and place were set, and when Jim came home that night to wipe off the blood—Willie's blood—he found in himself a grudging respect for his opponent's grit. Willie had been hit with several rights that Jim knew would have finished off the average fighter, but Willie had wiped off the blood and kept on coming. The session next day was the mix as before, but the crowd had grown larger.

During the thick of the mayhem a little Jewish lady cried out dolefully, "These boys are *killing* each other. Where are their mothers? Why don't their mothers come and stop all this bloodshed?" Jim smiled and went on fighting. He knew where his mother was: she was right there, in the front rank of spectators, urging her boy on. "Watch his left, Jim," she said over and over. In one spirited mix-up Jim broke four bones in his left fist, and a draw was agreed on until the hand was healed. Carrie took him to the hospital for splints, telling him she admired the way both boys had handled themselves. "Only, Jim," she said, "next time pick on someone your own size."

Carrie boasted to James Senior of Jim's valor, and he was pleased. He had made vague references at times to the "fighting O'Caignes," but when Carrie pressed him for information about his obscure family roots he grew even vaguer. "I forget what my mother told me about our family," James told Carrie, and likely this was true. About this time he began to have memory problems caused by his drinking.

As for Willie Carney, Jim was to hear from him again. In the early thirties, after Jim had attained fame, he got a letter from Willie: "Dear Jim, Maybe you remember when you and I hooked it up on Seventy-second Street and First Avenue. I'm over here at the Pilgrim State Hospital. My nerves are all shot, but I'm going to get out next spring. My sister is going to take care of me. If you have any old clothes you're not using, I'd appreciate your sending them on. Cigarettes, anything." Jim made up a package at once and sent it to Pilgrim State Hospital on Long Island and never heard from Willie again.

"Foolishly," said Jim, "I included cash in that package. I have no doubt that the kindly guards glommed on to it and the rest of the stuff, and that's why I never heard from Willie again. He and I never finished our battle because by the time my hand healed, Willie turned pro fighter and so left street fighting. He went on to holdups and murder, killing a fellow prisoner at Dannemora Prison, and then to Pilgrim. I still keep that letter from him over forty years ago, and I don't know why."

As Jim was growing into young manhood, his dad made periodic attempts to sober up. There was talk among friends of his taking the then popular Keeley Cure. But this cost money and required a long stay in a Keeley home, so James's life hardened into unremitting alcoholism. Jim always remembered his dad with love:

> Dad was a gentle, charming man. The way booze caught him was this. He had been a conventional drinker in his early days. It was the episode with Oppenheimer and the loss of those twenty-one teeth that did it. I never thought of it much, but as the years went on, I realized just how much pain the loss of those teeth brought Pop. We had no money for such luxuries as false teeth, so for years and years Pop went without them. Mom offered as an excuse for Pop's drinking the agony he went through with his teeth—and the ones remaining weren't good either—but we kids thought that she was just giving an easy excuse for him. But when I think about it, it makes perfect sense. He drank sip by sip all day to kill that pain, until he got hooked on the rye, and there was no way in those days for him to get unhooked.

The Cagney boys loved their dad but idolized their mother. Knowing that her husband was lost to alcohol, she took over the raising of her family, determined to educate them out of their poverty despite the pressures of her own bad health. She had severe gallbladder trouble most of her life and went to hospital free wards for brief but frequent stays. Carrie was to lose two children to early illnesses, Gracie, at ten months of pneumonia, and Robert, at thirteen months of meningitis in 1916. Carrie's bad health was the motivating factor in two of her boys, Harry and Ed, becoming doctors. Like Jim, she had an insatiable sweet tooth, a very bad habit because of her persistent diabetes. She grew heavy early, at thirty weighing 175 pounds and two years later reaching 240. The extra weight also brought on hypertension, which she battled the rest of her life.

She was conscientious in her churchly duties, seeing that the boys went to Mass every Sunday, and she was delighted that Jim volunteered early to be an altar boy. But it was education that she made the family theme for the future. She watched the bulletin board at the family's parish church, St. Francis de Sales, on East Ninety-sixth Street. She attended any free lectures in the neighborhood, always dragging one of her reluctant children along.

"But do you think the boys are old enough to follow those talks, Carrie?" her husband asked her.

"If they don't follow all of it, I'll fill in all of the blanks," she said.

On one such occasion she took little Jim along, and if he went unwillingly, he came back exulted in the grip of another life-changing experience.

The speaker was not difficult to understand, even for a nine-year-old. He explained, with accompanying color slides, that the United States was in serious trouble, first from misuse and overuse of farmland and next from destruction of the great American forests. "The answer to this devastation is simple," said the speaker. "For every tree you cut down, plant another." On the way home Carrie told Jim solemnly but warmly that the countryside should be held sacrosanct and not be marred. Fresh from his experience at Aunt Jane's, Jim took the lesson deeply to heart. She said that because this was the greatest country in the world, taking care of the countryside was especially important. "She told me all the storybook things," said Jim, "that just as ours was the greatest country in the world, where men were the freest, so this great country offered the greatest chances in the world to be successful. But, she said, we had to take care of this greatest of countries." Jim asked her how this could be done, and she told him: never take away a plant or tree without adding another in its place or nearby, keep all waters clean with controlled sewage ("I thought of the East River," said Jim), and put out with water every outside fire you start.

"That conservation lecture," he said, "was directly responsible for my becoming obsessed on conservation, and I'm proud to have that obsession. It led me to things like doing the voice of Big Brother for the Department of Agriculture's film *Ballad of Smokey the Bear* in 1966. Mom would have been proud."

From his earliest years young Jim developed a loner's reputation. This was partly due to his horror of things he saw on the streets. One day he heard the pounding of feet behind him and, turning, saw a boy collapsing, a butcher knife sticking in his back. Another time Jim saw a boy sobbing, walking down the street, holding his slashed testicle. These events were not isolated, and in old age he was still trying to forget them. "No wonder I tended to keep off the streets," he said. "But I think, really, this loner business was imbedded in me somehow from infancy." When he was barely able to crawl, he found his space under his mother's sewing machine. Here he sat on the treadle and rocked back and forth contentedly, singing a little song he had composed himself: "Doodle, doodle, doodle, / Doodle, doodle, *do!*" This he repeated endlessly, sitting and swinging. "I never had any trouble being alone," he said. "I was certainly no social bug like my brothers, although I must say I enjoyed their company, and my folks'!"

Jim never had a best friend as a boy, but the acquaintance he knew best, and most remembered, was Peter Hessling, known to all as Bootah. His family was even more poverty-stricken than the Cagneys were, forcing Bootah to do daring things for pennies. Once he took a dare that he would hang from the top coping of a five-story building for a nickel. Desperate for the money and needing to prove his virility, at ten years of age, Bootah accomplished the dare and won acclaim as a man.

"Bootah's need for a nickel," said Jim. "I've often thought of that. If only he'd gotten a few from his folks so that he didn't have to steal them. He was a totally nice human being, and he turned to crime just to get lots of nickels. It's so easy to understand why kids follow that path."

Bootah and Jim were ferocious baseball players. They started on a variety of scrub teams, then made a great advance in baseball circles by being asked to play for a local team called the John Jays. Bootah was in the outfield. A close friend of Jim's, George Mitchell, pitched, and Jim was the catcher. The John Jays were good players and did well in neighborhood school leagues, so well that Yorkville's best amateur baseball team, the Original Nut Club—so called because of the studied and at times unstudied eccentricity of key players—asked for a contest.

The John Jays were dubious at the prospect because the Nut Club boys were known to have engaged in hot after-game tussles with teams they had beaten. The natural tensions of rivalry during the game could easily explode into fistfights, and the John Jays agreed to the game uneasily. Said Jim:

> We skunked the Nut Club. Beat them fair and square, seven to four, and George Mitchell and I got the most hits. We were afraid that our victory could lead to a fight based on resentment. But not at all. The Nut Club guys were as nice as could be, and George and I soon found out why. They wanted us to join their team, which we were very happy to do. George and I were actually given free uniforms, not their custom, and I was very proud. I was sorry that Bootah wasn't asked. The fact is he was just an average ballplayer. But he was pretty skilled at petty and major crime. Because all the odds were against him. Because he didn't stay in school.

Jim, together with his brothers, went on to high school and a variety of odd jobs. His principal recreation became the Yorkville Nut Club, a team whose proficiency brought them into the best semiprofessional leagues in New York City, several of the Nut Club boys going into the major leagues.

Five years after joining the Nut Club, Jim went with the team on a special invitation to Sing Sing's player association, the Mutual Welfare League, among whom were several ex-pro ballplayers. This alone made the trip to Ossining a challenge. There was only one rule set down for the Nut Club: they were not to talk to the convicts before, during, or after the game. This was to prevent the passing on of contraband—shivs, dope, or possibly dangerous information.

Arriving at the field, Jim began to warm up the Nut Club pitcher, and as he was socking them in, he heard a familiar voice behind him. "Red, hey, Red." Jim tried to observe the letter of the law by ignoring the voice.

"Jesus, Jim, you getting stuck up? It's me, Bootah."

Jim swung around and shook his old pal's hand. "What are you in for, Bootah?"

"Five to ten. I shot a cop. In the arm only."

Before the game ended, Jim encountered three more pals from "the neighborhood." There was "Dirty Neck" Jack Lafferty, as well as Patsy Donovan and "Guts" Finster. It was the last time Jim saw Bootah, but he heard of him again a decade later.

I will always remember July 21, 1927. That was the night Jack Dempsey fought Jack Sharkey, it was the night I was playing in a Broadway show, and it was the night Bootah died in the electric chair at Sing Sing. I wept when I heard about him, and of all things to remember about him, I recalled something dreadfully ironic. I was sitting on our front stoop one day, reading a western pulp magazine. Bootah came by, sat next to me, and said, seriously, "Red, people who read those stories end up as killers." I inquired about why he went to the chair. Just like a bad movie script, he had decided to go straight but first he'd pull one more job for walking-away money. He went up to First and 102nd Street and held up a well-heeled Italian man. Just as Bootah was doing this, a policeman, who had been excused early from his beat to go home and take care of his sick wife and four kids, turned the corner on First and, in so doing, made a clicking sound with his shoe. Bootah turned quickly and, possessed of a hair trigger, killed the cop.

I thought to myself, That's what you get when you ride with the pack. Thanks to my mother, and not going with the gang.

That became a Cagney theme: never ride with the pack. Always be willing to be the rear support or fight individually as block champion, but never go with the gang.

"You could always count on Jim," said a classmate, Danny Walker. "He was there when you needed him: to fight your battle when you couldn't or to help the guys on the block. But he always did it his way, alone. The rear guard. The guy who finished things."

# 3 · Hard Knocks, Hard Knuckles

Jim spent the weeks following his three-day battle with Willie Carney nursing his broken fist and alternately stimulating and discouraging thoughts of becoming a prizefighter. His friends, as expected, praised his boxing abilities to the skies, and he sensibly discounted their praise as flattery. But a friend of his father's, Leo Linahan, who was not only a fight fan but one connected professionally with the game, told the boy he had the stuff to be a pro. "I know you're still a kid," he said to Jim, "but you really have the stuff to make it. But listen. You've got to give your heart and soul to it. No compromises, and if you do well, there's tons of money in it. Tons."

That phrase stuck in Jim's mind: tons of money. For him in a household where poverty was status quo the word "money" was magic. "Money" was the Cagneys' unalterable theme; their lives centered on the need and search for it.

Then came a marvelous season of prosperity. With money in part from James's gambling and in part from one of his few consistently employed friends, Harry Falk, in 1911 James opened his own saloon under the sponsorship of Eards Brewery. It was a modest but tidy establishment at Eighty-first Street and First Avenue. Jim went there every noon, sent by Carrie, with a hot lunch for his dad.

Carrie was both elated and horrified at the idea of her husband's owning, or at least managing, his own saloon. She was hopeful that the newly painted green and white sign in front of the place, JAMES F. CAGNEY, PROP., would give him dignifying pride in the responsibilities of management. At the same time, she knew his reputation as a bartender. He had been called Two-to-One Cagney, the barman who gave away two drinks for every one sold. But the early signs were mainly good; James seemed to be sprucer than ever and was drinking less. Moreover, aware that the pressures of city life were wearing down his beloved Carrie, he made plans to move the family to a nice house in Ridgewood, a New York neighborhood between Queens and Brooklyn. It was then almost a country town, and the Cagney house proved to be only one of nine on a quarter mile block. There were vacant lots in which to play. James visited on weekends, and all seemed uniquely harmonious. Jim was excited:

We were all agog, moving to Ridgewood. We were actually living in a house instead of a railroad flat with their noises above and below and screams down the hall and police wagons clanging down the block. We were only renting in Ridgewood, but for the first time we felt that the Cagneys were on the way up. I hadn't been doing too well at P.S. 158, what with my being Lord High Fisticuffer of my old neighborhood, but at Ridgewood that all changed. My marks went up. Markedly, you might say. I've had two great teachers in my life, Miss Hendrickson of Ridgewood, who told me once that I had a good brain, and Miss Eugenie Archer of Yorkville, who saw something in me that no one but my mom and Miss Hendrickson ever did: a desire to know all I could about the world. In Ridgewood, to top that off, there were thick trees to climb and, wonder of wonders, grass. Just like Flatbush. Do you know what it's like to live without grass, to live with concrete and asphalt all your young life? A part of life is missing. And here was fresh green grass in our front yard, where my brothers and I could play instead of on that unforgiving concrete full of doggy doo. But it was too good to last. We should have known.

The spanking new Cagney saloon in Yorkville foundered on the improvidence of its manager, who drank and gave away most of its profits. After his place's demise things were still not altogether bad for James because he soon found another good job bartending in a tavern at Seventy-sixth Street and First Avenue, and the family was able to stay on in Ridgewood until 1913, when James's fluctuating fortunes brought them back to Yorkville for good. Mercifully Carrie found a pleasant apartment for them on East Seventy-eighth Street.

Jim reentered P.S. 158 and found pleasure in a new interest, languages. All his young life he had been hearing foreign languages. Yorkville was the prime German colony in Manhattan, and on its streets young Jim heard not only German but Hungarian, Chinese, Spanish, Italian, Russian, Polish, and above all Yiddish, which he grew to love. He said:

Maybe I love Yiddish so much because it's the one great language of vituperation—fightin' words—something which we sure appreciated in that slugfest world of Yorkville. We Irish and German and other ethnic kids always envied our Jewish buddies their ability to insult. We only had the feeble clichés like "Fuck you, asshole," while the Jewish lads had such riches as what has now become my favorite way of telling someone to get lost: "*Gai kocken aufn yahm,*" which in essence means to "leave your presence and get the hell out of here." But literally it has the delicious meaning "Go shit in the sea." We Irish are pretty imaginative, but as far as I know, we've never come up with anything as earthly rich as that. And how about "*Zol vahksen tzibbelis fun pipek!,*" meaning "Onions should grow from your navel!" Another one I love: in English the word "jerk" is pretty good to describe a stupid lout. But a Yiddish word for them describes who they are very efficiently. In Yiddish a jerk is a *schlub*. Beat that. Beat the *sound* of that!

Jim graduated from P.S. 158 in 1913 and prepared to enter Stuyvesant High School later that year. Ever conscious of the need for family income and thinking that the world of words—stimulated in him by Miss Archer—was worth entering, he applied for a copyboy's job at the *New York Sun,* part-time. He was hired, but his contact with words was minimal. He took copy to and from the copy desk, but his job seemed more like an errand boy's.

The money he brought home was, as usual, consigned to Kitty, a large battered iron pot kept near the kitchen stove. Jim painted on the pot the smiling face of a cat. "In a very real sense," Jim said, "that pot kept us going. Kitty was our source, our symbol of need and replacement. We boys worked hard to make sure Kitty always had something in it." The only competition the Cagney boys ever had was in seeing which of them could add more than the next person. It was a common sound in the apartment. Part of the family would be in the living room, the kitchen screen door would open, slam shut, and a tinkle of coin thrown in the pot would sound. "No one," said Jim, "would advertise he'd put anything in it. We took pride in that. Just the noise of coins dropping into Kitty was the pleasantest sound in the world to us. Mom was the only person who looked into Kitty or of course took anything out."

When Kitty was notably empty, the Cagneys always had one dependable resource to fall back on: Carrie's jewelry. From her mother she had inherited four items: two diamond earrings, a lovely gold watch, and a solid gold chain. When Kitty got empty, usually in March of every year, Carrie would delegate Jim to take the jewelry down to Parliament Loan nearby and put it in hock. The items usually fetched between three and four hundred dollars, and this sum would keep the family in food and rent for the next two months. Then one of the boys would get a full-time job and Jim would take the ticket back to Parliament for redemption.

By 1914 the three boys had found something of a bonanza in part-time work at the New York Public Library. For ninety hours of work a month one earned $12.50. This seems scanty, but it was not inconsiderable pay in those days, and Harry, Jim, and Ed were happy to get it. Young Bill was only ten, but he made money in his own fashion, and rather good money too, finding discarded toys or crockery to refurbish and sell at a profit.

Part-time work for the Cagneys was always an adjunct of schoolwork. Carrie made sure of that. Study came first, and if she saw that one of the boys was getting poor marks in school because of a heavy work schedule, it either went or was whittled down. Jim would make another trip to Parliament Loan.

All the promise of James as his own boss had dissipated after his own saloon was taken from him by the brewery. He had no difficulty getting work because his personality was effervescent and his blarney unbridled. "Talk about charming the birds out of the trees," one of Jim's childhood friends remembered, "Cagney's old man could make them come down and do a chorus of 'The Rakes of Mallow.'" As the years went by and the alcohol began to afflict his brain, his "fits" grew more frequent, and seizures of delirium tremens became frequent. Carrie always knew when they were imminent, and she could hustle James off to their bedroom in order to hold him tightly in her arms. She was both bigger and stronger than her husband, and this was a control she had no trouble maintaining. The difficulty was that James would vanish from home, sometimes for days, and return genuinely vexed at his inability to remember where he had been.

His recuperative powers were astonishing. If he stayed off the whiskey for three or four days, as he did occasionally, he seemed totally renewed and ready for reform. In his early forties his hair was blue-black without a speck of gray, his face unlined, and his remaining teeth unmarred by alcohol. He was five feet seven and a half inches tall—the exact height Jim would attain. James loved to sing and, according to his son, "had the worst Irish tenor in history, a powerful and almost completely off-key voice with a vibrato that I swear shook the furniture." James was completely unaware of this, indeed rather fancied his singing abilities, and at times his children had to stifle their laughter when he overflowed his measure melodically. His favorite song was "I Don't Want to Play in Your Yard," which Jim interpolated in *The Oklahoma Kid* years later as a gentle tribute to his old man.

When James's fits began to occur daily, Carrie knew something serious had to be done on his behalf. She made inquiry at the New York Department of Health and was told that she had to apply to the Municipal Court as his nearest of kin for a court order forcing him into involuntary commitment to a hospital jail and "cold turkey" withdrawal period. Carrie got the order and was told to give it to her husband, who, out of deference to his family, had taken a room near their flat for several weeks of attempted recuperation. But she couldn't give the document to him and asked Jim if he would do it, knowing he was psychologically the strongest of her children. He hated the idea, but he would do anything for his mother.

He said:

Pop then had a room over on Eightieth Street, and I walked over there with this damned writ in my hand. I felt as if it were something unclean, but I knew I had to give it to him, for Mom's sake, for *all* our sakes. So I got up to the room and knocked on the door, and when I told him who it was, he told me to meet him downstairs in the hallway. I did that, and when he came down, all shaky and unkempt, I felt a surge of anger at him for making us do this thing to him: putting him away. But then, just as quickly, I realized he couldn't help what he had done, or he'd never have done it. I handed the thing to him and mumbled, "Sorry, Pop." His eyes filled with tears, and he said, "It's all right, Jamesie-O," his pet name for me, and I burst out crying, and we fell in each other's arms, sobbing. He looked a mess, but next morning in court he had scrubbed himself up, suit cleaned and pressed, nice shirt and tie, hair slicked back. He looked as if he had never had a drink in his life.

James was given sixty days at Blackwell Island and went through the withdrawal period in prescribed order. Carrie met him at release, and they held hands as they walked down East Seventy-eighth Street to their new ground-floor apartment at 420. He looked trim and healthy, and the family hoped and hoped. Less than a week later Carrie knew he was drinking again, but he was much more circumspect in that he remained mostly in the flat. Carrie's sorrow was poignant because she knew he had been devastatingly hurt by being sent to a common prison by the wife he adored. "But will someone please tell me," Carrie said to Jim, "in God's good name what else I could have done?"

In the early days of his adolescence Jim had a brief summer of respite from worries of any kind. His mother had encouraged the boys to take advantage of the opportunities offered by the nearby East Side Settlement House. One such chance was a six-week stay at the house's summer camp at Stepney, Connecticut. This was yet another taste of Aunt Jane's farm and the blessings of Ridgewood. Jim swam, marveled at cows in a nearby field, and for the first time wore boxing gloves. Carrie, helping out at the camp, herself supervised matches between the twenty-three children there, and Jim put on the gloves.

He found the gloves encumbrances; worse, he found them dangerous. He observed something that was going to be another lifelong obsession, one that became for him a crusade—a crusade not taken seriously by anyone but him. He saw that, paradoxically, even though barefisted fighting was bloodier than gloved fighting, it was safer. One could rattle an opponent's brains with the bulky gloves; one could not, with bare knuckles. As an adult Cagney seriously inveighed against the official rules that specified not only gloves but their weight. In 1976 he said, "John L. Sullivan was at his greatest and most skillful as a bare-knuckle champion, but he was forced to acquiesce to the Marquess of Queensberry rules that made fighters wear gloves, and thereafter he went downhill—and boxing injuries rose in number and potency." When Jim turned to oil painting in late middle age, his chef d'oeuvre, always on display in his study, was the disturbing portrait of a brain-addled fighter, arm raised in the ring. Jim called it *THE VICTOR—Chronic Progressive Fibrotic Encephalopathy—(Punch Drunk)*.

After the Stepney summer camp Jim returned to Yorkville's streets with the germ of an idea. The newspapers were full of stories detailing the great financial rewards of boxing. He knew he was uniquely qualified with his rearguard boxing background, and he sensed that although he found the gloves bulky and intrusive, he could likely use them to feed Kitty. He began practice boxing sessions open to the public at a nearby athletic field. In watching the boxing instructors, he saw over and over again that the best of them won more by having dexterous feet than powerful arms. Practical footwork became his emphasis.

By this time keeping Kitty fed was a serious business. James was virtually unemployable although he found occasional work as substitute bartender. Brothers Harry and Ed continued with Jim at the Public Library. By 1915 Jim—now called a book custodian, one who picked up discarded books on tables for return to the shelves—was given a raise to $17.50 a month. This was a night job. Days were spent at Stuyvesant High, and the nights he was not working at the library he found another job as "discipline orderly" (bouncer) at the East Side Settlement House. To top off this already punishing work schedule, he spent many Sundays, his day off, as a ticket clerk on the Hudson River Day Line. When not working at the settlement house, he gave himself the luxury of watching professional boxers in training sessions at a Yorkville gym, courtesy of a doorkeeper buddy. "I can do *that,*" Jim said to himself about almost every fighter he saw.

In the midst of this grueling exertion and punishing work schedule, Jim Cagney had his first profound intellectual experience:

> In one of my literature classes at Stuyvesant a teacher, in talking about great novels and the recent awarding of the Nobel Prize for Literature to Romain Rolland for his *Jean-Christophe,* said, "When you all get older, you'll be able to read that novel, and I hope you do." That rather pissed me off. When I got *older*? What was wrong with right now? I knew that *Jean-Christophe* was the most asked-for book in the library, with a long waiting list for the few available copies. Since I had "pull," I got to the top of that waiting list, and I settled down for a good, long read—sixteen hundred pages, and it was worth every page. I didn't get it all, of course. At sixteen I wasn't equipped to carry that load. But this story of a young guy, a musical genius, who leaves his home in the Rhineland for Paris and becomes famous, with the ideal of his art always foremost in his heart, moved me very much. Jean-Christophe needed beauty in his life, and for the first time in mine, I realized that I did too.

During this time Carrie, diabetically stout at thirty-eight, took on the big, certainly chancy burden of another pregnancy. Her family was well grown by 1916. Harry was eighteen, Jim seventeen, Ed fourteen, and spunkily independent Bill twelve. Carrie seemed to have no need for another child, but she had two good reasons. She and James had recaptured something of their first love, and she had the hope that he would find sobriety if a new child entered their life. Also, Carrie had always hoped for a little girl. Gracie had died in infancy, and that loss lingered. When, in 1916, Carrie became pregnant, she said a rosary nightly for a girl. It was a boy, Robert. He was a particularly beautiful child, and he became in quick order the family treasure. James's drinking abated. Carrie was fully happy. Then one evening, when the family was asleep, Robert began to scream—not the cry of a hungry or colicky baby, but the sharp yell of a child in deep pain. His spine began to curl into a sharp arc backward, and the screams persisted for hours. Next morning the doctor diagnosed tubercular meningitis. Robert died a few days later. Carrie was devastated.

Heart-struck as she was, Carrie grew determined to have her girl. She listened carefully to all the neighborhood female folklore on how to ensure this and in coming weeks followed all reasonable suggestions. Some of these, like sleeping only on your left side, seemed to skirt the edge of unreason, but Carrie changed her sleeping habits anyway.

Jim decided that he could scrap his odd jobs if boxing would bring him good money for Kitty. At this point he and his brothers, Bill excluded, had found better employment at a tearoom on 114th Street, Tiffin's, near Columbia University. The patrons frequently got confused about just who their waiters were, the three boys looked so much alike. Again, this was night work.

Leo Linahan, the Cagney family friend who had encouraged Jim to become a fighter, told him that there were openings in various fight bills through the city, and if Jim was interested, Linahan would put him up for a chance. Jim began to get up very early in the morning to do roadwork and strengthen his legs by running in a nearby park. Linahan got Jim an opening in a four-round bout at the Polo Grounds Athletic Club. This was to be his first professional appearance, and it would net him a sum large for him at the time, ten dollars.

Carrie did not much note Jim's early rising for roadwork because of the protracted nursing Robert required. But she noticed that Jim was getting thinner and asked why. Then it occurred to her that he had been leaving for school each day at a strange hour. Why so early?

"Not school, Mom. I'm in training."

"Training? For what?"

"A bout. Leo's got me set up for a prelim at the Polo Grounds. For *ten* bucks, just four rounds. Fifteen if I win. I can take this guy. I can lick him."

"Well, listen now," said Carrie. "Do you think you can lick *me*?"

"Whadda ya mean, Mom?"

"I mean you'll have to lick me first."

The Cagney boxing career was over.

# 4 · Farming Deferred

Cagney's entry to acting, like most of his life plans, was bred deep in circumstance. "I could have gone into several professions," he said. "My dominant drive was always the family. For them, I had to feed Kitty. Anything, I mean anything, which aided that I liked. Since boxing wasn't for me, I thought of the next-best thing I liked, and I didn't have to soul-search for that. Farming. But I, a tough gutter fighter, *do* farming? What the hell did I know about it?"

Carrie sympathized with Jim's ambition although privately she could not imagine her spunky little curb battler living on a farm, let alone working on one. Yet she saw he was in earnest, and the two of them set about investigating possibilities. Carrie, who had an artistic bent, hoped that Jim would want to amplify his sketching skills, but farming had seized his imagination. At the East Side Settlement House she found a brochure advertising the Farmington School of Agriculture on Long Island. Jim filled out an entrance application and waited eagerly for reply.

Instead of replying by mail, the Farmington School sent out an admissions counselor. Trying to hide it, the man was obviously incredulous about the Cagney mise-en-scène. In their crowded apartment the garrulous Cagney clan gathered about him, a disconcerting experience, and the man's few questions to Jim centered on his rationale for a career in agriculture. Jim was honest in reply. The reason he wanted to go into farming? He liked it. Any farming experience? No. Had he ever lived on a farm? No, just the two weeks at Aunt Jane's. What area of agriculture preferred? He didn't know; he liked the whole thing. The Farmington man shook hands all around and left, never to be heard from again. The idea of agriculture school went into abeyance.

Early in 1917 Jim made his first connection with show business, a peripheral one. A classmate's uncle, a member of the actors' club, The Friars, told Jim that there was a doorman's job going at the club and suggested that he go see about it. Jim found that the job was first-floor bellhop, that the salary was not great but the tips were. He got no titillation from close contact with the actors, well known and otherwise, for a very basic reason: he had never been to the theater in his life. He had seen a few amateur plays at the East Side Settlement House, he had been to vaudeville theaters, and he knew from newspapers that the great Broadway stars of the day were such people as George M. Cohan, Eddie Foy, Louis Mann, Raymond Hitchcock, Ed Wynn, Frank Tinney, and Charlie Winninger, all Friars. As a bellhop Jim got to know these people but only as a source of tips.

There, and there only, was he impressed with them. Without exception they tipped well, and the job was satisfying because it helped feed Kitty. Then a unique side advantage of the Friars job offered itself: free passes to Broadway shows from some of the actors. Jim was struck not so much by either the actors or the quality of productions as by the size of the salaries. He learned at The Friars that even actors in small roles were getting seventy-five or even a hundred dollars a week. He could scarcely credit it. For two and a half hours of work eight times a week? This would bear serious investigation. He began to read plays stacked on both the East Side and Lenox Hill Settlement House shelves. He found Bernard Shaw and began to understand more of Jean-Christophe's life journey.

Carrie had discovered that the Lenox Hill Settlement House on East Sixty-ninth Street offered unique learning opportunities for her boys. She knew Jim would always do well, but she worried about Harry, who had declared his intention of becoming a doctor. Harry was deeply shy, and Carrie knew this was poor qualification for one determined to be a family doctor. She heard of a free public speaking course at Lenox Hill and virtually forced Harry to take it. He found the course profitable and the company enjoyable. Lenox Hill staff people were warmly welcoming to anyone in their area who came in for self-improvement. Free lectures in many areas were standard, and communication skills were high on the list of things encouraged by the house for its largely ethnic clientele. In 1918 two new departments were added to the house's activities: dramatics, which immediately captivated Harry, and arts and crafts, which claimed Jim.

Heading dramatics was a skilled married couple, Florence and Burton James, who later went on to found the prestigious Seattle Community Theatre. Burton James pressed Jim into both designing and painting the sketchy scenery they were able to afford for plays. In arts and crafts Jim had already impressed the teacher by drawing exciting posters for the house plays and social gatherings of neighborhood people.

Harry developed his speech skills so well that he accepted Burton James's invitation to appear in several plays as an actor. In one of these he became ill, and because he had no understudy, James was frantic. "I've got an idea," said Harry. "I'll ask Jim to play it."

He played it, in a role as removed from his personality as salt from sugar.

He said:

I was a goddamned *faun*. That was the name of the play as I recall, *The Faun*. I wore a skimpy goatskin, my hair was marcelled, and I dashed about like a fairy in several senses of the word. A cut-rate Nijinsky from *L'Après-Midi d'un Faggy Faun*. I can recall some of my lines to this very day, and I wish I didn't. How about "Spring is running through the fields chased by the wynde"—that last is poetic for "wind"? And "Nay, sweet, give it me," and "The wayward wynde ran its fingers through the pine tree's hair." Nausea time, right? Wrong. I loved it. Not the words, but when I got out there before that audience, I could feel their approval or at least their *interest*. And for the first time I could see that there was something to this acting business beyond the money. I could see that there might be Jean-Christophes in the acting profession too. The approval of that Lenox Hill audience I truly felt, and that was Nirvana for little Jim, who of a sudden didn't feel so little.

Little Jim was regarded by Mr. and Mrs. James as something of a wonder boy. They knew that he as a volunteer, like his brother, would not be available for any kind of steady appearance. To keep his services, they asked Lenox Hill to hire him as doorman and general factotum at a salary that would allow him to quit his job at The Friars. He had found a wonderful new kind of home on the Lenox Hill stage. Mr. and Mrs. James were socialists and began to stimulate and influence his first political thinking.

One of the things Jim missed in the process of growing up was romance. His first love was at five in the person of Annie, a neighbor lass who won his heart by stopping him to lace up his perpetually untied shoes. He soon learned that keeping his shoes untied on purpose was a smart thing to do. When he was twelve, a girl his age named Norah propositioned him sexually, but he had no idea what she was talking about. Not long after, there was a sweet Jewish girl named Sarah who attracted him, but they engaged in nothing more than hand-holding and long talks. Next came a second Annie, who liked to run, and because he did too, that was an interesting relationship. "Never tried to catch her," he said. "We were platonic. No real dates, as one would call them today. Where would I get the money?"

His first real romance began when he was sixteen, a romance for which, in view of his multiple jobs, he barely had any time. This was Nellie Oliver, of whom he said:

An angelic blonde. The stuff of which dreams or at least my dreams were made at the time. Fairy princess type, blue-eyed and blonde, classic figure. I was working at The Friars then, and I'd get passes for the theater or the movies, both new experiences for me. I had seen little comedy movies in Ridgewood, but now I could watch the big stars—Doug Fairbanks, King Baggott, Bessie Barriscale, Marguerite Clark. Sessue Hayakawa. The thing I remember most about Nellie is that she loved to dance, and I didn't know how. But she taught me, and I began to love it too. We went only to parish and neighborhood dances. I couldn't afford taking her to dance halls, where we could have learned those great dances Vernon and Irene Castle were making popular: the one-step, the Turkey Trot, the Maxixe. Anyway, at the time, I thought they were cake-eater stuff. "Cake-eater" was current slang for "limp-wrist," the opposite of "manly." How wrong I was! When I saw Freddie and Ginger in *The Story of Vernon and Irene Castle*, I realized just how wrong I was. When I did *The Faun*, Florence James showed me some basic dance postures, which is where I first got the idea of line and extension. Then, God bless The Friars, I got passes to see Pavlova, and I sat there watching that beauty of motion so transfixed I could hardly breathe. I wept, it was so goddamned beautiful. I know that old wheeze "The Irish even cry at card tricks," and that is right, but this woman summoned up every emotion under the sun—just by moving.

Jim was to remember Pavlova and the superb simplicity of her movements and gesture when he began his life as a dancer. Some of those movements occur in the gentle, simple use of his hands, particularly in his early films. After the Pavlova performance he walked into the lobby with Nellie and for a long time was unable to speak. All he knew was that he had to see Pavlova again, and soon. Next day he asked at The Friars desk for two more passes, but the next time he brought Carrie. It was the experience as before. But intensified. "I couldn't explain it even to myself," he said. "But I sensed that this was something I had to do. Not in just that way. But dancing was in me." Nellie gradually faded from his life, and it was not easy for him because Carrie approved highly of the girl. He knew that this was not the one, and that is all he knew.

. . .

When Carrie discovered in early summer 1918 that she was again pregnant, she went to their church, St. Francis de Sales on East Ninety-sixth Street, for a prayer visit. She sat in the back pew one early afternoon and prayed that her baby would live and that the baby would be a girl. For the rest of her confinement she made sure she did not overdo housework or any other kind of activity. James was still not sober, but he was far from the drunkenness of earlier years, and this consoled her. James tried all he could do on Carrie's behalf. He shopped for groceries, ran the sweeper, and dusted the furniture. This pleased Carrie hugely. Her husband seemed to be coming into the orbit of a conventional life pattern.

The autumn of 1918 in the United States was a devastating one for the country. The drums of war in France were still sounding, and in New York and other large cities a devastating influenza epidemic had begun. Millions had already died of it across the world, particularly in Spain, and it was everywhere called the Spanish flu. It came to James F. Cagney with terrifying swiftness. He awoke one morning complaining of muscular discomfort and nausea. His usual hair-of-the-dog whiskey not working, Carrie insisted he go to Metropolitan Hospital. He entered the afternoon of October 9 and died the next morning.

An interesting fact attends the matter of Cagney's death certificate. The family was told that James died of the "Spanish flu," yet his death certificate reads "Cause of death: lobar pneumonia." The mystery is that influenza and lobar pneumonia are quite different things, the former being viral in origin, the latter bacterial. The matter is explained by the current *Encyclopaedia Britannica*'s article on influenza, which states, "Mortality is commonly low, resulting from complications such as pneumonia, usually among the elderly, who are weakened by debilitating disorders." Not-so-elderly James—he was forty-one—had his own virulent "debilitating disorder."

Carrie's sorrow was deep and exhausting. For all his grave faults, she loved James unshakably, profoundly. He was, she said, the only one in the world who could make her laugh when she didn't want to, and laughter was her only anodyne against the harshness of her life. Laughter, and her children. They promptly took over all duties attendant on James's death. Jim talked to the undertaker, then walked over to the parish church with several precious dollars in his pocket. It had been decided for reasons of economy that there would be a simple prayer service rather than the usual funeral Mass at the funeral parlor before James was taken to the Cagney burial plot in Calvary Cemetery.

When Jim arrived at the St. Francis rectory, he explained the situation to one of the assistant pastors, who agreed to come for services at the appointed time. Jim apologized for the modest amount and gave the priest two dollars. The priest said he would see him at the funeral parlor next day to conduct the prayer service. He did not appear, and the funeral director hastily took over the priest's duties. Jim took the priest's absence very hard. Apart from family christenings and funerals, he never appeared in a Catholic church again until his own funeral.

"My mother was not what you'd call an obsessive woman," said Jim in his maturity, "except on one point: education. She used to hammer it into us: 'A profession, a profession. You've all got to get into a profession.' She never stopped telling us that." Carrie had no need to urge her firstborn in this direction. From the time Harry became aware that his mother had health problems, he was determined to become a doctor. He won a scholarship to Columbia University and advanced rapidly in his studies.

Carrie fancied that Ed would do well as a teacher of languages because he had word facility and was a natural wit. He was the family jester. But he too felt the pull of medicine, and after Harry exposed him to the intricacy and scope of his studies, Ed entered medical school as well. Periodically he and Harry had to drop out of school to work for tuition money, but they always returned. Ed did not have to scramble for money quite as hard as his brother because by the time Ed was an intern, Jim was in Hollywood and could help out.

Carrie was certain young Bill, so glib of tongue and ample in vocabulary, would be a lawyer. Instead, following his long-established trading instincts, he became a businessman, entering a world in which he flourished. As for Jim's prospects, Carrie was frustrated and uncertain. When she saw him as a young child copying illustrations from newspapers, she rejoiced at the thought of his becoming an artist, and this hope was revived when he designed and painted the scenery at Lenox Hill. But when asked his intentions toward life, he said, "Oh, I don't know, Ma. I'd love to be in agriculture, but there's no way to get in that. I don't fancy signing on as a hired hand. I'd like to draw, but what future's in that?" He spoke vaguely of art school.

One day Harry came home from Columbia to tell Jim of the school's active recruitment of students in the Army-sponsored SATC, Student Army Training Corps, a forerunner of ROTC. There was an opening for those skilled in drawing as part of the military camouflage unit. If Jim stayed in the unit, he would receive a Columbia scholarship and become an Army officer on graduation day. He enrolled at once and, true to his interest in music, volunteered for SATC's band as a drummer. A drummer friend years before had shown him military rolls and beats on the snare drums. It proved to be fun in SATC. Even classes were fun for Jim, especially the German classes. His years in Yorkville were an advantage to him there, and he found learning the language easy. He enjoyed his distinguished instructor, Professor Mankiewicz, father of two brilliant sons: Herman J., author of *Citizen Kane*, and Joseph L., writer-director of *All About Eve* and other notable films.

Professor Mankiewicz found Jim's natural rapidity of speech fascinating. "Where did you learn to talk so quickly, Mr. Cagney?" he said.

"Upper East Side, sir," said Jim. "That's where you learn to walk fast, talk fast, think fast—and run fast."

"Well, this is Columbia, where we tend to think *slowly,* at least in our formulations. In any case, *slowly* is the way I would like you to read this passage from Goethe."

Jim read the first words at moderate speed, but his inevitable, inbuilt celerity took over. The class laughed.

"Mr. Cagney, please," said Mankiewicz. "It may interest you to know that you are a living example of the well-known phrase *geflügelte Worte,* 'winged words.' Now, do please slow down so we mortals can join you in your journey."

Jim's vocal rapidity he ascribed to his reading habits. He always read very quickly, the average book taking him two days to finish, and he remembered what he read. He thought rapidly, probably from the need in his early difficult years to be ready instantly for any emergency. He said, "I think in a way my winged words were not only milieu but my genes, the old blather and blarney my pop could do so well."

After his dad died, Jim left school, again to make money. He had had six instructive months at Columbia, but none of the Cagneys doubted that their concerted need now was to help Harry remain at his studies. Jim got a job wrapping packages at Wanamaker's department store, easy, if monotonous, work.

Family excitement was high in March 1919, when Carrie was approaching the end of her confinement. Her great wish came true on March 25, when her daughter, Jeanne Carolyn Cagney, was born, hearty and hale, the source of much happiness to mother and siblings. Jim put it graciously: "Mom saved the best for last."

With all the expenses attendant on a new baby, Jim felt added pressure to bring in a higher income. He was thus well disposed to something a

Back row, second from left: In drag for *Every Sailor*,
B. F. Keith's 86th Street Theatre, 1919

buddy of his at Wanamaker's told him. The fellow worker, a former vaudeville performer, mentioned that a friend of his was dropping out of an act
then current at B. F. Keith's 86th Street Theatre, and that the going rate for
the actors was a bountiful thirty-five dollars a week. For this, Jim learned, he
had to do "a little dancing and singing." Jim said:

> That sure described my performing talents at the time, a *little*, but
> I'm a take-a-chance guy anyway, so I went over to the 86th Street
> Theatre on the recommendation of my pal at work and saw the
> manager of the act, an act called *Every Sailor*, which was a pastiche
> of a popular wartime show, *Every Woman*, that had soldiers cast as
> women. Only this cast was sailors as women, and that was my first
> shock. This same troupe had gained a good reputation by enter-
> taining President Wilson at the Versailles Peace Conference, and
> when they came back to the States, a producer named Phil Dun-
> ning sharpened their act a bit and put it into vaudeville. The man-
> ager asked me if I could dance. "Sure," I said, although except for
> little skippings around on First Avenue when I was six, I didn't
> know a step except a popular dance of the time called the Peabody.

But I'm a natural-born mimic, and when he showed me the steps, I got them right away.

Jim was told to watch the others during a performance, "to catch the flavor." At first he was afraid the "flavor" would be epicene, but he was glad to be proved wrong, the humor of the piece lying in its quite masculine actors attired as and walking about as women, singing and dancing without swish. Jim got so adept at walking in high heels that it gave him what he called "a quick, jerky walk—a kind of occupational sea legs—and I got tired of my pals saying to me, 'Lengthen it out, Red!' to remind me how to walk properly."

Carrie and the boys came to see Jim's opening in the show, and she became a one-woman claque, even whistling loudly in approval. Jim stayed eight weeks with the troupe, making notable additions to Kitty. He then found a job as runner at a Wall Street brokerage house, picking up comparison slips—that is, going to other firms that had made deals with his company and waiting there to get verification that a sale had been made of the stock. It was, he said, the most boring job of his life, and it came brief weeks before the most interesting job of his life, the one in which he met the love of his life.

# 5 · Willie

*very Sailor* was a great success at the 86th Street Theatre, and plans went forward for it to go on tour in vaudeville houses across the country. Jim felt some inclination to go along because he had traveled very little in his life and it would have been fun. But he realized he was tired of playing a woman, however humorously. There was, moreover, the matter of Guy, one of the boys-as-girls, who Jim knew was a boy-wanting-a-boy. Guy had his eye, and sometimes a friendly paw, on Jim. "I think he really thought I was gay," said Jim. "I put up with his friendly little overtures because he was a very nice person, until I was forced to tell him that with me it was women, women all the way. Not that I'd had much experience in that department. But enough. Good old Guy got the idea."

Carrie was glad that Jim was leaving the troupe. She was dubious about show business as a career, and Jim was certainly of an age where school seemed mandatory. Yet the dominating fact of existence was maintenance of the family. Harry was still in college, Ed and Bill were in high school, and baby Jeanne was in need of many things. At this time Jim had not in any measure fallen in love with show business. But, in the Damon Runyon phrase, he more than somewhat loved the salaries. He knew he was now qualified, even if barely, as a chorus boy. Chorus boys in 1920 earned thirty-five to forty dollars a week in a day when a dollar would buy a five-course dinner.

One of the boys from *Every Sailor* told Jim of chorus boy casting in progress for an upcoming Broadway show, *Pitter Patter*, the musicalized version of a 1906 Willie Collier farce, *Caught in the Rain*. More than fifty young men were auditioned for the show on the stage of the Longacre Theatre, and as they waited in line to go center stage to perform a prescribed step, Jim made sure he was as far back as he could get. "My stratagem was fundamental," he said. "I made sure I had plenty of time to observe what the others did, then do it with what éclat I could."

He did what was required with an added spin of his own. Part of the popular dance step known as the Peabody that he knew required a quick, bouncy turn. This became the zippy little coda to his audition and was, he believed, the reason why he got the job. He knew that any number of the boys rejected were far better dancers than he; what he brought to his audition was a sense of kinetic excitement, of someone in motion even when immobile. Being the shortest of the boys, he was, as customary, placed at one end of the chorus line, the tallest boys being in the middle. As end man he got some automatic attention from the audience and from at least one of the chorus girls.

Frances Willard Vernon, the shortest of the girls, was usually paired opposite "the cute red-haired boy," as she described him to her girlfriends. She was known to them as Billie, and Billie Vernon was not much given to compliments. She was sweet, plainspoken, indeed candid to the point of bluntness, her personality reflecting something of her Scottish Presbyterian mother, wife of a farmer in Fairfield, Iowa, where Billie was raised. Born on June 19, 1899, in Des Moines, she had been sent at sixteen to live with her sister in Chicago, both girls under order to attend teachers' college there, as had two of their sisters before them. Billie had plans of her own. She took her tuition money to go to New York and dance upon the wicked stage. Her appalled parents ordered her home. She wrote a brief note to her mother, saying she could not go home because she had found her life's work in dancing, and she was sorry but there really was no use in discussing the matter further. Her mother disputed this, but she knew Billie had inherited her own staunch directness. In New York Billie worked as a waitress for a time, earned dancing school tuition, and mastered her art, especially wing dancing.* Her natural gracefulness, her good, if small, figure, and her piquant features ensured her continual work as end chorus girl.

Billie was intrigued by Jim Cagney because instead of playing cards, as most chorus people did between numbers, he read books. This was singular enough, but when she heard him discussing *Jean-Christophe* with another well-read chorus boy, referring to the book as a *roman-fleuve* (the French for "river novel," a story of a family over many years), she was, as she said later, "impressed that someone so cute should have so much brains." Years later she would kid him by saying, "Right then and there I decided that *you* were my *roman-fleuve.*"

---

*The "wings" Cagney did while dancing down the stairway in the White House in *Yankee Doodle Dandy* were the result of Billie's coaching.

With Wynne Gibson, sometime in the thirties, recalling an adagio they danced in
*Pitter Patter* on Broadway in 1920

Yet Billie saw there was nothing remotely bookish about Jim Cagney. He was lively of temperament, enjoyed a laugh, talked—if a bit too quickly for her midwestern ears—to everyone, and was innately shy. She tried to maneuver him into a date, but it seemed he never went out with the *Pitter Patter* gang. He didn't drink, although not a teetotaler. He wasn't gay—she had observed enough of his appreciative side glances at her legs to know that—yet he made no move in her direction.

Then she found out the uncomplicated reason why he never asked her out. He gave his pay packet to his mother, except for carfare and a few sundries. This made Billie even more determined to go out with him. She invented a story that her folks had sent her a goodly amount of cash for her birthday, and she wanted to be hostess at a celebration including her best friend and her friend's steady. Wouldn't they, she asked her girlfriend, please ask Jim? Done. The foursome went out for a pleasant evening, and during its course he asked her if she was going to a cast party the producers were giving the following week. "Only if you'll take me," she said, and Jim knew at once that this was inescapably the girl for him. "Not a doubt in the world," he said. He had felt free to criticize her the first time they met. She had rather underwhelmed him by the way she did her hair and her dress. The former emphasized spit curls, and the latter an excess of ribbon furbelows. Billie laughed but went rigid with inner embarrassment. Never again in her life did she wear ribbons or sport spit curls.

Billie loathed her baptismal name, Willard. Her parents, after having three girls, confidently yet prayerfully expected a boy, whose name was to be Willard. When a fourth girl came, they had her christened Willard anyhow, which did not sit well with her. In her adolescence, she prefixed it with Frances, in honor of the great American woman educator Frances Willard. When she began to go out with Jim, he called her variously Bill or Billie but, when they were alone, Willie, the name he liked best.

Jim and Willie were inexorably drawn to each other. They were alike: both small, wiry, good dancers (she better than he by a bit), intense, witty, and given to volatile displays of temper when crossed. At the time they met they were both going with other people. Jim, with Nellie Oliver, much approved of by Carrie; Willie with Ralph, a boy still in Iowa who planned to come east and marry her. One evening in her boardinghouse room, Willie smelled heliotrope on Jim's lapel, a scent she knew was not native to either of them. She demanded the source. Jim, never anything but forthright, told her of Nellie. Willie took Jim's framed photo from her table, hurled it across the room, grabbed a large jar of cold cream, and threw it vigorously at him. He ducked, and the jar splattered itself over a wall.

"I knew then that this was a serious matter," said Jim. "We both agreed to tell our respective inamorata and inamarato that we were serious about each other." This was done, and quite as expected, the rejected boy and girl were made very unhappy. Equally unhappy was Carrie, whose affection for Nellie was unbounded and whose dislike for Willie was pronounced. This resentment of the girl from Iowa was to have repercussions in the Cagney family even beyond Jim's and Willie's deaths.

"I can mostly understand why Mrs. Cagney resented me," Willie told this writer in 1980. "After all, I was from another world, an Iowa farm girl, who knew nothing about the city, particularly Mrs. Cagney's city. But more than that—much more than that—Mrs. Cagney disliked show business and all it stood for. What it stood for, I guess, was me."

One thing Carrie Cagney could not dispute about show business was the vital matter of income. Jim, hired for thirty-five dollars a week in *Pitter Patter*, most of which went to Carrie and her baby, augmented that income by twenty-five more dollars a week by performing extra duties for the play's star, Ernest Truex. That amiable little comedian, about to embark on a fifty-year career in films as the prototypical henpecked spouse, liked Jim and hired him as dresser and company baggage man on tour. "What a kind man Ernie Truex was," said Jim. "A great trouper, and professionally I learned from him one of his great skills: the take. He had great skill at this kind of comic-fright reaction, and I watched him every night from the wings when he did it."

One of the chorus boys in *Pitter Patter* was a cheerfully aggressive New Yorker, very fond of his beer, Allen Jenkins. Born Alfred McGonagle, he was to be a pal of Jim's all his days, particularly the Warner Brothers days, when Jenkins was typecast as an obstreperous loudmouth. "When Allen was on the sauce," said Jim, "which in the early days was frequent, you couldn't ask for a more troublesome guy. When he was off it, at the end of his life, you couldn't ask for a sweeter one. He certainly was fun for me."

The money Jim sent to Carrie from *Pitter Patter* she wisely banked when she could, believing—correctly as it turned out—that such largess couldn't continue. After a respectable Broadway run and subsequent tour, *Pitter Patter* closed, and Jim assessed his situation. He could not think of anything other than show business as such a fine income source. Moreover, his wife-to-be was committed to it. At the moment marriage was out of the question because as the only working member of the Cagney family, Jim owed first allegiance to them. Willie quite understood. She suggested that one way to make money was to set up their own vaudeville act, and he agreed.

They worked up what he called "a simple thing," based on the challenge dance idea, where two dancers in sequence try to outperform the other. "We had a little patter to go with it," he said, "but mostly it was dance, and that, unlike the patter, was pretty good. But overall the act needed funny talk. We needed a writer, and that was one thing we were not. We called ourselves Vernon and Nye, a scramble of our surnames."

Willie got word from her sister Jan, a housewife in Chicago, that their dad had died suddenly. Jan sent enough money for a one-way train fare to Iowa, and Willie left for the funeral. She stayed a month with her mother and went on to stay with Jan and her family in Chicago. Willie had no money for train fare to New York, and she thought that waitressing for a time would provide that. But that could take months, and she missed Jim desperately. She fell into despair. Then a most remarkable thing. She said:

It just had to be more than coincidence or luck. I'm not sure what you'd call it. No way to explain it. I'd been feeling down in the dumps in Chicago for so long, and I needed Jim so badly, that my sister said, "Look, I want you to go out and relax. Go to Loew's State and see vaudeville." She gave me the money for it, money she could ill afford. I went, enjoyed myself, and the closing act was two girls who sang and danced and played the piano. Cute act. I got out of my seat and was walking up the aisle to the exit when a woman behind me tapped me on the shoulder and said, "Excuse me, are you a dancer?"

I turned around, not believing what I heard, and I said, "Why, yes, I am."

"Did you see that last act?" she said, and I said yes. "Well, one of the girls is leaving the act, and we need a replacement." I walked with her backstage, sang and danced for an audition, and three days later left with the act for a tour to Milwaukee and New York. Now, how did that woman guess that I was a dancer? Maybe the way I walked? I asked her later—her name was Woodsie—and she said, "Honestly, I don't know." I can think it meant only one thing: that Jim and I were fated to be with each other.

Jim was making the rounds of vaudeville agents in New York and met the inevitable daily rejection that comes to all actors. He said, "You know deep down that the rejection is nothing personal, but that doesn't stop it from being rejection. After a while, when that keeps going on for months, you develop a sense of worthlessness, and in me that sense grew pretty strong. I would have taken any kind of job, but what else was I good for?"

When Willie got to New York, she saw how desperately unhappy and despondent Jim had grown. He told her he was willing to accept anything in the way of work: "shoe clerk, street car conductor, and permanently. I mean it." Willie gave him a severe talking to, saying that she had never heard of such nonsense and that he had better get his priorities straight once and for all. "You're going to dance; you're going to act. You're going to reach the heights, and I don't care how sentimental that sounds. It's the truth. You'd better get used to it. You'd better start working on it."

Years later the phrase "reach the heights" stayed in both their memories. The evening Cagney won his Oscar they returned home, and he placed the statuette on their dining room table. He said, "The *heights*. That's what you said. It couldn't have happened without you."

She looked very solemn and said, "Damned right, boy."

They both exploded into laughter.

In 1921 there was nothing to laugh about. Willie had no financial problems because she was constantly working, and she made sure that the Cagneys had food at those times when their income diminished. Bill was in high school, but his scrounging efforts always brought in a little money. Both Harry and Ed were in college, working their way through, and could not contribute.

Via the Broadway grapevine and close reading of *Variety* and *Billboard*, Jim was able to keep aware of auditions and miscellaneous actor calls. He was elated to be cast in a promising vaudeville three-act, Parker, Rand, and Leach, when Leach (Archie Leach, soon to be Cary Grant) dropped out. Parker, Rand, and Cagney was reviewed in *Variety:* "[They] begin with two boys and a girl in a skit idea that goes nowhere. It is a turn without semblance of a punch. There are no laughs and the songs mean little. One of the boys can dance. Small time is its only chance."

The "no laughs" was ensured by patter like the following:

PARKER: Do you know where I can always find money?

CAGNEY: Always?

PARKER: Always.

CAGNEY: Where?

PARKER: In the dictionary.

"*Variety* was right," Jim said. "We were good only for the small time like the Gus Sun time and the rural circuits, and not too hot even for them. But despite this, we did well enough, and I did plenty well enough by learning my craft." His partners could never understand why Jim spent most of his time in the wings instead of in the dressing room. What he was doing was uncomplicated: watching and remembering. The vaudeville acts were his dramatic education. Certain things, like the sense of control all first-rate vaudevillians possessed, impressed him indelibly. They not only knew what they were doing but did it with the least amount of effort necessary to obtain their effects. Moreover, they did it without distracting body movement so that one saw the act at its most functional: pure, focused, in utter control. He was to incorporate this into his acting. He noticed that this functional control was true of all the best acts, be they acrobats, animal acts, singers, jugglers, dancers, or clowns. This was his first important lesson in acting.

Parker, Rand, and Cagney quickly split up, but Jim grew to love vaudeville. In his old age he remembered the first years at Warners and vaudeville days as his most enjoyable, and of the two, vaudeville was the closer to his heart. In his last years the stories he told his friends were all about those difficult and ultimately most rewarding years. "Vaudeville is where I learned my business," he said. "And truth to tell, it's where I had the most fun."

After playing poky small-time vaudeville, Jim and Willie hit the near big time, a touring Lew Fields show, *Ritz Girls of 19 and 22*. Willie, as usual, was end girl on the chorus line; Jim danced and appeared in a few sketches. Fields, one of the most popular men in the American theater, was well publicized as producer and director of the production, but the theatergoing public across the country expected Fields as star and was badly disappointed when he didn't appear. He was at the time rehearsing for a reunion with his now old partner Joe Weber. Weber and Fields had separated and reunited so many times that George M. Cohan at a Friars dinner honoring them said, "I'll stop retiring if you two would stop having reunions."

*Ritz Girls of 19 and 22* opened on September 11, 1922, out of town just six days before Weber and Fields appeared in *Reunited* on Broadway to the fabled comic pair's usual critical acclaim. Both productions had come under the aegis of a powerful name, the Shubert brothers, who were now challenging the two giants of vaudeville producers, the Keith-Albee and the Orpheum circuits. Lee and J. J. Shubert were determined to break the virtual monopoly of these two giant enterprises on top-level shows. Since the Shuberts owned many theaters across the country, they reasoned that they could send out their own shows and revues to form a third powerful circuit. *Lew Fields' Ritz Girls of 19 and 22*, to give its final title, was one such, and early in its tour it played to many empty seats, but this changed as the weeks went by. Word of mouth helped compensate for the lack of Lew Fields in person. Reviews were good. Jim and Willie loved the people in the company, mostly musicians, singers, and dancers, headed by a skilled old Dutch comic, Harry Cooper.

Soon *Ritz Girls* was a profitable enterprise, and by the time it reached Cleveland for Thanksgiving it drew twelve thousand dollars, double its weekly expenses. But the new Shubert vaudeville circuit was falling apart, and the Shuberts closed *Ritz Girls* in St. Louis. Lew Fields wired the Shuberts indignantly, saying the show was not only profitable but well on its way to paying off the Shubert investment in it. Fields had expended money in St. Louis on the show, and creditors were closing in after the closing. There had been some talk among the cast that their salaries would be seized for Fields's debts, but the Shuberts honored their obligations.

As usual, when a good show playing to good audiences folds, the cast was despondent, but Willie and Jim were euphoric. *Lew Fields' Ritz Girls of 19 and 22* had been their honeymoon. They had gone to New York's City Hall on a Thursday morning, September 28, 1922, and got married.

# 6 · Vaudeville Variety

L ife had been exciting for the Cagneys during the *Ritz Girls* tour. Living
together in a variety of small hotels and boardinghouses was never dull
and always a challenge. But their return to New York precipitated a
challenge that Willie found hard to face.

For a number of reasons, all financial, she and Jim were forced to move
into the Cagney apartment on East Seventy-eighth Street. The Cagney family was used to crowding. Two-boys-to-a-bed, four-in-a-room had been the
operative mode for years, and no one felt badly used in consequence. It was
what had to be done, as was the daily hunt to feed Kitty. But the occupancy
of one of the bedrooms by a newly married couple, however much they
were "family," was another matter.

There were now, however one counted, two families living at 420 East
Seventy-eighth Street, and the heads of those two families, Carrie Cagney
and Frances Willard Cagney, were not in harmony. It was, no question, Carrie's household. She had been the life-sustaining matriarch of the Cagneys
during the lifetimes of Harry, Jim, Ed, and Bill. She was their guiding prin-
ciple, their rock, having given them the basic principles by which they lived.

Willie Cagney knew this well, and she realized the awkwardness of their
situation. She deferred to Carrie in everything, helped with little Jeanne,
cooked (but not very well) when needed, tried to be companionable to the
boys, who perhaps naturally resented her as an intruder. It was, at bottom,
an impossible dilemma, and out of it came the only unhappiness of any
depth in Willie and Jim's marriage. Willie was made to feel like an intruder,
and rightfully she resented it. Harry, Ed, and Bill were to manifest their
continuing dislike of her throughout their lifetimes. This tension was to be
exacerbated by one pervasive and unhappy irony: during much of the early
1920s Willie became the chief breadwinner of the Cagney family. As an old
man Jim bragged of this. "Willie was the one who put the groceries on our

table," he said. "Putting the groceries on the table" became Jim Cagney's prime leitmotif for his working existence, and if he became almost a bore in constantly repeating the phrase, it was nonetheless heartfelt.

Fortunately for Willie's state of mind, vaudeville tours took her and Jim away from the Cagney apartment for a number of weeks each year. And as time passed, Jim realized more and more how uniquely he and Willie were suited to each other. He said of her, "I was attracted to her for the good reason that she was pretty and she was bright and she liked me right away. All good reasons. Then I found a fourth and even deeper reason: she was a country gal. She was fascinated by my love of the country, which had begun when I was a kid." Jim pondered the paradox for a time. "Funny. She thought my country fixation was funny because if ever there was a city boy, it was me. Fresh, brash, New York accent, the works. I got such a kick from the fact that she was an original Corn Belt girl. 'What the heck, I'm a hick,' she used to say, and that endeared her to me very much. She became the country for me: the genuine freshness, a kind of knowing naiveté, the sweetness, above all the straightforwardness. No guile. She couldn't even *act* guile, and she was a hell of a good actress."

On the occasions when she and Jim couldn't get bookings as an act, Willie joined up with an old girlfriend, Wynne Gibson, before that strikingly attractive blonde went on to Hollywood to play tough dames and ultimately to become an actor's agent in New York. Willie regarded the act with Wynne her job insurance; if she and Jim couldn't work, there was always Wynne, and Kitty would get fed.

When Jim and Willie were out on the road, they felt the special comradeship that all vaudeville people felt for one another, sharing their experiences, good and bad, sad and hilarious. In his mid-years, after Jim had joined The Players Club in New York, he was fond of telling one story of his vaudeville days that his fellow members never tired of hearing. Peter Turgeon, a fellow Player, retells it:

Jim and Willie were out on tour with their dance act in a troupe which seldom played the big cities but rather the so-called tank towns named after the water tanks at the railroad tracks leading into town. The headliner in that particular company was an over-the-hill soprano who took her number one billing very seriously.

Traveling with her was an aging toy poodle with the inspired name of Frou Frou, whom the rest of the cast loathed. Not without reason. Number one, she smelled, and she did her best to bite people, and on overnight train trips she yapped incessantly, and she'd done all these things by the time she'd arrived for a week's engagement in Elkhart, Indiana, where a new act was to join the company featuring a huge, moth-eaten lion. As usual, the soprano proceeded to dominate the orchestra run-through. While she was out in front of the curtain arguing tempos with the conductor, the rest of the cast, including Jim and Willie, sat glumly backstage, waiting their turn. They had a clear view of that lion in his cage behind the scenery when, all of a sudden, out of nowhere, little Frou Frou appeared, having got the scent of the King of the Beasts, which was evidently even stronger than her own.

Jim and the others watched, fascinated, as the flea-bitten little pest danced daintily over and peered into the cage. Just as the soprano was trying in vain to get a high note out on the stage, the lion made his move. With one swipe of his enormous paw, he popped Frou Frou into his cavernous maw. The cast sat there, horrified, stunned by what they saw. No one said a word, nor did they say anything after the rehearsal, when they heard the late Frou Frou's mistress calling out to her. "What could we have said?" Jim pointed out. Plaintively the soprano spent the rest of the week going up and down alleys in her hopeless quest.

Many years later Jim and Willie were walking up Broadway when who should appear but the old soprano. As she recognized them, her face clouded over. Her eyes filled with tears. Then she managed, "Oh, my dear Willie and Jim, you were with me that awful week when my darling Frou Frou vanished into thin air." Well, the Cagneys knew it hadn't been thin air, but they hadn't the courage to tell her just where Frou Frou ended up.

For all their poverty in the vaudeville days, Jim and Willie had no lack of entertainment in the city. The young Cagneys were so well known in vaudeville circles in New York that they would go weekly to the Palace Theatre, ask the ticket taker if he "honored the profession," and the answer was invariably "Pass through."

It was at the Palace that Jim saw the first of the two performers who were to influence him artistically the most: Frank Fay. Jim said:

When I saw Frank Fay, it was utter revelation. I had seen wonderful monologuists before—Julius Tannen, Walter C. Kelly, James J. Morton—and they were great. But they couldn't touch Frank. Monologuists were the bravest vaudevillians because they went out there all alone—no gimmicks, no costume, no funny makeup—and they didn't sing, dance, or do cartwheels. They just *talked*. And how they talked, about anything under the sun, in such a whimsical way they made you roar. Frank's wit was legendary, the best-known example I guess being the time Milton Berle said to him, "I hereby challenge you to a duel of wits." Frank replied, "Please. I never fight an unarmed man."

Watching vaudevillians over the years, I came to understand and appreciate their sense of control, of true command over the audience with that control. Of all those great vaudevillians, I admired Frank the most because (a) he was the funniest, and (b) he had the most control. He never made an unnecessary move or facial grimace. He didn't need to wave a cigar around as a prop, and how he'd hate it (the way I do today) when some of these goddamned so-called comedians get in front of an audience and continually move the microphone up and down or drag it along and do everything with it but fornicate.

Frank let us see only *himself*, the quiet, droll gentleman who had a pleasantly acidic view of life, and mark those adjectives well. Later on, after vaudeville, I tried to keep in mind that constant composure he maintained. That was his secret.* A dynamic composure, if that's not a contradiction in terms. I tried to learn that. Cagney learned that.

After a long period with Wynne Gibson on the road, Willie returned to find Jim excited about a new revue Lew Fields was preparing, with an opening in it for them. *Snapshots of 1923* came to life in February of that year with Fields as the star, together with skits, dancers, comics, a line of girls (Willie on one end), and Jim as solo dancer. He also played eight different roles, juvenile to old age, in the hilarious Fields sketches. *Snapshots of 1923* toured three cities for six weeks. A tremendous psychological boost for him was his first rave review, from the *New York Star:* "Jimmy [Cagney] . . . is a dapper, smiling young chap, full of ambition to rise in his adopted profession. He will. Just watch his smoke."

The smoke began to settle. Jim and Willie returned to East Seventy-eighth Street, where it was soon apparent that the strain of Willie's presence

*Although his appearance is very brief, some of Fay's quality of control can be seen in his role as Master of Ceremonies in the film *Nothing Sacred* (1937). In vaudeville, Fay's jaunty walk onstage was a mix of sashay and swagger. It was imitated by Jack Benny and Bob Hope.

was finally too much for her mother-in-law. Willie told Jim they needed a place of their own, so they moved to a boardinghouse a few yards from Carrie's. Yet for some time they went on having their principal meals at 420.

Willie almost never stopped working because cute and petite chorus girls (called ponies) who could really dance were in demand. But during the spring of 1924 Jim entered the most depressing phase of his career. He had saved enough money from the Fields tour to put a small amount in the bank, but he was keenly aware that if it were not for Willie's jobs, the groceries would not be on the table very long for his mother and siblings. He made Willie keep a strict accounting of all the monies she had expended on his family's behalf—including a warm winter coat she insisted on buying him—so that in time he could pay her back. Willie had financial obligations to her sister in Chicago, and Jim knew Willie would never rest until they were met.

In 1924 the Cagneys were approached by an old friend, Charlie Leonard, former press agent for *Pitter Patter,* with a proposition. He told them that the best show business opportunities were in Hollywood, then attracting a flood of vaudevillians, many of whom were to stay on and become the great character people of the golden age of the sound film. It was, argued Leonard, the wave of the future, the coming haven of fabulous salaries and salubrious living. So convinced was Leonard of the Cagneys' ability to do well there that he offered to pay their train fare and expenses, the three of them going day coach. Sure they had nothing to lose, Jim and Willie agreed, having further reason to do so in that Willie's mother had just moved to a Los Angeles suburb, Hawthorne. At last Jim could meet his mother-in-law.

The four-day trip to California was excessively tedious, but they had great hopes, hopes that started to dissipate the day they arrived.

Hawthorne, they discovered, was more an exurb than a suburb, being almost an hour from Los Angeles by trolley. The three of them rented an inexpensive furnished bungalow near Willie's mother, but the daily journeys into town were debilitating to the two young men. Willie had determined not to go job searching until Jim was established.

Jim and Leonard soon found that apart from the cattle call pool for movie extras there was no way to get inside a studio without an agent. They had no agent and no way to find one. Jim had the address of an old vaudeville buddy, Harry Gribbon, looked him up, found him out of work as well, and suggested they put a comic dance act together out of bits and pieces they had seen in small-, medium-, and big-time vaudeville. "To give you some idea of how bad we were," said Cagney, "here is one of our chief gags in a rapid, cross-fire patter. Harry is supposed to be the bright guy, and he gives me comic answers to my dumb questions, until I really hang him up with this one, which I think goes back to antique burlesque: 'If is is is, or was was was, is is was or was was is, or is was is or was is was?' Harry does a double take, and the audience groans. But it was funny when Lew Fields did it, was my excuse."

The Gribbon and Cagney act was booked into a San Pedro theater and played a single, quietly dreadful performance. They were canceled in traditional fashion with the manager returning their display photographs. The partnership ended at once, Gribbon going on to years of success as a player with Mack Sennett and Mabel Normand. Jim wanted to go back to New York, and he found Willie willing. Her mother liked Jim, but she thought show business was no business and urged her daughter to take a secretarial course. The Cagneys decided to return to New York, and Jim wired an old Yorkville pal, by then a *New York Times* correspondent, Jim Fair, for what was known in show business as Hollywood medicine, fare back to New York after rejection by the movies. Fair wired them the money, and Jim and Willie set off and on the way to Chicago debated the wisdom of trying their luck there. The Second City, then as now, was a theatrical center, and a number of vaudeville booking offices flourished in the Loop.

Also in Chicago was the comforting presence of Willie's sister Jan, who had been so good to them in the past. She had always said, "If ever you're passing through, stay with us for a while. For a good while." The Cagneys thought this was the time. On arrival in Chicago they cashed in their tickets to New York and took a trolley to Jan's house, to be met by strangers. Jan had sublet the house and was away on an extended vacation. The Cagneys found a cheap boardinghouse and considered what to do. The only possibility was reviving Vernon and Nye, with a few new added gags from the Fields tours.

They picked up a few dates, but their money was almost depleted. Jim's worries about their future hardened into a stage fright he had never had before and would never have again. This brought on what he was sure were stomach ulcers, but he soon realized that this was part of a bigger fear: that he had chosen not only the wrong profession but the one profession as removed from his *true* profession, agriculture, as it was possible to be. He told this to Willie one evening after a prolonged dyspeptic vomiting. She told him with considerable passion that she wanted no such talk from him again: "I told you that you were going to hit the heights in this business, by God, and by God you will. So no more of that talk. *No more.* You understand me?" He did.

While in a Chicago booking office Jim ran into an old friend, Victor Kilian, a tall, long-faced comedian who was looking for a partner in an act he was creating. This constant partner-searching, partner-shedding process was endemic in vaudeville, resulting in some classic pairings, illustrated at its best by Gracie Allen and George Burns. Jim leaped at the opportunity to join Kilian, a skilled performer who in time was one of Hollywood's leading character actors. Again, and typically, an ad hoc comedy act with Jim dancing support was crafted, and Kilian, well known on vaudeville circuits, booked them straight through to New York.

It was Kilian who brought Cagney into the legitimate theater. When Kilian reached New York, he renewed contacts with old friends at the Provincetown Playhouse, who included Kenneth MacGowan, Eugene O'Neill, and Robert Edmond Jones, then casting the latest O'Neill play, *Desire Under the Elms.* Kilian told his three friends of the special talent Cagney possessed, and they sent him a notice about audition times for the play. Jim didn't want to go, having little interest in "straight acting," but since Kilian had taken such trouble, he went casually for an audition. There was no role for him in *Desire Under the Elms,* that grim New England rural tragedy, but director Kenneth MacGowan recognized Cagney's special quality and told him of an off-Broadway play he and his fellows would be producing next.

This project took shape in the coming months. It was a dramatization of novelist Jim Tully's autobiography, *Beggars of Life,* a look into the world of the hobo. It became *Outside Looking In,* by the soon-to-be-prestigious Maxwell Anderson, going into rehearsal in late July 1925. Like *Life with Father* years later, it offered great opportunity to red-haired actors, of whom, it seemed, there were few in New York at the time. Not only hair color but size mattered in the casting of the play. The two leading characters were named Oklahoma Red and Little Red, the former specified as big and burly, the latter as small and wiry. "You'd think Little Red was mine for the asking," said Jim. "But there was another small and wiry red-headed actor in New York, a talented one, Alan Bunce. I suspect I got the part because my hair was a bit redder than Alan's." Not so. Kenneth MacGowan chose Jim because of the vibrant quality of his acting and his tendency to remain concentrated in repose. One vital scene in the play demanded this.

For Oklahoma Red the producers cast another vibrant performer new to show business, Charles Bickford, and *Outside Looking In* was mostly his show. Burns Mantle's summary of the play in his *Best Plays of 1925–26* is to the point:

Cagney's first appearance in theatrical caricature—with Blyth Daly and Charles Bickford—in *Outside Looking In*, Greenwich Village Playhouse, 1925

Little Red, a hobo tramping the prairie country, meets and loves Edna, a youthful prostitute fleeing the law after having murdered her stepfather, who was her seducer. They run into a gang of hoboes dominated and led by Oklahoma Red. The hoboes organize a kangaroo court to try Little Red for being a "sissy." The court decrees he is unfit for hobo society and that he shall turn his woman over to the judge. Little Red fights off the gang, earns the admiration of Oklahoma Red and finally is helped to escape a sheriff's posse while the other hoboes go to jail.

The play opened on Monday evening, September 7, 1925, and won generally good reviews, the best going to Bickford, the next to Jim. Robert Benchley, drama critic of *Life,* the most sophisticated of New York critics, was unreserved in his praise of the two men:

You may object to *Outside Looking In* because the tramps use tramp language. If that is your objection, you needn't bother to make it because we shall be reading a book and won't even look up to acknowledge it. We know you and your ilk. . . . Which brings us to a statement of our reasons for liking *Outside Looking In.* It sounds true, in the first place. . . . It has drama in the second place.

We know that because we felt it. It has novelty in the third place, and that alone would make it for us. And in the fourth and a highly important place, it is as perfect a piece of casting in its two leading male roles as we have ever seen. Wherever Mr. MacGowan found two red-heads like Charles Bickford and James Cagney, who were evidently born to play Oklahoma Red and Little Red, he was guided by the Casting God. Mr. Bickford's characterization is the first most important one of the year . . . while Mr. Cagney, in a less spectacular role, makes a ten-minute silence during his mock-trial scene something that many a more established actor might watch with profit.

*The New Yorker* praised Bickford as being at times "gorgeously convincing" and at others as "almost circus clown in demeanor," while "Mr. Cagney is both plausible and less picaresque." The augustly humorous Percy Hammond of the *New York Herald Tribune* made the point that

if you are interested in mean, noble, cruel and witty vagabonds, there is a chance before [censorship] intervenes, to see one of them in *Outside Looking In.* Mr. Bickford as Oklahoma Red impersonates a frontier Villon, and he does it so well that you can renew your waning faith in the art of histrionism. He and Mr. James Cagney as his adversary, Little Red, do the most honest acting now to be seen in New York. I believe that Mr. [John] Barrymore's effective performance of *Hamlet* would be a mere feat of elocution if compared to the characterization of either Mr. Bickford or Mr. Cagney—both of whom are unknown.

*Outside Looking In* ran for only 113 performances because despite the discerning praise of the critics, enough was said of the play's hearty profanity to earn it the reputation of being a raunchy show. The short run was also partly due to half the newspaper critics coming to see the dress rehearsal and a number of them being put off by the heroine's detailed account of her father raping her. Maxwell Anderson, sensing their revulsion, hastily changed the script, and "my father" became "my stepfather" on opening night.

Jim and Willie were elated by the reviews, and she, more than he, felt that he had come into his own. Next, she said, was Broadway and stardom. His laughter in reaction was genuine, but that night as they went home to Yorkville on the subway, he pondered the idea briefly, then dismissed it. He said, "There were, as far as I knew, no Broadway stars five feet seven and a half inches in height. That, as far as I was concerned, settled the matter."

# 7 · Broadway

Counting on support from theatergoers who had read the Robert Bench-ley and Percy Hammond reviews, the producers of *Outside Looking In* moved the play a few weeks after it opened from the tiny 299-seat Greenwich Village Theatre at Seventh Avenue and Fourth Street to the capacious Thirty-ninth Street Theatre. More than half the actors had to be told to project their voices more strongly in this new venue. Jim had no such problem. He had at times compared his voice with a braying bull's, but he did need some vocal correction. Maxwell Anderson gathered his cast together in their new theater and emphasized that they must now speak twice as loud—"and twice as fast." He looked quickly at Jim. "Except you."

Transfer to the larger theater did not help ticket sales, and early in Jan-uary 1926 *Outside Looking In* closed. Jim said:

It was of course my first real experience in legitimate theater. And I was learning all the way, watching the more experienced actors particularly. I had already learned from great vaudevillians like Frank Fay the value of composure, and here in *Outside Looking In*, I got my second valuable lesson in acting. In rehearsal I particularly watched an experienced Irish actor—I think he was from the Abbey Theatre—named Barry McCollum, who played a crippled hobo. I noticed that Barry, with just a small role, nevertheless *lis-tened* to his fellow actors as they spoke, listened with great atten-tion. Then it occurred to me what he was doing. He was actually hearing everything being said *for the first time* each time. That really hit me. Of course that's what you have to do: listen to your fel-low actor just as you would in real life, hearing something for the first time. You just don't hear, waiting for your cue. You *listen*, liter-ally listen each time, as if it's the first time. I then applied that prin-ciple all the way through the play but particularly in the second act, when I was the subject of a kangaroo trial and had no lines at all for a long time.

This amplifies the reference in Robert Benchley's review to the way "Mr. Cagney . . . makes a ten-minute silence during his mock-trial scene something that many a more established actor might watch with profit." Among modern actors this is called "in the moment," the full engagement of the actor in attention to what the other actor is saying. It became a Cagney hallmark from *Outside Looking In* to his last film.

Lawrence Langner of the important production company, the Theatre Guild, saw *Outside Looking In* and was deeply impressed with Jim. He asked him to come down to the Guild for an interview, and this took place with some confusion on both sides. Langner thought Jim was anxious to become a Theatre Guild actor within a repertory framework, signing a contract for a variety of roles over a specified period of time. Jim thought he was being auditioned for a specific role Langner had in mind. When each finally realized the other's purpose, the meeting ended with a hearty handshake of farewell and good wishes. Privately Langner for the life of him couldn't understand how Cagney could turn down such a splendid opportunity. Jim, for his part, thought a Guild contract penal servitude at an insubstantial salary.

Jim was by now fully interested in acting as a profession but only as adjunct to his true calling: song and dance man. Although he had seen him only once on the stage, his idol was George M. Cohan, the song and dance man apotheosized, the kid with all the candy, the boyo who did it all: dance, sing (not well), write, compose, produce, and act. When Jim heard that Cohan was casting for the road company of one of his musicals, he went up to the casting agent, Chamberlain Brown, for an interview. By luck, Cohan was in the office and had a quick look at Jim. By ill luck, Cohan was in a fractious mood that day. Being a light-haired, short man, he tended to consider actors physically similar to himself unwitting Cohan mimics and cause for quick dismissal. In 1942, when *Yankee Doodle Dandy* was in production at Warner Brothers, Chamberlain Brown told Cohan he had rejected Cagney as a performer in 1926. "Goes to show you how smart I'm not," said Cohan.

Chamberlain Brown was able to do Jim a good turn, however: he brought him into contact with a talented sketch writer, Paul Girard Smith, who offered Jim and Willie a dance-comedy routine called *Lonesome Manor*, written on a percentage basis. It was ideal, said Jim, because "I was typecast as a city hick, a boy whose country was the city, and Willie was a hick hick, a girl whose city was the country." Willie fell in love with the act, which Jim describes in *Cagney by Cagney:*

The scene is Forty-third Street and Broadway, where the out-of-town papers are sold. I come on, and the newsboy asks me to hold down the stand for him while he goes to get a cup of coffee. When I'm alone, this little girl from Kokomo, Indiana (Willie), comes on, wants to buy the hometown newspaper. And the city hick, true to his city style, has to give her a nickname, so he says, "Well, Koke—tell you what to do." And such-like palaver with a cross-fire of jokes and then I sell her the paper, followed by both of us going into a dance—she singing "There's No Place Like Home" as her homesick counter-melody to my

> Oh, there's no doubt about it
> And I cannot live without it,
> So I simply want to shout it night and day;
> There's just one place to be
> And that's the place that's haunting me—
> > taunting me—
> And that's Broadway.
> Oh, a million lights, a million sights,
> A million ways to spend your nights.
> And when I die I surely want to go
> And join that gang below,
> For there'll be a bunch I know
> From old Broadway.

Then we wound up with a dance that got us off nicely.

With this act, called *Lonesome Manor*, the Cagneys were able to get better bookings than ever before. They were not yet a Palace act, nor would they ever be, but they were frequently on the bill with regulars from the Palace: Julius Tannen, Smith and Dale, Savoy and Brennan, and Bill Robinson. Jim stole dance steps from the latter and admired the comedic techniques of the former. "Incomparable people," he called them. "I'd laugh myself sick even though I'd seen them many times before: Smith and Dale and their malapropisms, Bert Savoy with his faggy way of punching a line, Julius Tannen and those great monologues with that sureness and control just like Frank Fay's. I loved those people. I wanted to *be* those people."

When asked whom he considered the greatest of all the performers he had ever seen, Cagney was emphatic:

Bert Williams. Not an actor in the usual sense, yet he was a *great* actor—who "just" sang funny songs. A quiet genius, and talk about control! He never made an unnecessary move or uttered a needless syllable. He was the greatest performer as far as Frank McHugh and I were concerned. Bert died an early death in 1922, and what a tragic loss. I saw him in the *Ziegfeld Follies* of 1919 on a pass, and I'll never forget it to my dying day. The stage lights dim, the great red plush curtains draw in, and the theater goes completely black. Then, almost like a shot—but it was totally silent—a white, white spot suddenly hits the curtain stage center. Four seconds of waiting, *just* enough to build up the proper suspense, and then out strolls Bert from behind the curtain, quiet, imperturbable. He looks at us with a gentle, quiet smile, bows to the orchestra leader, and says, "Professor, if you please." Then he sings his great songs, truly comic songs that make you howl with laughter and tear your heart out at the same time: "Nobody" and "I'm a Jonah Man" and "I'd Rather Have Nothin' All of the Time Than Somethin' for a Little While." Very funny and deeply sad underneath. For, as I've said, Bert Williams was a great actor, and that tragicomic mix I've never seen anyone do half so well. Also, once I saw him I was made aware for the very first time of the black man's plight in this country.

While the Cagneys were on the road with *Lonesome Manor,* a Broadway hit of some dimension opened, fittingly titled *Broadway,* a lively mix of melodrama, murder, and lovely girls, its dialogue all tarted up in the most recent slang. Alexander Woollcott hailed it as the play in 1926 "which most perfectly caught the accent of the city's voice, this play named after the great Midway itself, this taut and telling and tingling cartoon."

*Broadway*'s leading roles might have been written for the Cagneys. Roy, a streetwise song and dance man, in love with a country-bred girl named Billie [*sic*], finds she is also being sought by a charming but murderous boot-legger. Roy and Billie split up, several murders occur, and they are reunited, of all things, by love and their newly structured vaudeville-nightclub act. The prominent producer William A. Brady had first option on the play and, having seen Jim and Willie, had Jim in mind for the leading role. But the play's authors, Philip Dunning and George Abbott, fell victim to the beguiling talk of producer-director Jed Harris, who took over the show and gave the role of Roy to an excellent nondancing actor, Lee Tracy.

The authors themselves staged *Broadway* and, being competent professionals (director and stage manager), together with Harris's touch-up suggestions, produced what the not easily pleased Percy Hammond called "the most completely acted and perfectly directed show I have seen in thirty years of professional playgoing."

Inevitably Jim was bitterly disappointed with the casting. Lee Tracy, a year older than Jim, was in no wise a song and dance man, but he had made an auspicious Broadway debut two years before in *The Show-Off* and had a rollicking insouciance Jed Harris deemed vital for the play. The only dancing required of Roy was hoofing it off or into the playing area, and this Tracy did adequately. Jed Harris knew Cagney's ability, and when Jim came back from a *Lonesome Manor* tour, Harris asked him to audition for the role of Roy in the upcoming London production of *Broadway*. Phil Dunning, knowing Jim well from their *Every Sailor* days, told Harris that Jim was absolutely typecast as Roy. "He *is* the role," he told Harris. Jim got the role at a splendid three hundred dollars a week.

By the time rehearsals for London began, Jim had read the script carefully many times, had watched the show over and over, and knew that Roy was in his bones. He saw at once the key difference between his interpretation and Tracy's. The latter, who had a very ample quotient of charm, relied heavily on it to establish his character. Tracy had been told he had a winning smile, and he displayed it incessantly during the evening. His acting was solid, manly, thorough, but much of his Roy was personality display. Jim, while not averse to smiling geniality, conceived of Roy in realistic terms as an anxiety-ridden performer whose whole being, except for his love of Billie, was given over to the true vaudevillian's philosophy: get on, do it well, get off quickly.

During rehearsals for London he could see the specter of Tracy's performance hanging over his. Whenever he spoke certain lines or moved in the Cagney way, he was corrected. Harris and Abbott, either or both, would tell him to "do it the way Lee does, Jim." After a week of this, Jim realized Harris wanted a Tracy carbon copy, and he felt this to be egregiously wrong. "For one thing," said Jim, "although Lee was a good actor, he lounged around the stage, forever drooping himself over the furniture, and even when he was standing up, he hunched over, leaned on one foot, that kind of thing. Now, if there's one thing about dancers, they are proud of their stance. They don't droop about. Lee was the opposite of that. A little thing? No. Not when you're playing a dancer."

By dress rehearsal night, with Harris's constant nagging, Jim's nerves were in a frazzle. That night he was facing the most sophisticated audience in the world, his peers. On a night when most Broadway theaters were dark, Harris had invited the casts of those shows to see the London-bound company at work. Just before first curtain, Willie told Jim, "Do it your way, *your* way!" He did and got eight curtain calls from his discriminating audience. Harris was not pleased. Jim was overwhelmed in his dressing room after the show with congratulations from a wide range of actors and producers who, not knowing him, had no need to be anything but honest. Robert Montgomery, one day to become a Cagney confidant and partner, was typical of such people. He came to Jim and said, "Mr. Cagney, I'm just a beginner in this business, but if ever I get to be as skilled an actor as you, I'll be very proud."

There was just one more hurdle for Jim to clear before the company sailed to England. He was to play the lead for one evening on Broadway— on the night before they sailed. Nothing loath, even if apprehensive, Jim prepared to do so.

Ben Welden, longtime Hollywood actor and at this writing still hale at ninety-five, was a member of the original *Broadway* company and the assistant stage manager of the London-bound company. He remembers:

Jim was universally loved by the cast of *Broadway* for two good reasons. First, he had a big, big heart, and second, he was a superb dancer and actor, far better than Lee Tracy. Now, Roy Lane, the lead role in the show, was actually inspired by the life of a real song and dance man, a friend of *Broadway*'s author Phil Dunning, a guy named Roy Lloyd. Roy Lloyd was given a small part in the show. Then came Jim's being cast as Roy Lane in the London company, and we in the cast all loved that, and we loved his great performance in the dress rehearsal. And we were all waiting for him to play the lead in New York for just the one performance before sailing. The Cagneys had their luggage on the ship, all set to go, after Jim played the show on Broadway. Suddenly he was told that Roy Lloyd was going to play the Broadway performance. Not only that, but he was told—and this was just a few hours before sailing—that Roy Lloyd was going to play the lead in the London production. During a bon voyage party Jim was told this. He was directed to go over to Crosby Gaige's office, and did so with Willie. Gaige was a producer, the moneyman behind Jed Harris, and his office was where all the hiring and firing for Jed Harris shows was done. Harris didn't even have the guts to give Jim the bad news personally. He had Gaige do it. We, the cast of both shows, were of course absolutely stunned. Couldn't believe it. Neither could Jim.*

*Martin Gottfried in his *Jed Harris: The Curse of Genius* (1984) says *Broadway* stage manager Paul Streger told him Jim was given the bad news by Streger. Both Cagney and Ben Welden have testified to the contrary.

Neither, especially, could Willie. She looked angrily at Gaige and said, "I'd like to blow up your goddamned office." Jim wound up consoling her, but she refused to be. Jim had a run-of-the-play contract and was given a small role in the New York company, also, ironically, becoming Lee Tracy's understudy.

The psychological hurt to Jim was deep, devastating. It drained him of self-confidence. In his memoirs he makes light of it, but as the years went on, he faced that hurt more directly. He learned from his good friend Laurence Olivier what a consummate son of a bitch Jed Harris was. In his autobiography Olivier, who had worked for the man, calls Harris "the most hurtful, arrogant, venomous little fiend that anyone could meet . . . cruel, sadistic." Harris was indeed the villain of the piece, but there was another rotter involved whose identity Jim did not discover until his Warner Brothers days.

The *Broadway* company that went to London had success, playing for almost half a year. Roy Lloyd got respectable reviews, but not from Jim. In his not very objective view, Lloyd was "a skinny little man who couldn't dance, couldn't sing, couldn't do anything." Ben Welden, the assistant stage manager in London, had the job on arrival of posting the Cagneys' luggage back to them. Jim continued in *Broadway*, but the arrival of their luggage was to him emblematic of everything wrong with show business. He was, he told Willie, through. For good. He would go on to agriculture school.

Willie rebelled. She would, she told him, go to hell and back for him, and support him and his family while doing it, but he was not going to quit show business, on the penalty of her leaving him. She was especially appalled at the idea of his dancing talent going to waste. On reflection, she thought opening a dance school would be a good idea. She knew more about dancing than he, but in tap he was more skilled, and there was a demand for that training. Their combined incomes from *Broadway*—she had been hired as end of the chorus line—allowed them to open their school in Elizabeth, New Jersey, under one Gaelic form of Jim's name, the Cagné School of Dance.

They advertised in theater magazines, the first ad being "CAGNÉ SCHOOL OF THE THEATRE 60 Broad Street, Elizabeth, New Jersey Dancing and Acting by Prominent Professionals. Mr. Cagné has just completed staging of actor-managers, Grand Street Follies, Booth Theatre, New York." This printer's error raises a delicate image of incipient Beerbohm Trees and Henry Irvings in stately romp. It is actually a mangling of copy handed to the printer. The last sentence should read: "Mr. Cagné has just completed staging for The Actors-Managers Inc., *Grand Street Follies,* Booth Theatre, New York." The next advertisement, after the standard heading, was rather more inclusive: "Instruction in every phase of stage deportment. Acting— dramatic and comedie [*sic*]. Taught from the professional standpoint. Danc- ing of every description: Acrobatic Buck and Wing Eccentric Stylistic Under the personal direction of Mr. James Cagné and Miss Frances Vernon."

Near the school in Scotch Plains, New Jersey, was a single tax colony called Free Acres. Its founder, a socialist named Will Crawford, had been a Cagney acquaintance for three years, and Jim had helped his friend build the first log cabin in the colony. For some time Jim had been attracted to the principles of socialism; having lived in poverty much of his life, he was inevitably interested in any system that promised to abolish it. Moreover, Crawford was a kind and helpful friend. Now, in 1927, it was possible for friends of the colony to buy a simple but sturdy house for seven hundred dollars. All the houses at Free Acres shared in a single tax, and expenses were thus much lightened. The Cagneys bought one.

They loved their little house, and the teaching of dance was a joy. They had to scramble in the late afternoon from there to get to the Broadhurst Theatre in Manhattan, where *Broadway* was playing, and it was not easy to get back to Scotch Plains. The journey involved subway, ferry, and train, fol- lowed by a two-and-a-half-mile walk up a hill. "But we were young, and we figured it was good for us," said Willie. "We loved not only to dance but to teach dance because teaching always makes you a better performer. I know it worked that way for Jim, who enjoyed showing the process to the young- sters. I give that dancing school of ours a lot of credit for giving him that knowledge and sureness in his craft that he possessed."

After *Broadway*'s closing, Jim's friend William A. Brady called him in for a juvenile role in Daniel Rubin's play *Women Go On Forever,* which Burns Mantle called "a tough, rough drama of the cheaper boarding houses," in which its star, well-known farceuse Mary Boland, "fights fate, her boarders and her passions for thirty-six hours." Jim played, in his words, "a tough kid," which he admitted was not awfully hard for him to do. "But I learned some- thing from that play. Here was good old Mary Boland, who had played nothing but silly, vain old women all her life, trying a serious role. Same kind of bind I was going to get in at Warner Brothers. I had a hell of a time getting out of that bind. Same with dear old Mary. She tried hard, too hard, in this play. The result was that her trying too hard made her funny all over again."

It was at this time that Jim met and took to his heart two of the three closest friends of his life, Pat O'Brien and Frank McHugh. Pat met Jim by the very simple expedient of introducing himself. He had seen him in *Out-side Looking In* and was greatly moved by his acting, and when he saw him again in *Women Go On Forever,* he went backstage to compliment him. "I'm from Milwaukee, Mr. Cagney—"

"Jim. It's always Jim."

He liked Pat on sight, and so began a loving friendship that lasted till O'Brien's death, which Willie did not reveal to Jim until after he had recovered from a health problem.

"How typical of Pat, that coming backstage to tell a perfect stranger how much he liked the performance," said Jim. "Typical extrovert that he was—the exact opposite of me—and such a giving, warmhearted guy. Just like Frank."

Jim met Frank McHugh in 1928 at a Lambs Club Gambol at the Hudson Theatre when Frank, acting as a balcony usher, was suffering, in his words, "a brutal hangover." Frank's friendship with Jim was to last as long as O'Brien's and was of the same texture. "Irish actors are all made out of the same fun-loving stuff," said Frank. "Jim, Pat, and I—were I asked what kept us together for so long—had one quality we got from our ancestors, a love of storytelling, and I mean by storytelling *the telling of stories.* Not jokes. Anyone can tell jokes, and they are usually pretty boring affairs. But stories about real people, or people who ought to be real, they are the greatest and funniest things you can hear." Of the trio, McHugh was the funniest, closely followed by O'Brien.

Brigid O'Brien, Pat's daughter, remembers the occasions when Jim, Pat, and Frank got together at their house: "When those three were together, you never heard such laughter. Unending. They delighted in each other's company because those stories brought such happiness. Jim was himself a master storyteller, of course, but I know he would agree that no one could top Frank and Dad. Jim was their greatest audience, sitting there hooting with laughter and now and then unashamedly weeping at one of Dad's sentimental stories. The love of those three men for each other was like a great story itself."

*Women Go On Forever* ran fourteen weeks, and near its end an old Lenox Hill Settlement House friend told Jim that the Neighborhood Playhouse, a theater group connected with the Henry Street Settlement House, needed a choreographer for the current edition of its annual satirical revue, *The Grand Street Follies.* The *Follies* had no stars, but it rejoiced in the abilities of two brilliant mimics, Albert Carroll and Dorothy Sands. The *Follies* parodied every kind of Broadway and off-Broadway show, every style of theater and performance. Born in 1922, the *Follies,* in annual productions, moved from its settlement house setting to Broadway in 1927 and ended in 1929.

Jim was in the last two shows, the 1928 and 1929 versions, choreographing the principal numbers and acting in the sketches. In the 1928 edition at the Booth Theatre he effectively combined tap with tango in a number billed unsurprisingly as "From Tango to Taps," with Sophia Delza, and played in a musical burlesque of Max Reinhardt's production of *Romeo and Juliet,* in which he played Tybalt as danced by vaudeville star Harland

With Sophia Delza doing a tango in *The Grand Street Follies* of 1928

Dixon. The critics appreciated *The Grand Street Follies* of 1928, and it ran for several months. When it closed, Jim went on to summer stock in Massachusetts and Ohio. He returned for *The Grand Street Follies* of 1929, again at the Booth Theatre, but this time as performer only. He sang, danced, and acted in numbers satirizing the commedia dell'arte, the siege of Troy, Paul Revere's ride, the Garden of Eden, and Caesar's invasion of Britain as seen musically through the eyes of Noël Coward. It ran only fifty-three performances.

So busy had Jim become that the dancing school could not survive. Willie could not run it alone, and she did not fancy hiring staff. In any event she had decided she would work full-time in supporting Jim's career, becoming his unofficial agent. Her career was over. "For a while there," she said, "I thought of us as a kind of song and dance Lunt and Fontanne. But I was a shortie, and he was a shortie, and I think we'd have ended up as a sideshow act. The fact is, he was the real stuff, I wasn't. I mean, the stuff of stardom."

George Kelly had always been one of Jim's favorite playwrights. He loved Kelly's wonderfully natural dialogue and cogent characterizations. Now he read in *Variety* that Kelly was casting his new play, *Maggie the Magnificent*, at the Cort Theatre, and Jim was there on the day with fifty other young actors waiting for entry to the auditioning. Suddenly the door opened, and *Maggie's* stage manager leaned out and yelled, "Hey, Red!" as he pointed to Jim.

"Who, *me*?"

"*You.*"

Jim walked in, read a few lines from the script for the aristocratic Kelly, and was told to report for rehearsal next day. After a week of rehearsal Jim summoned up enough nerve to ask the playwright why he had been called in.

"I looked out through the stage door," said Kelly, "saw you in that crowd of waiting actors, and asked that you be sent in directly. Physically you seemed just what I was looking for: a fresh mutt. That is the essence of the role you are playing, Elwood." Jim was happy to have the job and all its bonuses, one of which was the girl acting opposite him, Joan Blondell.

Blondell, playing the role she played most frequently in her career—the wisecracking, nonchalant tootsie—became a close friend of the Cagneys'. She was a "great taker of direction," said Jim, "and she could have done many better things than the roles they gave her. Kelly told me that if she hadn't *looked* like a tootsie, she'd have made a great Lady Macbeth. He called her the 'undiscovered country,' and I think he was right."

Opening night of *Maggie the Magnificent,* a rather pallid play about a young woman's continuing troubles with her mother, Joan had a scene with Jim in which she walked about the stage as he followed her, arguing angrily. As he did so, he had to fight a strong temptation to laugh, and Kelly, in the audience, could see this. After the show Jim hurried up to Kelly and said, "I'm so sorry. I know you could see that I was about to break up, but do please come backstage tomorrow and watch Joan's backside from the rear window of the set and see what I see." Kelly did, and promptly broke up.

Blondell, whom Jim always described as having the most beautiful ass in Christendom, was wearing a tight black silk dress. As she walked around the stage, and visible only to anyone onstage, her lovely buttocks reflected upper stage lights so that two giant owl eyes stared at Jim as he followed her. Kelly corrected the lighting, apologizing to Jim for "taking away your fun."

The critics tried to be kind to *Maggie the Magnificent,* but it was tough sledding. Kelly, perhaps the best writer of women's dialogue in the American theater, was here not very good in plot. *Theatre Arts Monthly* called the writing "true" but lacking "the saving grace of arousing interest." All the critics conceded that Cagney and Blondell were the liveliest aspects of a thin drama. Brooks Atkinson of the *Times* spoke approvingly of "the scapegrace son played with clarity and spirit by James Cagney." Robert Benchley, although admiring Blondell, said her performance "was marred for me by the [Kelly] direction which made her keep her hand on her hip throughout. It is very seldom Mr. Kelly goes as bad as that." Benchley praised Cagney's playing, pointing out that "unless I am greatly mistaken, I once detected evidences of authoritative comedy in [his] tap-dancing in one of the smaller revues," a very prescient remark. Cagney's dancing was to grow increasingly spirited and comedic as his career unfolded.

*Maggie the Magnificent* ran less than a month, and both Jim and Joan were fortunate that William Keighley, director of an upcoming Broadway play, *Penny Arcade,* saw them in the last performance. "Manna from heaven," Keighley told Jim later. "I was looking for an attractive yet tough young cookie and a strong, beautiful broad, and here were you and Joanie on that stage, the living, breathing counterparts of the two I needed for *Penny Arcade.*"

*Penny Arcade* opened at the Fulton Theatre on March 11, 1930. Jim played Harry, the spoiled-rotten son of Ma Delano, proprietor of the penny arcade in a Coney Island–type amusement park. Harry usurps the bootlegging territory of a local tough during the latter's absence in prison, and on his return to freedom he is gunned down by Harry. Harry's sister sees the

With Frank Rowan in
*Penny Arcade,* 1930

killing, keeps her secret until Ma Delano tries to pin the murder on Sis's boyfriend. Sis tells the truth to the police, and Harry is hauled off to jail.

The dramatic highlight of *Penny Arcade* is Harry's confession to Ma that he has killed his bootlegger rival. Alternately sobbing and whining, the actor has not only to make this palatable to the audience but to win a degree of compassion for the boy who has been so badly spoiled by his indulgent mother. Jim accomplished this by the simple expedient of imagining Ma Delano as being what in fact she was: the opposite of Carrie Cagney. It gave him what he called "the boost" to reach the emotional heights needed in the scene. He would scorn calling this Method acting, the form in which the actor uses emotional experiences from his personal life to invigorate his performance. What Cagney did was purely to imagine a woman the opposite of his mother and play to her. However he did it, he did it powerfully.

One of the New York critics, Perriton Maxwell, said, "Cagney's confession of his crime to his mother stands out as the high point of the play." Brooks Atkinson added his praise, and one visitor to the play's opening night, Al Jolson, was also impressed. He liked Cagney and Blondell, but he was thinking more of the play as a suitable vehicle for his pals, Warner Brothers, just then adventuring into sound films with exciting backgrounds.

Jolson took an option on the film rights to *Penny Arcade* and, in selling the rights to Warner Brothers, urged Jack Warner to see the play before it closed, not only to assess its potential as a sound movie but also to judge the remarkable talents of James Cagney and Joan Blondell. Warner came and was convinced. He also went to a nearby theater, the Ritz, to see a play produced by an old friend, George Jessel. The play was *This Man's Town,* which had opened the same night as *Penny Arcade,* starring Pat O'Brien. Warner quickly signed Blondell, Cagney, and O'Brien to short-term contracts. *This Man's Town* and *Penny Arcade* quickly folded because of lukewarm reviews, but Jack Warner had a fondness for the latter play. It was to become James Cagney's first film.

# 8 · Warner Brothers

Jack L. Warner (1892–1978) fancied himself head of a quartet of brothers—Harry (1881–1958), Albert (1884–1967), Sam (1888–1927)—who came to Hollywood in 1915 from Pennsylvania to open film exchanges and their own movie studio. Their Russian émigré father instilled in them early the need for maintaining solid business principles, and they adhered to these rigorously, mostly under the guidance of Harry, whose seniority and sound commercial instincts inevitably made him president of Warner Brothers from its inception.

Jack resented this, even though he had the key job of making the films that were their product. Likable but personally crude, he fancied himself a wit. He wasn't one. On meeting Mme. Chiang Kai-shek, he apologized for not having any laundry to give her and wondered why she failed to laugh. He lied much of his way through life on the grounds that this was a necessary element of good business. Harry remained in New York as head of the corporation. Brothers Sam and Albert came to California to help Jack make films. Sam was in charge of the technical end of production—studios, equipment, and personnel. So engrossed was Sam with Warner Brothers' transition from silent to sound films that his supervision of its subsidiary Vitaphone's sound process cost him his life. In preparing the studio's first sound film, *The Jazz Singer*, Sam worked night and day and into such a state of exhaustion that he could not fight off pneumonia. He died the night before *The Jazz Singer* opened to enthusiastic reviews and the first great upsurge in the company's fortunes.

This left Jack Warner all the more firmly in the driver's seat at the studio. Brother Albert had none of Jack's push, and brother Harry had settled down firmly in New York to run the financial end. He and Jack had begun, ever so subtly, a management rivalry.

Jack had the astuteness to see that he could not make pictures without the help of a bright and skilled producer, a man he found in the person of Darryl F. Zanuck. Warners films became *sui generis* because, says Warners historian Clive Hirschhorn, the studio eschewed "the shimmery surface gloss of the films being made at MGM and the Continental sophistication that Paramount was peddling. Warner Brothers concentrated on realism. Its product echoed the headlines of the day, and its basic concern was for society's losers . . . it became known as the working man's studio . . . [reflecting] the harshness of the Depression." In effect, a studio where types like Cagney and Blondell would feel at home. Jim had been signed for a three-week contract at five hundred dollars a week plus transportation. Blondell received a bit less. They made their separate ways to Hollywood, Willie remaining in New York. At the studio the two new contractees were met by the director of *Penny Arcade*—now senselessly retitled *Sinner's Holiday*— John G. Adolfi, an actor-director who thought they had the dynamism to play the leading roles instead of the ones they had played on Broadway. But Darryl Zanuck, who had rewritten Marie Baumer's play into something more cinematic, disagreed, insisting that Cagney and Blondell play their former roles as the weakling son and the floozy girlfriend.

*Sinner's Holiday* retains the original plot of *Penny Arcade*, the weakling son as a murderer protected by his tough old mother, Ma Delano (strongly played by Lucille La Verne, who went on to speak the role of the wicked Queen in Disney's *Snow White and the Seven Dwarfs*). Ma shifts the blame to the hero, whom she dislikes, until her daughter, engaged to the hero, reveals her brother as the murderer. The film's heart is the mother-son love, and some of the dialogue is rather Oedipal, innocently. When his guilt is revealed, Cagney grows philosophic about his ma's attempt to aid him: "A good try. Forget it, old sweetheart. [*She sobs.*] You aren't going to quit me now, are you? Don't cry. You know I love you, don't you? I'll be back." Whereupon he kisses dear old Ma on the lips. Jim was able to bring himself to do this as an actor, but one line written by Zanuck he resolutely refused to say: "I'm your baby, aren't I?" The director insisted he speak it. Jim was adamant. The line was cut.

James Cagney's entrance scene to the world of movies is prototypical: rising gracefully from a chair and nonchalantly putting on a skimmer. He handles the hat with a casual elegance that, for him, was far from casual. Every movement he made in films was, if not choreographed, at least made with an awareness of line, a movement that had beginning, progression, and end, always in a smooth flow, even when jagged, as in the times when he played drunks.

*Sinner's Holiday*

Also, in his very first film he reveals the power and extent of his emotional thrust. Just before he murders the obnoxious bootlegger he works for (Warren Hymer, in an uncharacteristic serious role), Cagney, afraid of the gun his opponent holds, pulls a weapon of his own and, with quavering voice, says he has a gun and shoots. In this exchange, lasting not more than three seconds, he almost simultaneously expresses fear, anxiety, defiance, and incredulity. It is an acting tour de force one would expect of a veteran actor, not from a young song and dance man recently come to acting.

Slightly less than an hour in length, *Sinner's Holiday* still manages to tell "its little story compactly and credibly," said *Time* magazine, adding that "it is less a picture of action than of character, made so by the skill of Lucille La Verne and James Cagney." Mordaunt Hall of *The New York Times* praised the film generally, and its cast, "but the most impressive acting is done by James Cagney in the role of Harry Delano. His fretful tenseness is conveyed with sincerity."

Darryl Zanuck and Jack Warner quickly realized the worth of their three-week contract player. They extended his contract by three more weeks while trying to decide on a long-term contract. In the meantime they wanted

*Sinner's Holiday*

to get as much out of him as possible. *Sinner's Holiday* had been shot in two weeks, and a film called *Doorway to Hell*, already in production, became the next Cagney vehicle. Warners had begun its cycle of headline-oriented films with particular attention to the lives of leading American gangsters.

*Doorway to Hell* was preeminently one such, and for the role of gang lord Louis Ricarno, Zanuck cast the then widely popular Lew Ayres, barely twenty-two, handsome, and supremely clean-cut. This casting might have made some sense if Louis had been tagged "Baby Face" in the film. The viewer is asked to believe that this Boy Scout counselor is a much-feared czar of the underworld, so dreaded and respected indeed that gangs all over town congregate at his bidding to accept his control over them. They do, heartily, with the exception of a rat named Rocco. Within an extraordinary short time, Louis gives up his empire to go straight and retire to Florida with his new bride, Doris (played by a colorless actress, Dorothy Mathews), who is really in love with Mileway, Louis's chief lieutenant and pal, played by Cagney. Doris and Mileway are former, and perhaps current, lovers, and her reasons for marrying Louis—outside of his spectacular looks and huge fortune—are quite unclear. Mileway has been given Louis's fiefdom but is unable to control the internecine battles between the disparate mobs.

To get Louis back in the fray and control things, the ratlike Rocco inadvertently causes the death of Louis's little brother, and on Louis's return Mileway confesses himself out of the fray to the police and into jail. Louis is killed, and Warner Brothers gives us an uncomfortable coda in the form of a solemn epilogue assuring us that the gangster's way is a dreadful way and that the "doorway to hell is a one-way door."

In all this fuss Cagney has virtually nothing to do but stand around and observe. In hindsight he should have been cast as Louis, but production had begun before he was brought in—and after his memorable performance in *All Quiet on the Western Front*, Ayres was at the moment a "name" actor. In fact he was a most capable actor, and it is a tribute to his talent that not one reviewer remarked on his physical inappropriateness for the role of a domineering gangster and Cagney's appositeness for it. Nothing Cagney does as an actor is without interest, but one is hard put to find him very engaging in this part. There is a flash of gracefulness in one moment when he kisses the heroine. Fingers tightly together, his hand is slightly curved while he lifts her chin, as if it were a flower to sniff and admire.

After some days in Hollywood Jim's first impression of the town was that it was no different from any ordinary vaudeville stop, though the weather was

*Doorway to Hell*

nicer. It seemed just another place to hole up for a while and do another show. The money was excellent, and he happily signed a contract for one year, beginning June 23, 1930, at four hundred dollars a week, with options for his renewal of employment for six years following. He understood that Warners could drop him at the end of every year, but since show business was essentially a crapshoot anyway, this didn't bother him unduly.

His first task was getting Willie out to join him. He asked her to sell the house at Scotch Plains and was considerably distressed to hear that it had already been sold by an actor friend who had been leasing the place from them. This thievery was possible under the single tax structure of the colony and its semisocialist framework. It was also the beginning, the very faint beginning, of Jim's slow-growing disenchantment with liberalism. He had deep sympathy for the growing labor movement, markedly so as he began to observe working conditions at the studio. Directors of the films thought nothing of requiring actors and crews to work twelve hours a day seven days a week. Most directors knew that Jack Warner prized those who could turn out a picture in record time, and a number of these men vied with one another in this way, hoping to finish a film well before Warners' suggested deadline.

At first Jim didn't mind the extra work because he was living alone, and he wasn't a man for nightclubs. But when Willie arrived and they took possession of an apartment on Hayworth Avenue in West Hollywood, his attitude to overtime changed. The concept of pay for overtime was unborn, and Jim came to realize that he, like all studio personnel below the executive level, was in a form of servitude. He began to talk with fellow actors about this, and discontent spread.

One of these actors was Grant Withers, a tall and commanding leading-man type, who had played the hero in *Sinner's Holiday*. Withers regarded Jim as "an interesting little guy" and loved to listen to his stories of New York theatrical life. When the two of them began work on the third Cagney film, *Other Men's Women*, Withers took Jim under his wing, or tried to. He understood why his little pal was not a nightclubber, what with his wife newly come to town, but according to Withers, Jim was doing himself a disservice by not "being around." He explained patiently to his new friend that being around or at least being seen around was a vital part of the business. "Around" he defined as restaurants popular within the profession, the racetrack, studio parties, and the prizefights. "That's how they get to know you," urged Withers.

"I really would rather stay unknown then," Jim told him. "If my work doesn't make me known, to hell with being around." Withers was baffled.

*Other Men's Women* rejoiced in Joan Blondell's presence. She had taken to Hollywood rather better than Jim and saw a continuing future there. "And, God, the weather here," she told Willie. "How can you beat that? Good weather, and a decent paycheck. If only they didn't overwork us."

In *Other Men's Women* Jim plays a railroad gang foreman, almost an extra, with only one memorable line, an unconsciously comic one: "Jack will be all right after he gets used to the idea of being blind." Jim wondered if the studio realized that by giving him roles of this kind, it was not getting its money's worth. Then, luckily, he caught the eye of Warners' biggest star at the time, George Arliss. In his autobiography Arliss speaks of interviewing more than seventy contract players for his forthcoming film, *The Millionaire*:

> Just now and then I can feel sure of my man by one brief interview in the casting office. There was a small but important part in *The Millionaire*, the part of an insurance agent. The scene was entirely with me and was the turning point in the story. I knew it depended largely on the actor of this small part whether my change of mental attitudes would appear convincing. I saw several promising young

men without being much impressed one way or another, but there was one more waiting to be seen. He was a lithe, smallish man. I knew at once he was right. As I talked to him I was sure he could give me everything I wanted. He wasn't acting to me now. He wasn't trying to impress me. He was just being natural, and I thought, a trifle independent for a bit actor. There was a suggestion of here-I-am-take-me-or-leave-me, and hurry up. As I came to my decision, I remember saying, "Let him come just as he is. Those clothes and no makeup stuff. Just as he is." The man was James Cagney. I was lucky.

It is instructive in this little six-minute scene from *The Millionaire* to observe the past and future of twentieth-century acting: Arliss of the old artistic school of Beerbohm Tree and Henry Irving, cool, courtly, his voice taut with the faint ring of the elocutionist, controlled; then Cagney, controlled but in quite a different way—coiled steel set to spring, casual in tone, and quicker and more natural in speech pattern than Warners' then most prestigious actor, a man his senior by thirty years, yet both excellent of their kind. Arliss plays a just retired tycoon unhappy with his inactivity.

*Other Men's Women*

He wanders out into his garden and in self-directed anger knocks his outdoor furniture about. As an acting performance all this is done in carefully measured fury. It is *well* done, but it is anger premeasured and well cut—much too well cut.

Cagney, a brisk young insurance salesman, appears and in a charming comic scene tries to sell the old man life and accident insurance:

CAGNEY: You've got plenty of life insurance, I've no doubt. But not enough. Mr. Alden, you're a young man yet. Running what business?

ARLISS: I'm not running any business. I'm retired.

CAGNEY: Retired? Oh. *Oh.* I wasn't aware of that. Well—never mind life. What about accident?

When Arliss asks why not life, Cagney responds that they don't insist on life "when they're retired." In this scene Arliss is galvanized into coming out of retirement by taking Cagney's advice to begin a small business, an enterprise on which rests the prime plot of the film. Cagney conveys the ultimate sureness of the born insurance salesmen, who are also born actors. His cheerfully intense concentration is gently and quietly comic. It is alpha to the omega of his psychotic-killer roles and proof, if any be needed, that Cagney was as versatile as any actor in screen history.

That versatility was never more marked than in the contrast between this comic role and his next, the murderous Tom Powers in *The Public Enemy.* William A. Wellman, who had directed Cagney in *Other Men's Women,* was assigned to direct a new Warners film in the tradition of its newly set crime-headlines–to–life pictures, *Doorway to Hell* and *Little Caesar. The Public Enemy* was the dramatization of the novel *Beer and Blood* by two Chicagoans, John Bright and Kubec Glasmon, who knew their gangster-infested town well.

The story is both simple and sociologically penetrating, revealing a plague of the twenties, when Prohibition left an ugly scar on the land. Tom Powers (Cagney) and his pal Matt Doyle (Edward Woods) from their childhood as petty thieves grow up to be rum-running hoodlums who experience the high life before being killed, Matt in gang warfare, Tom in avenging his death. Eddie Woods, a pleasantly voiced actor of genteel background, had originally been cast as Tom, the leading role, but director Wellman and writers Bright and Glasmon came to realize that Woods had none of the gutter quality Cagney so patently possessed, and they protested the casting to Darryl Zanuck. Zanuck liked Woods but more than that appreciated the fact that the young man was affianced to the daughter of Louella Parsons, the powerful Hollywood columnist and female satrap of William Randolph

*The Millionaire,* with George Arliss

Hearst. However, Wellman and the writers stuck to their guns, and Cagney was cast as Tom.

The last scene in the film is perhaps its most memorable. Tom is in the hospital with severe wounds from the gang warfare, but a phone call to his family says he is on his way home. As they excitedly prepare the house for reunion, the doorbell rings. Tom's brother eagerly opens the front door, and Tom, in blood-soaked bandages, trussed up like a mummy, falls into the room, dead. The film ends.

Cagney presented this human ferret as such people truly are: amoral, instinctively vengeful, and without a shred of compassion. Dwight Macdonald, *Esquire*'s caustic film critic, defined this dazzling feat of acting: "Tom Powers is a human wolf, with the heartlessness and grace and innocence of an animal, as incapable of hypocrisy as of feeling; the smiling unreflective delight with which he commits mayhem makes Humphrey Bogart look like a conscience-stricken Hamlet. . . ." As for the director's contribution: "Wellman uses Cagney with subtlety, keeping him in the background much of the time while secondary characters occupy the foreground. (This development of secondary characters is usually a sign of a good movie.) So it is all the more powerful when Cagney moves up into the foreground at the big moments; our taste for this extraordinary actor has not been blunted by seeing too much of him."

As for Tom Powers, Jim said:

He was at heart based on a man I knew in Yorkville—not the character but the way I played him. This was Jack "Dirty Neck" Lafferty, a pal of my dad's. Youngish, but from childhood had white hair. Jack was lots of fun, could tell great stories, and then suddenly would become very morose, and I don't think he ever knew why. One time Pop asked him why, and Jack said, "I don't know why, Steam. Sometimes I feel very strange, like I want to kill somebody."

Pop said, "Ah, come on."

But Jack said, "No, I believe it. Someday I'm going to kill someone. I feel it. I know it."

The "someday" came when Jack stole a car, the owner jumped on the running board, and Jack blasted him off with a thirty-eight.

I saw Jack when our team played up at Sing Sing, and I think he just never knew what life was all about. Just change the adjective in "Ah, Sweet Mystery of Life" to "Damned." There are just some people who, for whatever reason, are damned souls, and Jack was one. I played Tom as a kind of tribute to Jack, but without his sense of humor. No time to do that.

It was the playwright Robert Sherwood who first noticed a Cagney singularity, that this actor could play a rotten human being yet elicit sympathy for him: "I doubt there is an actor extant who could have done what James Cagney does with the extraordinary character of Tom Powers. It is a performance to cheer for. . . . He does not hesitate to represent Tom Powers as a complete rat—with a rat's sense of honor, a rat's capacity for human love; and when cornered, a rat's fighting courage. And what is more, although his role is consistently unsympathetic, Mr. Cagney manages to earn for Tom Powers the audience's affection and esteem." This was the characterization, said Kenneth Tynan decades later, that "abolished both the convention of the pure hero and that of approximate equipoise between vice and virtue."

*The Public Enemy* is too well known for extended analysis, but its grapefruit scene is worth recalling as the progenitor of the sadism flavored by fun that became a staple of many gangster and lowlife films extending to this day. The scene derives from real life when a Chicago gangster named Hymie Weiss rubbed an omelet in his moll's face. Realizing how messy this could get, the authors of *The Public Enemy* changed the omelet

*The Public Enemy*
ABOVE: With Mae Clarke
BELOW: With Jean Harlow

*The Public Enemy,* with Edward Woods

to a grapefruit half. No scene like it had ever been offered in a film any-where, and it was both astringently funny and shocking. Tom, in the throes of a hangover, grows irritated at his mistress's fussy ministrations. His surliness to her provokes her martyred comment "Maybe you got someone you like better." With that, Cagney picks up the half grapefruit and twists it in her face.

There are varying accounts of the way this famous scene was shot. Mae Clarke, in an article for *American Classic Screen* in 1983, said that following the Glasmon-Bright script, the scene was shot with Cagney *throwing* the half grapefruit in her face and striding out. This, avers Clarke, was actually shot. Then Cagney and Wellman got together, discussed how the scene could be bettered, and asked Mae if they could do it again but this time with Cagney rubbing the grapefruit in her face. Would she mind? Yes, she said, she would, but she was willing to do it on the proviso that it be done only once, and there would be no retake. Agreed, and done.

Another version of the making of the scene comes from the film's co-author John Bright, as quoted in Patrick McGilligan's *Cagney: The Actor as Auteur* (1982). Bright claims to have been there during the scene's setup and shooting. He says the sequence was: Mae Clarke arrived to do the scene with a head cold and sore nose. She asked Cagney to fake the grapefruit push in deference to her sore nose. He agreed and in turn asked the cameraman to work a camera angle so it would only look as if he had pushed the grapefruit into her face. Director Wellman overheard this and angrily told Cagney that this, the best scene in the picture, a scene that would make him world-famous, had to be done full blast. Cagney thought it over, realized Wellman was right, and did it full out. After the shot Clarke, outraged and feeling betrayed, hit Cagney, called him an Irish son of a bitch, denounced Wellman as a bastard, and, turning to Bright, said, "You too, you goddamn writer!" She then left the set in high dudgeon.

Two versions from highly authoritative sources. Reader's choice.*

*The Public Enemy* had its quotient of real danger for Cagney. He recalled in *Cagney by Cagney:*

The picture had its hazards, among them real bullets. This was before the special effects boys learned how to make "exploding" bullets safe as cap guns. At the time, Warners employed a man named Bailey who had been a machine gunner in World War I, and this boy knew how to make that instrument perform. He sat with the machine gun on a platform above as I skittered along behind a "stone" wall. Seconds after I did this, Bailey opened up on the edge of the wall. It crumbled to sawdust, and so would I, had I been there two seconds before.

Cagney was to remember this incident a few pictures later.

Cagney began a career-long habit in *The Public Enemy* of adding what he called touches or goodies to his work, small bits of business that didn't alter the script and usually enhanced the uniqueness of his characterization. An instance occurs in the film when Tom enters their social club with Matt. He was directed to wave as he came in. What he does is simplicity itself but is arresting and sharply in character. He pushes his cap forward on his head in a gesture of assertiveness, then waves, but the wave is blended with his

*Mae amplifies her story in the recently published *Featured Player: An Oral Autobiography of Mae Clarke,* ed. by James Curtis, Scarecrow Press, 1996. She repeats her previous account but in more interesting (and convincing) detail. She seems to have heard of the Bright version, at least in part, and condemns it, particularly the cursing. "I don't talk that way," she says.

hand slipping by the tip of his nose to become almost the cocking of his snook. To blend imperceptibly a geniality with a thumb to the nose is subtle declaration of Tom's aggressively humorous independence.

The second touch occurs midway through the film, when, in an action most, if not all, of his audience had experienced, he reaches down his back, inside his pajama top, to scratch himself and finds his hand just slightly short of the spot he's trying to get at. He cannot reach it, and his frustration is palpable. Cagney does this unobtrusively at a moment in the movie when he must express dissatisfaction. This slight but common and potent irritation intensifies his unsettledness. We share it.

Director Wellman had great faith in Cagney's creativity, even allowing him to alter dialogue when he found it wanting. In the grapefruit scene Kitty, after turning down Tom's request for a drink, fondly agrees to get one for him:

KITTY: Yes, Tom. But I wish . . .

TOM: You're always wishin'. You got the gimmes for fair! I'm gonna get you a bag of peanuts.

Cagney altered this to the infinitely more pungent:

There you go with that wishin' stuff again. I wish you was a wishin' well—so that I could tie a bucket to you and sink you.*

*The Public Enemy* was enthusiastically received by critics and the public, but censorship boards in various states demanded some cuts, as did similar agencies abroad. What the film did for James Cagney was to make him a movie star of the first constellation. He was happily made aware of his increased fame at the same time that he came to realize that his seven-year contract was totally inadequate in salary. *The Public Enemy* was a box-office hit, and, said Jim, "I suddenly realized I was a star without a star's money." His agent, William Morris, complained to the studio. No response. Jim changed agents, and his new man, George Frank, went directly to Darryl Zanuck, and a heated dispute over money developed. Frank's argument was that *The Public Enemy* cost $151,000 and was currently making more than a million dollars at the box office with more to come.

While waiting, Jim made two more films, the first a slight but cheery effort, *Smart Money,* in which he played the pal of and second fiddle to Edward G. Robinson, the only time these superlative actors were ever paired. "I was playing pals that year and the year before," said Jim. "People

*The original script and emendations of *The Public Enemy* can be found in an edition by Henry Cohen (University of Wisconsin Press, 1981).

*Smart Money*
With Edward G. Robinson
and Noel Francis

*Blonde Crazy*

don't pay to see sidekicks." He then went on to make *Blonde Crazy*, a string of high improbabilities with *his* old sidekick, Joan Blondell.

Cagney, with Joan as his doxy, is a con man of high skills who wins, loses, and wins her. *Blonde Crazy* is suffused with that easily used, virtually indefinable word "charm." It shows Cagney and Blondell at their comedic best, perfect foils for each other. In Molly Haskell's words, "Blondell's beauty as a 'broad' is that she can outsmart the man without unsexing him, Cagney's beauty as a male that he can be made a fool of without becoming a fool."

Cagney's skill as a light comedian is here triumphant, a Cary Grant years before Cary Grant was Cary Grant, and this is all the more remarkable in that the film was shot scant weeks after Tom Powers met his messy, warranted end. In *Blonde Crazy* Cagney carries off—without embarrassment to anyone, let alone himself—the spectacle of himself holding Joan's extra panties against his middle and using one of her bras as eye blinders. To ridicule Joan's new boyfriend who adores poetry, Cagney reads a few lines of Browning to Joan in high affectation, ending with a high cackle of satirical laughter. He says, "Now, honey, I *ask* you," giving an effeminate sweep of his hair with his hand.

"Why, I think it's lovely," Joan says.

Cagney answers, "He may be a poet to you, but he's a peasant to me."

On completing *Blonde Crazy*, Jim needed only to read *Variety* to realize that the grosses from *The Public Enemy* made it a hit of the first order. The reviews of *Blonde Crazy* were enthusiastic, and he felt he had early come to a fork in the road of his career. He could continue making considerably less than he was worth to Warner Brothers, or he could go back to New York with Willie and find a nice little apartment in Greenwich Village. Which is what he did.

# 9 · Jack "The Shvontz"

It is apocryphal that Jack Warner and one of his underlings in contract talks over the table with Cagney discussed him in Yiddish only to realize that Cagney understood every word they said. The truth is simpler. At one such session, when the underling resorted to Yiddish, Jack replied in that tongue, "The Gentile understands. Stop." There was one Yiddish word Jim particularly enjoyed using. He had heard it frequently in imprecation among Jewish buddies since childhood: *shvontz*, "prick." He used the word unfailingly to describe Jack Warner.

In 1931, when Jim returned to New York, he was determined to out-wait the brothers Warner. He knew that it was impossible for him to work elsewhere under his current contract, but he had savings. He had obligations too—he still gave a monthly stipend to his mother for Jeanne's care and education—but he was betting that with the success of *The Public Enemy*, Warners would give in. It did, six months later, and he returned to Hollywood.

This time he convinced his brother Bill to come out with him, both to try his luck as an actor in pictures and to be his manager. "Can you imagine my relief," Jim said, "to have brother Bill always at hand to take over my business matters, contracts, anything to do with my money? One of the smartest things I ever did."

On the train to Hollywood Jim met an admirer, Moe Howard, linchpin of the Three Stooges, who asked him about the Warners. "How are you getting on with the boys?"

Jim replied, "All right. Now I'm going back to take up my job again."

"How about the shushy?" Moe asked. It was the first time Jim ever heard the word, and he used it a lot thereafter. Money.

He told Moe, "They're giving me a thousand dollars a week more."

"*Good* shushy," said Moe.

The first Cagney film after the suspension was *Taxi!*, and while Jim resumed shooting, Willie, now convinced that there was some degree of permanence in their lives, went out house hunting. She soon found what she wanted, a stucco-and-tile villa at 621 Hillcrest Drive, Beverly Hills. The Cagneys had long known that owning a car was *de rigueur* in that city of long distances. They had owned a secondhand Chevrolet during their first months in Los Angeles, but now brother Bill went out to find them a dependable car at a good price. He found a virtually new Buick, a "demonstrator," that was very cheap, and set about teaching Jim how to improve his driving. He was badly in need of it. When they first came to Los Angeles, Joan Blondell offered to teach Jim how to drive, but she discontinued the lessons when he seemed unable to grasp that one automatically slowed down when turning corners. Bill did his best but had to turn his brother over to a drivers' school, where Jim did little better. "I can dance up a storm," said Jim, "but I can't handle a goddamned box on wheels." He learned how to drive after a fashion but for the rest of his life depended on Willie or others to get places by car.

*Taxi!* (the exclamation point is a New York street sound) brought Jim into contact with exquisite young (nineteen) Loretta Young in a story about the then current taxi wars in New York. Unions were very much on the

*Taxi!*
OPPOSITE: With Loretta
Young

American labor scene in 1931–32, when the film was shot. Cagney plays
Matt, an aggressive young cabdriver, who rallies his independent fellow cab-
bies to resist the pressure tactics of a company owned by a villainous louse
named Buck. Sue (Loretta) loses her father and Matt his brother in the
ensuing combat, against which is set their growing love and Matt's pursuit of
the unspeakable Buck.

In *Taxi!* Cagney's acting reveals a new dimension: deeper emotional
depth. In one harrowing scene, on hearing of the death of his brother, he
pleads with the doctor, "Is there anything I can do? . . . He's my kid brother.
You know how it is." His voice begins to get ragged. "I'll do anything to save
him." Emotion chokes him. "Why did that have to happen to him? He didn't
have it comin'." Tears come, intensify. "That kid never hurt anybody in his
life." He cries starkly as Sue consoles him, his sobs now almost reaching the
rocking intensity of his lamentation for his mother in *White Heat* years
down the road, verifying that the ability to project deepest sorrow was his at
an early age.

One of *Taxi!*'s writers, John Bright, knowing Jim's fluency in Yiddish,
used that skill to construct an amusing opening scene for the star. It begins
with a foreign-looking man approaching a policeman to ask, *"Du farshtayst*

*Ellis Island*? [Do you understand Ellis Island?]," and the Irish cop not understanding, Cagney comes over and translates, a device to show off his Yiddish. Jim suggested that this be expanded into the "cute little scene," which it became. As the scene now stands, after the man approaches the uncomprehending cop, he fails to grasp why the cop cannot understand him. "*Oy gevalt*," he says, "*vos is der mir?* [Oh, for crying out loud, what's the matter with you?] *Ich hob a bruder; er shlept tsayner* [I have a brother; he pulls teeth]. *Vos is der mir mit dir; ir farshtayt nischt? A goyischer kopf!* [What's the matter with you? Don't you understand? A Gentile's head!] *Ich zog der plain in mamaloshen* [I tell you plainly in the mother tongue]. *Ich vil gayn tsu Ellis Island* [I want to go to Ellis Island]."

By this time the cop thinks the man is crazy, and Cagney in his cab asks the man, "*Vie vilst du gayn?* [Where do you want to go?]"

The man: "*Mein froy kimpt mit drei kinder fon Russland* [My wife comes with three children from Russia]. *A froy alayn* [A woman alone]."

Cagney says, "*Ich farshtay. Du vilst gayn in Ellis Island. Dan veib iz du* [I understand. You want to go to Ellis Island. Your wife is here]."

The man is delighted at this: "*Vu den—a Yiddisher yung?* [Of course—a Jewish youth?]"

Cagney: "*Vu den, a shaygetz?* [What else, a Gentile?]"

The man gets into Cagney's cab, and the cop, who knows Cagney, asks, "Nolan, what part of Ireland did your folks come from?"

Cagney smiles broadly and in a Jewish accent says, "Delancey Street, denk you!"

One burden making *Taxi!* imposed on him was the need to smoke cigarettes. Watching films of the thirties, one is fascinated by the prodigious amount of smoking done. It was part of the mores of the time, and an omnipresent one. For little other reason than that it has been ten minutes since anyone smoked, the hero—and frequently the heroine—would reach for a cigarette. Jim was able to avoid much of this during his career, and one rarely sees him smoking. But at times he was told to light up. He loathed smoking, and the anomaly was that the one dearest to him in the world was a cigarette fiend. Willie smoked a pack and a half a day for more than fifty years. However, she learned ways of keeping herself free of tobacco odor and smoked only in a special room at home. When Jim had to smoke in a movie, she would coach him in the essentials and how to fake inhaling.

Another problem facing him in *Taxi!* was a public ballroom scene in which a Peabody dance contest is held. This, Cagney's first dancing on the screen, was a matter of pride and particular concern for him, and he wanted it to come off well. He had no worries about his own Peabody dancing—he had been an aficionado of the step from youth—but he knew the scene needed the tension of a worthy dancing rival. No one at the studio seemed capable of dancing the Peabody well, and Jim was frustrated at the thought that he might have to spend hours teaching someone. Suddenly he thought of his friend George Raft, newly arrived from New York for a try at Hollywood and a superb professional dancer with ample knowledge of the Peabody. He asked Raft to play the competing finalist in the contest, and what is seen on screen was an actual contest and a study in easeful, beautiful ballroom dancing.*

The climax of *Taxi!* is Matt's ferreting out the dastardly Buck, his brother's killer, despite Sue's great efforts to prevent Matt from turning into a killer. Matt ignores her pleas and, when he finds Buck locked in a room, pours bullets into the door. But Matt is no murderer. The police arrive, enter the room, and find that Buck has fallen to death in trying to escape from a window. In later years Jim made much of the fact that he never, but never, uttered the words his mimics had him use: "You dirty rat!" "I never said it," he insisted. But he did, this once. In *Taxi!,* just before he empties his gun into Buck's door, Cagney shouts, "Come out and take it, you dirty, yellow-bellied rat, or I'll give it to you through the door!"

There is a touching tribute to Jim's dad in *Taxi!* In a love scene with Sue, he repeats his father's trick of placing his left hand around the girl's neck and softly grazing her chin with the right fist, saying, "If I thought you meant that—" Carrie Cagney, seeing the film in a Yorkville theater with her daughter, wept aloud when she saw the scene.

The critical response to *Taxi!* was uniformly good, and *The New York Times,* in an effort to describe Cagney's uniqueness, came up with something rather apt, calling him "the terrier of the screen." Lincoln Kirstein, for decades one of America's most discerning critics, did rather better. In the coterie magazine *Hound & Horn,* he found a totally new cinematic type:

> James Cagney, while he is neither typically strong or silent, does excellently as the latest title-holder of a movie type which either has become or is derived from a national type. Cagney, in a way, creates his own type. After the creation we can put it in its proper niche in the Hall of Fame of our folk legends. Cagney is mick-Irish. He was

---

*Young was as graceful as Cagney doing the Peabody, a quick-walk fox-trot performed in exhilarating quickstep. Essentially it is a one-step with a back-skip crossover every third step, here exquisitely done.

*The Crowd Roars,* with Ann Dvorak and Joan Blondell

trained as a tap dancer. He has had a small experience as a "legitimate" actor. He is the first definitely metropolitan figure to become
national, as opposed to the suburban national figure of a few years
ago, or of the farmer before that. . . . He twists a grapefruit in a
lady's face which is the reverse and equivalent courtesy of the older
"ladies first" school of etiquette. It delights and shocks us because it
is based on the reverse of chivalry. Cagney may be a dirty little lowlife rat, a hoodlum, a small time racketeer, but when his riddled
body is propped up against his mother's door, mummied in bandages and flecked in blood, we catch our throats and realize this is
a hero's death.

So *The Public Enemy* becomes a national treasure, or something like.
Kirstein goes on:

Cagney, in spite of the coincidence of his character with the American tough guy . . . is an independent actor in his own right and as
finished and as flexible an artist as there is in the talkies today. He
has resisted every attempt to have himself exhausted by being made
to act the same character in every play. Few new actors ever can

*The Crowd Roars,* with Ann Dvorak

survive the prestige of their first success. Cagney has an inspired sense of timing, an arrogant style, a pride in the control of his body and a conviction and lack of self-consciousness that is unique in the deserts of the American screen. . . . No one [in the movies] expresses more clearly in terms of pictorial action the delights of violence, the overtones of a semi-conscious sadism, the tendency towards destruction, towards anarchy which is the basis of American sex-appeal.

After being sent this by brother Harry, by then a prosperous physician in New York, Jim read it and handed it without comment to Willie. She read it, getting more and more excited, and, handing it back to him, said, "What do you think?"

Jim looked very soberly at her and said, "The *hell* he says!" and broke into laughter. "It's comforting to know I'm delightfully violent." She joined in his laughter, but she knew he was deeply moved and pleased.

The ironies in which Hollywood abound were never more comically manifested than in having Jim Cagney, perhaps the world's poorest driver, portray

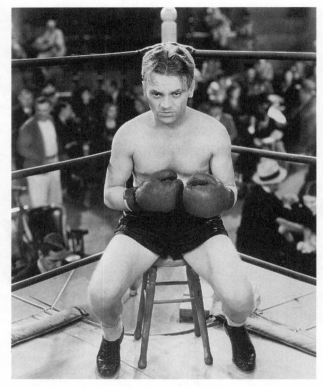

*Winner Take All*

a speed track driver in his next picture, *The Crowd Roars,* a totally predictable product apart from Cagney, made with a number of America's top
racing drivers, who as usual in such efforts appear periodically to say a few
wooden words. Much of the film was shot on location at Indianapolis and in
California at the Ventura and Ascot tracks. Cagney plays Joe, a national
champ, who tries to keep his kid brother, Eddie, from a racing career. In so
doing, he alienates both his brother and his girl and brings about the death of
a lovable sidekick who was trying to reconcile the brothers. Joe hits the skids
alcoholically but comes out of it to support his brother's try to win the
national championship by replacing him after an injury.

The Crowd Roars was an example of what Jim always called programmers, run-of-the-mill products with cliché plots and slapdash writing
redeemed only by their hardworking casts. The only pleasure Jim had in this
effort was the presence of pals Blondell and Frank McHugh, the latter well
on his way to becoming yet another Cagney sidekick. "Someone once asked

me if I minded being a Cagney supporting player," said McHugh. "It was a question sincerely meant, and I didn't take umbrage at it. I merely told this person that when you play the Palace, you are honored to be on the same bill with the star if it's a star of Jim's magnitude."

But Jim did not have even the consolation of Frank's and Joan's presence in his next, *Winner Take All.* He did find redemptive his occupation in the film, prizefighter, and his actual work in the ring with a real pro, ex-welterweight champ Harvey Perry. *Winner Take All* had yet another plus that took it mostly out of the programmer category, its coauthor, Wilson Mizner, fabled playboy-boozer-raconteur-writer. Jim, who loved the company of writers, sought Mizner out, and they quickly became friends.

The Mizner lines in *Winner Take All* are easy to spot: the fresh, original ones. When Cagney emerges from a bout worn out and battered, a little boy wants to know how he got hurt. "I fell under a lawn mower" is the reply. Later an etiquette coach asks him if he would like to read Shakespeare. "No," replies Cagney, "I don't want any part of that Shakespeare guy. He ruined Gene Tunney." Most of today's audience would not know that Tunney defeated Jack Dempsey in the famous long-count contest, going on to become society's darling, pal of Bernard Shaw, and at least a nominal fan of William Shakespeare. Punchy topical lines like this abound in *Winner Take All*, warming up the film—for those over sixty. These, and watching Cagney box, are the sum of virtues of *Winner Take All.*

In it, Cagney, an honest boxer, is temporarily turned into a phony and lounge lizard by a gorgeous and haughty society woman who fortunately rejects him so he can return to the winsome little ingenue who has been waiting around for him since the very first reel.

By now, 1932, Jim had become, and so very early on, an American institution. And a British one as well. Philip Hoare, Noël Coward's most authoritative biographer to date, tells of Coward's trip to California that year, a journey inspired in part by Coward's desire to meet Cagney. Hoare states:

> California furnished another diversion, in the shape of a Warner Brothers star, James Cagney. Originally a dancer, Cagney was now famous for his psychotic gangster roles, such as *The Public Enemy* (1931), in which he pushes half a grapefruit in Mae Clarke's face. The young Cagney was apparently engaging enough to inspire a song; when the composer Ned Rorem met Coward later, he "had heard that he and James Cagney were [lovers] . . . from many different sources. That the song 'Mad About the Boy' was written for

Cagney. I thought it was so incongruous, that's why it stuck with me." Coward's American agent, Charles Russell, said Noël told him "he had a rough and tumble with James Cagney, a wrestling match on the floor."

This encounter, about as likely as John Wayne's seeking a sex change operation, must be set down as one of the most desperately futile cases of wishful thinking in entertainment history. Years later Coward mentioned Jim briefly in one of his songs of the 1950s as "throwing those girls about." Jim, in speaking to this writer, said he was "introduced" once to Coward, and given Cagney's hearty heterosexuality, this is all it could have been.

During the making of *Winner Take All* Jim's mounting dissatisfaction with his salary surfaced again. Brother Bill had stimulated this in part, pointing out what any reader of *Variety* knew: that the weekly grosses of Cagney films were mounting higher and higher. There was also the matter of comparative value. Dick Powell, a talented singer but no powerhouse either as actor or personality, was making $4,000 a week at Warners in contrast with Cagney's $1,250. Something else irritated Jim: the en masse public appearance tours the studio was forcing on its stars. He found them pointless and boring. He sent a note to The Shvontz: "Dear Jack, Brother Bill will be in with my agent to explain my situation." Put simply, Jim wanted parity with Dick Powell. When The Shvontz refused indignantly, Bill announced Jim's separation from Warners. The trade press carried the story widely. A friend of Jim's, Lee Townsend, senior correspondent for England's leading film magazine, *The Picturegoer Weekly,* expressed the feeling of many people in Britain and the United States when he editorialized that it was a great shock that Cagney had walked out, this time vowing it was permanent. Said Townsend: "You and I and our neighbours were surprised and disappointed. For by one of those curious quirks of personality, this stocky red-headed boy, Jimmy Cagney, had come to mean something—and no little something—to all of us."

The interesting thing about this brouhaha was that it was no empty threat. Jim's anger at The Shvontz was formidable. He issued a press release, written entirely by himself, saying that he would

want to be paid in proportion to my current worth. When that worth declines, as it naturally will, I'll be content to grade my salary downward accordingly. This seemed a fair arrangement to me, but it met with a flat refusal. I then made this offer: that I would do three pictures for *nothing: Blessed Event, Twenty Thousand Years in Sing Sing,* and one other. That is, I would work a full year for no pay at all—providing [*sic*] that at the end of that year a new contract would be drawn up with terms in keeping with my value at the time—so there is nothing for me to do but quit the game entirely.

The "game" was acting, and he was entirely sincere. Even Willie backed him on this one. When he was asked what he would do without a chance to act, he said that he didn't care about acting that much, "I shan't miss trouping." He had ample money to go full-time to college, and he fully intended to become a doctor like Harry and Ed. His press statement concluded with "There will be something to look forward to later in life besides being a sort of superannuated man around a theatrical club."

The Shvontz was obdurate. He quickly cast Lee Tracy in *Blessed Event* and another Tracy, Spencer, in *Twenty Thousand Years in Sing Sing.* As for Cagney, The Shvontz said, "I have four words for him: see you in court."

It was just at this time that Jim met the second actor who influenced him greatly as a performer, Lowell Sherman. Frank Fay had taught Jim the value of control, of not doing anything but what was needed. Jim got to understand from Fay that most of the time in stress a performer need not storm. You were more interesting when you were the eye of the storm, where all was calm.

Lowell Sherman (1885–1934) was the star of a Broadway show Jim had seen in 1919, *The Sign on the Door.* Said Jim:

Unbelievable, but believable, that story, because of Lowell. He played a *rotten* rotter, I mean a bad bad guy, a no-goodnik, the worst sort of *putz* you could imagine. Lowell seduces an innocent lady who later marries a nice guy who is also the father of a nice girl. Years later Lowell tries to seduce the nice girl, and her father—who is already steamed at Lowell's having seduced yet *another* nice lady—goes to Lowell's rooms and, with more than ample reason to kill him, does so. He shoots Lowell, who drops on the spot, and so the curtain falls on Act Two. We have another act to go. But, as is still the custom sometimes those days, the audience applauded for a curtain call between acts. What they were clapping for, and I was with them all the way, was Lowell Sherman. Can you imagine? Here was this terrible, vile son of a bitch shot down, and justly so, and we *loved* him. He had to come out and take an individual curtain call. Why did we love him? Because he dropped the goodies.

For Jim, that was the answer to characterization. "Dropped the goodies" meant finding what was funny or touching or good in a villain and playing that without surrendering the nastiness. "Lowell told me," said Jim, "that you play the character, nasty as he might be, always from the character's point of view, not from your own. The man who is a son of a bitch doesn't know that he's a son of a bitch. He sincerely believes in himself. You have to as well. That is the actor's job. I already knew that, but a long, nice talk with Lowell confirmed that, and I realized that his performance in *The Sign on the Door* had left a most profound influence on me."

Jim's chief artistic exemplar was Lowell Sherman. Far from handsome (his nose was almost Durantesque), Sherman was still irresistibly attractive to women, deeply masculine, yet with a touch of mocking, feline swish that could become either comic or menacing. As a villain he was irremediably rotten but always nicely, almost regretfully rotten, implying that being villainous was simply his profession, his vocation, and that in Falstaff's assurance, "'tis no sin for a man to labor in his vocation." Lowell Sherman was the very real precursor of Tom Powers and Cody Jarrett.

In the early thirties Jim was given a questionnaire by a new friend, New York film and theater critic Robert Garland. Garland wanted to know Jim's choices in the "best" category of a number of things. The results show Jim very much a man of his time, essentially progressive, and, like many Americans, chillingly unaware of the inappropriateness of one of his choices. For Jim in 1933 the best in the following categories were:

| | |
|---|---|
| *Movie* | René Clair's *A Nous la Liberté* |
| *Poet* | Stephen Vincent Benét |
| *Movie critic* | Richard Watts |
| *Historical person* | Elizabeth Tudor |
| *Living American* | Mary Donovan |
| *Other country* | England |
| *Drink* | Sparkling burgundy |
| *Living human being* | Stalin |
| | Gandhi |
| *Composer* | Debussy |
| *Food* | Corned-beef hash |

Mary *who*? Mary Donovan was the leader of the pro–Sacco-Vanzetti forces in the country. Thirty-four-year-old Jim Cagney was a liberal, citing his reason for admiring Stalin as "his strength of purpose," a key Cagney trait then and forevermore. Jim stretched the truth a bit about the drink. He was hardly a drinking man, consuming perhaps two or three glasses a month, and he never altered that pattern the rest of his life. When shown this list at age eighty, he said, "I'll stand by a lot of that today, except the monstrous Stalin obviously. My God, how he fooled the world for so long! I think I'd plug Ireland now although I still have a lot of respect for England. Best living American? Not many heroes left. At least none that I can think of offhand. For the best living human being, it would be strictly a split vote. My choice would be Pat O'Brien and Frank McHugh. And I'm not kidding."

# 10 · The Mix as Before

As was to become almost a life pattern, Jim went back to New York vowing he was through with the Warners until decently paid, fully determined to enter Columbia University's medical school. In another predictable pattern Warner Brothers came through after bitter protest by The Shvontz. Jack Warner in his memoirs says that "Cagney filed so many suits against us that our lawyers went out of their minds. We had to settle each suit by giving him a new contract, but I suppose in the long run he was worth it." He dubbed Jim "the professional against-er," a title its recipient wore with pride. The 1932 suit was settled that September by arbitration with the Academy of Motion Picture Arts and Sciences in the person of Frank Capra. The new contract called for Cagney to receive three thousand dollars weekly with increments leading to forty-five hundred dollars weekly by 1935.

Jim's first picture on return was *Hard to Handle* ("the very definition of *that* son of a bitch," said The Shvontz about Cagney), directed by Mervyn LeRoy. From almost the first time he saw him, LeRoy was anathema to Jim, who after completing the film wrote a pungent couplet about this director:

> Where once were vertebrae is now a tangle
> From constant kissing at an awkward angle.

Jim believed LeRoy to be an utter sycophant as well as an inadequate director. The Cagney philosophy of directing was contained in these words:

> Direction is implicit in the writing, and if you've got a good script, competent actors, and a fine cameraman, you barely need a director. Not even hack directors can hurt a setup like that. I've had this happen more than once. I've seen these hacks point out to a good cameraman just where to put the camera, whereupon the cameraman would indicate to the second cameraman precisely where to put it, and it would be a good foot or so off from where the director

said. Then the cameraman would turn to me, wink, and walk away. Sure, there are some very good, some great directors, and it's been a joy to work with them. But too many of the ones I've worked with were phony baloneys like Mervyn LeRoy. The thing that irritated the hell out of me about him was that every so often just before the action began—but the camera rolling, mind you—he'd stroll into camera range, talk briefly to us actors with shit like "Now, boys and girls, I want you to give me your best in this. Lots of pepper." Or some such crud. Then he'd step out, we'd do the scene, and before calling, "Cut," he'd stroll back into camera range and say, "Great work, boys and girls. That's just the way I wanted it." Then he'd yell, "Cut." Why? Because he knew damned well the dailies would be seen by the big shots, Warner, Zanuck, and so our good script and the good acting would be seen framed by the bullshit of one Mervyn LeRoy, who would come out looking as if he had been responsible for the whole thing.

LeRoy always reminded me of an old decrepit general far, far behind the lines who had sense enough to hire only the best professional soldiers for both generalship and on the firing line as they did what was required. LeRoy was a very good promoter. Of himself.\*

Byron Haskin, one of Hollywood's great cameramen, worked with Cagney and noted his attitude toward LeRoy and his kind: "Jimmy's cynical viewpoint of the directors he had worked with during his career—and he was a top star at the time—was that most of the instructions he received were drivel. It didn't even have common sense to it. He would have to counteract this baloney and give a credible performance out of his unit [writer, actors, cameramen]. He was getting no help. Really. That's what his message was: that the general level of directing is phony, really."

One such efficient unit made *Hard to Handle,* and once again Jim had the joy of Wilson Mizner's companionship. As coauthor of the picture Mizner created in Cagney's character, Lefty Merrill, something of his own personality. Lefty is a promoter-publicist who is in a constant race to exploit anything exploitable: marathon dancing, public treasure hunts, fat-reduction cream, a

\*It should be noted that if LeRoy let others do his work for him, his procedures were efficacious. He was responsible for such good films as *Little Caesar, I Am a Fugitive from a Chain Gang, They Won't Forget,* and others. Cagney disliked him for the reasons stated but also because of what Cagney called "congenital sycophancy." LeRoy married the daughter of Harry Warner, the studio president.

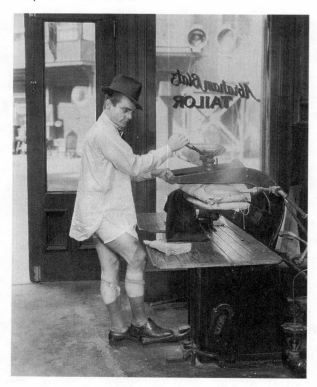

*Hard to Handle*

girls' college, and—teehee—grapefruit. It was only two years after the Mae Clarke episode, and Jim at first was adamantly opposed to what he considered an elephantine inside joke that went outside and offside, but Mizner made the entire episode so breezily nonsensical that Jim approved the sequence, which ends the film. Lefty, in order to sell grapefruit—which has become so huge a crop that much of it has to be thrown away—devises the idea of an eighteen-day grapefruit reducing diet. The country goes wild over the idea, and Lefty becomes a public relations hero. Cagney plays the role with ebullience, taking in stride such lines as "What do I know about grapefruit? I never even *saw* a grapefruit."

Jim was very fond of an old pro in the cast, character actress Ruth Donnelly, a George M. Cohan protégée, to whom Mizner gave the best laugh lines in the film. Donnelly is the only woman except Joan Blondell in all of Cagney's films to keep up with him in tone, intensity, speed, and comic flair. She loved the Mizner script, as well she might. Donnelly went on from here to play a series of tart-tongued pals of the heroine, in this case also being her mother. In response to Cagney's "Do I look like a thief?" she responds, "You look as if you'd steal two left shoes." Later she tells her daughter not to be dismayed at Lefty's seeming infidelity: "What did you expect? All bridegrooms are slightly used." Jim loved Ruth's performance and regretted that they would never costar again, as they do here in fact if not in billing.

In *Hard to Handle* Cagney uses his hands with more dexterity, style, and éclat than ever before. And, it must be said, almost to a fault. So trained had he been in balletic line by Willie, which emphasized the flow of arms and fingers, that in his early films he uses his hands very consciously to make points. In lifting up Loretta Young's chin in *Taxi!* to kiss her, he clasps his fingers together and curves his hand slightly so that the effect is like a blooming leaf raising that pretty chin. For all its real grace, it is just a shade too well done. He did the same thing, albeit with less emphasis, in *Doorway to Hell*. In *Hard to Handle* it is also slightly overdone.

In this film Cagney's hands function in the way a dancer uses his body.

*Hard to Handle,* with Mary Brian and Ruth Donnelly

The hands take on a life of their own, actually seeming to float (strains of Pavlova here), lifting sharply up in moments of anger as eruptive counterpoint, or in affirmation or beseeching. Halfway through the film, when Cagney uses both hands in a splaylike gesture of rejection, one is watching those eloquent hands more for their own sake than for the emotion they seek to convey. We have crossed over into Delsarte country.° Willie saw *Hard to Handle*, he did not, and when he asked her what she thought, she said, "Hands."

"Too much?"

"Too much."

Thereafter his hands retained eloquence but became more subdued and infrequent in use.

In 1933 the Screen Actors Guild was born, and Jim was elected to the board of directors. Here he began to work hand in glove with the man who was to become the third of his three best friends, Robert Montgomery. Montgomery, one of the powerhouse organizers of the guild, devised with Jim's help an efficient way to find supporters of the group. For the Screen Actors Guild Oral History project, Montgomery recalled how Cagney's quietly strong personality helped him enlist backers for the union:

> Cagney with his reputation for being very tough, a very tough fellow and a very tough operator, and I with a reputation for being a very smooth article in those days. And Cagney would simply sit in the room [with the potential backers] while I talked but would keep staring at the man to whom I talked—never took his eyes off him— while I begged and implored him to please give us an ad for one page or anything in order to raise funds for the organization. Cagney would simply stare at them. Little by little we became an organization.

Jim was heart and soul with the Screen Actors Guild, having seen, and many times experienced, the working conditions that made the union a necessity. Early in 1933, just before the guild was formed, many actors were being paid only sixty-six dollars for a six-day week, a week frequently ending with a Saturday workday beginning at 8:00 a.m. and continuing through to sunrise on Sunday. Chorus girls at Warner Brothers under the demanding

°François Delsarte, nineteenth-century acting teacher, advocated highly schematized outlines of gestures and bodily postures, each corresponding to a specific emotion. Delsartian teachers abounded in New York when Jim was young, and he knew their work.

Busby Berkeley got thirty-five dollars a week, usually for fourteen hours a day, six days a week. Continuous employment existed only for stars. The working body of performers might have nine days of work on a certain film pieced out over three weeks, being paid only for days actually worked.

Jim had intense sympathy for these supporting actors, and in his next film, *Picture Snatcher,* he was able to give some of them a break. He did this by a simple expedient. When he saw he had the opportunity to extend a customary one-day shoot into two, he did so, pleading late-afternoon ill health, thus requiring the actors in the scene to return for an extra day's work.

*Picture Snatcher* was based on Ben Hecht's first experiences as a Chicago newspaperman circa 1910, when he was called "the most adept and audacious picture thief" in town. When a sensational news story broke, newspapers vied with one another to get photographs of the protagonists, and when these could not be obtained honestly, any means became the means. In this story Cagney is a near-illiterate ex-convict who desperately seeks legitimacy in the newspaper business, and ultimately achieves it, as a photographer. He gets the girl and wins professional acclaim by taking a picture of a Ruth Judd kind of murderess at the moment of execution.

The film is conventional fun, and Cagney again has no trouble playing a lowlife. He always maintained that the highlight of the film was a little scene between himself and veteran scene stealer, the squeaky-voiced Sterling Holloway, who plays a fact-seeking journalism professor. Under the illusion that Cagney is a crack reporter and unaware of Cagney's prison stay, Holloway asks him who was the most difficult man he ever interviewed. Cagney replies, "The governor."

"What was the subject of the interview?"

Cagney replies, straight-faced, "I wanted to ask his pardon."

Keeping in mind Willie's comment about overuse of his hands, Cagney uses them here for dramatic punctuation but much more sparingly and increasingly with more reliance on his right thumb. With a tight-clenched right fist, the thumb does work of its own, almost independent of its base. When he wants to point to something with special emphasis, the thumb takes on a "let's-go-this-way" conformation, and he can also loosen it to a swivel, wiggling it comically to indicate nervousness or almost any other nuance to support the emotion in a spoken line. This is not Delsartian but lively counterpoint. Again he did not see the film, but Willie did and praised his gesturing.

Such things he regarded as little tricks of the trade, but in at least one quarter there was some regret. *The New Yorker's* critic called his performance in

*The Picture Snatcher*
BELOW: With Patricia Ellis

*The Mayor of Hell,* with Madge Evans

*Picture Snatcher* "competent, of course, rather too much so, perhaps, too assured of the tricks which he has found successful in the past. I wish he would acquire a few others to express the mannerisms of our hard-boiled youth."

Cagney's next, all about hard-boiled youth, was *The Mayor of Hell,* in which although a former racketeer, he wins a political post with crooked higher-ups to become a deputy inspector of state penal institutions. He comes on a once-a-year inspection to a graft-ridden boys' reformatory, where he is much taken with the school's nurse, and through her, turns the squalid place into a boys' republic. There is a mandatory reversal of fortunes until the villainous former school head, after a brief return to despotism, is killed and Cagney returns the place to former glory. But this film really belongs to the boys and their charismatic leader, Frankie Darro, with Cagney simply added as box-office insurance. As the *New York Post* put it, "The picture has been pulled out of proportion to force the Cagney role to the foreground."

*The Mayor of Hell* had one personal plus for Jim. For some time he had been after Warners to place under contract his old buddy from *Pitter Patter* days, fellow chorus boy Allen Jenkins. This was done, and in this film Jenkins becomes another Cagney sidekick, thereafter to be typecast in roles that are the very definition of scorn married to faithfulness.

For some time at the studio there had been a growing meeting of minds between Cagney and the Warners about his doing a full-fledged musical. *Taxi!* was a slight move in that direction. Warners' musical genius was the unflappable and quixotic Busby Berkeley, who knew Jim's background well and had earlier suggested a more active role in musicals for the star who was now in the top ten of the most popular Hollywood performers nationwide. Warners had entered the field of movie musicals wholeheartedly by 1933. Its previous efforts, *Forty-second Street* and *Gold Diggers of 1933* (shot in 1932) made tremendous profits in the midst of the Depression, and plans were set for a continuing series of them.

On Sunset Boulevard in Los Angeles, close to Warner Brothers, were the offices of Fanchon and Marco, where vaudeville units and musical shows were cast, written, and produced, to be sent out into the few surviving vaudeville houses or to the large movie palaces that used the shows as half-hour-long prologues for the feature movie. Warners writers Manuel Seff and James Seymour came up with a story based directly on the Fanchon and Marco enterprises. Their hero, Chester Kent—Cagney's role— was based even more directly on a musical producer of the time, Chester Hale. The nub of *Footlight Parade*'s story is the desperate attempt of Chester to produce three new prologues in three days to satisfy the requirements of a theater chain owner. This is done with all the glitzy magic only Busby Berkeley could display—interestingly, with only a single camera— offering wide, expansive shots like sixty chorus girls with flash cards creating a photograph of Franklin D. Roosevelt and similar wonders.

The obstacle to Chester's putting the shows together is the backstage sabotage of his efforts by a rival prologue producer. But all is well even when Chester is forced to dance the lead in the last sequence because the leading man is undone by booze. The number is called "Shanghai Lil," written by Warners' indefatigable songwriting team Harry Warren and Al Dubin. Like all of their music, "Shanghai Lil" is poundingly danceable and exhilarating. In the sequence Cagney is an American in white tie and tails visiting a Shanghai café, singing despondently in rhymed couplets that he has covered every highway and is climbing every hill, looking for his Shanghai Lil. She is, he allows, a little devil but also something on the level. A variety of the café's

*Footlight Parade*
ABOVE: With Joan Blondell and Ruby Keeler
BELOW: With Joan Blondell and Claire Dodd

clientele, both sexes, comments on Lil's extraordinary popularity, which seems to make her a compound of angel and tart. A forthright gob says that Lil is every sailor's pal and everybody's gal—and is knocked down by Cagney for his trouble. A melee ensues. The Shore Patrol arrives and cleans things up. Cagney goes behind the bar, vanishes, and immediately and inexplicably reappears in full U.S. Navy garb.

Also now from behind the bar comes the notorious Shanghai Lil, but what's this? She is the most innocent-looking creature in God's world, Ruby

*Footlight Parade,* with Ruby Keeler

Keeler, made up with slanted eyes and looking about as sexily languorous as Shirley Temple at her kewpie-dolliest. Ruby's reunion with her boy is brought about in a whirligig of numerous gobs marching off in military patterns "To Station" while darling little Ruby taps merrily away on the bar. Here, in her dancing, the contrast with Cagney is strong, and not to her advantage.

In all her Warners musicals Ruby taps efficiently and she has nice legs. From the waist down she rates an academic B or B−. From the waist up, C− or C. As a dancer she is almost a disaster technically because her arms are used as if she were balancing perilously on a tightrope. Those arms have no grace at all; they are leaden. What saves her from complete awfulness as a dancer are her sweetness and Irish colleen charm. Cagney, in vivid contrast, dances with his usual brio, his arms free-floating and in total consonance with the lithe movements of his body.

When asked what he thought of *Footlight Parade* and Ruby Keeler, Jim said:

> Never met the lady. [*Incredulous look from interviewer.*] No, really. I was never introduced to Ruby Keeler. If that doesn't show you the impersonality as well as the factory approach to work those days at Warners, nothing will. I showed up to rehearse the "Shanghai Lil" number a few times, and we nodded friendly enough, and we had some lines earlier, but it was all work, work, work, and I think we were mutually shy, so we never met. We did the number, and that was it. I saw Ruby at a couple of parties after that, but we were in separate groups, so we just nodded and smiled. As to *Footlight Parade,* it was one of the few of my movies I've ever seen, and I liked it, having seen it just after it was made. Then I saw it years later on television and hated it. Now [1980] I think it's fun.

At this time *The Martha* came into Jim's life. It was a superb forty-three-foot sailboat, launched in 1907 and at a recent date still afloat in charter. *The Martha's* importance to him cannot be overstated because it meant not only release from the Warners' factory but from the land itself. "I honestly think," he said, "that the genes from some Norwegian forebears of mine lodged in me. I loved taking *The Martha* up the New England coast with its fascinating little inlets, all wonderfully different, easy to get into with *The Martha's* scant draw of three feet, nine inches. It was less fun with *The Martha* in California after a bit because it seemed to me the whole coast consisted of bathing beaches, private yacht clubs, or large municipal marinas."

Jim's privacy was always compromised by the latter. Casual sailing as the years went on became almost impossible on the California coast. He confined himself principally to the area at Balboa and Newport Beach, where eventually his brother Bill and sister, Jeanne, were to live.

Jim never hid the irony of his odd brand of seasickness. "It is a joke, really," he said. "Here, in me, you find a guy absolutely devoted to the sea and rejected by it consistently. Or rather, *in*consistently. Because at times I'd be out in my boat with the wind bucking her up to a fare-thee-well, and I'd feel as if I were in my own library at home. Then sometimes I'd go out there, the water flat as a mirror, with barely enough wind to get her crawling, and the mal-de-mer would knock me speechless."

Jim felt a special affinity with *The Martha* and her builder: "It was built by a man named Johanson in 1907, a man with a premonition he'd die at sea. He was equally certain that as long as he was on board *The Martha,* he'd be utterly safe, just as I do. Then one morning Johanson took his boat's dinghy out to the far side of the harbor to do some fishing. A sudden squall upset the dinghy, and Johanson drowned in full view of *The Martha.*"

The Cagneys were fond of inviting close friends on the boat. They were not party givers as a rule, but they had sailing weekends with their old pals Pat and Eloise O'Brien and Frank and Dorothy McHugh. Just as their husbands felt a strong affinity for one another, Willie Cagney, Eloise O'Brien, and Dorothy McHugh became the closest of friends. Brigid O'Brien, Pat's daughter, recalls:

They had such fun, those three gals. They were like kids. My God, they *were* kids. Once down at Del Mar, when we lived next door to Lloyd Bacon, the director, Mom and Willie wanted to try absinthe, which they had never tasted. And they knew the Bacons had some. Bacon was over, visiting us at the time, and the girls asked him for the absinthe. Fine, he said, but he and his wife, Doris, were on the outs, and she wouldn't let him in the house. So, nothing daunted, Mom and Willie went over to the Bacons', knocked on the door, which Doris answered, and the girls said, "Hi, Doris, we've come over for the absinthe." Which they promptly got. They sat out on the beach, their heads under an umbrella, sipping the absinthe over ice, through straws. Mom said that's the last thing she and Willie remembered for days. I remember also when the three of them were playing canasta near a pool, and Dorothy kept losing. Finally she got so fed up that she said, "If I don't win this hand, I'm going to jump right into the pool." She didn't, so she *did,* fully clothed. Those three went everywhere together, shopped together, gossiped together, and, above all, *laughed* together.

Jim was put next into *Lady Killer,* a curious film that cannot make up its mind whether it's a serious account of a man's reformation or a thriller or a comedy. Whatever it is, it's fun, and Cagney as Dan, a crook in hiding from New York police in Hollywood, unexpectedly but not untypically becomes a movie star. His old gang from the East appears and tries to force him to help them rob movie stars' homes. The film marks his reunion with Mae Clarke, now a con lady and would-be seductress. (In her come-on to him she offers Cagney a drink, then "Chaser?" "Always have," is his reply.) Later in the film he makes *The Public Enemy*'s grapefruit assault on her look like very small potatoes by hauling her out of bed by the hair and pulling her twelve feet down a corridor. ("Not to worry," Mae wrote a concerned friend. "If you look close enough at the scene, you'll see I have a firm grip on Jim's hand, and the hand is bearing all the brunt.") After some potent gunplay, Cagney is united with his true love, played with almost glacial friendliness by Margaret Lindsay.

Lindsay was something of a mystery to Jim: "She was certainly a lovely lady. Very nice to look at, but I could never quite get on her wavelength. For all her beauty, there was a coldness in her acting, I felt. She was personable and pleasant offscreen, but on—I don't know. She was an Iowa gal, like my Willie, but Margaret had gone to acting school in England, and it showed. Inappropriately, I thought. For instance in *Lady Killer*, she said 'ahsk' for 'ask' and 'bahthroom' for 'bathroom.' I was waiting for Roy [Del Ruth, the director] to correct her, but he never did. Margaret did that a lot, putting in unexpected and unwarrantable Britishisms, and they stuck out like a sore thumb."

Notwithstanding, Cagney's coziest scene in *Lady Killer* is with Lindsay. Working as an extra in the movies, he is attired as an Indian chief, accidentally falling asleep in movie star Lindsay's dressing room trailer. She returns from shooting a scene and gently inquires who he is, as she stares at his Indian war bonnet. She asks, "What are you made up for?" He: "Big Chief Es-Tut-Mir-Vay-in-Tuchas" (Yiddish for "Big Chief Pain-in-the-Ass"). This was a gag that necessarily passed by Gentile viewers. Cagney inserted it himself but never saw the picture. Again he had Willie report on it, and she said the laugh he planted was, as he anticipated, confined to a small portion of the audience. "But those who got it howled like crazy," she said.

Around this time Jim received the sobriquet that, in the opinion of his close friends, best suited him. Pat O'Brien called to remind him of a dinner being given at the Masquers Club for a friend of theirs. "Don't forget," Pat said. "You said you'd come."

"What makes you think I won't be there?" Jim asked.

"Ah, I know you, Jim. You're one of those faraway fellas."

Jim knew the truth of that. The tail of his gang at eleven, he had followed that pattern of existence all his life. Gregarious and clubbable among his few close friends, he was of them yet not of them.

"Faraway fella" translated into his politics as well: concerned, but at a distance from most things. Under the influence of Mr. and Mrs. James at the settlement house, and Will Crawford, his socialist friend in New Jersey, Jim had become a liberal. "As a faraway fella," he said, "and that's an

*Lady Killer*
BELOW: With Mae Clarke

accurate description of me by Pat all right, I was wedded to theory rather than practice. What the hell did I know about the ebb and flow of political movements or even what they meant? At first it all seemed so sensible: take from the overrich, give to the poor. Distribute the wealth. How does one do that? I hadn't a clue. In any case, at the time, left seemed right, in several senses."

In the thirties Jim came under the influence of two friendly liberals, John Bright, screenwriter and author of some brilliant Cagney films, and Samuel Ornitz, also a screenwriter, both ultimately members of the Communist party. Jim was unaware of their political affiliations other than that they were on the side of the underdog. Bright and Ornitz got Jim interested in the plight of the unjustly accused Scottsboro boys, the nine black youths sentenced to death in Alabama in 1931 for supposedly raping two white women on a freight train. They also got him to attend a few meetings of the Marxist-oriented Film and Photo League, a liberal moviemakers' group. Bright and Ornitz were personable and intelligent, and Jim enjoyed their company.

Willie loathed them. Whenever they appeared at the Cagneys', as they occasionally did, she did not hide her dislike. "Those boys are going to be trouble for you," she told her husband. She was right.

# 11 · More Troubles
# in Our Native Lan'

Faraway fella though he was, Jim Cagney was always a citizen of the world. From Carrie Cagney he learned the Donnean philosophy that no man is an island and that mutual responsibility was part of what it meant to be both American and human. He sympathized with all human trouble, having had so much of it. Whenever it came, he tended to use an old Irish phrase of his dad's: "More troubles in our native lan', is it?"

In his Scotch Plains days at the single tax colony, Jim had ingested some semisocialist ideas and in part believed them. His friend Will Crawford had been particularly kind to the Cagneys, lending money when needed. Most of the people at the colony were socialists of one stripe or another, and "it would be odd indeed," said Jim in *Cagney by Cagney*, "given my age [twenty-one] and sense of gratitude, if I hadn't imbibed some of their philosophy. . . . It was just a question of lending my voice to the protests of the very troublesome times of the Twenties. . . . As my life interests grew, I assumed what might in general be called a liberal stance."

By 1933, through his new Marxist friends Bright and Ornitz, Jim had become friendly with the famous muckraker Lincoln Steffens, at times called the American Socrates, who wrote the influential book *The Shame of the Cities,* which with its devastating overview of civic corruption sounded a new note of reform advocacy in the land. It quickly became one of Jim's bibles. Steffens was married to Ella Winters, also a writer and a social revolutionary, who in the early thirties wrote a series of articles on a cotton workers' strike in the San Joaquin Valley, detailing the death from starvation of a striker's baby, which she had witnessed herself. Jim immediately sent a check to help relieve the workers, all Mexicans, of their plight. He was not aware that the strikers were receiving support from the Communist party. It would have made no difference if he had known. He knew the strike was justified.

In 1934 Sacramento's district attorney, Neil McAllister, was gathering evidence against Communist sympathizers in a sensationalistic proto-McCarthy–era publicity splurge. McAllister gained access to some of Ella Winters's letters in which she mentioned Jim's contribution, adding, "Cagney was fine this time and is going to bring other stars up to talk to Stef about Communism." Her husband, who was adamant that he belonged to no political party, was yet well known as the man who had gone to Petrograd in 1919 and had written back to a friend, "I have been over into the future, and it works." The Sacramento DA was a hearty advocate of guilt by association, in the same style as Senator Joe McCarthy a few decades later. The DA told newspapermen that he was going to "prove" that Cagney was a Communist. McAllister further blustered that he would obtain a Superior Court injunction restraining Cagney from giving financial aid to Communists.

McAllister's cardboard case collapsed when a list of contributors to the strikers was published; they included prominent Mexican-American actors like Ramon Novarro, Lupe Velez, and Dolores Del Rio supporting their countrymen. Cagney counterpunched McAllister by calling him the publicity hound he so manifestly was. Still, as in the case of Senator McCarthy later, this episode left lingering doubts in some minds about Cagney's patriotism. It was a fire that never quite went out, and it burned again in the unholy days of the House Un-American Activities Committee of the forties.

In 1934's *Jimmy the Gent,* his next picture, Jim began his long and mostly rewarding connection with Michael Curtiz, whom he both admired and despised. Jim said:

> Mike was a pompous bastard who didn't know how to treat actors, but he sure as hell knew how to treat a camera. He was one of those few directors who could, at need, place a camera where it would do the most good. So I give Mike respect there, and when you got through a picture with him, you could be confident that it was well done. But, as I said, he just didn't know how to treat actors. He left me alone because he knew I'd knock him on his ass if he didn't, and I left him alone until our last picture, when I had to tell him a few home truths.

Distressed by now in his fourth year of Warners employment by its almost invariable casting of him as a hoodlum or worse, Jim decided to show up for *Jimmy the Gent* as hoodlum *in situ.* "They want hoodlum, I'll give them hoodlum," he told Willie, and went to the makeup department the first morning of the film's shooting with some specific ideas in mind. The makeup artist was directed to shave the Cagney head to the Prussian model and place bottle scars all over his pate. Jim arrived on call precisely at the hour Curtiz had specified. Curtiz was horrified. "Why, Jeemy, why?" he said, in the strong Hungarian accent he never lost.

"You wanted hoodlum, you got hoodlum," Jim said, knowing this would be communicated directly to The Shvontz, thereby irritating him inordinately.

In the film Cagney is Jimmy the hoodlum who would be a gent. He runs an agency that finds heirs for people who die intestate "for a small commission . . . never more than fifty per cent." One of his employees asks what happens when the legal heir can't be found. "Ah," says Jimmy, "we can't let all that nice money go to waste, see?" All his employees do see, and the agency prospers. Then Jimmy encounters, at his only rival in town, a smoother, more efficient, above all much classier operation—with tea served around the clock. Bette Davis has left Jimmy because of his lack of ethics but is unaware that her new employer, although more sophisticated,

*Jimmy the Gent,* with Bette Davis

*Jimmy the Gent*

is an even bigger scoundrel. To convince her that he is not, in her description, "the biggest chiseler since Michelangelo," Jimmy contrives to prove to Bette that her boss is a phony and that he, Jimmy, is morally salvageable. Done, and done.

This is the first of two Cagney-Davis teamings and although better than the subsequent one, *The Bride Came C.O.D., Jimmy the Gent* is 50 percent Cagney, 25 percent Davis (she loathed the role, and it shows), and 25 percent supporting players, especially chirpy Alice White, a dumb-blonde specialist, who has the best line in the film. When Jimmy asks the sweet, sexy flibbertigibbet what she would do for five hundred dollars, she says, "I'd do my best."

If Cagney tried hard to ugly himself up for *Jimmy the Gent*, he went the other way in preparing for his next, *He Was Her Man*. He tried to soften the sting of playing another bad guy by wearing a Ronald Colman mustache, which unattractively shortens his already short lip. Despite this, Joan Blondell as a reformed whore adores him, and he, even if he is an ex-con safecracker, nobly pretends he doesn't, sending her off to become the faithful wife of a goodhearted fisherman. Cagney further ennobles himself by turning himself over to two vengeful henchmen to spare Joan a similar fate.

When Jim read the negative review of *He Was Her Man* in show-wise *Variety* calling him and Joan "two pieces of human flotsam [whose actions] may both alienate and confound the patrons," he said, "And yet more troubles in our native lan', is it?" Quite agreeing with the review, he was prepared to do a walkout from the studio on the basis of his persistently being cast as a hoodlum, when The Shvontz offered him a picture to be shot mostly at, near, and on the sea—a picture, moreover, to be made with buddies Pat O'Brien and Frank McHugh. Pat starred with him since they were well qualified as antagonists, and Frank was the inevitable and truly jolly comic relief.

*Here Comes the Navy* is an amalgam of all service films, past and to come, out of the Warners repertoire. Cagney is the feisty malcontent, and O'Brien the all-for-the-corps superior, McHugh their loyal sidekick. The pattern for these films was set by the enormously popular 1924 war play *What Price Glory?*, with its battling but fiercely codependent servicemen, Captain Flagg and Sergeant Quirt. O'Brien and Cagney in parallel roles in *Here Comes the Navy* are so inimical that Cagney actually joins the Navy to get at his opponent. Inevitably Cagney proves to be a hero, even saving O'Brien's life and finally going so far as to marry his sister.

In the lifesaving scene there was real hardship for Jim and Pat. While helping to land a Navy dirigible, Pat as head of the ground crew is suspended from the dirigible, handling a rope. When the ship rises suddenly in an updraft, Pat is lifted high into the air, still clutching the rope. Cagney, in the dirigible cabin, climbs down the rope in defiance of orders and, wearing a parachute, lashes himself to Pat, and they chute down. In *Cagney by Cagney* Jim explained the complication that occurred:

> This was being shot from the ground up against the sky, giving the illusion that Pat, the rope and I were well up in the air. As he was dangling there and I came down the rope, I put my legs around him and suddenly he completely lost his grip. I couldn't support his weight and mine too, so we both went straight down. Somebody said they could see the smoke coming from my hands as I slid. They put medication on both our hands. Pat's were burned too, but mine looked like hamburger because I was hanging on tighter.

There is a sad note to this exuberant film, which was filmed in and around San Diego and on the USS *Arizona*. The *Arizona* was destroyed at Pearl Harbor, and a number of the chipper young sailors seen in the film were killed on that merciless Sunday.

If Jim thought that being a Navy hero would stop the studio from casting him as a brawling malcontent, he was wrong. The very title of his next film, *The St. Louis Kid*, made that clear. He rather liked the plot. He and

*He Was Her Man,* with Joan Blondell

sidekick Allen Jenkins are truck drivers on the St. Louis–Chicago run who become involved in a squabble between trucking companies and striking dairymen. Anything having to do with unions was now of great interest to Jim. He had just been elected vice-president of the Screen Actors Guild, and he began to see the labor movement in all its colorations, as unions both gathered power and were denied it.

He soon discovered that once again he would be fighting from the very outset of the film. He was disheartened. "Honest to God," he said, "when I found out that I'd be slugging my way from the very start of *St. Louis Kid,* I got so frustrated I made sure I didn't have to do it the usual way. I went to the makeup people again and had them put splints on my fingers and bandages on my hands, and in the scene where I had to fight I did a kind of double whirl fadeaway and bopped the guy with my head, knocking him out."

The reviewer for *Variety* seized on this: "If *The St. Louis Kid* is the criterion, there's only one thing for James Cagney to do, and that's to start

*Here Comes the Navy,* with Pat O'Brien and Frank McHugh

knocking guys out with a dirty look. In the past he's made good and frequent use of hands and feet. In this one he KOs them with his head. . . . The system is to stand directly in front of an antagonist, make believe you're going to lead with a left, but cross him by snapping your head forward so that it meets with his chin. As Cagney does it, it's a surefire punch, for they all go to sleep immediately."

*The St. Louis Kid* was nothing if not topical. In 1934 the nation's newspapers were full of the Milk War. Dairymen were stopping milk trucks and pouring their cargoes out onto the ground because many milk companies were cheating farmers of their due, a decent price. It was only when the film was finished that Jim realized that he and Allen were actually playing scabs—decent ones, but scabs—and it horrified him.

The one deep boredom quotient for Jim was the interminable waiting between setups—the moving of camera, microphone, and lights and actor placement before the camera rolls again. There are usually a large number of these setups during the working day, and they take up most of the time. As a result, the average film is lucky to shoot five minutes of usable footage a day. The actor has nothing to do during setup time except read, study lines, or doze. Jim chose to write verse. He put it simply:

Making verses I cannot help
As a pregnant female her brood must whelp.
Each will come in its given time,
So there's naught to do but write and rhyme.

During one setup Joan Blondell walked past Jim and noticed the notebook in which he was jotting down a few lines. "Whatcha doin'?" (Yes, she talked that way.)

"Oh, writing a few bits of corny verse."

"*Honestly,* Jim Cagney! What won't you think of next?"

The notebook was also used for impromptu sketches of the things he saw about him, including on one occasion Joan's fundament. He showed it to her and said, "How's that for a beautiful ass?" She did not recognize it and, when told it was hers, beamed proudly.

He was very good at describing ad hoc situations. Once when Willie was driving them down their street in Beverly Hills, they stopped at a red light where in the lane facing them was Humphrey Bogart in a new sports con-

*The St. Louis Kid,* with Allen Jenkins, Edna Bennett, and Patricia Ellis

vertible, industriously picking his nose, a long-standing habit. Jim composed the following and put it on Bogie's dressing room table next day:

> In this silly town of ours,
> One sees odd primps and poses,
> But movie stars in fancy cars
> Shouldn't pick their famous noses.
>
> —Jim Cagney

There was no reply.

In the early thirties an actor who was a close acquaintance of Jim's was working on a movie starring Constance Bennett. Something of a chip off the old block—her father, Richard Bennett, was an old actor of prodigious irascibility—she fancied that Jim's friend had made a mistake during the shooting of a scene and rounded on him viciously and before the whole company and crew. Entirely innocent in the situation, the actor, a very gentle soul, took the indignity hard. Jim took it harder. Although he never sent Bennett a copy of his descriptive verse of her, he told his friend it was perfectly all right if *he* did so, authorship clearly stated. The friend chose not to.

> The Artiste
> One views the form and finds it fair,
> The face decided comely,
> Though without a jot of stick and pot
> They say she's rather homely.
>
> Performancewise, there's ne'er a change,
> No matter what the part is.
> When one perceives so spare a range,
> One wonders what the art is.
>
> By dint of constant labor,
> She parlayed little into much:
> There were stocks and bonds, annuities,
> Real estate and such.
>
> She handled each transaction
> With shrewdness and with tact,
> But she'd give it all up happily,
> If only she could act.*

---

*To give the lady her due, Constance Bennett was adept at satirical light comedy, as witness *What Price Hollywood?* (1932) and *Topper* (1937).

But the Cagney verse was not always comic by any means, as evidenced by this plaintive quatrain:

Plea

Sweet haunt, I hear the clatter of your chains,
Whose links make song, whose strength detains
This heart wherein your heart rests uppermost.
Sweet haunt, why must you remain a ghost?

There was one bit of verse, the first he ever wrote, a simple couplet he penned during a backstage wait in *Outside Looking In*, that was to stay with him the rest of his life:

Each man starts with his very first breath
To devise shrewd means for outwitting death.

He made it the epigraph of his autobiography, and it reflected his feelings throughout his life. In talking of friends long gone, he frequently assessed them in terms of their skill in encouraging life and discouraging death. Once when Frank Morgan's name came up, Jim sighed and said, "What a wonderful man! What fun to be with!" Then, in anger: "Absolutely refused to take care of himself. Unbelievable. It upsets me to this day. Used to stash liquor all over his house so he could take quiet nips whenever he wanted to; then, feeling quite juiced, he'd go down to the local high school and play a vigorous game of basketball someone was promoting among his pals. He did his friends the outrage of dying at fifty-nine. Unforgivable."

Jim's close friends were not many, but he grappled the few he had to his heart with hoops of steel. From the earliest days in Yorkville he remembered and kept in touch with George "Specs" Torporcer, a boy who despite poor vision went on to be a professional baseball player with the St. Louis Cardinals. Others Jim remained close to were Artie Klein from Seventy-eighth Street, who subsidized Jim and Willie when they were reduced to eating soda crackers and water in vaudeville days, and Jim Fair, who was also generous with money when the Cagneys had none. Throughout the years he called these three men at least once every two weeks and visited them whenever he could.

Of people in his profession, Jim had equally fond memories, and his Christmas card list of old vaudevillians was huge. His closest friends were the seven members of what columnist Sidney Skolsky called the Irish Mafia and its members called the Boys Club, founded in the late thirties. Frank McHugh on its founding:

I was sent an autograph book from a church in Hartford with a request to Spence Tracy, Pat O'Brien, Jim Cagney, and me to sign it, then return it to be auctioned off at a church benefit. Pat and Jim being with Warners were easy targets, but Spence was at MGM, and I didn't have his home address or phone number. So I sent a blank page of the autograph book to him [at the studio] asking him to sign. He did so, returning it with a note that he thought it sad that old friends living in the same town had to reach other by mail, suggesting that the four of us get together for dinner. Jim and Spence got together first for dinner, then the four of us, and I became sort of secretary, making the reminder phone calls.

Lynne Overman was our first added member. Then Ralph Bellamy and Frank Morgan. That was our regular roster, but we would have guests from time to time. Bert Lahr was always welcome, and Lou Calhern, and others whom we'd invite. Or not invite, as the case may be. Once Zachary Scott came over to the table when we were holding forth and stood there, smiling, looking very glamorous, single gold earring and all. "How do you join this Irish Mafia?" he said.

I'm afraid I replied, "You don't *get* to. You are asked."

Then Lynne Overman ended Mr. Scott's hopes by saying, "And we have just run out of *asks.*"

As for the function of the Boys Club, McHugh defined it:

Our purpose was just to get together for conversation and laughs. Generally the conversation was about wine, women, and song, just boys getting together. Once in a while it would be an exchange of opinions about a picture or a role. Once when Spence was considering *Dr. Jekyll and Mr. Hyde,* he asked the group if he should do it. Lynne said no. Spence asked why, and Lynne said, "You wouldn't be good in it."

Spence bristled at that and said, "Just *why* wouldn't I be good in it?"

Lynne replied in his quite matchless way, "Nobody ever is."

And he was right. Spence went ahead anyway, did the part, and failed. Most of us were from different studios and had simply gotten out of touch. From each other we learned about the pictures and the trends, and most of all, we kept our friendship alive. And had a lot of fun in the bargain.

Perhaps the most memorable evening the Boys Club ever had was the evening of Lynne's potatoes. Jim's recollection of it was:

Now, get this. There were seven of us, four of them Irish, all of us performers, so there had to be a lot of excitable talk, stories, memories, what the hell have you, all done with a lot of spirit, and once in a while with some quiet wisdom. The latter usually came from one of two sources, occasional guest Jimmy Gleason, whom we all revered, and our local pundit, so to speak, Lynne Overman. He always had the right thing to say, with perfect timing, in a dry, offhand, but memorable way. We really listened when Lynnie said something. Well, Lynnie died at the damnable age of fifty-six, and we felt that our heart as a group had been cut out. We didn't meet for a while, and then, when we did, the first order of things was to memorialize Lynne. Lynne used to drink a potent cocktail called a Rob Roy, made of scotch, sweet vermouth, and bitters, so when it came time to order drinks, Pat, eschewing his beloved Cutty Sark, ordered Rob Roys all around the table.

No good. I never drink cocktails, only a glass of wine once in a while. Spence was then on the wagon. So was Frank, little Frank, McHugh, because he was ill with tummy trouble. Frank Morgan had an early studio call and couldn't drink. And so on. There was no one to drink Lynne's health but Pat. So Pat got what seemed like an inspired idea. Lynne's favorite dish was lyonnaise potatoes, which he always ordered two dishes of, one for him and one for us to pass around so he wouldn't be bothered by people wanting to taste his. Lyonnaise potatoes, I must explain, are fried in heavy fat with lots of onions. So Pat ordered two dishes of lyonnaise potatoes and passed them around so we could toast Lynnie with a spoonful of his potatoes. We went around the table doing that, feeling a little silly, but it seemed a good idea. When the potatoes reached McHugh, he said politely, "No, thanks."

Pat got indignant. "What do you mean—you won't toast Lynnie? Didn't you love Lynnie?"

"Yes," said Frank. "Of course I loved Lynnie, but every time I taste those lyonnaise potatoes, I have to puke. I love Lynnie, but I don't want to join him."

Ralph Bellamy tells of a memorable occasion when Cagney's wealth and the newly built Motion Picture Country Home for retired actors and technicians were mentioned in the same breath:

On [one] occasion Jim, after having done *Yankee Doodle Dandy* from which he had acquired a bob or two, was thinking out loud at a Boys Club meeting: "We're all in a precarious business—profession if you will. I wonder if, God forbid, some unforseen tragedy arose, how would you go about gaining admission to the Motion Picture Country Home?" At this point there was a lengthy Macready [the English actor known for the long dramatic pauses he took].

Then Tracy leaned across the table and with a King Lear whisper replied, "Buy it, you bum, and we'll all get in."

The attrition of time and circumstance dissolved the Boys Club. Overman and Morgan died, Cagney and McHugh moved back east, O'Brien returned to the stage, Bellamy and Tracy alone remaining in California. But there are very few two-man clubs.

In his old age Cagney remembered: "Those were the finest and dearest men I ever knew. How honored and privileged I was to know them."

# 12 · Easier Trouble

When Jim was told that another service epic was to be his lot, he told Willie he thought that at least he couldn't be required to wallop anyone in *Devil Dogs of the Air*, a film that turned out to be something of a mate to *Here Comes the Navy*. He was happy to be starred with Pat O'Brien, and as was to be expected, in the old Captain Flagg–Sergeant Quirt framework, as rivals for the same girl, played in her usual gelid fashion by Margaret Lindsay.

As always in a service picture, someone has to be in mortal danger and saved in the last reel, and here Cagney and O'Brien are in equal peril, with the latter unexpectedly given the palm, having held together the severed wing of a plane they are flying. Frank McHugh was again comic relief, playing a medical attendant who is extremely disappointed when his services are not needed for crash calls that turn out to be false alarms.

Said Jim about McHugh:

All right, you can say I'm prejudiced. He's one of my best friends. But I'm telling God's truth when I say Frank McHugh brightened more dark corners of Warner Brothers pictures than they could ever give him sufficient credit for. He did it in such charming little ways. In *Devil Dogs* he made his laugh just plain fun. He took "ha, ha, ha" and deliberately spaced the words out, into what he called his one-two-three laugh. It is really three sounds that burlesque laughter. Made no sense at all, but that little bit of nonsense made people laugh—and he did this sort of thing over and over. He was worth his weight in platinum to Jack Warner, and give the old Shvontz credit, he realized it.

Not long after *Devil Dogs of the Air* was released, Jim was announced as one of the top ten moneymakers in Hollywood, and it was a matter of record that every one of his films made in 1934 had earned more than a

*Devil Dogs of the Air*
BELOW: With Margaret
Lindsay

million dollars. This kind of news story made Jack Warner very nervous indeed. He could just see Cagney preparing a brief for a salary increase. The Shvontz was always in charge of production, but he relied heavily on his chief deputies, first Darryl F. Zanuck, who left Warners in 1933, and then Zanuck's successor, hardworking, imaginative Hal Wallis.

Wallis not only put scripts into production but rode hard herd on all the company's directors, advising them after seeing the dailies that vital things needed to be stressed or unstressed. In 1935, when he cast Cagney as a idealistic young lawyer in a stunning new Warners picture, *G-Men,* Wallis told director William Keighley in an office memo to "harden Cagney up a little." Several days later Wallis scolded Keighley again by memo, saying, ". . . you are still playing Cagney too much of a gentleman." Cagney meanwhile was having the time of his life being a gentleman. Wallis told Keighley further: "I can't seem to get you to let the fellow be a mug from the East side. After all [in *G-Men*] he is supposed to be an East side mug who was put through law school by a lot of crooks, and he is playing it like a white-collared gentleman in a drawing room." What Keighley could not possibly convey to Wallis is that no one was going to tell Jim Cagney how to play an East Side mug with some education. Moreover, Jim did not much care for Keighley, regarding him as a poseur and a nice guy–phony from their early days together in New York, when Keighley had staged *Penny Arcade.*

Jim had hoped Wallis would appear on the set to give him instructions on how to act his role in *G-Men* (initially known as *The G-Men*). "Had that happened," said Jim, "it would have given me exquisite pleasure to tell Mr. Wallis to fuck off. I liked the way I was doing it, and I played it just the way I felt it."

To step from a bad guy to a good guy, and the best among the good guys—a crusading FBI agent—exhilarated Jim. He called Carrie to tell her, "Honest at last, Mom!"

Jim worked hard at his role of a lawyer turned agent to avenge the death of a pal by gangsters. Coolly ignoring Wallis's suggestion that he drag in a touch of the gutter, Jim played Brick Davis as the brisk, nice young man Jim was in real life. The film's climax is the agents' raid on a gangsters' country hideout where Brick's girl, Kay, is being held hostage. Here director Keighley gave Hal Wallis all the biff-bam-bang he wanted. It was ten minutes' gunfire for its own sake, serving the urge in all of us to watch a full spray of firecrackers just for the rackety hell of it.

Warner Brothers that year (1935) had signed a new and powerful actor to play bad guys: Barton MacLane, *G-Men*'s prime villain. Jim was delighted:

*G-Men,* with Robert Armstrong

Every tough guy they hired made it easier for me to evade those parts. Bart MacLane was also a guy easy to know, utterly natural, and the cause of pleasure for Pat, Frank, and me off camera. Because he was the most *naturally* profane man we had ever met. He cursed without giving it a thought; he cursed as he breathed. The marvelous thing about him was that he didn't realize this. Had no idea in the world how many profanities came out of his mouth. One night Willie and I went to the theater, a rarity for us because we were homebodies. But the road company of a good Broadway show came to town, so we decided to see it. It was pretty good, and we enjoyed it. We sat in our favorite seats, tenth row, all the way over on the right. After curtain calls we were walking up to the lobby, and then I heard this voice, "Hey, Jim!" I turned around, and there was Bart and his wife, walking up the middle aisle toward the lobby amidst a large portion of the audience.

"How'd you like it?" I shouted to him.

"Best fuckin' show I ever saw," he shouted with utter sincerity.

Willie and I practically choked, trying to hide our laughter. He meant it. It was the best fuckin' show he ever saw, and so he said so.

He loved that adjective. Pat, Frank, and I used to ask him innocent questions just to see how many times he'd use his favorite word. "Howya doing, Bart?"

"Fuckin' OK."

The last shooting day of *G-Men* was March 28, 1935, and in an intracompany memo an assistant director, Chuck Hansen, reported to Hal Wallis that Cagney seemed to be up to his old tricks again. On orders from above, Hansen dismissed the performers—Cagney, Ann Dvorak, and eight extras—plus crew and director, at 5:40 p.m. with instructions to be back at 6:45 p.m. so they could shoot the very last bit of script. Cagney is quoted in the memo as replying, "Not me. I told you last night I wouldn't work tonight. I'm going home and won't be back." Hansen's complaint was that the studio had "to carry on salary the entire *G-Men* [crew] and part of the cast one day beyond completion date." The most interesting part of the memo is a listing of the daily pay of the key people involved. For a day's work, at a time when the dollar was very robust indeed, the pay rates were: Keighley, the director, $108.33; Cagney, $666.67; Ann Dvorak, $183.33; eight crew members and extras, $5 each. It paid to be a star.

What Hansen did not know was Cagney's habit of extending production an extra day for the benefit of extras and crew. As an indigent actor he too well remembered his meals of water and soda crackers.

Making *G-Men* was a pleasure because of his role. The only irritation, by now distinctly bothersome to Jim, was Margaret Lindsay. One of her lines was spoken in pure American save for the last word: "Every time I see you I wonder if it's going to be the last!" "Last" came out "lahst," then unaccountably in the next line, after saying "chance" in American, she pronounced it "chahnce" minutes later. Cagney could never understand why director Keighley allowed these little aberrations.

*G-Men* won much critical favor. *Time* magazine called it "enormously exciting." *Liberty* magazine pronounced it "violent, sanguinary and highly exciting," and William Boehnel of the *New York World-Telegram* said, "Mr. Cagney has acted any number of superb characterizations . . . but I think that here, as Brick Davis, he gives his most satisfactory performance." What Boehnel applauded was James Cagney playing pretty much James Cagney, a quiet, intelligent, yet potentially volatile man. The *Times* of London said that Cagney, "who has often found himself toughly and coolly resisting law and order, is here their champion—and a very vigorous and courageous one he is." It went on to point out perceptively that switching from bad guy to good guy diminished not a whit "his air of having every situation well in hand, however loaded the dice may seem against him, his self-confidence and his gift for repartee. It has only limited them, and the very discipline of limitation has, oddly enough, given them an added significance."

Only one movie critic, the still-obscure but brilliant Otis Ferguson, writing for the *New Republic,* saw *G-Men*'s failure to address, as it so ostentatiously seemed to, just what crooks and national crime were all about. National morals keepers, being who they presently are, said Ferguson, have forced the writers of *G-Men*

> to show the underworld from the top looking down, dissolving finally to the hint that old Joe Crime, he dies herewith. . . . The big-time gangster as a sort of inverted public hero (not enemy), a lonely, possessed and terrible figure . . . is not shown here. In *G-Men* he is simply a dangerous bad man who would have gone on nefariously forever if the government had not come along, with the aid of love and that delightful man Cagney put a stop to him for good. All gone now, all better. It not only makes a flabby evasion of the rather cruel truth, but it makes a flabby picture, and a disappointment.

Ferguson is right. *G-Men* is flabby aesthetically, utterly lacking in core truth. It is also infinitely watchable, and it made millions. Ferguson conceded in his review that the public for *G-Men* was "breaking down the doors at its first New York showings," a clear sign "that the public has been dying for a little dish of crime."

Someone high at Warners must have gotten the message that Cagney came from an East Side Irish family and would particularly enjoy doing a comedy set in that framework. *The Irish in Us* possessed for its three stars the virtue of sharing the main work. This is not a Cagney vehicle; it is a Cagney-McHugh-O'Brien vehicle, and though the film is creaky in plot and cursorily written, the combined force of these talented Irish boyos playing brothers holds it well together. It is hard to conceive that writer Frank Orsatti did not know of the brace of Cagney brothers and their love-'em-and-keep-'em-in-line Irish ma. Such mas have been a staple of Irish drama since before Boucicault and Lady Gregory. "Having the three of us throwing ideas about was just what the writer wanted," said Jim. "Our director was Lloyd Bacon. He told us, 'Go to it, boys!' and we did. We thought something worthwhile would happen, and mostly it did."

There was one initial difficulty in putting the picture together. When the cast was announced, Cagney and Pat O'Brien were appalled, privately,

*The Irish in Us*, with Mary Gordon

at the casting of Mary Gordon for the role of their mother. They knew Gordon's thick, double-burred Scots accent would be fully intelligible only to residents of The Gorbals, Inverness, and John o' Groat's. For years Gordon had been cast in Hollywood Irish roles to the increasing dismay of bred-in-the-bone Irish film actresses like Una O'Connor and Sara Allgood. The latter, although living in England at the time (1935), told Pat O'Brien years later that had picketing by actors been in vogue, she would have resorted to it in this instance at Warner Brothers' London office. "Mary Gordon was a perfectly good actress," Allgood told O'Brien, "but the dear lady's accent wasn't anywhere *near* Irish. Certainly not to Irish ears, and to those who know Irish voices and real Irish accents. Her casting in your picture was an insult to Irish actresses."

Jim insisted that some reference to Gordon's obvious Caledonian quality had to be made in the script. He was given the line "Uh, uh, that wee bit o' Scotch comin' out again" when he and Gordon discuss money. "*Wee* bit indeed," said Allgood testily to O'Brien. *Time* magazine's review said that "Mary Gordon's brogue is so strong that, to the possible improvement of the picture, half her lines are virtually unintelligible."

Fortunately for Cagney in *The Irish in Us* he is typecast as a man who loves boxing. Here he has the pleasure of playing an out-of-work fighter and promoter whose "boy" was lunkhead Car-Barn Hammerschlog, bouncily played by Allen Jenkins, who drinks a bottle of gin to solace a toothache, forcing his mentor to take his place. Cagney got in the ring for the second time in a Warners production and with Harvey Perry, his opponent in *Winner Take All*. In the making of that film, Tommy, a pug friend of Perry's, watched the protracted rehearsals with Cagney, then told Perry, a redoubtable welterweight, that Cagney was a "pro," and he was willing to bet on it. Perry explained Cagney's street fighter background, and Tommy still refused to believe it. It took Jim himself to explain that his skilled footwork came from being a dancer. "You ought to give lessons," Tommy told him.

The leading lady of *The Irish in Us* is Olivia De Havilland, and here, said Jim, "was a delightful lady. Beautiful, like Maggie Lindsay, but warm, warm, warm. A joy to work with." As in most of his pictures, Cagney gets the girl, this time winning her from Pat O'Brien, and McHugh gets most of the laughs. In *Cagney by Cagney* Jim recalls with special fondness a scene "where Frank comes in, having been to a formal affair at the Firemen's Ball. He returns home at midnight wearing a full-dress suit and a white cap. Pat looks at the cap and says, 'You didn't wear that to the ball?' to which Frank improvised the great reply, 'Shoulda been black, huh?' "

Lloyd Bacon, director of *The Irish in Us*, was personally esteemed by Cagney, McHugh, and O'Brien. The son of the distinguished actor Frank Bacon, whose tenure as the star of *Lightnin'* established a Broadway long-run record in 1918–21, Lloyd was one of the few directors Cagney liked or trusted. He said, "Lloyd knew his business, but he rushed everything. He liked to get it done—and as soon as possible. My God, there were times when we rehearsed scenes before the camera, and he would surreptitiously film and print those rehearsals. But he always let us do our own thing, and the three of us, Pat, Frank, and I, used to ad-lib the dialogue to no one's discontent as far as I could see. We called those pictures cuff operas because so much in them was done off the cuff. That helped rather than hindered."

The next Cagney picture released was *A Midsummer Night's Dream*, which had actually been filmed between *Devil Dogs of the Air* and *G-Men*, the delay occasioned by the long editing and special musical track of the Mendelssohn music scored for the film by the authoritative Erich Wolfgang Korngold. *A Midsummer Night's Dream* is a Cagney film in that his name heads the cast list, but he gibed at the designation when he first heard it used by a Warners flack. The man was ordered to desist. The billing proportions based on 100 percent were title, 100 percent, Shakespeare 50 percent, Cagney together with Joe E. Brown and Dick Powell, 80 percent; Mickey Rooney and Victor Jory, 20 percent. Something was seriously out of whack when the greatest writer in history got only 50 percent.

Cagney had no desire, then or later, to play Shakespeare. It was not, he said, his cup of tea. He had not even read *A Midsummer Night's Dream* when casting began. But Bottom, the bumptious Elizabethan weaver, with his gargantuan vanity and invincible belief in himself, is one of the world's great comic creations, and Cagney knew it was at least worth the trying. Several top Warners executives wanted Guy Kibbee for the role and mercifully were argued down. Kibbee's specialty was general befuddlement, not a characteristic of Bottom, and it is highly unlikely that Kibbee would have been able to suggest any of Bottom's volatility. Hal Wallis particularly wanted Kibbee, but Reinhardt insisted on Cagney.

In explaining his choice, Reinhardt spoke of the actor's "mysterious, dangerous, terrifying uncertainty that never allows an audience to relax." The director did not explain how those three adjectives, absolutely inapplicable to Bottom, qualified Cagney to play this mindless buffoon. There is no question Reinhardt thought Cagney the best actor in Hollywood, because he said so on a number of occasions, adding, "Few artists have ever had his intensity, his dramatic drive. Every movement of his body, and his incredible hands, contribute to the story he is trying to tell." In the event, they contributed virtually nothing to *A Midsummer Night's Dream*.

The entire production derived from a variety of Max Reinhardt's productions of the *Dream* in Austria, in England, and most spectacularly at the Hollywood Bowl in 1934. Here he emphasized spectacle, in close consonance with Mendelssohn's score, and the production was seen and admired by most prominent filmmakers in Hollywood. But only Hal Wallis had the imagination and (some said) the nerve or guts to bring Reinhardt's vision of the *Dream* to film. The result is, in Otis Ferguson's phrase, "fairly tedious," at least it is for those who love Shakespeare. In the tripartite plot of the lovers, the fairies, and the homespun tradesmen, the latter are far the best in this film for two reasons: they do not have to worry about the great lines of poetry since they all speak prose, and in their number are some of Warner Brothers' most skilled character actors. Cagney does Bottom poorly, but his ebullience would make the Nile stand still, and Joe E. Brown as Flute, a bellows mender, is riveting in his childlike mental opacity. Frank McHugh as Quince, a carpenter, almost steals the show with his earnest, plodding, concerned stupidity, and Hugh Herbert, if, as always, overdoing his giggle, is nonetheless consistently in character as Snout, a tinker. Dewey Robinson, Otis Harlan, and Arthur Treacher as the other "mechanicals" all contribute something, however small. *In toto* they convey the essence of "men which never labored in their minds till now."

The fairies, especially their monarchs, Victor Jory and Anita Louise, are not very lyrical. Puck, as bountifully, beautifully played by Mickey Rooney, does steal what show there is to be stolen. But his physicality was severely limited by his breaking his leg while tobogganing at Big Bear early in the shooting and by the necessity of having to wheel him about in most of his scenes on a disguised tricycle.

The lovers, except for Olivia De Havilland, are weak. Dick Powell's cutesy-pie smirking as Lysander is shame-making.

A disappointment for this writer is Cagney as Bottom. Not his fault, it might be said. He had no experience in Shakespeare. Yet either he or the studio had the option of furnishing him with an acting coach for this specialized role. His energy as always is enormous, and one cannot resist its consummate directness. He does have one brilliant moment in the film; the rest is simply profitless overacting, particularly in the Pyramus and Thisbe scene at court. In that, he and the others overdo an already spectacularly overdone play within a play. Burlesquing a burlesque undoes the burlesque, which must always be played with great sincerity. "Now this overdone, or come tardy off, though it make the unskilful laugh, cannot but make the judicious grieve," Hamlet tells the Players. "Overdone" is the word here— for the film's direction or more likely for the lack of it. Reinhardt was nominally the director, but all details of shooting were in the hands of his former student and assistant William Dieterle, an intimidating man, six feet five inches, who rather unnerved the actors by constantly wearing white gloves. He was in fact in awe of Cagney's reputation and hardly spoke a word to him. Hal Wallis, watching the dailies, knew full well that Cagney was overdoing it, and in a February 12, 1935, memo to Henry Blanke, German-born and -speaking production supervisor of the *Dream,* chewed him out: "Also, while it is too late to do anything about it, I am telling you that Cagney overacted too much in the last scenes in the palace. He used his hands too much and generally hoked it up too much, even though he was supposed to be burlesquing what he was doing."

The indictment is true. Moreover, the Cagney performance is also flawed by his incessant, extraneous laughter. It is rather as if he were saying to himself as performer, "What the hell do I do now? Ah, to hell with it.

Since I've got to do something, I'll laugh." This he does endlessly and prof-itlessly. He also throws away one of the biggest laugh lines in the play. Bot-tom, like any number of Shakespearean clowns, is given to malapropisms, and there is none funnier than his injunction to his fellow mechanicals to follow Quince's instructions for them to rehearse in the palace wood lest they be observed and be "dogged with company." Bottom concurs, adding, "We will meet, and there we may rehearse most obscenely and coura-geously." Bottom has heard "obscenely" before and thinks it means "obscurely." Cagney gives the word the same tempo and emphasis as the other words, without the needed stress to punch up the gag. He says the entire line quickly, in typical Cagney style. The laugh due here is a big one in the *Dream,* and it is gone, the victim of underemphasis, a rare charge against Cagney.

Cagney told this writer that he was not directed in any sense by Dieterle and only once by Reinhardt. But a very good bit of business that once was. When Bottom awakes after Titania has been restored to sense and his ass's head has been removed, he yawns and begins, "I have had a most rare vision. I have had a dream. . . . Methought I was, and methought I had—" He holds out his hand twelve inches from his face. Dr. Reinhardt directed him then to move trembling hands up to feel the ass's ears. Not there. He laughs with delight, laughs again—a laugh that sounds like a donkey's bray. Now in earnest he begins to feel for snout and ears, cannot find them, walks away, trembling still, but exalted.

Yet Cagney would not be Cagney if there were not a moment of special skill entirely his own, and in this instance it is the most moving moment of his performance. After imposing the ass's head on Bottom, Puck throws a stone at his neck, Bottom scratches, discovers his hairiness, and bit by bit searches out his elongated ears. Then, sadly, comically, his traveling hands find his snout. He drops down to look at himself in a stream and then rises to croon a single, sad note to himself. The tears course down his hairy cheeks, and as he sings his little nonsense song, "The finch, the sparrow, and the lark . . . ," he achieves pathos, something notably hard to do with a don-key's head covering the most expressive part of one's body. His wobbly tonal-ity as he sings (Cagney's singing was always uncertain unless he talked his songs) serves him perfectly here. It is a broken voice in more ways than one, and for a few seconds Bottom becomes both funny and richly poignant.

*A Midsummer Night's Dream* did not reap much critical praise, the reviewers concentrating in most cases on Cagney's worth or lack of it. His favorite critic, Richard Watts of the *New York Herald Tribune,* as expected,

*A Midsummer Night's Dream*

*A Midsummer Night's Dream.* ABOVE: With Joe E. Brown

liked him, saying Bottom "was excellently played . . . because [Cagney] really is a first-rate actor. At the same time, he did disappoint me slightly. I thought he would be something more than just effective." André Sennwald of *The New York Times,* after praising Joe E. Brown and Mickey Rooney as the best performers in the film, found Cagney "too dynamic an actor to play the torpid and obstinate dullard," adding that the actor "belabors the slapstick of his part beyond endurance." Sydney Carroll of *The Times* of London said definitively, "The most lamentable mistake in the cast was the Bottom of James Cagney. He seemed to me to misconceive the character and only became tolerable where he discovers the ass's head on his shoulders."

After a number of films with Lloyd Bacon, Jim would kid his now-close friend, "Are we going to run with this one, Lloyd? Do you get a bonus if we finish in three weeks?" Bacon would grin, but he never denied the bonus charge. *Frisco Kid* took more than three weeks to make, but not by much. Jim's appraisal of it was "that stinking piece of junk, made up of tissue paper and spit." It was an obvious copy of Samuel Goldwyn's recently successful *Barbary Coast,* and when Jim was given the outline of *Frisco Kid*'s plot, he said to Warners executive Robert Lord, "Goldwyn wouldn't even sue you for making this pile of *dreck.* Are you really going to make this thing?"

Lord replied, "Jim, for Christ's sake, it's already sold. We've got a million dollars in the bank from it right now. You can't quarrel with that, can you?"

*Frisco Kid* is notable, if that's the word, for more exhortatory mob scenes than almost any other movie ever made. Someone is forever standing up and stepping forward to urge a feckless group of faceless people to revolt, hang someone, wipe out dens of iniquity, or burn down a town. Despite Margaret Lindsay's being cast as his girl, Jim agreed to play the penniless sailor, Bat Morgan, who rises to opulent power on San Francisco's Barbary Coast, once more engaging in a violent fight, this time with Fred Kohler, prime screen villain of the thirties. The fight is the only memorable thing in *Frisco Kid.*

Kohler plays Shanghai Duck, a brute of a man who makes his living by selling men as sailors for ships en route to China. His very sight is intimidating: massive of build, and in place of a right hand there hangs a heavy, sharp hook. When he and Cagney go at it, it is gladiators to battle stations, and the watching crowd is all for Cagney. After his inevitable triumph Lloyd Bacon yelled, "Cut!" and Jim walked to his supine opponent to help him up. But Kohler waved away the proffered hand. "Thanks, Jim, just let me rest," he said, breathing heavily. Jim walked away, worried. One of his pet dicta to

*Frisco Kid*, with Lili
Damita and Fred Kohler

friends was "Never surprise your heart," and he chastised buddies who failed to get proper exercise. His apprehension about Kohler was well founded: Kohler was to die of heart disease at forty-nine.

Graham Greene in his film critic days found *Frisco Kid* "stale, sentimental, worthless," but he thought its fight scene deserved to be placed in an anthology "of the excellent scenes that can so often be found in the worst films," citing it as the most brutal and convincing "I can remember seeing on the screen." One scene Greene doubtless found "stale" was one Jim also found so. The last scene in the film was a conventional "kiss and fade." He could not bring himself to kiss Margaret Lindsay in the usual manner. Instead he kissed her on the brow; her head rests on his manly chest as the music swells and the scene fades.

If *Frisco Kid* was predictable and derivative, the next Cagney film, *Ceiling Zero,* was the first of these but not the second. The mixture, as before, was Cagney the bad boy getting in trouble and doing something redeemingly heroic. But the theme of *Ceiling Zero* is that and something more, uniquely more: the weather. This trip out, Cagney had no fears about either vehicle or director. *Ceiling Zero* had been a successful Broadway play, and the film version was directed by Howard Hawks. Hawks, himself a master pilot with combat experience in World War I, selected *Ceiling Zero* for its nostalgic appeal. It was written by Lieutenant Commander Frank Wead, who went through World War I as a naval flier, returned home, fell out of an office chair, became paralyzed, and turned to writing. Every technical detail in the film's action is rivetingly authentic. The film's action is chiefly the changing weather. "Ceiling zero" meant total fog or similar atmospherics that prevented flight but that some daring fliers ignored, usually to their peril. One such is Dizzy Davis (Cagney), wearing (alas) a Charlie Chase mustache, who is chief pilot and frequent heartache for Federal Airlines and is an underling of old flying comrade Jake Lee (Pat O'Brien), head of the company's Newark airfield. Dizzy and Jake have a pilot cohort, Tex (Stuart Erwin), who was in their outfit in the war, also stationed at the field.

Dizzy is the dashing scapegrace type, Tex is the amiable comic relief, and Jake is the stern but only human paterfamilias who must maintain a balance between his loyalty to the airline and to rule-breaking Dizzy. Dizzy feigns heart trouble to keep a date with a lady flier, and Tex takes his place on a flight. Ceiling zero occurs, and Tex crashes to his death. Later guilt-

*Ceiling Zero*, with Pat O'Brien, Isabel Jewell, and June Travis

ridden Dizzy in similar weather, defying orders, takes up a plane to test a new de-icer, he too falling to his death.

The critics ranked *Ceiling Zero* as near-prime Cagney and certainly a good example of its genre. The *London Daily Telegraph* defined this with a faint trace of condescension: "The Americans are unsurpassed in the contrivance of films which bolster up improbable events and crude psychology with plausible detail. These films have little or no relation to art, but they are undeniably entertaining." Sniff, sniff. Cagney said his films were not in any fashion concerned with art, a point he made several times, echoing the opinion of his friend Fred Astaire, who regarded the use of the word in respect to his films as akin to personal injury.

Jim had once asked a mutual friend for an introduction to Astaire and was told by the friend to be at a certain RKO sound stage by 3:00 p.m. Jim arrived early and hid as best he could in order to watch Astaire at work. Jim marveled and called it a high point of his life. The two became good friends and shared many memories of various vaudeville theaters they had known. Jim said, "Freddie had one characteristic: he was the best. Not one of the best. The *best.*" Astaire, who had been in show business from early childhood, once shocked Jim by using a number of raunchy oaths. "You know, Freddie," Jim told him delightedly, "you've got a touch of the hoodlum in you."

With the completion of *Ceiling Zero,* Jim's money itch began again, stimulated in part by brother Bill, who by now had retired from acting and was Jim's full-time manager.\* Warners, said Jim, "was still consistently interested in paying me only a very small percentage of the income dollar deriving from my work." He had an excellent opportunity to express his dissatisfaction. One of the specifics of the Cagney-Warners contract was that he was always to receive top billing in all his pictures. The manager of a Los Angeles Warners-owned film house, the Beverly Theatre, for no one knows what reason, set out on his marquee "PAT O'BRIEN in *Ceiling Zero.*" A reporter pal of Cagney's saw it and telephoned Jim, who immediately sent a photographer to record the aberration. The Cagneys were jubilant. Jack Warner raged. He knew what this little mistake portended.

---

\*Bill Cagney's acting career consisted of four films: *Ace of Aces* (1933), *Flirting with Danger, Lost in the Stratosphere,* and *Palooka* (1934), mostly for Monogram Pictures.

# 13 · Out of the Factory

I thought to myself, three strikes and out," said Cagney, "when the *Ceiling Zero* billing thing came up. I was really fed up with The Shvontz and the whole damned Warners setup. And I know they had no fond thoughts of me. I had the fullest confidence in brother Bill, and so I left it all up to him. We let my agent go, our lawyer go, because I knew Bill would get me the best deal possible. No more factory work for me was the way I felt. Warners had become just that for me, a factory. A place to churn out product. I wasn't going to be churned out anymore."

He and Willie drove East and found a temporary apartment at the Gramercy Park Hotel a few feet from his beloved club, The Players, where he could hold forth with old pals. Among them he had a particular favorite, Ed McNamara, a rotund ex-cop from Paterson, New Jersey, who had a singing voice that, said Jim, "could charm the angels and anyone else in hearing range." McNamara, although not much more than a journeyman actor—whom Jim tried to put in as many of his pictures as possible—held top rank as a singer who remained unsung. "Maybe it's because he looked like John L. Sullivan gone to seed that he didn't make it as a singer," said Jim. "But the likes of his voice I have heard only a few times in a lifetime."

Ed could have been, averred Jim, one of the Metropolitan's great stars had he started younger and given himself over to the task. But Ed was really given over to his friends. "He was, for me, the perfect example of the man who could have had it all but didn't want to pay the price," said Jim. Marc Connelly said of him, "Ed McNamara is the greatest container of affection I have ever seen." A senator of Ed's home state, Billy Hughes, was a friend of Caruso's and told the great tenor of Ed's talent. After Caruso had heard Ed sing, he called that voice the most natural organ he had ever heard and urged him to get a good teacher. Ed said, "Fine, what teacher?"

Caruso thought a minute, then said, "Don't take a chance on a teacher. I'll teach you," and he did, Ed becoming Caruso's only pupil.

"So this great voice came into existence," said Jim, "and sadly, only his friends knew it or ever heard it."

Ed McNamara became a Cagney traveling companion and was, from the testimony of all who knew him, the greatest company in the world. When Jim asked him why he didn't enter the world of show business whole-heartedly, Ed said, "I am in the hands of my friends. They're the best company a man could have, and I suppose I'll always keep it that way." One of the friends was a well-known cartoonist of the time, Denys Wortman, who lived on Martha's Vineyard. Ed suggested he and Jim go up to visit Denny for a little holiday since Jim's future looked very open in 1936.

When Jim saw the beautiful Massachusetts island in all its summer lush-ness, quite unspoiled by tourists then, he was enamored. He drove about the island, examining it all appraisingly, and lost his heart to a little agricul-tural area in the island's center. It all seemed so unlikely, the things he loved most: a farm and near the sea. It was irresistible. He bought a hundred-acre farm with an old, extremely decrepit, yet obviously durable house on it, accessible only by a dirt road. The inaccessibility comforted him a great deal. The house's deed went back to 1728, and all this was his for an incred-ible seventy-five hundred dollars. Willie, like Carrie Cagney, was indelibly a city girl, despite her rural origin, and she was very loath even to visit the place. Jim prevailed. She went up reluctantly and remained reluctant until she went rooting through the jumble sale mélange she found in the attic.

Willie was a history buff, and in a mess of papers in the attic she found to her considerable and delighted surprise a newspaper announcing Lin-coln's second Civil War draft together with old journals of similar age and value. She found letters to the farm family from sailors who had jumped ship in California and been caught up in the gold rush. She discovered a ladle made of bone once used on a whaling ship, and a hundred other pieces of history. She was captivated. Their farm on Tea Lane, Martha's Vineyard, became their retreat from Hollywood. To be accurate, Jim's retreat. All their lifetime Willie went agreeably enough to where her husband wanted to go, but at heart she was always Ruth amid the alien corn whenever she left their California home.

Harry Flynn, a prominent Hollywood publicist, met Jim in 1939:

I come from a Martha's Vineyard family, and we still live there. When Jim arrived in 1936, there was an automatic caution sign lit up by natives who judge new arrivals on the island not by their celebrity or wealth but by what kind of people they are at heart. Right away they became very fond of Jim. The island is used to celebrities; indeed it's amenable to them if they fit in. He did at once. He was a landowner, had his own farm, whereas most celebrities came down on a big boat or rented a place. Jim was straightforward, no airs. I loved the guy. We all knew he loved the land and was very serious about working it. Indeed that's why he finally had to leave the island after years there because he couldn't get the farm labor he needed to really work his land.

One story that has anecdotal preference in our family is of Jim coming to stay with us one of those rare occasions when he didn't have time to open the farm and stay awhile. On such fleeting visits he always stayed with us. We kept his old wool lumber shirt and corduroy pants in a back closet. On one particular visit he brought Allen Jenkins with him, and those two took on themselves the very serious and arduous job of opening one of our ponds. Our oyster pond has to be opened two or three times a year into the ocean because the tidal movement brings salt water back into the pond and keeps the clams and oysters alive. So the opening of ponds on the Vineyard has been a tradition for hundreds of years, and our family still does it.

So here are Jim Cagney and Allen Jenkins, guys I don't think who have a lot of shoveling in their schedules, working away at this pond opening, which in places means digging deep and digging a lot. It is one hell of a lot of work, and they did it, getting very sunburned in the process. Jim, especially, with his fair skin. They opened up that pond and in consequence were terribly proud of themselves, as they had good reason to be. So Jim Cagney was a legend to us, not as a movie star but as a kind, caring, and compassionate man. As a neighbor, a good neighbor.

While Jim was being enchanted with his island, brother Bill was carving out a little happy enclave for them that had promise of growing into a company all their own. Edward L. Alperson, formerly of Warner Brothers' Sales Division, had learned his lessons well at the studio and, knowing that a successful film studio needed hefty financial backing, good directors, and a box-office star, approached Bill Cagney with an offer. Alperson had the first two of the three essentials. He offered the Cagneys $100,000 a picture and 10 percent of the earnings. The Cagneys took it, and a contract for those terms was signed with Alperson's company, Grand National Films, Inc.

In the interim there was the matter of Jim's walkout from Warners to be settled. Early in March 1936 he appeared in court to testify that Warners had violated his contract by its failure to keep an oral agreement Jack Warner had made with him that Jim would appear in no more than four pictures a year. Jim was called to the stand and, in dilating his experience of contract talks with Warners executives, began with quoting comments made to him by Darryl Zanuck, specifically one in which Zanuck "asked me where I got such ideas of money." Jim continued: "He said in effect 'what do you mean by asking for so much money?' He said he wasn't getting much more than that himself. I told him that his career was a different type than mine, because his was of a much more lasting nature. I said he shouldn't object because he himself had well over his share of worldly goods. 'You should see my bills,' he told me."

In court on March 5, 1936, Jim went on to reveal a personal discussion he had had with Jack Warner just before his last contract was signed: "Jack Warner said he could not understand why Darryl Zanuck ever signed me. [Warner] said he didn't like me and could not understand why Zanuck wanted a mug like me around the place. Mr. Warner also said that because of my lack of drawing power I wasn't as important as I thought I was, and that therefore the studio could not possibly use more than four of my pictures a year." He and Warner, continued Jim, went on at length to discuss the limiting of the number of films he was to do. "J.L. [Jack] said he didn't have to put [the four-pictures-a-year specification] in the contract because his brother Harry [president of Warner Brothers] would think he was completely off his nut. [Jack] said, 'Just accept my word for it that we can't make more than four pictures or sell more than four [Cagney] pictures a year."

The next day in court the Warner Brothers attorney brought to the stand Jim's former agent George Frank, who had just been fired by Bill Cagney. Frank testified that Jack Warner had never committed himself to the number of pictures a year Cagney would make. In quick cross-examination Frank's strength as an objective witness was considerably lessened when the Cagney lawyer got him to admit that he would receive $35,000 in commissions if the Cagney suit was dismissed and Warners won, thus maintaining Frank's original contract. There was personal unhappiness here because Frank and Cagney had been close friends, but both understood the necessary tensions of a contract dispute.

Next day in court Jim made a final plea that twice since the 1932 contract had been signed, the studio had forced him to make five pictures within a twelve-month period. The studio lawyer, in turn, denied that any oral agreement on limitations had ever been made, additionally pointing out that a section of Cagney's contract specified that no oral understanding had been reached outside the terms of the contract itself.

Ten days later, March 16, 1936, the Cagneys appeared in court to face, together with two Warners attorneys, Superior Court Judge Charles Bogue, who ruled:

1. Cagney's contention about the four-film limitation was not valid because he had automatically waived his right under the alleged oral agreement when he went back to work for the studio after making a protest.

2. However, Warner Brothers had breached the Cagney contract when it violated a section providing that he should always receive star billing. The studio failed to do so in the Pat O'Brien/*Ceiling Zero* instance, as well as on one occasion when Cagney's name was second to Joan Blondell's in a *Footlight Parade* ad.

James Cagney was now a freelance actor, fully entitled to enter the employ of Grand National Pictures. One of the plums in the contract was that he would have final approval of all films made.

It was not an accident that his first film for Grand National was titled *Great Guy* and that its protagonist was a squeaky clean inspector for the

*Great Guy*, with James Burke

city's department of weights and measures. The only further away you could get from gangsterdom was to enlist in the clergy. Even more, was it not an accident that Cagney's leading lady was Mae Clarke, who lovingly bullies him throughout the film? Reversal intact. The new Cagney regime does not eschew rough stuff often, but offers it only when rough stuff is needed against bad guys. Jim's character is the hero of a series of *Saturday Evening Post* stories: Johnny Cave, fighting precursor of Ralph Nader and other friends of the housewife.

The plot is fairly predictable, concerning as it does a faithful civic servant who must be offered bribes and upon his refusal be set up and placed in compromising situations until, after losing his girl, he regains her by uncovering graft and governmental malaise. The Cagney acting style is unchanged. All the gestures are in place, but particularly the floating, air-sculpting hands, this time not overdone. In later years the use of his hands as dramatic punctuation diminished considerably, but in this yet early phase of his career they are deftly and fascinatingly employed. In moments of stress his right hand becomes a lithe snake's head that writhes and lunges in anger, changing with the sudden lift of an admonitory finger to make its own emphatic, intimidating statement. In quiet contrast, his hands can float softly, and not at all ostentatiously, as they gently lift up Mae's chin for a kiss.

When asked about this in old age, Jim said, "Where I lived as a boy, with so many different languages spoken around you, you not only learned how to talk with your hands instead of words, you learned how other people talked with *their* hands. Everybody, from the guy selling fruit on the corner to your neighbor to the guy cleaning the street to the kids you met in school, all talking a different lingo—you couldn't possibly communicate unless you had hands and used them well. I just kept on using them when I started to dance and when I got in pictures."

Despite plot predictability, *Great Guy* is briskly paced and well written. At one point Cagney expostulates to Clarke: "My best friend gets hit by a streetcar, there's Civil War in Spain, we have an earthquake in Japan—and now you wear that hat!," pointing to a saucy creation on her head. Ed McNamara is in the cast and quite typecast as a police captain, bringing his infectiously robust charm to the role. The mother of *The Irish in Us,* Mary Gordon, also appears as an orphanage head, her Scots' burred *r* ("in all my yearrrs of serrrvice") strong enough to unskin a mammoth. "Nice old lady," said Jim, "but I could barely understand her. They brought her in at the last minute when the actress originally cast couldn't make it."

Cagney is as cheerily truculent as ever but now on the side of the law. When one lawbreaker argues and swings at him, Cagney gives him a hard right and drops him at once. The reviewers all noted this, and *Variety* was disappointed: "It's all typical Cagney stuff, and that's the trouble with it. An actor of Cagney's ability should not be typed, either at the studio or in public estimation." The reviewer evidently missed the point that Cagney was now playing a sweetheart for a change. The reviewer for *Time* magazine called it "vintage Cagney, [going] a long way to disprove the Hollywood theory that, given a free hand in selecting stories and casts, an actor's vanity is sure to lead him astray. . . . [The picture] sets the industry an example of what a young company can do by spending its money on good actors and good writing instead of big names, ponderous sets and over-pretentious publicity."

It was at this time that Jim had one of his most curious Hollywood experiences. Out of the blue came a personal phone call from Charlie Chaplin, hoping that Jim and Willie would join him and consort—if that's what she was—Paulette Goddard for a visit to Chaplin's home. "Do come," said Chaplin. "I'd like to talk over business matters and to have a pleasant day." Jim said:

On the phone he asked me if I played tennis. No, I didn't play tennis—my sport was dancing—but I wasn't against trying. It was that "business matters" that intrigued me. What the hell could we have in common? So I said yes, and Willie and I went there to his mansion in time to have lunch—a very good one, well served—and after an hour or two we drifted out to his tennis courts, Willie talking to Paulette, I to Chaplin. Or rather he to me, because for all the hours we were there I swear the man never stopped talking and putting on his little sideshow pantomimes. I have never seen a guy pour on the charm as relentlessly as he did—and I have never been so goddamned bored in my *life*. He'd be explaining some pretty peripheral matters—peripheral to him and me anyway, I thought—or talking about something I knew or cared nothing about, and for chrissakes, he'd *act it out for me*. I guess I was supposed to marvel at his ability to do this. Anyway. He finally got around to what we were there for. He had just written a screenplay about Napoleon, and would I be interested? I told him politely that no, I wouldn't, thinking to myself that I'd be interested in Napoleon just about as much as I'd be interested in playing Little Lord Fauntleroy. He pointed out that I'd make "a splendid Napoleon," what with my "forceful personality" or something like that. I made it very clear, again very politely, that the answer was no. That didn't stop him from entertaining us, though. He was "on" all the time we were there, and I can say truthfully that I have rarely had a duller, more misspent day.

One can understand Chaplin's interest in the role. As David Robinson says, "Napoleon offers a uniquely rich role for an actor of small stature." Chaplin and Cagney were at least as one in being short.

Ed Alperson, head of Grand National, was very pleased with its first Cagney film. *Great Guy* seemed to have all the potential of a hit, and the new studio began the difficult and complex task of getting it distributed. There were then five major studios, and they did not take kindly to thoughts of a sixth. This meant not only another slice of the market pie gone but complications that would (in the words of a film business scholar) "have seriously altered the complex system of cooperative bookings then common in Hollywood." Notwithstanding, Grand National went bravely ahead with its second Cagney vehicle, *Something to Sing About,* a musical.

In his eightieth year, when Cagney was asked which of his films, outside of *Yankee Doodle Dandy,* he would like to see again—he had seen just under half of his output—he selected *Something to Sing About.* A sixteen-millimeter print was obtained and shown him. "I like the songs. They're damned cute," he said. More particularly, he yearned to see his old comrades-in-dance Johnny Boyle and Harland Dixon, two men integral to the making of the film. Johnny Boyle was, if anyone can be so credited, the creator of the Cagney dancing style, a style at once highly eclectic and uniquely street Cagney, a mix of George M. Cohan (whom Boyle had worked for), semiballet, and down-to-earth vaudeville hoofing. Jim had worked with both Boyle and Dixon in vaudeville and deeply admired their work. He loved their style, based on walking cadences emphasizing frequent turns and gentle, floating use of the arms. They do this splendidly in *Something to Sing About* with Jim in the center of their routine, happy to be between his old friends. Jim had several films made of both men in their best routines and would watch them for hours.

Dancing, much more than acting, was in those years Jim's greatest creative joy. As he points out in *Cagney by Cagney,* he considered dancing "a primal urge coming to life at the first moment we need to express joy. Among pre-language aboriginals possessing no music and the most primitive rhythm, I suspect dancing became their first expression of excitement. And an extension of that idea is embedded in my belief, quite applicable to myself, that once a song-and-dance man, always a song-and-dance man."

Johnny Boyle was Jim's living connection with the greatest song and dance man, George M. Cohan. Boyle had been featured in *The Cohan Revue of 1916* on Broadway and became a choreographer for a number of Cohan shows. Jim had seen Cohan perform only once and was curious about

*Something to Sing About,* with Johnny Boyle and Harland Dixon

the great star's stiff-legged dance, a staple in which Cohan would in effect prance across stage in measured beat, arms swinging briskly. Boyle taught Jim the dance, and it is used briefly in a few of his films before finding functional use in *Yankee Doodle Dandy.*

Jim said, "I have had highlights in my career like any performer, but inevitably there are some higher than others, and I am pretty sure that there is almost no greater moment for me personally than in the middle of *Something to Sing About* when I had the great honor, the very real privilege, of doing that number with Johnny Boyle and Harland Dixon."

*Something to Sing About* is in part spiritedly autobiographical. Jim plays Terry Rooney, a song and dance man and an orchestra leader who becomes a Hollywood success but, in high improbability, fails to realize it because of the machinations of a wicked studio head. When Terry grasps the truth, he and his songstress wife agree to his signing a seven-year contract, during which, for the sake of American womanhood, he must pretend to be a bach-

*Something to Sing About*

elor. Because of a scheming leading lady, Terry almost loses his wife but comes to his senses, reclaims her, and lives happily ever after, with wife and orchestra, in New York.

The nasty head of the studio is a barely disguised caricature of Jack Warner, who bears the interesting name B. O. Regan, well played by Gene Lockhart. B.O. in show business parlance is "box office," and at this time Lifebuoy soap was featuring ads urging purchase of that product to defeat nasty B.O., "body odor." Hollywood is gently and effectively satirized in the film with ogreish leading lady, fussy makeup men, insulting wardrobe men, and a diction coach with a foreign accent. Cagney's leading lady was Evelyn Daw, a tall, demure, baby-faced soprano, fresh out of a North Dakota high school, with an excellent voice. She is the chief musical talent of *Something to Sing About,* together with the film's multiskilled director, writer, and composer, Victor Schertzinger, who wrote five charming songs for the picture. Jim, again, cannot resist throwing in a little Yiddish. At one point, bidding his orchestra farewell and good luck, he says, "So now—*auf vi der kocken!*" *Kocken* is Yiddish for "defecate," and the expression is the same as the current show biz good wish, *merde.*

One of Cagney's key characteristics as a performer is too briefly and tantalizingly touched on in *Something to Sing About:* his essential status as a comedic actor. There is no performance in the first two thirds of his career that is not marked by comedy, even if sardonic and bitter. In the present film, as he and his wife are walking down the street, he is explaining film comedy and brilliantly illustrates five of its staples: a double take, a triple take, and a triple take with a slow burn and one-eyed fadeaway, this last done in the style of its great master, Jimmy Finlayson, Laurel and Hardy's prime stooge. Cagney then caps these with veteran Keystone comic Charlie Murray's famous mouth-ends-down grimace, which causes a lady passing by to scream in fright. With regrettable brevity we glimpse Cagney the Clown, of whom, alas, we see little in his career.

Critical praise for *Something to Sing About* was not muted but not extensive. Nor should it have been, given the film's unpretentious intentions. Otis Ferguson in the *New Republic* was the only one wise enough to note that "much can be done by good people who break away and bring the industry up short by independent accomplishment." Ferguson, who called *Something to Sing About* "about the happiest experience we've got in the last few months," is adept at explaining the essential Cagney one sees on the screen: "the basic appeal he has for the audience as a person—under all that tough surface and fast talk people glimpse a sweet clarity of nature, a fellow feeling and rightness and transparent personal honesty. It makes all the difference in the world, and when he rips out a statement you sense without stopping to question that it is the living truth spoken through him, and not a line rehearsed and spoken on the set any longer."

Despite the sweetness and charm of *Something to Sing About,* the handwriting on the wall was being written for Grand National Pictures. To make money, one's films have to be seen, and here Grand National was at a large disadvantage. It has been suggested that in the matter of bookings the five major studios closed ranks behind the scenes to ensure that Grand National had nowhere to go.° But Cagney did.

°Grand National merged with a short subject maker, Educational Films Inc., in 1938.

# 14 · The Factory Gentrified

During Jim's halcyon days out of the factory, brother Bill was preparing for his return to it under comfortable working conditions together with a hefty raise in salary. Warners offered him a contract in which he could do only two or three pictures a year for five years for a total of eleven, got a twelve-week vacation annually, could refuse any script he didn't like, all of this at $150,000 a picture plus 10 percent of the grosses over $1.5 million. The factory was becoming homelike.

During his time at Grand National, Jim brought into focus at meetings of the Boys Club a matter that began with John Barrymore. In Jim's early Hollywood days he occasionally dined at the Brown Derby with Ed McNamara and his good friend columnist Sidney Skolsky. The three were sitting together in a booth, Ed on the outside, when they heard a famous voice sounding forth: "Pissant, pissant!"

Ed looked out and down a few booths and saw Barrymore indicating Cagney with repeated turns of his head. "It's John Barrymore. He's saying 'pissant,' and I think he means you, Cagney."

"Well, we'll find out," said Jim, and walked down to see Barrymore, whom he had never met. "You sent for me?"

"Yes, I sent for you," said Barrymore.

"What have I done?"

"That's just it. It's what you *haven't* done. Play it, goddamn it. Play it!"

"Play what?"

"*The Playboy of the Western World.* You were born to play it. Play it! Goddamn it, why don't you do it?"

"Nobody ever asked me to do it."

"Oh, so that's the kind of pissant you are!"

Jim, taking no notice of the liquor-fired rudeness, said he might give it some thought and returned to his booth. Next day he read for the first time

J. M. Synge's comic masterpiece and was intrigued with the idea of playing a character not in his usual range. The Playboy is Christy Mahon, a shy rural lad in the far province of Munster who comes to a village in County Mayo a self-proclaimed fugitive from justice. Christy believes he has killed his father and in telling of it becomes a figure of some regard in the Mayo village. Even the town beauty is enchanted with him. Suddenly his father appears. Christy is at first intimidated but rises to dominate his bullying father and goes away with him, having attained manhood at last.

Jim was greatly taken with the play but wondered if satiric Irish comedy was quite his cup of tea. He debated it with himself. While he was about it, he read a number of other Irish plays, by Sean O'Casey, Paul Vincent Carroll, Lady Gregory, and William Butler Yeats. Then he brought the idea up at the Boys Club and met with mostly a favorable response. Pat O'Brien was enthusiastic, and Frank McHugh liked the idea but cautioned that their work schedules would prevent most of them from giving extended time to an Irish repertory company, Jim's ultimate plan. Spencer Tracy didn't feel ethnically bound to the idea, but older Irish actors in Hollywood were sounded out and became excited: Barry Fitzgerald, Ed McNamara, J. M. Kerrigan, William Gargan. Even cautious businessman-actor Robert Montgomery was caught up with the concept.

In the end the matter of scheduling and availability killed the project aborning, although from time to time Pat O'Brien and Bob Montgomery resurrected the idea until eventually it died.

Going into what he thought was to be a new leisurely life at Warner Brothers, Jim was surprised, then angered at an acceleration of his work coming not from The Shvontz but from Hal Wallis, and this through the director of Jim's first picture on return to the lot, the recent Broadway hit farce *Boy Meets Girl*. The director was his old friend Lloyd Bacon. Wallis, going on the chancy assumption that all farce must be fast, in watching the dailies with Bacon found place after place where he thought the action dragged, and Bacon had to reshoot, something he rarely did and certainly did not enjoy.

He had a superb cast: Cagney, Pat O'Brien, Ralph Bellamy, and other Warners veterans and a newcomer, the zanily attractive Marie Wilson. *Boy Meets Girl* is the story of two screenwriters (loosely based on Ben Hecht and Charles MacArthur), played by Cagney and O'Brien, who seize on a dumb but sweet studio waitress's pregnancy to make her baby the studio's newest star. The boys' foil is a vain and ponderous-thinking studio head

*Boy Meets Girl*, with Dick Foran, Pat O'Brien, Ralph Bellamy, and Marie Wilson

(well played by Ralph Bellamy) who is led up and down a variety of garden paths by the boys until the baby's unwed mother is well married off to an English lord, and the studio head's own baby is destined for the stardom planned for his predecessor.

Both Cagney and O'Brien knew that the unremittingly swift pace Wallis had imposed on their director was too much and that in farce, as in everything else, one had to grant moments of rest. Jim was in special need of caution because of his natural tendency to talk fast. He never watched dailies as a rule but did one day in Ralph Bellamy's company. As they came out of the projection room, Jim turned to his friend and said, "Would you tell me what I just said? I couldn't understand a word." Pat O'Brien, also a man given to ripping off the dialogue, found himself going at an unwonted pace. Jim thought he would argue the point with Wallis but reasoned himself out of it; if the reviewers noted the undue pace, perhaps Wallis would learn a lesson.

As Jim hoped, one critic the studio respected, Archer Winsten of the *New York Post,* wrote, "A machine-gun pace explodes wise cracks and comic situations so fast that you have to sit forward for the laughs. . . . Cagney's staccato delivery is particularly at fault." This bad review, Jim told Pat, is one he treasured having, and he made sure that Wallis saw it, sending it through interoffice mail. Wallis, in his autobiography, does not mention *Boy Meets Girl,* but he says of Cagney: "We had major problems with James Cagney, who became our house rebel. He fought endlessly over everything through-out the Thirties. . . . He and I never became friends. He was cold to me, and I wasn't particularly fond of him. Nevertheless, he was very talented, and few could equal his energy and drive."

Wallis went on to say that Cagney's best acting of those years was in *Angels with Dirty Faces,* an assessment few people would contradict. It was in this film that Jim immortalized a real-life Yorkville pimp. This was a com-paratively young man, a debonair pimp dressed in an electric blue suit and fancy straw hat, who would stand on the corner of First Avenue and Seventy-eighth Street observing the fortunes of the four girls of his stable. He stood with his arms down and his fists pressed against his abdomen, then lifted his fists in a constant hitching motion, usually accompanied by a roll of the shoulders. He greeted friends with "Whadda ya hear?" or "Whadda ya say?" or to those specially favored, "Whadda ya hear? Whadda ya say?," continually looking around for cops who might interfere with his trade.

This physical sequence Cagney incorporated into his characterization of Rocky Sullivan in *Angels with Dirty Faces,* and Cagney mimics have been repeating the movements for over fifty years. "I did that maybe eight times in that one movie," said Jim, "and they've been doing it in those imitations of me ever since. I wonder if that guy—I think they called him Smoke—ever got to see that picture, and I wonder what he'd think of all those mimics and impres-sionists doing *him.* Last I saw of him, he was running up First Avenue, pur-sued by an angry husband. Years later, and I don't know if this is true, I heard a very vicious rumor to the effect that he had reformed and settled down."

Warner Brothers did not scant production for the film. The largest set-ting in the picture, the tenement street, covered four city blocks, and fifty-six pushcarts were brought from New York to dress the set. Four genuine hurdy-gurdies were also imported. "I thought I was back in Yorkville of 1910," said Jim. "Truly exciting. I was right at home. Those pushcarts were full of real vegetables too, hundreds of them, and they were distributed after each day's shooting to local charities. I'll say this for Warner Brothers: when the studio put its heart into doing a thing, they went all the way."

*Angels with Dirty Faces*
ABOVE: With the Dead End Kids; BELOW: With Ann Sheridan

*Angels with Dirty Faces* is the story of two men and six boys. The men, Rocky and his childhood pal and coeval Jerry Connelly, grow up to be crook and priest respectively. Father Jerry tries to keep the boys in their old neighborhood free from the moral taint of their admiration of Rocky when he returns to the place of his youth, but to no avail. Rocky becomes their idol, and his influence on them grows, to Father Jerry's increasing dismay. After Rocky kills several rivals and is condemned to the electric chair, he is indifferent to his fate. Father Jerry pleads with him to make the boys despise his memory by turning yellow on his walk to the chair. Rocky refuses contemptuously. Then, at the very end, walking the last mile with the priest, Rocky pretends—or does not pretend—to turn yellow, crying out, seemingly in agony, "I don't want to die. I don't want to die. Please! Don't make me burn. Oh, please. Let go o' me. Don't do this, please." He begins to sob and utter inarticulate cries of fear and terror while being dragged to the chair. And mighty strong is the viewer who is not moved to emotions of pity and terror when listening to Cagney's agonized shrieks. Father Jerry affirms to the boys what the headline of the newspaper they are reading says, ROCKY DIES YELLOW, and he asks the boys to go with him to say a prayer for their former hero.

*Angels with Dirty Faces*, with Pat O'Brien

Does Rocky die yellow? It was a question Jim was asked unendingly, and his reply was undeviating: "I think in looking at the film, it is virtually impossible to say which course Rocky took—which is just the way I wanted it. I played it with deliberate ambiguity so that the spectator can take his choice. It seems to me it works out fine in either case. You have to decide."

Hal Wallis in his autobiography says of this ambiguity that the "script's directions were very specific on this point, and I believe the audience understood it perfectly." Understood, that is, that Rocky was pretending to be yellow.

The electrocution scene, the most vivid and memorable in the picture, took three days to shoot, and Jim lost four pounds doing it. The art department copied the famous chair at Sing Sing, but it was never photographed, only its shadow being seen. The death cell and the corridor to the chair were also exact replicas of those at Sing Sing, and as he walked the last mile, Jim thought of his old pal Bootah making the same journey. The death cell scene between Cagney and O'Brien was the longest take—twelve uninterrupted minutes—that either actor ever made in his career. They did it without mistake, and on the first take.

For the second time in his career Cagney barely missed death during filming. The same expert studio machine gunner who had just missed him with live bullets in *The Public Enemy* was assigned to gunnery tasks in *Angels*. As the director, Michael Curtiz, planned it, Cagney was to stand at an open window, shooting down into the street below. Machine-gun bullets would then traverse the right side of the window, just missing him. Curtiz explained that it would all be perfectly safe. Jim demurred, telling him to do the sequence in process, a superimposition method. Curtiz argued again that it was all "perfectly" safe, but Jim refused. The machine gunning was done without him, and one of the bullets hit the window's steel border, deflecting it to the wall where Cagney's head would have been.

For his Rocky, Jim was nominated for Best Actor of 1938 in the Oscar race, but it was won by Spencer Tracy for his Father Flanagan in MGM's *Boys Town*. Even so, *Angels with Dirty Faces* was one of the top moneymakers of the year, and Jim was named Best Actor by the New York Film Critics and the National Board of Review. He enjoyed making the film, despite a slight dustup with Leo Gorcey, the leading Dead End Kid of the boys in the picture. Just before Jim gave one of his lines, Gorcey ad-libbed one of his own. "I gave Gorcey a stiff arm right above the nose," said Jim. "Bang! His head went back, hitting the kid behind him, stunning them both momentarily." He told them to cut out "this goddamned nonsense," and thereafter there were no problems.

One of the reasons Jim became a wealthy man is that in the late thirties he began to buy property. In 1938 he bought his own island, a small one, Collins Island, a showplace of the Newport Beach area at the western tip of Balboa Island, California. Here he had been harboring *The Martha* for years. Later he bought even more property on Martha's Vineyard as well as in the desert at Twentynine Palms, California. This pattern was to continue most of his life, but he did not stay long at any of his homes except for the one he bought in 1939 in Beverly Hills when he was working and the farm at Martha's Vineyard when he was not. He visited his mother every year at her fancy but efficient apartment in Queens, New York, where she lived close to Harry and Ed Cagney, both of whom had thriving medical practices in that borough.

In the late thirties on one of the trips east he was approached by Iris Barry, curator of the Film Division of the Museum of Modern Art in New York, to see and comment on a revival it was sponsoring of *The Public Enemy*. The showing was attended by fifty Columbia University Extension students, and Jim agreed to a question and answer period. He watched the movie appalled by what seemed to him to be its interminably slow pace. He said, "We made that picture in 1931, but in seven years movie technique gained speed and pace. As a result, I sat there, my face burning, and I watched myself hamming up scenes. The camera would prolong each close-up by two or three seconds as it dollied up or dollied back. It is incredible in view of what is done today. I don't often blush, but when the lights came up, I was red as a beet."

He spoke for a few minutes from notes, talking about scripts, of their general poor quality in his experience, and of directors and actors generally being unable to have any say about their scripts. In respect to skills, some directors, he pointed out, "are frankly unable to tell an actor what to do and they admit it. One fellow [Lloyd Bacon] said to me, 'I wanted to be an actor, and I was lousy. Now, wouldn't I be a sap to try and tell successful actors how to go about playing a scene?' That man got more out of his actors than anybody I know."

Jim went on to praise the Hollywood artisans he prized above directors:
The cameramen are a very expert group, really marvelous. I found that out when I first got out there and also that they are very sympathetic and understanding. Not knowing what was required, I found myself with my back to the camera, doing all sorts of things, wandering off instead of staying put. The head cameraman would whisper in my ear and say, "See that light there? Now, when you don't feel that on your face, you are out of camera." Or he would

break a matchstick in his hand, drop it where I was to stand, and say, "See that there? Well, stay on it." Which is very nice. I mean, you can't ask for more than that. I had a bad habit—it started out as a definite trick—of outguessing the cameraman. This consisted of starting off one way, stopping and wondering whether the door was there or here, then going off the other way. Well, you will admit that is something for a cameraman to follow. We had a man on one particular scene, a very nice little fellow, and after I had done this a couple of times I heard him muttering to himself, "This so-and-so." Finally he did it again, so I asked him what the trouble was, and he said nothing at all.

But when I heard him saying it again, I said, "Am I doing something?"

And he answered, "Well, I wish to hell you would make up your mind which way you are going!"

I told him I was sorry and marked my spots off, so after that there was no trouble at all.

When Cagney's next film, *The Oklahoma Kid*, came to the screen, there was much critical complaining, mostly humorous, about the dese-dem-dose kid becoming a cowboy by the two simplistic devices of donning a ten-gallon hat and mounting a horse. In fact the only thing foreign to Jim was the hat. "It truly pissed me off," he said, "when the critics went on about the East Side kid remaining the same with just a change of costume." *Variety* called most of the film "unbelievable," citing Cagney's playing "without variation of his Hell's Kitchen manner" and his incongruity in the chaps and spurs setting. Jim was irritated that not one of the critics noticed how well he sat his horse: "By 1938 I had not only owned good horses, but I had a good seat and could ride as well as the best of them. Yet because of all the pictures I had done before, I was supposed to have made a poor Western hero. As we say in Yiddish, '*Er kricht oyf di gleicheh vent*' "—literally, he thinks he can climb up straight walls.

This, Cagney's second picture with Humphrey Bogart, was bound to have strengths and tensions not to be found in the average Western. Kenneth Tynan, decades later, said it was basically "a laconic Hemingway hero up against Studs Lonigan. . . . The contrast of styles was beautiful to watch. It was Bogart the wily debunker versus Cagney the exultant cavalier."

Graham Greene thought that Cagney took "perhaps a little less kindly to the big hat and tight breeches . . . than Mr. Humphrey Bogart as the bad man in black. But Mr. Cagney can do nothing that is not worth watching. On

*The Oklahoma Kid*

his light hoofer's feet, with his quick, nervous hands and his magnificent unconsciousness of the camera, he can pluck distinction out of the least promising part—and this part has plenty of meat." Greene goes on to describe the film as concerning the new Tulsa:

built by pioneers in the Cherokee strip of Oklahoma, where the bad man has established by trickery his monopoly of vice centers, and has corrupted the law with bought juries. There's a lot of gun play around the sinister Mr. Bogart before he frames the fine old man with white whiskers and has him lynched by saloon loungers. That's when the Oklahoma Kid [Cagney] begins to make good—the dead man's worthless son with a price on his head takes the law into his own hands and disposes of his murderers one after another. His brother is the new reforming sheriff who, at the end of the last magnificent slug feast with Mr. Bogart, dies with a bullet in the stomach after telling the Kid that he has procured his pardon. So the Kid is free to marry his brother's girl [Rosemary Lane], the dumb plain pure creature in gingham with little filly ways—you expect her to whinny whenever she opens her mouth. Apart from one scene in which Mr. Cagney sings "Rock-a-bye Baby" rather unconvincingly to an Indian papoose, this is a direct and competent picture.

Hal Wallis had some trouble getting Cagney into what Wallis thought was the appropriate mood for the characterization. In a memo to director Lloyd Bacon, Wallis pointed out: "I just cannot get any kick out of him playing the scenes with that grin on his face in the serious moments when he should be grim, and I know definitely that if he plays them with a grimness and with a definite purpose, they will be twice as powerful. . . . Somehow or other, Cagney grinning all through these scenes doesn't particularly characterize him as the happy-go-lucky dashing bandit of the early days. . . . Let's play it straight for drama."

This advice on acting by one not remotely his peer Jim happily ignored, and *The Oklahoma Kid* is infinitely the better for it. Frank Nugent of *The New York Times* caught this flavor: "Mr. Cagney doesn't urge you to believe him for a second; he's just enjoying himself—and, if you want to trail along, so much the better for you."

Jim was in no doubt about keeping the film's atmosphere light and untouched by graver matters. As was usual with these off-the-cuff works, he inserted his touches to perk up the action when it was not very active. One such moment in this film is his praising the country air, reaching up with his thumb and forefinger while saying, "Just feel that air." This Jim got from a friend of Ed McNamara's who had a habit of doing it. Another Cagney interpolation was a quiet tribute to his father. In the funniest scene in the picture the Kid asks the saloon pianist to play "I Don't Want to Play in Your Yard," James's favorite song. The pianist in the scene does not want to, but the Kid persuades him with a sharp snarl and "*Play* it!" As the pianist swings into it with enthusiastic fear and the Kid leans over the piano to sing it, a Bogart henchman (Ward Bond) taps Cagney on the shoulder for attention. The Kid gestures "not now" to him and goes on singing. Bond does it again, gets the same response tinged with annoyance, and the Kid goes on singing. Angered, Bond reaches around to grab the Kid's collar, and without missing a beat, the Kid slams a barrelhouse right into Bond's jaw, knocking him down, still singing the song with great enjoyment. Jim said, "No one knew why I asked for 'I Don't Want to Play in Your Yard' to be played, but when my family saw the picture, they knew who it was for."

One reference in *The Oklahoma Kid* has a strong modern resonance. The Kid, in speaking of his not enjoying civilization, has a long speech explaining why, which says in part: "In the first place the white people steal the land from the Indians. Right?"

His brother replies, "They get paid for it, don't they?"

The Kid says, "Paid for it? Yeah. A measly dollar and forty cents an acre, price agreed to at the point of a gun."

At this time, on a trip to New York, Jim experienced something remarkable, recalled later in an Ed Sullivan column. Asked by Sullivan what his life's biggest thrill had been, Jim said, "The greatest thrill I ever had occurred outside the business. In New York one night I was invited up to Dorothy Parker's apartment near East 86th Street. Here, on the lots and waterfront where all my gang had played as kids in Yorkville, were those magnificent apartment houses. I don't know if anything has stirred me so deeply as that. That's a great city, New York." It was for him a defining event: little Jim Cagney, the tough little scut of his tough little gang, finding himself, on the very site of their brawls, in the company of a literary elite he loved and honored. He said, "To realize as I sat there, chatting with Bob Benchley and James Thurber, that these men, my heroes, actually wanted to meet me—never mind what for, that didn't count—was the greatest thrill of my existence up till then. It will always remain a pinnacle of my life—a reminder to me, a great *proof* to me, of my country's greatness. That I, an ordinary little guy, could buddy up with the smartest and the brightest."

It was on this trip that Jim was able to convince his mother and sister to move west. At the unlikely age of eighteen Jeanne had just graduated from Hunter College, where she made Phi Beta Kappa. She had majored in languages, specializing in German and French. Jim had hoped she would continue academically toward a doctorate and teach German, at which she was unusually adept, but from her first year in college Jeanne had appeared in plays at school, not at all because of her brother, indeed despite her brother. Jim had gone through enough job-seeking traumas to last several lifetimes, and he knew that even though he could help initiate her career through his influence, she would have to pull her own weight artistically. She knew this too and told him so when she finally announced her determination to become an actress.

She started out, as did most neophyte actors then, in summer stock, appearing in *Brother Rat* in the East, thence to San Francisco for *Tonight at 8:30.* She acted in radio, doing one of the wives in *Ceiling Zero* as well as several other programs, showing a well-developed comedy sense.

Jeanne and her mother settled down in a business district of Los Angeles, Carrie pointedly ignoring Jim's request that she occupy a house he wanted to buy for her in Beverly Hills near his place in Coldwater Canyon. For her summer living he had already purchased a country home for her near his on Martha's Vineyard, but she would have none of it; she thanked him but said that if she could have her druthers, it would be to live in an apartment at Broadway and Forty-second Street with one glass wall so she could sit in her rocking chair and watch the heart of the world go by. In Los Angeles Jeanne lived with her until she married an actor named Kim Spaulding. About this time Jim had enticed brothers Harry and Ed out to California as well, pointing out that with Los Angeles's constantly growing population, they were needed.

Jim's house in Coldwater Canyon was studiedly unpretentious. There were only two bedrooms, a kitchen, a knotty-pine paneled living room, and a library. The three bathrooms gave the only hint of luxury about the place. In his library he hung a collection of pipes despite the fact of his nonsmoking ("pipes are nice to look at") as well as an antique cobbler's bench; he told friends he did not make shoes either. In time he commissioned a set of four carved and polychrome-decorated wood panels by his old friend and artist Will Crawford. The first showed Willie as a young ballerina; the second concerned *The Public Enemy,* Jim's springboard to fortune; the third honored Abraham Lincoln, a hero of both Cagneys; and the fourth celebrated Jim as Bottom in *A Midsummer Night's Dream,* wearing a purple and orange costume.

*Each Dawn I Die* brought Jim once again in touch with his old friend George Raft, for whom he had great admiration as both dancer and authentic tough guy. Raft, a product of New York's Hell's Kitchen, had grown up with gangsters, as Jim had, but unlike Jim, Raft stayed close to them, purely on the social level. "Curious thing about George," said Jim, "he was *of* the underworld yet not *in* the underworld. From Al Capone down, he knew them all—the worst hoods you could imagine—yet George had no part of lawbreaking. An amazing man, a superb dancer, and I didn't mind a bit his stealing *Each Dawn I Die* from me."

This is overstatement—no one ever stole a picture from Cagney—but an understandable one. Raft here is steely silken as the gangster whose life Cagney saves after the latter has been railroaded to prison by a corrupt district attorney. As Ross, an innocent newspaperman caught in the maws of prison life and psychologically bludgeoned into becoming a hardened criminal, Cagney plays softly, quietly, for the most part low-key. In one sequence it is not too much to say that he does the finest acting thus far in his acting career.

Just when it seems as if Ross has a chance through parole for freedom from the appalling hellhole into which he, an entirely innocent man, was

*Each Dawn I Die*, with George Raft

thrust, he faces the parole board, headed by Grayce (Victor Jory), the venge-ful man responsible for his imprisonment. Grayce, knowing just how to rub Ross the wrong way, scores him for not feeling "properly penitent." At this, weighed down by the searing injustice of it all, Ross, driven to angry frus-tration, calls the board—all men of probity save Grayce—"you sanctimo-nious, mealy-mouthed—," then catches himself in an agony of reversal. With a driving need to control himself, Cagney is able in the span of two minutes to combine fear, anger, sorrow, desperation, and the need to show "proper" penitence.

He weeps, crushed. "I'm sorry," he says. "I didn't mean what I said. Give me another chance. I just couldn't stand it." He speaks between gulping sobs. We, the viewers, are embarrassed at seeing the dignity of a man torn apart by injustice masquerading as its opposite. "I can't do any more time," he says in pleading that goes beyond pleading. "Please turn me out of here," as he fights to regain breath and control. By now the viewer is ravaged too with pity and needs relief. It comes in the form of a kindly-faced board member who says gently, "We'll do what we can for you. Go along now." We have just seen a man with his soul ripped cruelly in half before strangers.

This is acting far beyond the competence of George Raft, but Raft shares a strong quality of Cagney's: control. Some might describe Raft's control as poker face, but his facial impassivity is grounded in some form of inner thinking—fundamental emotionalizing, doubtless—that provides good counterpoint to Cagney, who maintains a different kind of facial restraint. Cagney's slight grimaces of amused resentment or obduracy reflects the quietness of a great actor who is actually listening to his fellow actor, not just waiting for his next cue.

With the exception of moments like these by Raft and Cagney, *Each Dawn I Die* is melodramatic hodgepodge until Raft is finally killed in a prison break, sacrificing himself so Cagney can find freedom. Otis Ferguson says "the story is of the kind you would have to see to disbelieve." It is also a sterling example of how bricks can be made of straw through good acting. You are prepared to believe the impossible tale when the teller is credible.

One bountiful bonus from the making of *Each Dawn I Die* was the saving of Jim's life. At the time the picture was made, a disreputable labor racketeer, Willie Bioff, was holding a number of Hollywood studios hostage because he headed the stagehands' union, the International Alliance of Theatrical Stage Employees, where chicanery at the top level reigned unchecked. Either Bioff or one of his colleagues would go to major film industry leaders like Harry Cohn and Joseph Schenck and demand payoffs or threaten to close the studios by making all stagehands stop work. Bioff, who seemed to have had total access to most Hollywood sound stages because of his "boys," the gaffers, grips, and other technicians, appeared one day on the set of *Each Dawn I Die*.

Raft saw him there, and they exchanged nods, Raft having known Bioff as an underworld figure. A few days later Raft saw him again on the set, this time looking angrily at Cagney during the shooting of a scene. Cagney had the reputation of being unfriendly to labor goons, whatever their eminence. Raft observed Bioff closely, saw him looking up into the flies where the gaffers (electricians) worked on pipe bridges to set the big klieg lights for the set below. Bioff gave a signal to one of the gaffers. Raft did not like this, although it could have been just a sign of greeting or an instruction.

After the picture was finished, Raft went to New York, where quite by accident he met Bioff again. Bioff said, "You did pretty good with *Each Dawn I Die*. You can thank me for that."

"What do you mean?" Raft asked him.

Bioff said, "The studio wasn't going to pay off, and we were planning to take care of Cagney. But I got word to lay off because you were in the picture."

"You son of a bitch," Raft said. "It's a good thing nothing happened to Cagney. Jim's one of the greatest guys in Hollywood, and if you had hurt him, you would have hurt me."

Bioff later went into forced hiding from his Mafia associates. Sixteen years after the making of *Each Dawn I Die* he was in the grocery business in Arizona under an assumed name. He went out one morning to start his pickup, and it exploded, killing him. His killers were never found. It is to be doubted that anyone strove very hard to find them.

It was while making *Each Dawn I Die* that Jim came to a rounding out of his 1927 traumatic experience, his firing from the lead role in the London company of *Broadway*. Ben Welden, privy to the entire disreputable story, said:

There was real live drama on the *Each Dawn I Die* set. (I was acting at Warners then.) Jim had not long before discovered that the real reason he had been fired from the London company was the machinations of an actor-producer, John Wray, a leading player in *Broadway*, who was a close friend of Crosby Gaige, coproducer of the show. Wray prevailed on Gaige, and Gaige in turn prevailed on partner Jed Harris to fire Jim. Now, in one of those great reversals of fate, John Wray lost his money as producer, came out to Hollywood as a mere actor, and got a job as the sadistic guard in *Each Dawn I Die*. Jim was aware of this, naturally, and those of us in the know wondered just what he would do in confronting Wray either off or on the set. Well, Jim encountered him—the man responsible for Jim's heartbreaking loss—and what did Jim do? He treated him as he did every other actor—with courtesy and no ill will at all. Just another proof to me that Jim Cagney was what he always was: a very great gentleman.

# 15 · In Function

As Jim went into the major phase of his career, he found life good indeed. By 1940 he, with the wife he adored, had the house that she at least proposed to live in forever. He was content with that. He enjoyed his work at Warners—even The Shvontz was cordial when they met—and Jim had the blessed prerogative of picking his own scripts. More, he had the sharp business acumen of brother Bill always at hand. His family was now all in Los Angeles—mother, sister, brothers—and there they remained. Carrie much preferred living in the East, but as always, her family came first.

There was one cloud in the sky, but yet a faint one. Carrie had never much liked Willie, and this attitude had gradually seeped down to the rest of the Cagneys. Willie did not much care, but at times it stung, although she almost never communicated this to Jim. Still, it was a good life; she well knew it and savored it. She had found two best buddies in Eloise O'Brien and Dorothy McHugh, delightful women with robust senses of humor.

When work was finished for the year, or for most of it, Jim went out to Martha's Vineyard, sharing the cross-country drive with Willie, sometimes in two cars because of her smoking. He loathed flying, and she disliked it too. His friendships with Pat O'Brien and Frank McHugh continued vigorously and would do so for a lifetime. He also found increasing comfort in the company of Robert Montgomery. Montgomery was an instinctive aristocrat, born to wealth and private schooling, but when his father lost his fortune, Robert easily adjusted to near penury. He became in turn a railroad mechanic, oil tanker deckhand, short-story writer, and finally actor, this last because it paid so well—the precise reason why Jim had become one. Neither man was ever fully committed to acting because of artistic need.

The two complemented each other effectively. Montgomery envied Cagney his elemental toughness and common touch; Cagney admired his friend's easy and natural gentility. "They were a pair," Willie said in her old age. "One supplied the other with what he had and the other hadn't. I believe that deep down the one thing that connected the two of them most, though, was their Americanism. Without being show-offy about it, they were both great patriots—even though I never heard them talk about how much they loved their country. But they both did, and very much too. To top it all off, as far as Jim was concerned, was the fact that Bob was a war hero. Jim honored him so much for that." Montgomery in World War II had enlisted as an ambulance driver for the American Field Service in France, where he remained until Dunkirk, when he joined the U.S. Navy. He served at both Guadalcanal and off Cherbourg on D-Day, finally receiving the Bronze Star for meritorious service.

Jim had hoped that Pat O'Brien would be in his next picture, but since they both were leading men, costarring roles were less available for them as a team. Frank McHugh, though, was always working in his tidy, humorous supporting parts. It was Frank who gave Jim's new picture, *The Roaring Twenties,* its leadoff scene. Mark Hellinger had written a less than competent script for this zingy recap of the twenties, and his opening was particularly turgid. So, at any rate, felt Jim and Frank before they got together with director Raoul Walsh in his first picture for Warner Brothers. He asked them what they thought of the opening scene, which took place between them. They both agreed it was blah. "You're right," said Walsh, "but I can't tell that to Hellinger. But I'll happily make up one of our own, if you like. How about this for a start?" He outlined what he had in mind. "Not so good, huh?" Jim and Frank nodded. Jim suggested a variation on it and was halfway through when he realized it had no interest even to himself.

Frank then came up with the workable one. The story opening was simple: Jim and Frank in a postwar reunion after two years spent apart, Frank in the States, Jim in the Army of Occupation, Germany. How to make this functional and interesting? Frank said, "Well, I'm in my room in the old boardinghouse, dozing over a bubbling coffeepot. Jim comes in without my seeing him, of course, and he serves me the coffee, chatting away as if I had seen him an hour ago, and I go along with this, talking at a great rate before I realize when I suddenly get out of my doze that it's him, my old buddy back from the war." So begins *The Roaring Twenties,* this initial episode set in 1919, beginning a story of the American way of life during the calamitous era of Prohibition. Throughout the shooting of the film, Jim and Frank vied with each other constantly, adding touches to what they both knew was rather a watery script.

Bill Cagney remembered: "Each night McHugh and Cagney would go over the next day's shooting, with the script girl writing down the dialogue and with each person in the scene ad-libbing." This, despite the assignment at various times of eleven studio writers on the script. Yet, said Bill Cagney, referring to two of Hollywood's Poverty Row studios, "It was a typical Republic script, the worst kind of Monogram cheapie. But there was *heart* in the picture. Somehow or other heart crept into it with all their ad-libbing." *The Roaring Twenties* became a vividly interesting picture because of its actors and their cooperative, action-obsessed director, Raoul Walsh, but it took some doing to get there.

By now in his films Jim was so tired of knocking people down that he tried either to discourage the action or to offer an interesting variation. He said, "I was running out of variations when I reached this goddamned piece of malarkey. But I found something. In the script two hoods come up to me, one says something that prompts me to bounce him, and down he goes. I varied the scene by placing the second hood behind the first, and when I belted number one, his head went back, hit number two in the chin, and they both went down."

Cagney plays Eddie, a mechanic who comes home to New York after a stint in the Army of Occupation to find his old job filled. In need, he turns to bootlegging. The vagaries of this stressful work are thoroughly explored in *The Roaring Twenties* in a clichéd story: Eddie becomes a big shot, loses the heroine to an honest pal of his, vies for gangland supremacy with a dishonest pal (Bogart), kills him, and is in turn killed by his pal's pals. All this is sustained only by the quality of the acting, a point critics at the time made endlessly. It presents an interesting anomaly. The piece is junk, made worthy by the acting and consequently no longer junk, yet it is junk. Certainly Cagney thought so. He called it "wind acreage" and chalked up another one to the hoodlum image he was trying to shed. He blamed no one but himself. He did think *The Roaring Twenties* had a historical integrity, at least, and happily the reviewers, for all their demurs, liked it, as did the public. A good summation is Pat McGilligan's: "Unoriginal, yes—superficial, yes—but flaws notwithstanding, *The Roaring Twenties* is superb; exciting spectacle, moving lifelike drama."*

Jim badly needed a change of pace in characterization, so through brother Bill's memo to Hal Wallis late in 1939, he asked to play John Paul

---

*The Cagney films are given a good overview in McGilligan's *Cagney: The Actor as Auteur* (1982).

*The Roaring Twenties.* ABOVE: With Gladys George and Humphrey Bogart
BELOW: Cagney as ganglord

Jones, a role that Jack Warner had actually suggested for him a few months before. "Naturally," said Bill to Wallis, "he would like to do this character-ization because of the succession of hoodlum parts he has portrayed." Bill went on to say that he had seen his brother recently "on some color film and found that in color he is just about five times as vital a character because of his red hair and green eyes."

For reasons of expense, and the fear that the public would never take to Cagney as a legendary American hero, however combative, Jack Warner put John Paul Jones in permanent abeyance. But he thought Cagney capable of

*The Roaring Twenties,* with Gladys George

playing a less exalted but nonetheless durable American hero, Knute Rockne, Notre Dame's great football coach, who had perished in an air crash eight years before. Cardinal to the success of the picture, Warner felt, was obtaining an actor of top rank with big box-office viability. In a word, Cagney. Approval of the casting was needed not only from Rockne's widow but from the Notre Dame president, Father Hugh O'Donnell, because the film was to be shot mostly on the Notre Dame campus. Both Mrs. Rockne and Father O'Donnell were sounded out about Cagney's casting, and both rejected him in favor of Pat O'Brien.

On hearing this, the film's writer, Robert Buckner, wrote to Father O'Donnell, explaining frankly and confidentially why Cagney was to be preferred over O'Brien. The body of the letter is as follows:

Dear Fr. O'Donnell:

I would like to present the "interior" situation here at the studio which motivated our preference of James Cagney to Pat O'Brien, in hopes that you, as a part-time business man, may understand the vitally important economic reasons for our position.

Frankly, and this is of course confidential, Pat O'Brien possesses only a fraction of Cagney's popularity, both in this country and abroad. Cagney is now among the first three or four male stars in the industry. Pat is not among the first fifty. The picture's cost has been estimated at $750,000, with the strong possibility that it may run higher. The studio could not afford the extremely dangerous gamble with Pat. In fact, it is a certainty that neither our sales organization nor the thousands of exhibitors would react favorably to the idea. In effect, it is a simple matter of arithmetic. Cagney would insure the picture's success, O'Brien would not.

So much then for the purely economic angle. Now, as to the faithfulness and effectiveness of the characterization of Rockne. . . .

It is a common and easy mistake to identify an actor with the type of roles which he has made famous. It is also a great tribute to his acting ability. The studio sees *The Life of Knute Rockne* as the first big step in a new career for Cagney. The next picture for him is *John Paul Jones*. We agree entirely with you that one of the basic ideas in the picture is to show Rockne as he was in life, a great hero to the youth of the nation. But knowing both actors intimately, through years of experience with both men, we believe that Cagney can give it all the heart and warmth and sincerity that any friend of Rockne's could wish. Cagney realizes his responsibility and believes strongly in his ability to give the best performance of his life.

Mrs. Rockne and Father O'Donnell were not moved. Cagney, they said, was associated with gangster pictures and would be totally unsuitable for a man of such high rectitude as Knute Rockne. It would have to be Pat O'Brien, and this for Pat was the turning point in his career. Both his popularity and salability soared after *Knute Rockne—All American* was made. He was a resounding success in the part, playing it with all the verve and style required. Jim was delighted and sent his buddy a wire of congratulations which said in part: CONGRATULATIONS, PADDY-O. I COULDNT HAVE TOUCHED THE PART IN A MILLION YEARS THE WAY YOU DID.

*The Fighting 69th,* as recalcitrant hero

Cagney, O'Brien, and McHugh were solidly reunited in *The Fighting 69th,* a wartime parable of New York City's crack Irish regiment. From Civil War times on, the 69th was called the Fighting Irish, and its accomplishments on and off the battlefield were legendary. The chaplain of the outfit was also legendary, Father Francis Duffy, whose name now adorns Times Square, a role for which devout Catholic Pat O'Brien was perfectly suited, the first of a number of priest roles he played in the forties and fifties.

There was nothing for Cagney to do but assume another "Cagney-type" role, which meant mostly one who, if not in defiance of the law, at least lingered about in defiance of someone. In *The Fighting 69th* he is in rebellion against the very regiment itself. As Jerry, a loudmouth braggart, he is despised by every man in the outfit. After revealing himself to be a coward in battle by raging hysterically, thus alerting the Germans to rain death down on his comrades, Jerry is court-martialed and sentenced to the firing squad. His jail is bombed, and in escaping, he overhears Father Duffy leading some wounded men in prayer. This brief excursion into pietism instantly gives Jerry the courage to launch an attack on the enemy with a trench mortar, thus making him a hero of the regiment before receiving a plot-needful mortal wound.

The film, typical of its genre, resounds with martial derring-do, but it is blessed with stalwart character actors from the Warner Brothers stock company, which was headed essentially by Cagney, O'Brien, and McHugh. One of the best scenes in *The Fighting 69th* was another cuff creation of McHugh's in the victory parade at the very end of the film after reels and reels of bitter carnage. The script had a soupy ending. Frank was asked what he thought would pick it up. He said, "Why not end it with me in the parade, foot strongly bandaged? A guy'll ask how I got it, and I'll say I sprained my ankle getting off the ship." Done.

McHugh said to this writer:

What a bunch of people we had at Warners! Handsome, intelligent leading men like George Brent, great menaces like Bogart, and

*The Fighting 69th*

character actors who were in the main real *characters,* like Tommy Dugan, who knew every vaudeville gag under the sun; Guinn "Big Boy" Williams, who was so strong that once he picked up a horse and set it on its feet; Allen Jenkins, always a riot onscreen and off; Alan Hale, a physical culturist who drank nothing but the purest scotch. You never heard such laughter as when those boys got going. Sure I'm prejudiced when I say Warners had the best supporting actors in the business, but I don't care. Almost all from vaudeville, all different types, ranging from Chester Clute to Franklin Pangborn, freelancers the lot of them. All gone today from pictures [1980], and no one to replace them. Our character actors these days seem to be wise-ass kids from comedy clubs. If you call foulmouthed put-downs comedy.

As usual, the critics' approval of Cagney was strong with perhaps the best assessment of his situation, in terms of career and of *The Fighting 69th*'s worth, coming from *Time* magazine, which, after speaking of the Warners' longtime efforts "to refine through suffering the character of their ace triggerman, James Cagney," goes on to evaluate the film: "Aficionados who know a first class carnage when they see and hear one ought to like this picture. There is seldom a dull moment. Others will be willing to take James Cagney's word for it. Asked during a lull in shooting the picture what was going to happen next, Cinemactor Cagney eyed his questioner, demanded incredulously, 'Are you really that interested?' "

It was during the shooting of *The Fighting 69th* that Jim asked his good friend George Brent to dinner with the Boys Club, and Brent was happy to be their guest. Said Jim:

I don't know what the hell got into me that evening, but I got going on the subject of Hollywood's having gained the reputation of being the divorce capital of the world. I got a little indignant and I fear a little stuffy about it. I said this was an undeserved reputation among many people in the industry. I said, "Pat, look how long you've been married, and to the same woman. Frank, you too. Spence, you. Me. Why, there are scores and scores of people who have the same wives they started out with—" Then I gulped. There, sitting before me, was George with a funny look on his face. George, who had been married a number of times. I said, "George, me and my god-damned big mouth. I'm sorry."

"Forget it," said George, and he meant it. "It's very unimportant." Then he grew serious and a little pensive. "You know, boys," he said, "I married four of them." He paused, then went on reflectively. "And I didn't like a damned one of them!" Well, we all fell to pieces after that. George went on to marry two more "of them," and not long before he died, he told me number six was the one he should have married in the first place.

Jim's marriage was as strong as or stronger than ever, but he did miss children, Willie not quite so much, although she had maternal instincts. She did volunteer work at an orphanage near their home and enjoyed helping the youngsters in their recreational pursuits. The Cagneys were envious of the O'Briens and their growing brood. After a few years of trying to become pregnant, Willie sought medical explanation. Jim went with her for tests, and it was established without doubt that he was sterile.* Willie first suggested the idea of adoption, and Jim was pleased at the thought. He had always been fond of children, and the idea of a family for himself stirred old memories.

In 1940 Willie, through the orphanage where she worked, arranged for the adoption of a baby boy, to be called James Junior, followed in short order by a baby girl, Catharine, to be known as Casey.

Not long after their adoption, Willie made a decision for the children that must surely have had a profound psychological effect on Jim Junior and Casey. In view of Jim's need to study his roles—he insisted on being letter-perfect in his lines, even though he knew he tended to paraphrase them—Willie decided that it was impractical to have the children live in their house. Accordingly she had another, smaller house built on their property, perfectly fitted out, where James Junior and Casey would be raised.

An old family friend of the Cagneys' says:

This was certainly an outré arrangement, or at least that's what we, the close friends of the Cagneys, thought. From one aspect, it made a lot of sense. Jim did need to be alone and secluded when he was learning lines. And let's face it, the learning of lines is the biggest part of your job outside of the acting itself. It is your essential preparation. Also, Jim had to have it quiet and restful when he came home from a hard day's work at the studio. And Willie was a demon when it came to taking care of her husband, making sure that he got the proper rest and nutrition. But think of those kids and their position. How could they be expected to be part of a so-called

*Since Cagney's death, long-undiscovered "sons" of his, unaware that their "father" was incapable of their conception, have appeared on the public scene.

normal family situation, living as they did with their own house-keeper in another building? I think, in any case, the life history of movie stars' kids in general has not been a happy one. Look at the Crosby kids, Eddie Robinson's boy, and others. At the Cagneys' their first years with the kids were happy, but I cannot believe the later years were. That living in another house—I can't think Jim Junior and Casey could do anything other than resent it.

Of the two parents, it seemed to good friends of the Cagneys', the one closer to the children was Jim, although he saw them less. Willie devoted herself to making her husband comfortable. In view of his frequently erratic hours and location shooting, this was not easy. Willie, like Jim, was always in a sense on call, and she frequently had to accommodate to his hours at the expense of the children. She made sure that he always had a hot meal when he got home and that family tensions were avoided in whatever way possible.

Notwithstanding, Jim always tried to have a little time each day with the children, at least in the early years, and this he accomplished by going to their house after work and reading to them. He recalled, in *Cagney by Cagney,*

> the wonderful, wonderful feeling of having them sit on my lap as I told them stories. I told all the great traditionals, Little Red Riding Hood, the Three Bears and Goldilocks, but I made a great melange of them. To this day [1975] Jim and Casey talk about those stories. For example, I dreamed up an account of the three and a *half* bears. In this version the three bears had a cousin who came to visit them, but he was a half bear only because he had length and width, no thickness. In fact when this bear cousin turned sideways, you couldn't see him. Now, this little cousin bear was walking through the woods one day when he saw Goldilocks being followed by the big bad wolf. The wolf obviously being up to no good, the little bear challenged him. The wolf went on the attack, but the smart bear out-foxed him—to mix animal images a bit—by turning sideways. Naturally the wolf couldn't see his prey and he was very upset. And so on. This was a typical incident in those fairy tales I told my kids and they, I'm glad to say, are now telling the same stories to their kids.

Jim was very sensitive to the nuances of intelligence in his children and was delighted when he found them. He remembered that

> one day I was walking down to the barn with young Jim, and in a perfectly clear and beautiful soprano he began singing the Marseil-laise in French. He didn't realize I was paying any attention. Later

I started to sing "Allons—" and I stopped to ask him the next word. He didn't know what I meant. I explained that I had just heard him sing the song in French. He said he didn't have any idea, and he didn't. Never sang it again, couldn't get him to sing it. Now figure that one out if you can. When Casey was little, we didn't even know she'd taken the trouble to learn The Lord's Prayer. But Willie heard her one night as she knelt beside the bed, "Our Father, who art in heaven. *Hollywood* be thy name. . . ."

Jim tried to include the children in all home activities at Coldwater Canyon. He owned ten acres there and had put up a racing oval with full accoutrements for the new horses he kept buying. He fell in love with Morgans, a beautiful breed of American saddle and trotting horses, and developed a great interest in sulky racing. The Coldwater property became too small when Beverly Hills began to develop, and he took his horses to a farm he bought from Louella Parsons in Northridge in the San Fernando Valley.

Bill Cagney had become an associate producer at Warner Brothers, a blessing both to him and, whether they knew it or not, to Hal Wallis and Jack Warner. Bill was the buffer between both these volatile and busy executives and his excitable brother. After the success of *The Fighting 69th* and the apparent shelving of *John Paul Jones,* there should have been available for Jim a script of some substance. Instead, as Bill said, in a memo to Wallis he submitted "most respectfully":

Mr. MacEwen sent me 103 pages of *Torrid Zone* which I have read and must report that this is just the type of story that made Cagney want to leave the studio upon the expiration of his last contract. There is no real substance or importance in the entire 103 pages, and I know that Jim will only be enthused by plot and development that is worthy of his talent. I can't go to too great a length to explain the importance of our realizing the necessity of submitting material that is dramatically sound and worthwhile to Cagney. In addition to all the previous reasons which you know about, he is constantly besieged with offers to do the most important vehicles at other studios and therefore would naturally feel that if we don't supply him, others will.

The front office ignored him.

Since there was nothing else available at the moment, Jim decided to do *Torrid Zone,* which he always called *Hildy Johnson Among the Bananas* because it was a crude rewriting of the Hecht-MacArthur play *The Front Page. Torrid Zone* costarred Pat O'Brien and featured Ann Sheridan, a girl

*Torrid Zone*, with Pat O'Brien and Ann Sheridan

Jim had found very pleasant when they did *Angels with Dirty Faces*. Purely to spite Wallis and The Shvontz, Jim kept a pencil-thin mustache he had grown just to put some kind of change in the "atmospherics" of the picture, as he called it. Wallis asked the producer of the film, Mark Hellinger, to ask Jim why he had wreaked this curious disfiguration on himself; it made him less tough, they said. Jim said simperingly to Hellinger, "Tell Hal that just *once* in my life I'd like to play a gigolo." Hal was not amused.

The only bit of fun Jim had in connection with *Torrid Zone*, apart from working with Pat, was a radio appearance plugging the film on the Edgar Bergen and Charlie McCarthy radio show. Jim had appeared in vaudeville at the same time Bergen had in the early twenties. (Charlie McCarthy, for those too young to know him, was a snappily impudent and charmingly lecherous little dummy.)

BERGEN: You know, Charlie, Jimmy and I are old friends. In years gone by, we played many of the same vaudeville theatres.

CAGNEY: Yes, we did, Edgar—but we never appeared on the same bill together, did we?

BERGEN: I wonder why. No, we didn't.

CHARLIE: Well, the public can only stand so much.

CAGNEY: Ah, but we had a lot of fun in those days. Too bad vaudeville died, eh, Edgar?

BERGEN: Yeah, but things really got tough that last year. I was at liberty an awful lot of the time. How about you. Jimmy?

CAGNEY: Well, I successfully lived in a trunk for eight years and the last year things got so bad I had to rent out the upper tray to a team of acrobats.

BERGEN: You know, Jimmy, we went to see you in *Torrid Zone* just the other night and liked it a lot.

CHARLIE: Yeah, and especially that "Oomph" Sheridan. Oomph! She's pretty nice, huh?

CAGNEY: Oh, yes. She's a nice girl.

CHARLIE: That's what I thought. Say, is she—is she—huh?

CAGNEY: You really want to know, Charlie?

CHARLIE: Yeah!!!

CAGNEY: Well, Charlie, I'll tell you. She's a very intelligent girl. She's very well read and a devoted student of philosophy.

CHARLIE: If you're going to give me that stuff—let's drop it. Sorry I asked you.

CAGNEY: But what did you think of my acting in it?

CHARLIE: Mr. Cagney, I thought you were very intelligent, well read, and a devoted student of philosophy.

This was followed by a send-up of *Torrid Zone* called *Horrid Zone*, a title Jim appreciated, in which Charlie played Cagney's boss, chastising him for bananas arriving rotten and concluding with Charlie and Cagney in duet singing "Strolling Through the Park One Day."

The most searching review of *Torrid Zone* came from Otis Ferguson, who said, "Mainly, this version of Quirt and Flagg belting natives and getting out the fruit sees no reason to believe for a minute in any one of the diverse plot turns it has borrowed. Neither will you."

During the making of *Torrid Zone* Jim shot himself—accidentally. Coyotes were prowling over his ten acres at Beverly Hills, and he was determined to frighten them away from his well-stocked henhouse. He bought a .22-caliber pistol, and one evening when he heard his hens cackling excitedly, he went out to investigate, saw a coyote, and aimed at it, holding the gun with both hands. "Don't know how I did it, but the bullet grazed my left hand, and I had to get a tetanus shot and a stitch-up. I never held a gun in my hand again. Except in the movies."

Jim was proud of his henhouse and all his property in Coldwater

Canyon. Ralph Bellamy described Jim's pride in an interview with Timothy White of *Rolling Stone:*

> Jim hates this story but I'm going to tell you it anyway because it says so much about the earnest nature of the man. He loves the outdoors and is an accomplished naturalist and an informed conservationist, right? Well, back in the mid-Thirties, he got himself eleven acres in Coldwater Canyon, just over the hill from Hollywood, in a place that had no house near it for a mile in any direction. He was going to create a paradise. He builds a stable for trotting horses, including a track, and buys ducks and geese and makes a pond for them. Then he gets some goats to run up and down the hillsides, and he puts up a chicken coop and fills it with twenty-six hens and four roosters! He goes up one day to check everything out, but he's still not satisfied. It's not quite right, and he wants to find a way to improve it. He goes down to the henhouse and sees that he's got just four roosters and figures, "Well, this won't do," so he goes and gets another twenty-two of them, so that every chicken will have a mate. The next thing you know, there's a commotion you wouldn't believe, with every chicken on the place on the roof of the coop and the roosters diving at them from the sky. It was hilarious! There were feathers all over every *inch* of Coldwater Canyon. The story spread around town, and he still [1982] isn't over the embarrassment.

In the summer of 1940 on his way to Martha's Vineyard, Jim stopped off in Rutland, Vermont, to watch some harness racing. A local reporter came up to ask him if he had read the day's news, which said that Cagney, along with other Hollywood people, had been cited to the Los Angeles County Grand Jury by District Attorney Burton Fitts as one who had shown interest in Communist activity. After verifying this with his brother Bill, Jim drove to New York and, terrified of the air, boarded a TWA Stratoliner for San Francisco, where the Dies Committee was holding forth as a precursor of the appalling House Un-American Activities Committee. Jim called a press conference and before a large room of reporters made quite clear his political commitments: he was a Democrat, he intended to campaign for Roosevelt in the upcoming election, he had never been a Communist and could not possibly become one because he was a passionate believer in democracy. He concluded: "The source for these accusations of my being Communist stem, I have no doubt, from my giving an ambulance to the American Abraham Lincoln Brigade fighting for the Loyalists in Spain, and for my contributing to the relief of some starving cotton pickers in Salinas years ago. Look, I

*City for Conquest*
ABOVE: With Frank
McHugh, Donald Crisp,
and George Tobias
BELOW: With Ann
Sheridan

belong to the Screen Actors Guild, and we're a *labor* union. I was trying to help some workers."

The next day Jim appeared before Representative Martin Dies and told him the same story, followed by Dies's telling newspapermen that he had "every confidence in Mr. Cagney's veracity." That ended that. But inside, Jim was seething. He not only regarded himself as a a good American but considered himself a devoted and committed one. That feeling was to intensify.

As an omnivorous reader he missed little of quality in any current literary season. In 1936 he read and very much liked a best-seller of that year, *City for Conquest* by Aben Kandel. A multiplot novel with New York City as its theme, it treats of a dozen or so characters over a span of years, all in some measure influenced by a great city that at first seems indifferent to their lives and destinies. Kandel's theme, in his words, was "There's no welcome in New York—no farewell. . . . The city is deep and high and angry. Come in and you're swallowed. Leave, and you're not missed." But there was also a feeling of love for the city that gave the different stories a unique vitality.

Jim was so impressed by *City for Conquest* that he periodically reread parts of it. The story's principal locales are the Lower East Side (where Jim was born), Greenwich Village (where he and Willie lived for a time), Battery Park, the Bronx, Brooklyn, and Yorkville (where he grew up). He enjoyed the sweep of the novel, its pungent characterizations, its almost poetic realism. It was about home, the home he knew well.

When in 1940 he was told not only that Warners had bought the screen rights to the book but that it was to be a vehicle for him with brother Bill as associate producer, he was "thrilled, and that's not a word I use very often." Moreover, he was pleased that the screen adaptation was to be done by a prominent New York playwright, John Wexley, author of the well-crafted hit play *The Last Mile*. Jim was also pleased that the film's director was to be his pal Raoul Walsh. Everything was set, at which point things began to unravel.

The front office decided that for a prestige picture it must have a so-called prestige director, so Walsh was yanked, and Anatole Litvak, Tola to his friends and enemies, was substituted. Jim loathed Litvak, a director given to endless retakes and peculiar shooting methods. The shooting script by Wexley also turned out to be unacceptable to the brothers Cagney. In a memo to Bill detailing the faults in the script, Jim summed it up: "It is quite apparent that Wexley knows nothing of show business, of what went on during the period covered by the script and apparently knows less about the fight business. The dialogue throughout is completely phoney and will have to be redone if there's to be any honesty in the finished production. The fact that it is still interesting speaks more than well for the Kandel yarn."

The script was rewritten with the help of Robert Rossen and, although not fully what the Cagneys wanted, was at least acceptable. Shooting began, and fortunately a young actor and soon-to-be-great director was in the cast. Elia "Gadge" Kazan plays the small but tremendously alive role of Googi, gangster pal of the Cagney character, Danny Kenny. In his autobiography Kazan tells of watching Cagney ("one of my heroes") being directed by the imperious Litvak. Kazan observed the antipathy between the two and concluded it was the result of the way Litvak shot the film: "Litvak's method was not straightforward, like that of Raoul Walsh or Jack Ford; it was showy and somehow European. [It was a method that would] try to get as much of the scene as possible in one shot by moving in and out and panning right and left." This required tedious and extra work by the actors, requiring that they be in an intricate multiplicity of places for a moving camera's benefit. Jim hated this. Kazan wrote:

> The crew liked and respected Cagney—they were off the street too—but they didn't like the way [Litvak] spoke to them, and Jimmy didn't either. Tola had an abrupt way of giving orders, and was always dominating and impatient with objection and error. I was to hear the same bullying tone of voice in Europe when I worked there, particularly in Germany. Directors from there—certainly at that time—thought of their crews as laborers who didn't eat in the same cafés. American stars and directors tend to make a democratic show; they buddy-buddy with their crews.

Kazan found another, more interesting reason why Cagney didn't care for Litvak:

> I could also see that Jimmy didn't like Tola's reputation as a lady-killer. I've noticed that many "big" stars of that day, despite the glamour of their public images, were rather prudish sexually. Fonda was an exception, but he was reserved and private about his personal life; Errol Flynn was another, but he was British. I never saw a woman around Jimmy, never met his wife, even after months of working with him. Scenes with men came naturally with Jimmy; his love scenes with Ann Sheridan, a lovely girl, were perfunctory. I don't know if Jimmy had a problem with women.

Jimmy's "problem" with women was a simple and traditional one: he adored his wife. One need only wait for his next film, *The Strawberry Blonde,* to see how convincingly Cagney could make love on camera.

Kazan goes on to say that Litvak "tolerated" Jim's scorn because he had to get the job done per schedule and also because in the pecking order Jim came first. Kazan, the finest director of actors in the American theater, accurately analyzes Cagney the professional:

Jimmy was a completely honest actor. I imagine he'd have figured out each scene at home, what he'd do and how he'd do it, then come to work prepared. But what he did always seemed spontaneous. Not only didn't he need direction from Tola; he didn't want it. He had no schooling in the art of acting, although he had tremendous respect for good actors. If the Actors Studio had existed then, I'm sure he would have despised it. [Later he did.] He didn't do an elaborate preparation for a scene before the camera rolled; I concealed my own so he wouldn't think less of me. Jimmy didn't see scenes in terms of great complexity; he saw them in a forthright fashion, played them with savage energy, enjoyed his work. He believed in himself and didn't need to be praised constantly. He was a complete actor. He raised many doubts in my mind about the artistic snobbery of some actors in the Group [Theatre].

The only preparation Jim did at home was (a) read the script, (b) seek out the author's intention, one of his obsessions, (c) learn the words, and (d) go to the studio and do it. He made no preparation, elaborate or otherwise, and said so for over sixty years. Who is to doubt him? He possessed the spontaneity of experience.

In working on *City for Conquest,* he was in home territory because his character, Danny Kenny, a truck driver turned prizefighter, was a boy of the streets seeking to better himself. Danny turns fighter, is successful, but ultimately loses his sight when an opponent grinds an acid chemical into his eyes and is reduced to running a newsstand. Eddie, his beloved younger brother, a musician (well played by Arthur Kennedy), after succumbing for a time to Mammon, becomes a successful composer. The last and quite moving scene in the film is of Danny and his once-strayed girl friend (Ann Sheridan) at the newsstand listening to Eddie's symphony playing on the radio from Carnegie Hall.

Jim did make elaborate preparations, however, for his fight scenes. As sparring partner he again had Harvey Perry, and the two entered a professional fighter's training regimen. Jim was up each morning by five-thirty, ran ten miles, took just enough wholesome food to keep him going, shadowboxed and wrestled, slept ten hours a night. He lost ten pounds and felt better than he ever had in his life—until he began to undergo Litvak's direction.

*The Strawberry Blonde,* with Rita Hayworth

"A squirrely son of a bitch," Jim described him. "There are some guys who are just natural-born assholes, and Tola was one of them."

Nevertheless, Jim completed the picture with high hopes for the completed product. What he saw was one of the bitterest disappointments of his life, purely because of injudicious cutting. The most poetic of the episodes filmed were excised in order to emphasize the soap opera tendencies of the script. *City for Conquest's* multiplot story had to go, and everyone understood this; otherwise the novel could only be realized in about six hours of film. But the more poignant and soul-revealing aspects of Danny Kenny's story were gone. "I'll never see another picture of mine again," Jim said, a promise he mostly kept.

Despite his animadversions, *City for Conquest* is not at all a bad film. It is certainly heartfelt in its sentiments, which is also an accurate description of the next Cagney picture, *The Strawberry Blonde,* taken from the Broadway play *One Sunday Afternoon.* The story is simple, if a bit tired: hardworking Biff Grimes (Cagney) loses the beautiful strawberry blonde (Rita Hayworth) to his venal boss, Hugo (Jack Carson), who compounds the injury by allowing Biff to go to prison for something Hugo has done. Biff marries sweet Amy (Olivia De Havilland) on the rebound. In prison Biff becomes a correspondence school dentist, and when he returns to Amy, he realizes he is the luckiest guy in the world for having her. He revenges himself on Hugo by getting him into the dentist chair and extracting his abscessed tooth without anesthetic.

Set in the 1890s, the screenplay is adorned with turn-of-the-century locutions like overripe plums: "Tell it to Sweeney," "That's the kind of hairpin I am" (which Jim, having heard it from his father, inserted in the script), "all the fudge," "twenty-three skiddoo." Cagney not only doesn't fight in this picture but receives a series of unreciprocated black eyes. One obvious but interesting flaw in the film is that Olivia De Havilland is supposed to be the plain girl of the story. She is by any reckoning fully as beautiful as Rita Hayworth, if not more so. *Time* magazine, which called the film "a blithe turn-of-the-century buggy ride," liked Cagney very much, adding that "Rita Hayworth takes the picture away from him and dark-eyed Olivia De Havilland takes it away from both of them." It is a just evaluation.

Jim enjoyed making the picture so much that he invited his mother to come down and watch the shooting of the title song scene, set in a period beer garden. "Casey would waltz with the strawberry blonde, and the band played on . . ." goes the song from the nineties, thematic to the film. An extraordinary coincidence prevailed here, Jim told director Raoul Walsh. In her late girlhood Carrie Cagney, a beautiful strawberry blonde, was dating a man named Casey, and they had gone waltzing the very week the song was introduced to the New York public. Walsh was delighted and asked Carrie if she would like to be an extra in the beer garden scene. "Oh, I'm too fat," she said, and would not listen to Jim's attempts to persuade her. When asked if the beer garden setting and props were authentic, she said, "Yes. With one exception. You've got pretzels on the table. They didn't come in until later."

Walsh was greatly taken with Carrie's hair. She was overweight and in her early sixties, but her hair—which Jim used to stroke as a little boy, admiring its coloration and sheen—was still gorgeously red with tiny shimmering highlights of blue and orange. "Mrs. Cagney," Walsh told her, "if this picture had been in color, I'd have kidnapped you to be in it."

Cagney in this comedy was so well received that Warners decided on another for him, this time with its by now leading female star, Bette Davis. She had been in a Cagney film seven years before, and the two of them blended well, two toughies. *The Bride Came C.O.D.* is, if not Cagney's nadir, mighty close to it. The premise is good: Cagney, a Hollywood honeymoon pilot, who flies couples to Las Vegas for a fee, agrees to kidnap the eloping daughter of a Texas oil baron at regular baggage rates, $10 a pound, back to Papa. The fee in Bette's case adds up to $1,180, a very good sum at the time. The comedy in the film is sclerotic, its highlight being Cagney's picking cactus quills from Davis's behind. But taken purely on the basis of diversion, *The Bride Came C.O.D.* is worth seeing once. Cagney and Davis together, just standing together doing nothing, are not without interest, but there is no kind of real action between them. They do have at least one charming scene. They are in a deserted mine shaft without food, and she believes they are doomed. He doesn't tell her he has access to food because he must keep her alone for a few more hours to complete his mission. He eats surreptitiously; touchingly they realize their growing mutual attraction. They kiss. A moment of sweetness as their lips meet. Then she jumps up and screams, "Mustard!" accusingly at him, and romance ends temporarily. "We both reached bottom with this one," said Davis in her autobiography. Not quite.

By the summer of 1941 much of the world was at war, and the United States was only six months away from Pearl Harbor. Service pictures, a Warners staple in the early thirties, were now making a comeback. In the

*The Bride Came C.O.D.*, with Bette Davis

*Captains of the Clouds*

vanguard of these was *Captains of the Clouds,* with Cagney as a rakish Canadian bush pilot who volunteers to train pilots under the strict discipline of the British Commonwealth Air Training Plan. His old character of the rotter who straightens up and flies right metaphorically is trotted out, and one can almost chart the path of his defiances of law, order, and "common decency." Inevitably, after disgrace he flies off into the blue, a heroic figure condemned to die by the inexorable law of such scripts.

Despite difficulties, Cagney enjoyed his Canadian jaunt. He said:

The plot was the same old crap: I'm a no-good who winds up doing good. On the positive side, after our doing *Angels with Dirty Faces,* Mike Curtiz was not only used to my adding to the dialogue or changing it, but actually encouraged it, and it was fun doing that. Our cast and crew started out living in a cheesy hotel on location, but the tourists and fans used to crowd the lobby so much, trying to see the cast, that we were moved to private homes. But all the Canadians were so nice to us. At North Bay, where we were, Warners built a whole little town which I understand remained that way after the war. Ed McNamara came up to visit me, and I got him a little part in the picture, so there was wonderful company, what with George Tobias, Dennis Morgan, and Alan Hale.

There was only one bad moment during filming. Jim did not like the idea of doubles doing his stunts, and when a scene called for him to be knocked from a pier into the water by a seaplane propeller, he insisted on doing it, because all the safety guards were in operation. He fell off as required and suffered a small concussion. In the end the scene was scrapped because it was found that the propeller in that situation would have been turned off long before reaching the pier. This cured Jim of volunteering to be his own double.

What made (and makes) *Captains of the Clouds* worth seeing is that not only did it give insight into Canada's war preparations, soon to become *de rigueur* below the border, but it was the first chance for Americans to see— and in Technicolor—the breathtaking beauty of Canada. Mike Curtiz and a special crew of Warners cameramen took exquisite footage of the Far North's lakes and forests.

A key scene in the film is of an actual Royal Canadian Air Force wings awarding conducted by Air Marshal William A. "Billy" Bishop, Canada's great air ace from World War I. It is a most moving ceremony, and RCAF recruiting personnel estimated that several score young Americans enlisted with them because of *Captains of the Clouds*.

Said Cagney:

That Billy Bishop. He was something. Why the Canadians have never made a movie biography of him, I'll never know. Smart, masculine as hell, honest, a true hero with just the tiniest bit, and very proper bit, of arrogance, and above all, he was the epitome of that old cliché, a born leader of men. That is one terrific scene, the pinning of the wings, and we had one hell of a time getting it because of the weather. I love Canada, a great place, but we forget sometimes it's the home of an awful lot of weather.

Patriotism was astir in both countries, and vitally so for several reasons in the hearts and minds of Jim and Bill Cagney.

# 16 · A Dandy Yankee Doodle

In Cagney's Museum of Modern Art *Public Enemy* colloquium, one of the Columbia students brought up the ephemeral matter of actor as personality:

STUDENT: Mr. Cagney, to what do you ascribe the fact that your films can be sold on personality, in the main portion?

CAGNEY: It depends on the kind of story it is. If it is a personality story, it is one thing. We depend entirely on that—little bits of business, touches here and there. But if you have a good story, you don't have to get in front of the story. You can stay back and let the story speak for itself. But generally when the story is not a good sound one, you have to get in front of it, which means the personality does the work.

STUDENT: Why can't you do that on the stage?

CAGNEY: But it has been done. By George M. Cohan, for instance. For years.

STUDENT: In a film, though, every star maintains his own personality throughout most of his pictures, whereas George M. Cohan is the exception rather than the rule.

ABBOTT [the moderator]: You are supposed to be asking questions, not telling what you think. I mean, state the thing in the form of a question. Does George M. Cohan change his roles?

CAGNEY: Primarily, Cohan is a personality. The thing that projects itself is Cohan's personality, regardless of anything he says.

This is virtually Cagney's self-description. He was in those last words unconsciously describing both himself and a goodly proportion—certainly more than half—of his films. He would be too modest to admit this, but the results of his person on his work—on the cuff operas especially—is unquestionable and indelible. The audience goes to see "a Cagney picture" as specifically as it goes to see a Clark Gable picture or a Fred Astaire picture.

Of the theater personality as distinct from the film personality, comparison cannot handily be made. The former vanishes in time; the deeds of the stage actor are writ in water. Only a few apt, well-turned phrases from critics like Bernard Shaw, James Agate, or Kenneth Tynan preserve the stage personality, and that perforce scantily. George M. Cohan, one of the most entrancing stage personalities of this century, lives on only in the memories of septuagenarians or older and in a 1932 film, *The Phantom President*, which Leonard Maltin correctly dismisses as a "musical antique . . . interesting only as a curio." It no more reveals Cohan's unique abilities as dancer and actor than shadow does substance.

George M. Cohan (1878–1942), accurately described by Gerald Boardman as "the first enduring figure of the modern American musical comedy stage," set forth for that musical stage, and for the first time, its present distinguishing marks: songs with lively, uncomplicated lyrics set to simple, memorable music and action and dialogue that were clearly American in essence and spirit, astringently sentimental and mostly comic in tone, and staged at a brisk, unflagging pace. Cohan, an entertainment polymath, was best described by his friend the classic farceur Willie Collier: "George is not the best actor or author or composer or dancer or playwright. But he can dance better than any author, compose better than any manager, and manage better than any playwright. That makes him a very great man."

Despite Jim's dislike of Cohan's antiunion stance, Cohan grew to be his idol: "When I worked at the Friars Club and what-have-you as bellhop and doorman, I must have seen him. But I never really met him until I was an actor, and then I think he just had to take a look at me when I was applying for work to realize I wasn't the type he wanted." So it was. What Cohan preeminently did not want was another Cohan, and Jim Cagney in his early twenties was as close to Cohan as one could be: small, fair-haired, light-complexioned, a performer who danced well, sang poorly but brightly, acted superbly, was well possessed of a typical Irish mug. Cohan brooked no rivals, and it is not to be wondered at that he dismissed Cagney quickly after hearing him read a few lines. The wonderful irony is that decades later the little red-haired actor immortalized Cohan and gave him and his life an admiring audience of millions.

Jim was first approached to do a film of Cohan's life by Hollywood columnist Sidney Skolsky in the mid-thirties. Skolsky had been an admirer and friend of Jim's almost from the time he arrived in Hollywood and had given him considerable publicity in the newspapers. It had always seemed to the columnist that the resemblances between Cagney and Cohan were striking. In bringing the subject to Jim's attention, Skolsky asked that he be allowed to pursue the matter as producer or assistant producer of the film. Jim said he saw no objections to that, if it could be worked out. As time passed, however, and brother Bill took over Cagney's destiny, the Skolsky connection did not seem feasible, and in later years Cagney had only vague memories of the Skolsky connection. Skolsky grew resentful that his role as initiator of the idea was never acknowledged by the Cagneys, and it was only in their old age that the Skolsky-Cagney friendship was renewed.

In 1940 the Cagney brothers were on the hunt for something memorable to establish Jim's bona fides as an American. The ludicrous charges that he was Communist or Communist-friendly had received wide circulation, and Bill particularly was anxious to dissipate the impression. What better way than to make a musical about the biggest flag-waver in show business? Cohan, who was born on the Fourth of July,* was unashamedly, overwhelmingly patriotic almost to the level of jingoism, and his songs were suffused with love of country and well lodged in the consciousness of many Americans.

Cohan at this time was highly conscious of his own mortality. He had been diagnosed with intestinal cancer although he had not been informed fully of the disease's seriousness. His doctor (an inadequate one, according to Cohan's beloved daughter Mary) did not keep his patient well informed of his condition. But Cohan was realist enough to guess that he was in a bad way, and when friends told him they thought his life should be filmed, he listened. Among the friends was Ed McNamara, Cagney's old chum, who told Jim that acting on this advice, Cohan had approached Samuel Goldwyn with the idea of producing a Cohan musical biography starring Fred Astaire. This, on the face of it, was a naive idea—not unlike William Powell playing Mickey Rooney. In any case, when approached, Astaire politely rejected the idea of playing a turtleneck-and-derby song and dance man.

Ed McNamara told Cohan that Jim Cagney would be perfect to play him. "Can he dance?" Cohan asked anxiously.

"Dance?" said McNamara. "Why, for God's sake, he's almost as good as you are, George." As a rule one did not compare other actors favorably with the egotistical Cohan, but Ed knew what he was doing. He knew that although the old man's ego was formidable, he valued talent.

---

*His first biographer, Ward Morehouse, discovered a baptismal certificate for Cohan dated July 3. I cite vital reasons why this is a clerical error in my *George M. Cohan: The Man Who Owned Broadway* (1973).

"Can Cagney sing?"

"Well, so-so, George."

Cohan was relieved to hear that. "About like me, Ed?"

"About like you, George." Cohan was pleased.

Meanwhile Jack Warner, through his old friend Abel Green, editor of *Variety*, had heard of Cohan's interest in a biographical film with music. He, together with Hal Wallis, had long admired George M., and the idea of Cagney's playing the role in a full-scale musical excited both men. This coincided beautifully with Bill Cagney's intention to have his brother portray a paragon of Americanism. Initially Jim did not think he could do Cohan satisfactorily, but Bill convinced him, both personally as to its being a needful antidote to his so-called overliberal reputation and professionally as a nonpareil opportunity to play a great American showman. Jim agreed, on the condition that a satisfactory script be written. Hal Wallis became the film's executive producer, and Bill the associate producer, in this case the man who did most of the producing. Wallis asked a skilled writer, Robert Buckner, to do the script in close cooperation with Cohan himself. Buckner went to New York for some weeks and began a friendly working relationship with Cohan that proved very fruitful.*

For weeks Cohan and Buckner worked several hours a day, the old man pouring forth memories of his childhood, youth, and middle age, all spent in the theater. Buckner was able to write a complete script, which, after being approved by Hall Wallis, was sent to Jim at Martha's Vineyard.

He was astounded. "I read it with incredulity," he said in *Cagney by Cagney.* "There wasn't a single laugh in it, not the suggestion of a snicker. And this was a script purporting to be about a great American light entertainer, a man who wrote forty-four Broadway shows, only two of which were not comedies." Jim told Bill he absolutely would not do it as written, but if the script could be gone over thoroughly "by the Epstein boys," he would give blanket approval of the script then and there.

Julius and Phil Epstein, a brother team, were former radio writers in their native New York before going to Hollywood in 1935 to write screenplays for Warner Brothers. They were frequently employed as trouble-

---

*Years later Buckner said he believed this part of his closeness to Cohan resulted from Buckner's being a Gentile because Cohan, according to the writer, "had some anti-Semitic tendencies." This is incredible to the present writer, Cohan's authorized biographer, with full access to Cohan's widow and Mary, his closest child. Cohan was known along Broadway as a *pro*-Semite. His best friend, partner, and brother-in-law, Sam Harris, was a Jew, as was Cohan's son-in-law.

shooters, taking bland scripts and infusing them with vigor, with color, and frequently with humor—a service they had already rendered *The Strawberry Blonde.* Not only were the Epsteins comedy writers, but their career chef d'oeuvre was *Casablanca,* which brought them an Academy Award.

They set to work on *Yankee Doodle Dandy* with a bit of aid from a gag writer friend, Ed Joseph, and came up with a script based on the Buckner effort which Jim liked. It was not shown to Cohan, who had already turned in a script of his own to Buckner, a manuscript both ponderous and unfunny. From it Buckner could extract only a few items of value. Including Cohan, there were now five contributors to the *Yankee Doodle Dandy* script. There would be one more, Jim Cagney, who restructured lines that would suit his style of delivery and who, as usual, added bits of business appropriate to the story line.

Cohan had given Buckner a list of taboos, first among them being no mention of Cohan's first wife, singer Ethel Levey, who left him in 1907, after George M. had fallen in love with Agnes Nolan, a chorus girl in one of his shows, with whom he spent the rest of his days. Ethel, who was still performing at the time of the film's making, was threatening litigation if she was not treated fairly in the film. (She did sue Warner Brothers after the film was released on the charge of invasion of privacy and lost.) Cohan sensibly suggested that the vital matter of his love life be handled by giving his one and only wife in the film the name of Mary, thus tying in with the singing of one of his greatest songs, "Mary."

Cohan also stipulated that there be no explicit love scenes in *Yankee Doodle Dandy,* a specification Jim was happy to honor. He was never one for "mushy" scenes, he said; they very much going against his screen personality, and his offscreen personality too, for that matter. He said:

This taboo on love scenes didn't bother me, for the way I do a love scene, it's never a necking party. To me, a panting and grappling love scene is embarrassing when I see it on the screen. So when I sang "Mary" to the girl who played Cohan's wife, I just told her the lyrics as she played the melody. I poured coffee, put sugar into it, stirred it, and handed it to her. Then I sat down, drank the coffee, and she sang the lyric back to me. The way we did it, it was an effective love scene—without any lashings of goo.

Singing Cohan's songs was a joy for Jim. His confident, tonally uncertain baritone resembled Cohan's confident, tonally uncertain tenor in that both men recognized their vocal limitations and relied a great deal on talking their songs. Cohan wrote all his songs in a major key, using simple, natural progressions, the way a person's speaking voice does. The songs did not emphasize flats or sharps, and they were sparing in the variety of their notes. "As a composer," said Cohan, "I could never find use for over four or five notes in my musical numbers." This was a great relief to Cagney.

In setting about to play Cohan, Jim had the help of a trusted few pros who knew the Cohan style—most of the Boys Club. From *Cagney by Cagney:*

> When it was decided that I was to do the job, I sat down with Lynne Overman, Frank McHugh, Spencer Tracy and Pat O'Brien to find out what I could about the man himself. They all had known Cohan. I was the only one in our group who hadn't worked with him. I had seen him in *Ah, Wilderness!* and from that I keyed the mannerisms. He was a fine actor and often did very much with very little. The dancing I got from Johnny Boyle. . . . In any case George M was quite a fellow, and in summing up, I have said many times that we took fifty years of a very troubled life and set it to *his* music. That it turned out well was because of the material we had to work with— and he did it. Happily for all of us, he liked it when he saw it.

His approach to Cohan was not mimicry. Cohan had a unique physical presence. Onstage he tended to strut in rhythmic fashion when he walked, his head bobbing. He frequently looked out of the corner of his eyes at people when speaking, his head cocked, not facing them straight on. He stretched his vowels in New England fashion, usually speaking out of the side of his mouth. In effect he became something of a bantam rooster. Cagney adopted most of these characteristics for Cohan onstage, but he played himself in all other scenes because he knew the script had no time for the essential George M., who was a rather exotic bird met directly. Cagney certainly did not try to define the inner Cohan, not only because he didn't exist in the script but because putting him into it would have been a monumentally difficult task. The real George M. was once precisely described by a woman who had known him all his life: "A complex and amazing man, George was, and one of a million contradictions. Vain and violent-tempered, childish at times, sulky and temperamental, but a man with a heart and a soul, one who was easily hurt and one who could be a great friend. There was a wistfulness always about George, and there was never another Irishman born in the world who had his unfailing charm."

Cagney did rather well in the charm department in *Yankee Doodle Dandy,* conveying much of his elemental self: a buoyantly confident, multi-talented professional, complex in the sense that like many actors, he was an introvert in an extrovert's game. For Jim Cagney, playing George M. was a professional homecoming. To play the best, the most thoroughgoing song and dance man in American history was an honor, *the* honor, of his life.

*Yankee Doodle Dandy* is a career-long life reminiscence by Cohan, framed by his being informed by the White House that the president, Franklin D. Roosevelt, wishes to see him down to FDR's bestowal of *a* congressional medal of honor—not *the* Congressional Medal of Honor (which the film implies)—for "his contribution to the American spirit" as evidenced by "Over There" and "You're a Grand Old Flag." The film concentrates first on Cohan and his family, known as the Four Cohans, a prime vaudeville act at the turn of the century, the family well played by Walter Huston as dad Jerry, Rosemary De Camp as mother Nellie, and Jeanne Cagney as sister Josie. There was little nepotism involved in casting Jeanne. The film's director, Michael Curtiz, was aware of Jeanne's good stage and film experience as well as her dancing and singing abilities. The idea of Cagney's sister playing his sister fascinated Curtiz, and he auditioned Jeanne personally, then awarded her the role on merit.

Filming of *Yankee Doodle Dandy* began on an astonishing day in history. Rosemary De Camp recalls:

The camera and the crew were standing still with grave faces. Jeanne Cagney, Walter Huston, and I, made up and elaborately costumed, were standing at a little radio emitting the sound of President Roosevelt's voice along with a lot of static. Mike Curtiz . . . and Jimmy Cagney came in through the freight dock and walked toward us. When they reached the set, Mike started to speak, but Walter held up his hands. The president finished with the grave news that we were now at war with Japan and Germany. Then the national anthem blared forth. Some of us got to our feet and sang the words hesitantly. At the end Jimmy said, clearing his throat, "I think a prayer goes in here. . . . Turn that thing off." Someone did.

We stood in silence for a full minute, and Jeanne and I dabbed our made-up eyes. Mike bowed and with his inimitable accent said, "Now, boys and girls, we have work to do. We have had bad news, but we have a wonderful story to tell the world. So let's put away sad things and begin." That began our first day on the film, *Yankee Doodle Dandy,* the day after Pearl Harbor, December 8, 1941.

Cagney set the pace for all the others. He was always on time for a call, as he had been always in his career, but this time he made special efforts to do what "was required," a favorite phrase of his all his life. Rosemary De Camp says:

> Throughout that picture we all worked in a kind of patriotic frenzy, as though we feared we may be sending a last message from the free world, because the news was very bad during those months in the winter of 1941–42. We had three weeks of dance rehearsals, during which Jimmy was a great example for all of us. He came through the main gate every morning at six-thirty in his modest old car, wearing his sweatsuit, with his lunch in a paper bag. He worked out dancing, creating most of his own choreography, until noon. He took a half hour to eat, a half hour to rest, and then was back dancing tirelessly until five. We all tried to live up to him.

An interesting dichotomy on the pronunciation of "Cohan" obtains in the film. Jerry and Nellie pronounce it "Co-HAN," which is the traditional pronunciation of the name; George and Josie say "CO-han," the pronunciation common among most Americans. George M. always said "Co-HAN" early in life until his last years, when it became "CO-en" in tribute to his Jewish friends. In the film supporting actors say either "Co-HAN or "CO-han," with the exception of veteran actor George Barbier (playing Abe Erlanger), who in one line says "CO-han" and moments later resorts to "Co-HAN."

Cohan's professional life is accurately portrayed overall, with proper emphasis given to his partnership with Sam Harris and their subsequent amicable breakup after fifteen years together. In the film the reason given for the split is George's disenchantment with play producing because three of the Four Cohans are gone and George wishes to travel. In life the split-up with Harris was caused by their divergent views on unionism. Sam knew labor unions were here to stay. George, stubborn to the last, after having defied the actors in their memorable strike of 1920 for their union's recognition, wanted nothing to do with unions. This attitude had been fostered in him by his father, and George thought his father was the greatest man on earth. So Cohan and Harris dissolved.

Cagney was intensely curious about Cohan's personality, asking this writer many questions about him. He was told that the "real" Cohan was a curious mix of sophistication and childishness, this last the result of never having had a childhood. Cohan was a performer from the time he could walk and exhibited precociousness in terms of personality and creativity from the age of nine. He was running his family's act by the time he was fifteen, doing this with the loving approval of his father, mother, and sister. When George at last married the woman he loved, he was uxorious to a fault. Little of the real Cohan's personality appeared in *Yankee Doodle*

*Yankee Doodle Dandy*
ABOVE: With Jeanne Cagney, Walter Huston, and Rosemary De Camp
BELOW: With S. Z. Sakall and Richard Whorf

*Dandy,* and in retrospect Cagney preferred it that way. He said, "It was a sad story, in a way, but there it goes, right back to one's childhood. George M. running his family's act at fifteen for a very good reason: he knew how to do it better than anyone else. A sad story but a happy one too because he brought so much happiness to others, and not the least to me. I have great compassion for the man, and it makes me realize what a tremendous blessing I had in my mother. Without that great woman the Cagneys would have been carried off in the tide."

In the making of *Yankee Doodle Dandy,* Jim as always was kind to all the people he worked with, cordial, helpful. He was especially kind to Joan Leslie, the seventeen-year-old actress given the heavy burden of playing the wife, Mary. She recalls the improvisatory attitude Cagney believed he had to take with a subject on which he and no one else within hailing distance knew anything about, the life and work of a song and dance man. She says:

It was the scene in the publisher's office when we sang "Harrigan." On most occasions we were given the script before the movie began, but on this picture we would get a new script every day. Jimmy would make the changes. We would get on the set, and he might say, "This isn't quite right."

Mike Curtiz would say, "Whatever you say, Jimmy."

Then Jimmy might say, "I think the girl should say this . . . and turn up her nose and turn around. . . . Then we'll go on singing." Then he would turn to me: "Joan, now you say this to me, and I'll say . . ." The script girl was taking this all down, and a new script would be forthcoming.

Finally the set was being lighted, and we had a piano player to run through it. Jimmy said, "Suppose I do the first four or five lines of the verse, and you do the second, and then we go into the chorus, start out together. When we come to this line, I'll take it. You do the second line." With that, we would go into it and do it.

It gave me such confidence. He made me feel as though I could do whatever he said, which was an extreme compliment. He was asking a great deal of me, but he believed I could do it. He put it all together in about fifteen minutes before we shot it. There was no LeRoy Prinz [Warners' head choreographer] there. I felt as though I had rehearsed the routine a hundred times, because he made me feel so secure. I don't remember more than one take on anything with him. We just did it. Then Mr. Curtiz came over to hug Jimmy and tell him how wonderful it was, and I of course basked in that kind of approval because I was part of it.

*Yankee Doodle Dandy*

The great success of *Yankee Doodle Dandy* was due to a consummate blend of subject material, workable script, Cagney's added "touches," superb performances, and the firm, guiding hand of its director, Mike Curtiz. Jim did not like Curtiz as a man but much admired him as a director. It has been said of Curtiz that in making this picture, he said to an actor, "Don't do it the way I showed you, do it the way I mean." This is apocryphal. What he said was: "I couldn't show you the way to do it, so don't do it that way. Do it the way I mean." It is true that he called *Yankee Doodle Dandy* the "pinochle of my career." That career went back to the silent days in 1926, when Warner Brothers brought him to Hollywood from his native Hungary. He made more than a hundred films for the studio, and always with thoroughness.

*Yankee Doodle Dandy*, with Jeanne Cagney, Joan Leslie, Walter Huston, and Rosemary De Camp

He was, says one of his chief cameramen, Byron Haskin, "a tremendously visual man. He had no command of any language that I could find out, not even Hungarian, which he was supposed to be. His verbiage was loaded with four-letter words. He drove his Packard car one year and never knew it had any other gear but second, let alone reverse. I don't know how he got around with it. But he did have a visual sense. . . . He visualized a shot. 'I poosh my extras across here and I do this.' He was a kind of Busby Berkeley of the drama."

Cagney said:

I had great respect for Mike as director. But that's where it stopped. He didn't know how to treat actors. He gave me no trouble because he knew I'd give him trouble right back. I saw him mistreat actors right and left, so I had to tell him off at times. One day when we were doing *Captains of the Clouds* up in Canada, he gave one of the actors a hard time for no discoverable reason. I took Mike on the side and started to lace into him but good. He said, "Jeemy, I am a sheet-heel, no?" I said, "You are a sheet-heel, yes!" I really came down on him for his meanness, which in this instance was ample and quite deliberate. I saw that he was hurt by what I had said to him, but it had to be said. This was the only moment I ever had with him when I realized he *could* be sensitive and sorry. Through the years I've always contended there was no such person as Mike Curtiz *himself.* There was only Mike Curtiz the director. He somehow became that, and that was all there was. Sad. But whatsoever a man soweth—! A bright man. Intelligent. Yet he never learned one of life's—and art's—basic rules: be good to your actors, and they'll be good—in several senses—to you.

Jim had trouble with only two fellow actors in his entire career: a young man in *One, Two, Three* and the other, an old man, in *Yankee Doodle Dandy.* S. Z. "Cuddles" Sakall, the pudgy, flabby-jowled comic actor who

*Yankee Doodle Dandy*

began to play numerous roles at Warners in 1940, when he arrived from Hungary, was the particular nemesis of a Cagney pal, Alan Hale. Hale did not like "Cuddles" for two reasons. Pat O'Brien described their enmity: "Sakall started to get a number of roles that ordinarily Alan would get, and on top of that Sakall used to keep his foreign accent nice and sharp, which absolutely drove Alan up the wall. When in his cups, Alan would yell at him, 'Sakall, you old bastard. You can speak English as well as I can. Why do you keep on going into this old cutesy-pie foreign accent thing?' Sakall came right back at him, deliberately exaggerating his accent: 'My dear Alan, mine agzzent iss money in de bank!' "

In *Yankee Doodle Dandy* Sakall, playing a moneyed potential backer for a Cohan play, has a scene in which Cohan secures his interest in a new musical by suggesting that he wouldn't be interested in it. Sakall, as Schwab, a girl-crazy old roué, is immediately interested and listens avidly as Cohan explains the virtues of the musical to partner Sam Harris. Sakall's function in the scene is to listen with fascination to what Cohan says, but in the shooting of the scene, Sakall kept interpolating little ad-libs of his own. This angered Jim for a very practical reason. He got Curtiz on the side and said, "Mike, this scene with Sakall is, for chrissake, a *plot* scene. We have to hear what the hell I'm saying, and now this old bastard keeps muttering and repeating everything I say. I know he's doing it for comic effect. For *his* comic effect. I've got plot to get over, and I want him to stop it. If he does it again, I'm really going to tell him, so to forestall any unpleasantness, I want *you* to tell him."

"Oh, no, I couldn't tell," said Curtiz.

"Why not, Mike?"

"Because Sakall was such a big star in Budapest. Oh, no, I couldn't correct him."

"Then I'm going to tell him."

"No, Jeemy, please. I'll have to do it my own way."

The correction was made, Sakall was given a line with which to express his reaction, but a bit of the mumbling repetition of Cagney's line remains in the film. Cagney disliked Sakall from then on.

Cagney's favorite scene in *Yankee Doodle Dandy*, the one that he said he could more or less watch over and over, occurs during a scene that reproduces Cohan's musical play *Little Johnny Jones*. There is a moment in it that for him represented the zenith of the film and, by logical extension, the zenith of his career. As jockey Little Johnny Jones, falsely accused of throwing the English Derby, he is at Southampton Pier, where a pal tells him that he hopes to find on the ship now leaving the evidence proving Johnny's innocence and that if he finds it, a rocket will be fired from the ship when it is out in the bay. The ship, rear deck only visible, pulls away, and Johnny sings "Give My Regards to Broadway" softly, sadly. He pauses reflectively as the chorus takes up the song's refrain, then walks, dejected, into the shadows of the darkening stage.

Moments later, in miniature cutout against the ocean backdrop, the ship appears in the distance, moving in the harbor, its lights twinkling in the gloom. It progresses slowly, and at just the moment when the tension must be relieved, there suddenly arches up from the ship a shivery, sparkling white rocket.

Johnny looks out at the audience with a warm, delighted smile, holding out his left arm with a gesture of satisfied accomplishment, tilting his head back in happy triumph to shout, "Aha!" as he goes into Cohan's stiff-legged yet curiously relaxed dance, arms in perfect counterbalance to his body, while the orchestra thunders out "Give My Regards to Broadway." Jim said, "I think—hell, I *know*—that was my happiest moment in pictures because I was doing what I best liked in a part that I loved. You can't do better than that."

Another moving moment for him was the father's death in the film. Mike Curtiz had asked Phil and Julie Epstein for a heavily emotional scene at this point: "Give me the tear in the eye." Julie Epstein says, "So we wrote the death scene with the Cohan trademark: 'My mother thanks you, my father thanks you, my sister thanks you,' and so on. We thought it was hilarious. We thought they would never use it. But they did, and it was one of the best scenes in the film."

The death scene is dignified by the restraint of another great actor playing the role of Cohan's father, Walter Huston, who in his delirium talks of the booking office's wanting the family to play Des Moines. Sitting on the bed, George tells him he has canceled the engagement, and "we'll pick it up on the way back." Jerry is suddenly back in the days when George was a kid, playing the title role in *Peck's Bad Boy,* when his cockiness caused them all trouble. Jerry now tells him sternly, "Don't upstage your mother or I'll whale the tar out of you!" George says, "I'll never do that. I'll play the whole show with one foot in the trough [footlights]." Jerry asks how many curtain calls there were. Six. "That's pretty good for a drama. Make a speech?" At this point, barely able to hang on, George says softly, "Uh-huh. I thanked them for us. I said my mother thanks you, my father thanks you, my sister thanks you, and I—" His head comes down; he cannot go on. Jerry puts his hand on the back of his son's neck. George, weeping, holds his dad's hand, puts his hand over his dad's, kisses his father on the forehead, and Jerry dies.

As this scene was shot for the first time, Jim, caught up in sorrow for his own father, played the scene with deep emotion, then suddenly heard behind him the sound of weeping. It was hard-boiled Mike Curtiz, tears streaming down his cheeks. "Cheeses Chrisdt, Jeemy," he said. "Beautiful. Beautiful." It was, thought Jim, the ultimate tribute. He had planned not to weep but simply to lower his head on Huston's chest. Then, as the scene progressed, the memory of his own father's early death possessed him.

Jim had to repeat the scene five times to accommodate the variety of camera placements needed: long, far, and medium shots and close-up. One take was ruined because the script girl was weeping too loudly. It is a tribute to Cagney's talent that the fifth time he did it, the scene was as emotionally powerful as the first. But there was no "emotional memory" process à la the Method school of acting. He had expended his emotional reaction in the first take, and the four subsequent ones were done quite as well as the first without any inner emotions, done simply with the pure certitude of a great professional.

When *Yankee Doodle Dandy* was finished, a special showing was arranged at the studio for Edward C. Raftery, one of Cohan's lawyers and the man who represented him in all Warners contract and procedural matters. Raftery, a hefty poker-faced man, watched the film stolidly sitting on a chaise longue, unsmiling at even the lightest moments. Near the end of the film, when George M. leaves FDR's office and dances a wing step down the White House stairs, Jack Warner, who was on the chaise with Raftery, felt it begin to shake. Blasé Ed Raftery was sobbing.

A print of the film was dispatched to Cohan at his summer home in Monroe, New York, and his son, George M. "Mike" Cohan, Jr., watched his dad closely during the showing. At the end Mike said, "What do you think, Dad?"

Cohan shook his head in wonderment and said of the Cagney performance, "My God, what an act to follow." Next day he sent Jim a wire of congratulations on his "wonderful job." Cohan had been apprehensive that his wife, Agnes, would resent his wife in the film being called Mary.

His daughter Mary Cohan said:

Not a bit of it. Mom was delighted. There were a couple of non-family people there when they saw it together, so she followed that quaint old Irish custom of formal address in their presence, and she said to Dad, "Oh, Mr. Cohan, I always knew I was Mary to you!" Dad thought Cagney was just terrific. I talked to him about it sometime later. Dad was not much of a moviegoer, but somewhere he had seen Cagney in a picture or two and of course had him pegged as a gangster type, so he was a bit dubious when Cagney's name came up to play him. Dad wanted Fred Astaire, but after seeing the movie, he realized how wrong Fred would have been. Dad said about Cagney, "I can understand how he could do my dancing, what with Johnny Boyle teaching him the steps the way I did them, but Johnny couldn't show him how to play my *attitude*. That Cagney got on his own, and for the life of me I can't imagine how he did it." Dad was a vain man—with a lot to be vain about—and he was a great actor. To me, the wonder was that Cagney had the imagination and talent to really become George M. Cohan

The premiere of *Yankee Doodle Dandy* was held in New York City on May 29, 1942, as a war bond benefit for the Treasury Department, raising $4,750,000 in war bonds sold that evening. The film was a success everywhere. It was nominated for eight Academy Awards, winning three: Best Sound (Nathan Levinson), Best Musical Scoring (Heinz Roemheld and Ray Heindorf), and Best Actor.

On Academy Award night the Best Actress Oscar was given to Greer Garson for her portrayal of the title role in *Mrs. Miniver.* When called to the podium, this lovely but verbose lady held forth endlessly saying (said Cagney) "as far as I can remember absolutely nothing except thank you eighty-four million times. A dear girl—but my God!" When Gary Cooper, the previous year's Best Actor, opened the envelope for that category, he looked bewildered. He smiled, realizing he was holding it upside down, then shouted happily, "James Cagney—for *Yankee Doodle Dandy!*" The applause was tremendous. Jim came up to the microphone, and an off-screen voice demanded, "Stay there with him." Jim said, "I want you to, old boy." More applause, flashbulbs going off, and Cooper withdrew. Jim said, "Ladies and gentlemen, I'm very happy." There came cries of "Louder, louder!" He raised his voice. "I've bent [*sic*] into my work here. Very happy. Very happy. Because of the highly personal quality of our business, I've always had the feeling, ever since coming into it, that you can only be as good as the other fellow thinks you are—or, I might add, as bad. And it seems that quite a number of people have thought that a good job has been done, and that makes me very happy. And just one added thought: I might say it was a pretty good part. Thank you."\*

\*This transcript is taken from the Hearst International Newsreel footage of the ceremony. His speech is not quite as he cited it in *Cagney by Cagney,* but he was then (1976) recalling it from memory.

The applause was overwhelming, both for such welcome brevity and out of affection for a master of "the business." The next day Jim presented his Oscar to brother Bill, leaving it on his desk. Bill returned it within an hour, and it remained in Jim's bedroom until his death.

The critical approval of *Yankee Doodle Dandy* was abundant and unstinting. One of the first to see it was Cohan's daughter by his first wife, Ethel Levey. Georgette Cohan said, "Lovely. This is Daddy's life as he would liked to have lived it." Bosley Crowther of *The New York Times* marveled that there "was not a maudlin note struck in the film," which, he said, "magnificently matches the theatrical brilliance of Mr. Cohan's career." Archer Winsten of the *New York Post* said that "front and center is James Cagney, whose personal dynamism is a letter perfect conception of the George M. Cohan the public has known." *Time* magazine called it "probably the most genial screen biography ever made."

The review Jim was waiting for proved to be the happiest of all. Abel Green, the clear-sighted and tough-minded editor of *Variety,* said at once that it was a box-office triumph, a sure hit, and "for Cagney, a personal triumph, easily his top cinematic performance. He hoofs like one demented, he troupes like a lammister from The Lambs, he does Cohan like a relative. If he forgets the side-of-the-mouth droop after the initial impress, it's little noticed and perhaps better liked. Thus, in celluloid, Cagney has immortalized Cohan for all time. There can be no more fitting climax to any career."

One of the reasons for the film's success is that there was no interference in the film's making from Warners' front office. Anxious to placate the Cagneys, who were again feeling restless about their home base, Jack Warner and Hal Wallis had allowed the team of writers, performer, and director to make the film very much their own way.

But for Jim and Bill Cagney the taste of such artistic freedom was irresistible. On March 30, 1942, Bill announced to the trade papers that he and his brother had formed Cagney Productions,° created to make their own films, to be financed by the formidable Bankers Trust of New York, for theatrical release by United Artists.

This time the Cagneys were determined to go it alone.

---

°Technically William Cagney Productions Inc., but the brothers always called it by these two words.

# 17 · The War

Jim's love of country, first instilled by his mother, was an essential part of him. He said:

I can recall when I was a tiny one, how much my mom talked of how great a country this was. Just as she taught us about Christ and the need to be good. She never preached—that was never her way—but she never ceased talking in one way or another of how great the United States was. I think that much of this was due to the contrast between her folks' early days in Ireland, the hunger and poverty there, and the wide sweep of opportunity available when they reached the States. In any event, Mom never stopped praising this country. I know I have never stopped, and I never will, until they pat the sod over me.

He said this in his eighty-first year.

An FDR Democrat in his early days, Jim had become increasingly aware of the way the world was turning in the late thirties. He was a faithful reader of a variety of newsmagazines and *The New York Times*. "At the Boys Club," said Pat O'Brien, "Jim would be almost the only one to bring up contemporary and social matters. Not that we didn't talk about such things, but usually he and Spence Tracy were the only serious ones in our bunch. The rest of us were there to wing-ding it. Of course, when the war came along, we were all truly concerned and found ways to help out by going on USO tours and the like. But Jim, I think, was the only one among us who could see the war clouds gathering early on."

In 1939 the motion-picture industry sponsored a nationwide program over NBC Radio deploring those war clouds and urging an emphasis on true Americanism. Newsreel footage of that program exists showing its chief participants: Cagney, Edward G. Robinson, Walter Connolly, Pat O'Brien, Paul Muni, Edward Arnold, Donald Crisp, and a few child actors, among them

Bobby Mauch and Judy Garland. Jim was asked to write "a few sentences" and speak them as prologue. Introduced by Robinson, the master of ceremonies, Cagney said: "Millions throughout the world envy us the privilege and the right to call ourselves Americans. Let us prove our deep appreciation of that privilege by rededicating ourselves to true Americanism—with faith in God, faith in man, faith in liberty, and faith in America." He felt the need for those faiths more and more in the next few years as he saw the world drift toward war. He was horrified by the 1939 Hitler-Stalin nonaggression pact.

In 1942 he was elected president of the Screen Actors Guild, this giving him heavy responsibilities in the direction of Hollywood's participation in the war. He attended numerous meetings of the Hollywood Victory Committee, of which he was chairman, and appeared in bond-selling one-reel films.

The best of these, *You, John Jones,* was shot at MGM. This ten-minute short was to have been done by Spencer Tracy, who became ill two days before shooting. Eddie Mannix, MGM executive, at Tracy's suggestion, called Jim to see if he would be amenable to taking over. "Name the day and hour," Jim said. The lines were not difficult to learn; the setting and photography, as usual with Hollywood's top studio, were impeccable. The only irritation Jim felt was with the director assigned him, his old nemesis Mervyn LeRoy, but since he believed LeRoy had never directed him anyhow, this was no great problem.

It is instructive to look closely at *You, John Jones* both as an example of American propaganda for home consumption in wartime and as a model of how very good acting can vivify cloying dialogue. *You, John Jones,* which Cagney called "a pretty dull thing," was made by MGM as its 1943 contribution to United Nations Week of that year and was written and produced by studio veteran Carey Wilson, the man responsible for both the Andy Hardy and Dr. Kildare series. John Jones (nothing more elementally American than that name, placing us at once in a morality play) is foreman at an airplane factory. His pet phrase in response to good news is "Ain't it the beautiful truth!" After work he comes through the white picket fence into his beautiful house where Mary, his beautiful wife, played by Ann Sothern, is watching their child, beautiful Margaret O'Brien, reciting Lincoln's Gettysburg Address in preparation for her school's elocution contest. "Isn't she wonderful?" Mary asks John.

"Ain't it the beautiful truth!" says John.

The phone rings. John is suddenly called away to his air-raid warden post. He goes there, and as he sits on a park bench jotting down the time in his notebook, he sees the moon above and says, "Hello, God. It's a wonderful night, isn't it?" Even God would hardly deny that manifest truth. John goes on: "Bright, clear, and shiny. Wonderful night for an air raid. [*Pensive music begins.*] I don't think there's going to be an air raid. Not here in our own United States of America. I suppose that some of the people on our side are being bombed somewhere—like England, Russia, China. Terrible. But I just wanted you to know we appreciate not being bombed here, in our own country, in our United States."

Onto the sound track comes an ominous voice-over, solemn, portentous, asking John Jones if he *does* appreciate, asking him to suppose that his home, his wife, and, above all, "*your* baby, John Jones, *your* baby" (a phrase repeated eight more times in the film with mounting solemnity) were situated in "those other places." Whereupon we see beautiful little Margaret O'Brien in eight manifestations: as an air-raid victim in England; as a one-legged refugee in Greece; as a starving child in China; as a crying child in Yugoslavia; as a fugitive child in occupied France; as an Australasian child in a Japanese prison camp; as a victim of the massacre at Lidice, Czechoslovakia; as a dead child in a bombed-out Russian house, each of these visitations prefaced by "*your* baby, John Jones, *your* BABY," the voice-over becoming more dramatic and whispery each time. Then we are back with Cagney on the park bench.

The voice-over now demands to know if John Jones realizes how lucky he is and if he realizes that if the conquered people of this world were to accept their conquest, "were to collaborate with their cruel conquerors, your side wouldn't win this terrible war. Did I say your side? Excuse me, John Jones. I meant *our* side."

Suddenly an air-raid siren sounds, a bomb falls, smoke swirls up, and Cagney shouts, "This is *it!*" We hear beautiful Margaret screaming as Cagney runs to his house. It is no longer beautiful. "*Your* baby!" the voice-over insistently intones.

Then with equal suddenness, we are back with John Jones on his park bench. It has all been a daydream. Everything is quiet, as John continues writing in his report book, in calm consternation. He walks home, sees that it is still beautiful, closes his eyes in prayerful thanks, enters, and asks his wife if she is all right. "Of course, dear." The phone rings, and John learns that there is no red alert (danger).

"All clear, Mary," he says to his wife. Then he goes to the door, opens it, and, looking at the moon, whispers, "Thank you, God."

"Oh, Daddy," Margaret says, "you didn't hear all my recitation, so I'll finish it now, please." She goes on, "The world will little note . . ." to the end of the Gettysburg Address: ". . . of the people, by the people, and for the people shall not perish from the earth."

He kisses her and, with his arms around wife and child, exclaims, "Ain't it the beautiful truth!" as the music swells up. The End.

It's easy to sneer at the necessary pietisms of wartime propaganda years after the fact, but this is truly relentless cutie-pie sentimentality. Yet in the viewing it rings not a single false note, purely because of the acting. Cagney takes this jingoistic confection and gives it authentic life, and he does it by the simplest yet most difficult of acting devices: listening to and honoring the author's intention. "If you accept an author," said Cagney, "you must give him the truth of what he means." *You, John Jones*'s innate air of superiority—thank God we're all right, and thanks, God, for preserving us, which, after all, is our just entitlement—jars today. But it didn't then, when the United States was just flowering into world power, maturity, and self-knowledge.

The Hollywood Victory Committee, under the aegis of the Screen Actors Guild, had been formed by members of all the trade guilds in the industry— actors, writers, producers, and directors—to support the armed forces in every way possible. This inevitably resulted in shows, touring and otherwise, that appeared at service camps and USO centers. An adjunct of this was the Victory Caravan, consisting of more than a score of well-known entertainers from Hollywood, venturing cross-country for three weeks of personal appearance bond selling. The stars were Desi Arnaz, Joan Bennett, Joan Blondell, Cagney, Claudette Colbert, Jerry Colonna, Bing Crosby, Irene Dunne, Cary Grant, Charlotte Greenwood, Olivia De Havilland, Bob Hope, Frances Langford, Bert Lahr, Laurel and Hardy, Groucho Marx, Frank McHugh, Pat O'Brien, Merle Oberon, and Risë Stevens, together with a group of Hollywood starlets, seven pretties, to spruce up the scene. Hope and Crosby had to leave at various times for previous engagements, but the others were fully committed. They began to form a cohesive unit, mostly all new friends with one another, very much enjoying one another's company. There were also cliques formed, clusters of people who felt a special affinity for each other, the most striking one being Cagney, McHugh, O'Brien, Lahr, and Merle Oberon. She attached herself to the four early on, and the group invariably had dinner together. She listened avidly to their wealth of theatrical reminiscences and was enchanted. As the days went by, one member of the general party asked Oberon why she was with such an unusual crew, and she said, "Oh, I love baggy pants comedians."

The Southern Pacific Railroad donated nine cars, including a dining car, a lounge car with a full bar, and Pullmans, each star having his or her own compartment. The schedule was Union Station, Los Angeles, to Washington, D.C., for a reception on the White House lawn given by Eleanor Roosevelt, followed by a meeting with the president. This was capped by a three-hour show in Constitution Hall, then back to the train for war bond–selling stopovers in New York City, Boston, Philadelphia, Detroit, Cleveland, Chicago, Milwaukee, St. Louis, St. Paul-Minneapolis, Des Moines, Dallas, and Houston.

The amount of bonds sold was prodigious, and the stars reveled in the chance to have fun and do something tangible for the war effort. Sexual frolic was severely limited by the presence of chaperons occupying a no-man's-land between the male and female sections of the train. But there were attempts made. Jim noticed Charles Boyer sneaking over into the ladies' area and knocking at a door, where he was admitted. Jim quickly waved a group of pals together, and they assembled outside the compartment, which was occupied by a very pretty starlet. Jim motioned for silence, and the suave, courtly tones of one of the screen's greatest lovers could be heard distinctly through the door: "My dearest, please. I was taken by your beauty the moment I saw you."

"Oh, Mr. Boyer, don't."

"But please. If you only had some idea of just how much you mean to me!" Sounds of scuffling.

"Oh, please, Mr. Boyer. We only just met a few days ago."

"Time means nothing when two people truly care about each other." The scuffling sounds grew louder. "Please!"

"Really, Mr. Boyer. Really! I want to sleep alone!"

By this time Jim and his crew were stuffing handkerchiefs in their mouths to choke down their laughter. To help the girl inside, Jim took command of the situation. He knocked on the compartment door and in a gruff voice said, "Western Union for Mr. Boyer!"

The scuffling stopped, and a strangulated voice said, "Wrong compartment. There is no Mr. Boyer here."

In the same gruff voice Jim replied, "The people down the hall here said they saw Mr. Boyer go in here."

This time the girl replied sternly, "Mr. Boyer has not been in here. Will you kindly go away?"

With that, Jim waved dismissal, and everyone retired, including Mr. Boyer presently.

Then in a curious twist of fate Jim found himself caught in a bizarre romantic drama, one very much not of his own making. One fascinating and disturbing thread had run through his stay on the train: the well-displayed seductiveness of Merle Oberon toward him. She was clearly besotted, following him about, trying to sit next to him whenever she could. In his presence she would show off her lovely legs to the point of near immodesty. One of Cagney's closest friends who does not wish to be identified in this instance was on the train and remembers:

Jim was well aware she was chasing him. He enjoyed her company when she was with people in her presence, but he avoided her otherwise, when she was by herself. "Don't leave me alone with her," he told me.

Then one afternoon she pulled a coup. She bribed a porter to let her into Jim's compartment, where she undressed and got into bed. Jim returned a few minutes later and found her there. The bedclothes were loosely draped about her, and she looked her most beautiful, which was *very* beautiful. He had conscientiously tried to keep away from her, but he had not had sex for a long time, and here was this great beauty offering herself. So he got into bed with her. A few minutes later Merle in her excitement suddenly cried out, "Ooohh, Jimmy Cagney's fucking me!"

At that Jim stopped. Stopped cold, got up, and dressed.

"Why?" she said.

"Nothing," he said. "This is my fault. I guess I'm not the type."

He told me later that the minute Merle uttered those words, he thought of his wife and felt sick with shame. "I'm not the type," he said. That's right. He wasn't the adulterous type. He blamed only himself, but in my view, the blame—whatever blame there was— was not his. I think it took a real man to do what he did. How many guys would have had that kind of strength to resist such a gorgeous dame?

Thereafter Jim treated Oberon just as he had before, with the greatest cordiality and friendship, and she continued to be one of the Lahr-McHugh-O'Brien-Cagney coterie. But there was no more leg flashing, and he successfully avoided being alone with her.

"All these people," said Jim, "added up to a real troupe, reminding everyone of the good old days. Once on the train we had no towels for three days, so four of us used one of my old sweatshirts. The hotel rooms were small, stuffy, and noisy. . . . Lahr said every room we slept in was an iron

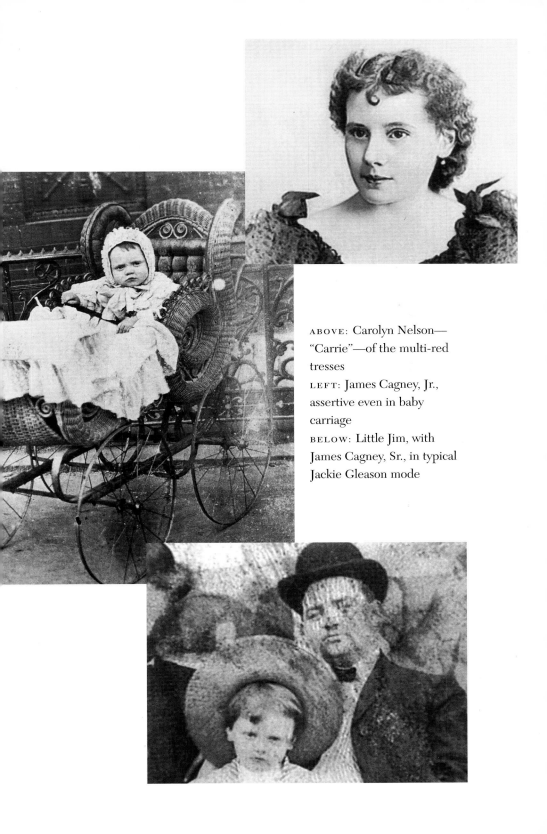

ABOVE: Carolyn Nelson—
"Carrie"—of the multi-red
tresses
LEFT: James Cagney, Jr.,
assertive even in baby
carriage
BELOW: Little Jim, with
James Cagney, Sr., in typical
Jackie Gleason mode

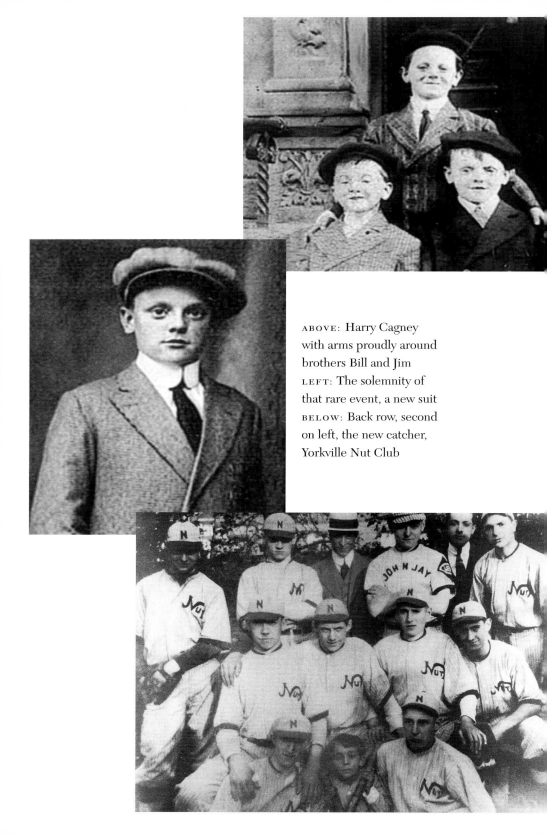

ABOVE: Harry Cagney
with arms proudly around
brothers Bill and Jim
LEFT: The solemnity of
that rare event, a new suit
BELOW: Back row, second
on left, the new catcher,
Yorkville Nut Club

ABOVE: Cagney, archetypal
vaudevillian, smile and skimmer
RIGHT: The Cagneys' passport
photo, taken for their aborted
trip to London, 1927
BELOW: "Willie," Francis
Willard Vernon, little lady
of the chorus, 1919

On the set:
RIGHT: With Joan Blondell
BELOW: With Loretta Young

Horsing around, onscreen and off
BOTTOM: With Buster Keaton,
Harpo Marx, and George Burns

LEFT: With Bing Crosby and Carole Lombard
BELOW: At home

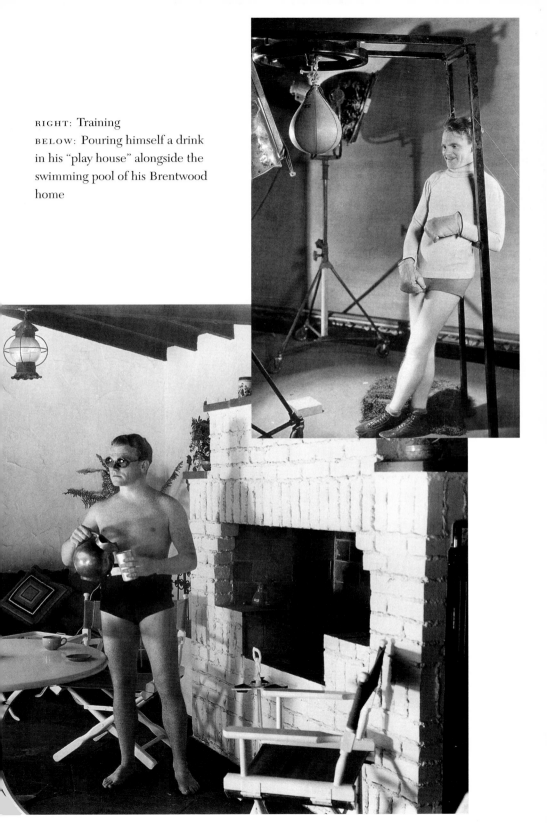

RIGHT: Training

BELOW: Pouring himself a drink
in his "play house" alongside the
swimming pool of his Brentwood
home

LEFT: With his mother, his sister, Jeanne, and his brothers Eddie and Bill
BELOW: With his two children, Catherine ("Casey") and James Junior
BOTTOM: The four Cagney brothers, left to right: Eddie, Bill, Jim, and Harry, 1943

ABOVE: With Frank Capra,
Darryl F. Zanuck, and
Jack L. Warner
RIGHT: With his brother
Bill, facing Lowell Sherman,
at the Beverly Wilshire Hotel
BELOW: With Spencer Tracy,
Pat O'Brien, Frank McHugh,
and Lynne Overman

RIGHT: The Cagneys arriving in
New York to attend the premiere
of *Yankee Doodle Dandy*
BELOW: Jim and Willie, Martha's
Vineyard, 1937

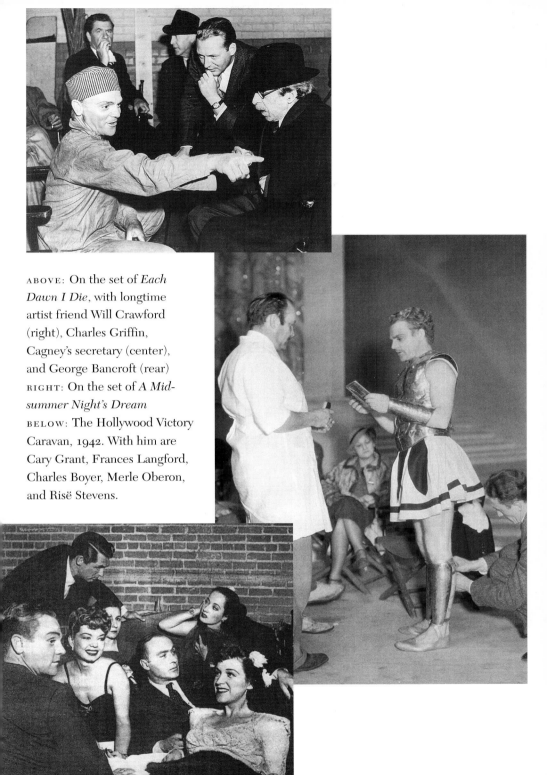

ABOVE: On the set of *Each Dawn I Die*, with longtime artist friend Will Crawford (right), Charles Griffin, Cagney's secretary (center), and George Bancroft (rear)

RIGHT: On the set of *A Midsummer Night's Dream*

BELOW: The Hollywood Victory Caravan, 1942. With him are Cary Grant, Frances Langford, Charles Boyer, Merle Oberon, and Risë Stevens.

The Cagneys photographed by
Eve Arnold at the farm in 1955

ABOVE: With Charlton Heston and Ronald
Reagan at the AFI tribute to Cagney, 1975
RIGHT: With Mae Clarke, thirty years after the
"grapefruit incident"
BELOW: With Marge Zimmermann at the tribute to
Fred Astaire at the Beverly Hilton Hotel, 1981
OPPOSITE: *Man of a Thousand Faces*

Jim and Willie on the RMS *Queen Elizabeth*
sailing to England for the making of *Ragtime*, 1980

lung." The dressing rooms were even worse, reminding Jim of the verminous ones in old vaudeville theaters. In San Francisco he and his pals were in a dressing room abutting the stage, and everyone had to walk through it to get onstage, "even when we were only partly dressed," he said. "Some girl came around with free sandwiches and orangeade, but we never found out who she was. The camaraderie was wonderful, though. When it was all over, we just looked at one another and knew that there was never a troupe like that and never would be again."

The Victory Caravan's great success was due to the opportunity it gave average folk not only to see famous stars in the flesh but also to see these people provide first-rate entertainment. Pat O'Brien called it

*Your Show of Shows* years before they invented that name. Imagine, on the same stage in one evening, Bert Lahr singing one of his great songs with Cary Grant as his stooge, Groucho Marx doing an insult routine, Charlotte Greenwood with her high kicks dance, Bing Crosby singing "Blues in the Night," then trading ad-libs, *funny* ad-libs, with Bob Hope, Jim Cagney with a line of those pretty girls doing "Yankee Doodle Dandy," Laurel and Hardy doing one of their great routines. It was one of those occasions, those three weeks, that really in my lifetime deserved that much-overworked adjective "fabulous." It really was, nothing less. Fabulous.

Pat and Frank McHugh did a World War I song and dance and then followed the rest of the troupe into the dressing room, where Stan Laurel and Oliver Hardy were holding court with a large bottle of scotch, set forth for relief of postshow jitters. Pat was generally acknowledged to be the life of the caravan. Jim, as usual, retired early, but as he said, "Our two stay-ups were Pat O'Brien and Al Newman [conductor of the orchestra]. They'd be up all hours of the night, talking and drinking. After about three days of this Pat, who always managed to look fresh, went into the barbershop to have his usual shave. 'Where's Newman?' the barber asked. 'Oh,' said Pat, 'I drank him at four o'clock this morning.' It never hurt Pat that I could see. He went on well into his eighties, still the life, and I mean the lively life, of the party."

The quintet of Cagney, Lahr, O'Brien, McHugh, and Oberon also went on to the end of the run. In Chicago "the boys," as Oberon called them, took her a number of times to dinner at the swank Pump Room of the Hotel Ambassador. "She was beautiful, just beautiful," said Frank McHugh. "When we'd go into the Pump Room, this gorgeous creature would enter, followed by our unlikely crew. Everybody looked at her and then at us, and you could hear them saying, 'What's going on?' "

Bert Lahr remembered: "Everybody called at our table, just to see her, but she never asked anyone to sit down."

Oliver "Babe" Hardy all his later days remembered the Victory Caravan as one of his life's highlights. "That's the saddest part of show business. A company forms. You meet great people, you have wonderful times, and then inevitably it breaks up, and you know you'll never get back together again. They were special people doing something special. Such fun, the time of your life, and the icing on the cake was that we were all together for the sake of the boys in service."

After it was over, Jim went on to Martha's Vineyard for a rest and had been there for several weeks when the USO approached him about a personal appearance tour at Army bases in England. He was happy to go. The idea of making an extended sea trip on behalf of his country, even with submarines lurking below, was exciting. He rousted out his old pal Johnny Boyle from retirement to help him construct an act. "It was a big favor Johnny was doing me," said Jim. "He had worked so hard on *Yankee Doodle Dandy* with me that he scragged part of his leg, but as usual, he came through. We whipped up an act called, pretty fancily, the *American Cavalcade of Dance,* but I think it was all to the point, and I had the great joy of imitating Fred Astaire. I was of course a poor shadow of the greatest dancer our country has ever produced. But I enjoyed it, and I think the boys did."

The boys did. As always, the showstopper was dancing and singing Cohan. Cagney was reviewed by several British critics informally as he made his way across England and Wales, and scarcely a newspaperman could refrain from commenting on his lack of tough guy accent and his gentle appearance. Jim said:

My God, you'd think people would get the idea that I am an actor and that even though I was born on the East Side, I never in my life said "dese" and "dose" and "dem" except in a movie. But when I played before the boys and would go into the tough guy routine as a gag, I'd get howls of recognition. That was fun. It was also terribly sad too because I knew some of those fine young guys I played to were going to be dead in a few months, and that thought was almost unbearable: looking out at those fresh young faces and wondering how many of them would never get back home. One spunky young guy came up to see me after I had played a show at his base and told me he was from Yorkville. "No kiddin'," I said.

"No kiddin'. Seventy-eighth and First Avenue."

"My God," I said. "That's right around the corner from where I lived when I was a kid."

So we exchanged the old did-you-know and whatever-happened-to talk, and he gave me his mom's name and address, and would I please drop her a line. She'd get such a kick out of it, et cetera. So I did that first thing I got home, saying he was a great little guy and was fine. His mom answered me with a lovely little note.

Then some weeks later I got another note from her saying her boy had been killed in action. By Jesus, that just took the mickey out of me, that letter. I was reading it at my desk, and I dropped my head down and started to weep. Willie came in the room, alarmed, wanted to know what was wrong. I handed her the letter, and she cried too. I'll never forget that little guy, Tony. He was just as big a hero as any of them that won all the medals, and I know the boys with the medals would agree. Tony is one of the reasons I'm so proud to be an American, and I don't give a goddamn how senti-mental that sounds. Next time I got back to New York I dropped by Tony's place in my old neighborhood, but his mother had moved, leaving no forwarding address. Every time I drive by East Seventy-eighth and First, I think of him. An authentic American hero.

Jim spent most of the war years in California. He frequently gave his place on Martha's Vineyard over to the recreational use of servicemen, mak-ing sure there was always plenty of beer on hand. A nearby unit of Navy pilots and a company of enlisted men had a standing invitation to drop in for beer whenever they liked when he was in residence.

As supplemental service to the war effort, Jim appeared whenever asked on the Armed Forces Radio Network show *Command Performance*. It was a weekly show that featured movie stars in comedy skits supple-mented by musical numbers, all specified in requests from servicemen. One mid-1944 show Jim particularly enjoyed featured him and Jack Benny, a comedian Jim treasured. On the program Jack's braggadocio and all-around fecklessness are explored by means of contrast with Cagney's tough guy rep-utation. Jack boasts to announcer Don Wilson that he actually beat up Cagney on the way to the station. Don says, "You wouldn't sneeze if Cagney threw a handful of pepper in your face," and Jack goes on to say that Cagney's car bumped his, "and that's all I needed, brother." A witness to all this was Ginger Rogers, who promptly enters to explain that Jack smacked into Cagney's fender, jumped out of his car, followed by Cagney jumping out of his car, followed by Jack jumping back into his. Jack then dressed Cagney down after securely locking his doors and rolling up the windows. Jack denies this, saying there isn't a window in his car.

GINGER: Not now there isn't. I'll never forget the look on Jack's face when he saw Jimmy's fist coming through the windshield.

BENNY: Well, he didn't hit me.

GINGER: How could he? You had your head in the glove compartment.

Jack threatens to fix Cagney's "wagon," and when MC Deanna Durbin tells Jack that Cagney "is standing right in back of you," Jack says, "Well, that's just—yipe!" Deanna introduces Cagney. Jack blusters:

BENNY: Listen, don't try to laugh it off, Cagney. You know you smashed my fender, and it's going to cost you about three hundred dollars to have it touched up.

CAGNEY: Who's doing the painting for you, Rembrandt?

BENNY: That happens to be his name, Morty Rembrandt. Eighteen-twenty Temple Street. Open evenings.

The sketch continued for fifteen minutes, revolving around the reputed request to Cagney from five Brooklyn servicemen (says Deanna) that he "pick somebody on *Command Performance* tonight and punch them in the jaw." Jack tries to argue his way out of being the recipient, but he must accommodate. Cagney is too tenderhearted to do it, and Jack calls him a coward. There is a smack sound effect, and Ginger Roger says, "And will the gentleman in the audience who caught Mr. Benny kindly return him to the stage?" Deanna Durbin comes in to say, "While the ushers are reviving Mr. Benny, it's time to say we've had an awful lot of requests to have Jimmy Cagney sing a few songs from *Yankee Doodle Dandy*." He obliges and thanks "all the servicemen in the ETO [European Theater of Operations] who treated me so wonderfully when I visited them recently. I really got a great bang out of it, and that's no fooling. And for me to tell you that you're doing a great job is like telling Abbott and Costello who's on first. Anyhow, with a bow to George M. Cohan, here it is: the songs you requested." He then sang "It's a Grand Old Flag" and "Yankee Doodle Dandy."

The program concluded with Jack Benny's return to say that the Cagney punch was just a gag but adding, "I'd give that Cagney a Mickey Finn if I didn't think he'd enjoy it. Good night, fellas."

# 18 · The Lone Cagneys

The combined euphoria of freedom from the Warners factory and of delight in the Cagney brothers' self-governance was almost enough to turn Jim to drink. "For the very first time in my life," he said, "I gave serious thought to hanging one on. I had never been drunk in my life, and for maybe eight seconds I seriously considered it. Then I thought of my dad, and that thought flew out the window. In any case, I guess I was giddy enough with happiness to get about the same effect. We were a happy pair of Irish boys."

Jim and Bill were the chief officers of Cagney Productions Inc., with controlling interest. By the time the company was ready to make movies, they had added to the board of directors brothers Harry and Ed, both successful physicians but increasingly interested in show business. With Carrie and Jeanne settled permanently in Los Angeles, the idea of the four Cagneys with their own producing unit, with Jeanne as a featured player, was irresistible to Harry and Ed. Jim would be the focus of most but not all of their films. Bill would produce them, and Harry and Ed would act as studio aides, admittedly amorphous designations, but both men enjoyed creative work, were intelligent, and took Bill's word that they would be functional elements of the organization. Jeanne not only was truly pretty, but could act.

Cagney Productions Inc. had what the family believed were exciting plans for their non-Cagney pictures. There were plans for buying worthwhile literary properties, dramatizing them, putting appropriate stars under contract, and, above all, supervising the genesis of their films closely so that abortions of good material like *City for Conquest* could not occur.

The Cagneys had learned from their experiences with Grand National that extensive distribution of their films was vital, and a tiny outfit like Grand National could hardly find the distribution it needed. Grand

National's dissolution told its own sad story. The key to success for a small studio was affiliation with one of the eight large motion-picture distributors in the country, and here the Cagneys got a break. Seven of these distributors were also large producing studios like Warner Brothers and Metro-Goldwyn-Mayer. Of the eight, one did not produce films. United Artists didn't have its own studio. Its name stated its origin: a group of artists—originally Charlie Chaplin, D. W. Griffith, Mary Pickford, and Douglas Fairbanks—who separately produced their own films, then turned to their parent company to release and distribute them. Other vital figures in the film industry joined them through the years: Samuel Goldwyn, David O. Selznick, and Walt Disney. All became shareholders.

In time this ideal arrangement began to unravel, with the departure of some of the stockholders like Goldwyn and Griffith. United Artists began to experience hard times. Fortunately in 1941 Edward Raftery, the man who approved *Yankee Doodle Dandy* for George M. Cohan, became president of United Artists. He and the Cagneys began to discuss the possibilities of affiliating. At this time United Artists had never given direct production financing to nonshareholders, with one exception, Walter Wanger. But in 1941 UA needed product badly; its released films at this time were few in number and not exceptional in content.

Under the agreement between United Artists and Cagney Productions, the former would help the latter get production financing from wealthy banks like Bankers Trust of New York as well as give the Cagneys preproduction money for script purchase and operating expenses directly from UA coffers. The Cagneys, for their product, were to receive 25 percent of the gross up to $800,000 and 10 percent on any income after that. These were extremely generous terms. The Cagney boys were officially in business with United Artists as an affiliated, independent producer beginning in 1942. They were to have six eventful years with UA.

Bill Cagney was asked by a *New York Times* reporter about his new company's policy. He made it vitally clear that the mix would not be as before, that above all, Jim would not be a toughie, citing *The Public Enemy* as the cause of his brother's persistent public image:

Suddenly Jimmy clicks as a strictly "dese, dem and dose" guy. A tough mug, so tough that every gangster in the country was nuts about him. They'd look at him up there on the screen and they'd say to themselves, "There's the guy who's tops in my business." If they weren't too scared they'd try to shake hands with him whenever they happened to see him in person anywhere. Jimmy was made, but that wasn't all. He was typed—typed as exactly the kind of guy our mother had tried to push us farthest away from. So for ten years Jimmy makes five pictures a year and all along the same Warner Brothers formula—Jimmy is a heel for eight reels, then clean him up in the ninth. You don't like it, you argue, you're suspended, you get a reputation as a difficult actor—so usually you give in.

Bill went on to tell the *Times* that after he had become Jim's producer at Warners, under the new contract script approval was granted the Cagneys, but Warners persisted in trying to force the old formulas on them, hence the need to form their own company. Bill was asked if Cagney Productions had a definitely formulated policy about upcoming Cagney films. Bill said: "We've got a very definite policy on 'don'ts'; the 'do's' are wide open. There won't be any more gangster pictures for Jimmy, no more cocky arrogance of the old Warners formula kind. On the positive side, there are just a couple of simple rules." He summed these up by saying he had an obligation to find good scripts, scripts that were meant for audiences above the twelve-year-old age range. But there is, he said,

> another thing too. The audience is your customer, and the customer is always right, damn it, because you're making pictures for them, not for yourself. Now I've been watching Jimmy for ten years. It's kind of peculiar putting your own brother under a microscope but that's what I've had to do—analyze what he had to sell, what he had to be careful of. And one thing we can't get away from. Jimmy has a kind of electricity that makes audiences expect action from him; even the way he moves is a sort of promise. And we can't let the audience be disappointed too much. Most of Jimmy's pictures probably will be romantic action pictures of some sort.

"Action" is an extremely elastic word, and it must be stretched full width to describe the first Cagney Productions film, *Johnny Come Lately*. Jim had sought friendships all his life with writers, and in 1940 he had cultivated the acquaintance of the popular novelist Louis Bromfield. Bromfield's work has not lasted, but in the early years of this century he was one of America's best-known novelists, writing mostly for popular magazines like *Cosmopolitan* and the *Saturday Evening Post*. In addition, he was a professional farmer and writer on agriculture. It was in these areas that Jim was first attracted to his work. Bromfield won a Pulitzer Prize for his novel *Early Autumn* which postulated that industrialization was ruining America and that home farming was mandatory to preserve national greatness.

Jim, as he did so frequently with people he admired, wrote a fan letter to Bromfield, and Bromfield answered. When Cagney Productions began to search out literary properties, it was inevitable that Jim would think of Bromfield. He selected one of the novelist's gentlest stories, *McLeod's Folly,* featuring a protagonist as unlike the standard Cagney screen persona as it was possible to be short of a hermit. The Cagneys obtained the services of the London and Broadway playwright John Van Druten to transmute a mild little novel into what unfortunately turned out to be a mild little movie, *Johnny Come Lately.*

The year is 1906. A small town. In the town square Tom Richards (Cagney), a soft-spoken, Dickens-loving itinerant newspaperman, is sitting cross-legged on the plinth of the town founder's statue, dry-shaving himself, chuckling over his copy of *Pickwick Papers.* This first shot of Cagney is emblematic of the film's "action." We have already met old Vinnie McLeod, gently sweet but tough-minded owner-publisher of the town's second news-paper, heavily mortgaged to W. W. Dougherty, owner-publisher of the town's leading newspaper. (No one ever explains why such a small town has two newspapers.) With mention of mortgages we are already in the environs of melodrama and will there remain until the end of the film. Yet it all man-ages to be quietly plausible because of the acting. Cagney is excellent play-ing this bookish, gentle intellectual because he is in essence playing himself. Vinnie is acted with calm authority by Grace George, one of America's lead-ing stage actresses, whose only film appearance this was to be.

Now that Jim owned the production company he could hire whom he wanted, and it gave him great joy to cast Ed McNamara in one of the lead roles, the crusty W. W. Dougherty, the piece's villain. As an actor McNamara tended to bark his lines, and he is woefully out of his depth trying to play on the same level with Cagney and Miss George.

Oddly, Ed McNamara was a very able actor—off camera. A magnificent raconteur and superbly talented singer (tantalizingly brief excerpts of his singing flash by in the film), he was grievously afflicted with stage fright, which frequently set him, during performance, in the mold of a rigidly pos-tured, unblinking monolith. In *Johnny Come Lately* he looks impressive, and when his stage fright can be used as stimulus for his anger, he is fine. The rest of the time his stance is stiff, his voice monotonous and largely uninflected. On camera he was a talented amateur.

The plot of *Johnny Come Lately* is the tired one of the gentle stranger who comes into the lives of troubled people, stirs them into reversal of their downward course, then, having revitalized them, leaves as suddenly as he came. Hi yo, Silver. Good-bye, Shane. Still, *Johnny Come Lately* is living

*Johnny Come Lately.* ABOVE: With Hattie McDaniel, Marjorie Lord, and Grace George; BELOW: With Edward McNamara

stuff, has blood and flesh—if brittle in its bones—because added to Cagney and Grace George is a list of supporting actors who keep the faith dramatically and give the conventional dialogue the life it so badly needs. This is a very old Hollywood story. Jim all his working life and beyond insisted that the supporting players were the reason for the thirties and forties being the golden age of the American film. "Without the Frank McHughs, without people like Chester Clute, Franklin Pangborn, Donald Meek, Clarence Kolb, Margaret Hamilton, and Russell Hicks, there would be no golden age," he said. "I had great fun casting the supporting players in the Cagney productions. You can't fault us there." An accurate assessment. *Time* magazine said of the "small" roles in *Johnny Come Lately:* "Bit players who have tried creditably for years to walk in shoes that pinched them show themselves in this picture as the very competent actors they always were: there has seldom been as good a cinematic gallery of U.S. small-town types."

One such actor in *Johnny Come Lately* is Robert Barrat, a tall, hawk-nosed character actor, who shares with Cagney perhaps the best scene in the film. Barrat, a political boss in the state capital, is approached by crusading editor Cagney for support in bringing the nasty McNamara to account. To prepare for his encounter with Barrat, Cagney has learned that the man adores ketchup, reveres it, indeed lost his old girlfriend, Gas House Mary, snobbish keeper of a genteel bordello, because he even put ketchup on her homemade peach ice cream. (We are not dealing with profundities here.)

Armed with this information, Cagney, offered lunch with Barrat, says he will have only coffee and, when it arrives, casually pours ketchup in it. Looking at Cagney with delighted incredulity, Barrat says, "That's something I've never tried. Is that *good?*"

With cool proprietary confidence, Cagney replies, "Ketchup is pretty good with anything, isn't it?"

Barrat tries it and shouts triumphantly, "That's *good!*"

Another of the Hollywood small-role versatiles in the film is Victor Kilian, the old Cagney friend responsible for giving him the tip leading to the role in *Outside Looking In.* In a boxcar scene, not set there by accident surely—*Outside Looking In's* chief locale—Kilian, as a tramp, addresses Cagney, who has the look of one, and says of his own life journey:

There's a road that passes cities, and it leaves them on the side,
It goes across the mountains and takes them in their stride.
You can meet with friends along that road or travel on alone.
It's the open road of freedom where you call your soul your own.

"Not good," says Cagney, "but I can see where it has a point. Who wrote it?"

"A fella by the name of Tom Richards. Just a tramp." Cagney, as Tom Richards, has no comment.

The point of the verse is the theme of *Johnny Come Lately* and of Jim's own life at that juncture. Like Tom Richards, who overcomes the bad guy and forces the big competing newspaper to give way, Jim was sure that he was showing the Warner Brothers that he could do what he wanted to do competently and very much in his own way. Brother Bill in a newspaper interview at the time explained again their rationale for making such a quiet start: "We started out with *Johnny Come Lately* because it doesn't try to compete with the drama in the newspapers and isn't a big spectacular job. It's just a story about a hobo and an old lady with plenty of guts way back in 1906. I think it's got charm and that you can be intelligent and still like it. Jimmy thought of *Johnny Come Lately* as the title. I gave him three dollars for it. That's so you can't sue the company, I told him." There is clear defensiveness in this, and it is warranted.

On the picture's release the most discerning of all the reviewers was John T. McManus of *PM*, the invigorating New York newspaper that spoke the liberal viewpoint. McManus did not begin kindly:

> *Johnny Come Lately* is almost the kind of business that might result if James Cagney, the immortal movie star, had returned to play the lead in the annual production of his old high school's Masque and Film Club. . . . [The film] is so palpably amateurish in production and direction, so hopelessly stagy, uneven and teamless in performance and so utterly pointless that it is bound to cause raised eyebrows wherever it is shown. This is the same Jimmy Cagney of *The Public Enemy* . . . and the recent magnificent *Yankee Doodle Dandy.*

McManus concluded with a shivering blast that must have made Jack Warner chuckle if ever he read so radical a paper: "It is a backward shot for Cagney Productions, indicating if anything that Warner Brothers old studio knew lots better than William Cagney what was good for brother James."

This sentiment was echoed by Alton Cook of the *New York Mirror*, who praised the acting but not the vehicle: "Cagney brings the full force of his dramatic swagger to this fluffball of a role and the results are effective. This is a long step below the full length characterization of any of his recent pictures, so let's just say Johnny is played about as well as any such flimsy hero." Jack Warner would have been delighted at the words of Archer Winsten of the *New York Post:* "[The film] is not dreadful—Cagney is still the unique Cagney—but it is far below his standard. To put it bluntly, it is an old-fashioned story told in a very old-fashioned way. Please, Mr. Cagney, for the benefit of the public, yourself and Warners, go back where you made pictures like *Yankee Doodle Dandy.*

The august *Times* of London went so far as to head its review A SUBDUED MR. CAGNEY. It said: "[The film] has something of a feel of a faded photograph. . . . Everything seems drained and remote from life. Even Mr. Cagney, that most virile and assertive of actors, suffers from the general devitalizing atmosphere . . . but it is not without a certain dim, old-fashioned charm." Similar reviews proliferated, but despite them, *Johnny Come Lately* did well at the box office.

During the filming of *Johnny Come Lately* Jim made the acquaintance of marvelously competent Margaret Hamilton, today best remembered as the Wicked Witch of the West in *The Wizard of Oz.* He had the pleasure of casting her in *Johnny Come Lately,* and over lunch one day she said, "You may think this is heresy, Jim, but I've always thought of you as essentially a comedian."

It was, he said, one of the most sensible and searching remarks ever made about him. "I told Margaret that it was not only not heresy, it was gospel. My gospel. You can name any part I've played, from the cowardly boy in *Penny Arcade* through Cody Jarrett in *White Heat* right down to the police commissioner in *Ragtime,* and all had comedy in them, and not just incidental comedy either. I have too much of Frank Fay and Lowell Sherman in me not to have a comedic attitude at the base of my acting."

After his tour of duty of the Army camps in England and Wales, Jim returned to work on Cagney Productions' new film, *Blood on the Sun,* and to do what he could toward the reelection of President Roosevelt. On November 6, 1944, the Democratic National Committee presented a program on CBS Radio offering the cross-section testimony of Americans who expressed the need for FDR's election the next day. Among its show business highlights, Judy Garland sang a song urging all to get out and vote for FDR and Humphrey Bogart expressed his faith in him. This was followed by a variety of working-class Americans testifying on behalf of their commander in chief. Then:

> This is Jim Cagney, member of Screen Actors Guild. I guess I'm just an old sentimentalist about these bygone days when those gangsters I used to play in the movies were rum-running all over the place. But under the first Roosevelt administration, Prohibition was repealed and bootlegging became a lost art. Soon afterwards Roosevelt's Department of Justice took care of the mobsters in general. Well, as I say, I feel pretty mellow about the dear old days, so

I hope you'll understand if I break down and sing a song with two other sentimentalists, Keenan Wynn and Groucho Marx.

Jim sang the first verse:

>Do you remember those dear old days
>Of the rugged individual? And the dole, dole, dole?
>Remember Herbie Hoover? And his sweet old-fashioned way?
>And Harding with his record black as coal?

Keenan Wynn and Groucho Marx then joined Jim in the chorus, to the tune of "In the Good Old Summertime":

>In the good old Hoover time,
>In the good old Hoover time.
>Lots of jobs for everyone, bootleg booze and crime.
>Buddies singing everywhere, "Can you spare a dime?"
>Don't go back with Dewey to that good old Hoover time.

The three performers followed this up with a parody of "East Side, West Side" with phrases like "stocks tumbling down," followed by a song to the tune of "I Want a Girl": "We don't want a depression / Just like the depression / That ruined dear old dad." Other election songs and testimonials were given by a variety of nonprofessionals.

Jim greatly admired Franklin Roosevelt, crediting him with giving the country much-needed leadership, but when FDR died, Jim felt less comfortable with Truman. A key reason for Jim's increasing conservatism was his admiration of his now very close friend, Robert Montgomery, a Republican. Moreover, Bill Cagney was a committed Republican, and this left its mark on his admiring brother.

Jim was not anxious to get back to work after reading the lukewarm reviews of *Johnny Come Lately.* Bill had worked out an excellent deal with Darryl Zanuck at 20th Century–Fox for Jim: director and story approval, the then astronomical salary of $350,000, and the film to be shot in just six weeks. Jim turned it down. Bill phoned him at Martha's Vineyard, where Jim was happily cooking mulligatawny soup, one of his prize recipes, aromatic with Indian curry. Bill explained the deal, and Jim asked him if he could smell the mulligatawny on the stove.

"You mean, screw it?"

"Screw it."

"That's the way he felt," said Bill. "He didn't want to work. He wanted to be on the farm. He was only happy on the farm. Good scripts were so far and so few between, and everything conspired against your getting a good script because there was a dedication to seeing that we did not succeed as a production company."

This dedication, according to Bill, came of course from the major studios, which would inevitably discourage independent production. But the work habits of Bill Cagney himself were not conducive to helping his company's reputation as a dependable business entity. Bill was the polar opposite of Jim, being something of a playboy. A nightclub habitué, he possessed in full the gregarious qualities his brother so signally lacked. Bill began to spend great amounts of money on literary properties for their company. According to Kevin Hagopian in his study of the Cagney studio, in one case "the Cagneys spent $200,000 on screenwriters before even choosing a usable subject. Further, the Cagneys entered into bidding wars with major studios for choice literary properties and insisted on endless revisions of scripts. . . . But it was the Cagneys' generosity toward actors that provides the clearest evidence not only of free spending but of poor industry savvy."[*]

The Cagneys had only one major star, Jim. Their other contractees were not "names": Grace George, Marjorie Lord, and Jeanne Cagney. The Cagneys gave one-picture contracts to featured players like William Bendix, Robert Armstrong, and Wallace Ford, again people not of star caliber. The Cagneys could not even borrow name stars for any price because the major studios wouldn't lend them.

So it was not until the dust had really settled after *Johnny Come Lately* that Jim could be persuaded to get his creative juices flowing again with their new enterprise, *Blood on the Sun,* calculated to cash in on America's fear and hatred of the Japanese in that war year 1945. The script promised genuine action. Jim played Nick Condon, American editor of a Tokyo newspaper in the 1920s who, angered by what seems the senseless murder of a valued friend and his wife, discovers that there is a "Tanaka Plan" of world conquest by Japanese militarists. Nick is helped by Iris Hilliard, a Eurasian girl well played by Sylvia Sidney. The two of them manage to steal a copy of the plan in order to show the world. Only incidentally do they plan to conquer each other. So it is Cagney and gal against the bad "slant-eyes," especially the dastardly Tojo, acted with hissing hamminess by Robert Armstrong.

Jim enjoyed working with Sylvia Sidney, one of the few people in the movie industry who could speak Yiddish with Jim's fluency. To this she added a piquant wit. One scene for the film involved Sidney's wearing a beautiful Japanese costume and modeling it in front of a variety of light changes. There were rhinestones on her dress, her eyes were carefully made

[*]Kevin Hagopian, "Declarations of Independence: A History of Cagney Productions," *Velvet Light Trap* (Nov. 22, 1986).

up in Oriental fashion, and as she paraded before the camera, she made a convincingly beautiful Eurasian. To tease her, Jim said from behind the camera, "*Zee kikt aus vi a chinkeh!* [She looks like a Chinese lady!]"

With utter aplomb and without interrupting her walk before the camera, Sidney said, "*Fa vus nit?* [Why not?]"

*Blood on the Sun* gives us the good old action-happy Cagney, but with a new twist. Instead of hammering people with his fists, he does all his slam-banging in judo. At first he was delighted because there seemed to be less physical injury attendant on this new form of traditional Japanese jujitsu, which applies principles of balance and leverage. Jim said at the time, "I got hold of a judo expert and worked with him. I didn't know it then, but there are grades of judo. My first teacher, Jack Hollaran [who plays a Japanese captain in the film], was a third-degree black-belt judoist; he became a fourth degree. My last teacher was a fifth-degree black belt by the name of Ken Kuniyuki. Both are really great teachers. I grew so fond of judo I used to keep in shape with it until a back injury I picked up doing something else put me on the sidelines."

The judo, and the cut and thrust of melodramatic escapes, are at the heart of *Blood on the Sun,* and for those desiring a push-and-shove Cagney they were sufficient. The *New York Post* put it bluntly enough: "It is the most violent workout Mr. Cagney has had since *The Public Enemy,* and it ought to be fine for those who admire a good ninety-minute massacre." *Variety* affirmed that he was "the same rough and tumble character he's always been." And the public agreed, the picture earning more than a million dollars, excellent profit for the time.

Peter Turgeon, an actor who was a close Cagney friend, came to the Music Box Theatre, Los Angeles, with the Louis Calhern–Dorothy Gish company of *Life with Father* in the early forties, when he met Jim's family:

What a bunch of charmers. Of course I lost my heart to Jeanne right away, but I think, as they say, that she was fixing to get married to an actor, Kim Spaulding, so that let me out. But we were still friends, and one day she came to see me. *Life with Father* was sold out, and Jeanne wondered if there was anything I could do on behalf of two tickets for her and her mother. I had already met Mrs. Cagney, and I can still see her—pale, heavy, lovely blue eyes, and confined to a wheelchair. (The Cagneys when they aged ran to weight.) That wheelchair was going to be a disadvantage in my getting those tickets, I thought, but no, I asked our stage manager, and he said that for Jim's mom we'll fix something up. So they got her into a spot allowable by the fire laws, and there she sat with Jeanne all through a matinee.

Naturally I was anxious to hear how she liked it, and after the performance Jeanne came backstage and said, "I want you to know my mother just loved it. She cried through the entire play." Well, I'd been in *Life with Father* for two years, and this was the first time I'd ever heard of anyone *crying* through it. But of course I should have known why Mrs. Cagney did so. As Jeanne pointed out to me, here was this dear old sentimental Irish lady, and there, on the stage, there appeared one after another *four red-haired boys.* Exactly her family, red hair and all, minus a girl.

Carrie Cagney was not bored with California, but she was not thrilled with it either. When Jim first bought property on Martha's Vineyard, he bought her a large house on the water a few miles away from his farmhouse; it was hers, he said, for any and all family use. She gamely tried occupancy for two weeks, then called him up. "Jim," she said, "you've got this place because you love it, and it is beautiful. But." She left no doubt that country living was not for her.

*Blood on the Sun,* with Jack Holloran

. . .

When Harry and Ed began their medical practices in Woodhaven and Woodside, Queens, Carrie moved to that borough, but reluctantly. She had always liked the jangle of streetcar bells and the buzzing roar of the city. When necessity forced the move to Los Angeles—she had no recourse once all her children had moved there—she would have no truck with suburbia, and in her downtown Los Angeles apartment she could hear the comforting sound of traffic. "It's got a nice sound to it," she told Jim. She even liked the blare of fire engines and the whine of police sirens.

Carrie had constant medical care, with two doctor sons always at hand. She deliberately used herself as a case history for them. "I must emphasize" said Dr. Harry, "that she did not do this in any hypochondriacal way. She simply kept note of her illness symptoms rather proudly so she could share them with Ed and me. She was very objective in all this because she thought her boys could learn thereby."

Education continued to be Carrie's obsession. She had been deeply disappointed when Jim left Columbia for show business, though she never voiced this explicitly. In time she came to realize that perhaps she had not

*Blood on the Sun*, with Sylvia Sidney

shown Jim the appreciation due one so eminent in his field. She never showed favoritism to any of her children, but it was an open secret that Jim was her special one. There was a unique connection between them. A year before she died she suffered a stroke and was forced to communicate to everyone through pantomime. Jim became her translator when she could not fully use her gestures to express herself. He always knew what she meant.

It was felt by her other children that Carrie might have been severely upset by her little Jim's being the first to leave the warm nest of the mutually supportive Cagneys in 1920. Jeanne Cagney told of an incident a few months before her mother died: "Once when Jim came to visit her, having just come from the beach looking very young and boyish, as he always does when he is sunburned, Mom motioned to him that she wanted him to sit beside her on the bed. He did, and she took him in her arms and rocked him, as though he were a little boy. Jim had sometimes wondered if Mother had resented the fact that he had been the first to break away from home and to get married, and in that moment he had his answer."

The last Cagney movie his mother saw was *Johnny Come Lately,* and its quiet ambience suited her perfectly. During the making of *Blood on the Sun* she suffered a number of small strokes, and it became apparent that she was dying. Her five children came, and without planning it, the boys arranged themselves according to age: Harry and Jim on the right side of the bed, Ed and Bill on the left. Jeanne sat at the foot. In her last use of pantomime Carrie did not need Jim to explain her meaning. From *Cagney by Cagney:* "She indicated Harry with the index finger of her useless hand, she indicated me with her second finger, she indicated Eddie with her third finger, and with her fourth finger indicated Bill. Then she took the thumb, moved it to the middle of her palm, and clasped the thumb tightly under the other four fingers. Then she patted the fist with her good hand and made a single wordless sound. We understood at once that Jeanne was the thumb and we four boys were to take care of our girl."

Carrie died a few days later, at the age of sixty-seven. Jim was devastated. He said, "I knew this day would come, inevitably. When it did, I understood for the first time what the word 'sorrow' truly meant. It meant pain, pain, pain."

Tensions between the Cagneys, who were overspending, and United Artists, which rightly resented it, were mounting. When the opportunity came for Jim to make more money for the Cagneys by loaning himself out to 20th Century–Fox, he promptly did so. His first Hollywood producer, Darryl

*13 Rue Madeleine,* with Annabella

Zanuck, was now the kingpin at Fox, and he asked Jim "as a favor" to do a movie for $300,000, and for less than two months' work. The result was 1947's *13 Rue Madeleine,* based on the wartime spy work of the U.S. Office of Strategic Services. The producer was Louis de Rochemont, one of the founders of *The March of Time* and a dedicated documentary maker. The result is fairly hokey melodrama all dressed up in the fresh garments of realism, which it wears very well. It is a film well worth seeing. Cagney as Bob Sharkey, described in the voice-over narration as a "widely traveled scholar and soldier of fortune," teaches carefully selected candidates for work behind enemy lines in secret operations. Cagney is persuasively literate and intelligent, as is his spy opponent among the candidates, Richard Conte, here named O'Connell. Why someone in OSS did not notice that Conte-O'Connell looks about as Irish as Rossano Brazzi is its own special mystery.

To offset German double agent O'Connell, Sharkey must land in occupied France, where he will gather intelligence on the German V-1 rocket depot. When he is captured by the Gestapo, his superiors order the Gestapo headquarters at 13 Rue Madeleine in Paris destroyed by bombing, lest Sharkey be forced to reveal his secrets.

Jim had heard that the director of *13 Rue Madeleine,* Henry Hathaway, a veteran filmmaker, was difficult. "When I hear evaluations like that, I always reserve my judgment until I work with the man." Production began, and Jim experienced absolutely smooth sailing. He discovered that the people who had complained about Hathaway were a few disgruntled crew people who had failed in their work and were given hell by the veteran director. In particular there was a wardrobe man who, knowing Jim's friendliness with crew people, had complained to him. Jim did detective work and found that the man hadn't done his job. "You didn't do what was required," he told the man. "And what else is there?"

The reviews for *13 Rue Madeleine* were uniformly favorable, and Jim was pleased. He felt comfortable on the Fox lot and was disposed to return if wanted. Cagney Productions had by this time acquired some properties it thought were excellent. One of Jim's favorite writers was Thorne Smith, author of the *Topper* books, and Cagney Productions took an expensive option on a Smith book, *The Stray Lamb,* in which Jim was to play (according to a Cagney press release) "his first Gaelic speaking role. . . . The fabulous character of The Russet Man, a 30,000 year-old bearded Irish wizard who transforms people into kangaroos, horses and dogs." For the production, to be filmed at the Goldwyn Studio, the Cagneys imported at considerable expense from Australia two prize kangaroos, Joey and Harris. The kangaroo in *The Stray Lamb* (Harris was to double for Joey) had to box, wear costumes, and ride in a convertible. An Australian was hired to coach Joey, and the animal did very well, but Harris stolidly refused to cooperate, and this aspect of the film was endangered when Joey died suddenly while trying to leap a fence. This was typical of the entire *Stray Lamb* project. The Cagneys were to begin shooting on a certain date when an impending carpenters' union strike forced cancellation. Goldwyn insisted that the Cagneys honor their contracted start date; in honor, they could not. Goldwyn sued them, and the Cagneys lost a fortune in preproduction costs. *The Stray Lamb* was dead.

For their next picture the Cagneys were determined to film a first-rate work, if not a masterpiece, at least something thought to be one. They found it in William Saroyan's 1939 Pulitzer Prize–winning play *The Time of Your Life,* a relentlessly whimsical yet charming visit to a San Francisco saloon. The dominant figure of the play is Joe, a wealthy, genial alcoholic who enjoys watching over the destinies of his friends in the place. These are a naive young man in love with a former whore, also present and now dependent on Joe's largess, a workman, a cop, a dancer, a youth continually trying to reach his girlfriend on the phone, another youth who unendingly plays a pinball machine, a black piano player, the cheery bartender, a villainous detective head of the vice squad, and a Falstaffian drunk who calls himself Kit Carson.

Cagney, playing Joe, inevitably dominates the film, which he and Bill determined should follow the stage play faithfully. This was a considerable risk because the play is an essentially formless excursion into the lives and hopes of the characters, each eliciting Joe's philosophical comments, these being neither deep nor very apropos of anything. Brooks Atkinson, drama critic of *The New York Times,* said Saroyan in this play lacked "artistic discipline," using "material impulsively, just as it pops into his head," living "exclusively off the top of his emotion, [and as] an erratic writer . . . any contact he makes with the mind of the theatregoer is chiefly accidental." In consequence, *The Time of Your Life* is about very little, but that very little is exquisite.

What the Cagneys produced was something not extraordinary but exemplary. Even lacking a first-rate director, their film manages to convey the spirit of the play, principally through that old standby of valid dramatic enterprise the unflagging spirit and talent of their actors. The spirit of *The Time of Your Life* Saroyan defines quite simply and beautifully in one of his stage directions:

> *The atmosphere is now one of warm, natural, American ease; every man innocent and good; each doing what he believes he should do, or what he must do. There is deep American naivete and faith in the behavior of each person. No one is competing with anyone else. No one hates anyone else. Every man is living and letting live. Each man is following his destiny as he feels it should be followed; or is abandoning it as he feels it must, by now, be abandoned; or is forgetting it for the moment as he feels he should forget it. Although every one is dead serious there is unmistakable smiling and humor in the scene; a sense of the human body and spirit emerging from the world-imposed state of stress and fretfulness, fear and awkwardness, to the more natural state of casualness and grace.*

This is both windy and profound, and the Cagneys had a fascinating time trying to bring the profundity to life. Certainly for Cagney in the leading role it was a formidable challenge to be "dead serious" in the spirit of "unmistakable smiling and humor." Unending spoken philosophy was his assignment, this for an actor naturally prone to action, one coiled like a steel

*The Time of Your Life*
Cagney as table-bound philosopher

spring. Kenneth Tynan speaks of Cagney's "clenched, explosive talent," a man "who moved more gracefully than any actor in Hollywood." Yet in *The Time of Your Life* Cagney sits at a table through 90 percent of the film, even admitting at one point that he cannot dance. At all. On top of which he is playing a soul in stasis, literally and figuratively. One reviewer in France said of him in this film, "The tiger of the screen sits down."

Yet Cagney not only manages to remain an interesting figure throughout but dominates—whenever, that is, James Barton, a legendary stage actor, is not reeling off his lying boasts as Kit Carson, the Falstaffian figure. As always, Cagney dominates by listening to the other actors with total intentness. As he attends to the grievances of all the others, his receptive listening becomes ours, and we are brought close to the problems in the film. The chief of these is the presence of Blick, repulsive head of the police vice squad (his profession in the film is changed to freelance blackmailer). It is the confounding of Blick that caused the only substantial change the Cagneys made to Saroyan's original.

In the play Blick is killed by the liar, Kit Carson, who for the first time proves to be a doer instead of a talker. Two pistol shots are heard offstage, and the bartender runs in to say that Blick has been killed. This comes as a relief to the audience since Blick has been consummately nasty and cruel throughout. Carson enters and Joe tells him, "Somebody just shot a man. How are you feeling?" Kit replies, "Never felt better in my life. [*Loudly, bragging but somber.*] I shot a man once. In San Francisco. Shot him two times. In 1939, I think it was. Fellow named Blick or Glick or something like that. Couldn't stand the way he talked to ladies." A few more lines, the play ends, with everybody waving to Joe as he exits, waving back.

The Cagneys shot this ending for the film and took *The Time of Your Life* out to previews at theaters in Pasadena and Santa Barbara. Jeanne Cagney, who played the whore in the film with gentle understanding, vividly remembered the audiences' reactions: "The original ending just went off like a sweet sad song. There was no resolution of any kind. It was very avant-garde for the period. And the audience was spun by it. You could have heard a pin drop in the theater. There was a kind of sense of 'what is it?' " I just don't think audiences were ready for a philosophical play."

In other words, the preview audiences didn't get it, couldn't follow it, wouldn't accept it. What a sophisticated Broadway audience welcomed, the average movie audience of 1948, used to sweet, conventional endings, did not.

Realizing that Saroyan's ending was not working for movie audiences— or so they believed—the Cagneys resorted to Cagney slam-banging for a new ending. Instead of Blick's being killed, Cagney beats him up, and the blackmailer, half groggy, is marched outside by the bartender (warmly played by William Bendix) while Joe settles down to talk chummily with Kit Carson, taking over one of Kit's best lines and merrily directing it to him: "I don't suppose you ever fell in love with a midget weighing thirty-nine pounds?" There is no semisweet sadness of Joe departing, as in the play. The film ends on a distinctly non-Saroyan note. First comes an establishing shot of the saloon's exterior and a close-up of a sign in the window: COME IN AND BE YOURSELF. JOE. The last shot of the film has Joe taking the sign down, ripping it up, and saying, "Enough is enough!" The concession to popular taste has been made; importantly, from Bill Cagney's point of view, the audience has witnessed the Cagney fist efficiently at work, and all is well.

It disturbed Jim deeply to have the seriocomic poetic justice of Saroyan's ending destroyed. "But what the hell else could we have done?" he said to this writer. "The public just didn't get it at the previews. Funny, verbose Kit Carson an out-and-out murderer? Today [1980] they'd eat that kind of thing up. I wish we could release it with the original ending, and maybe someday we will. But I'm glad we did it. In hindsight, knowing what I do now, would I do it again? Likely not. I see that Joe never really had any innards. Joe is a character who charms his way through life, and charm is pretty hard to convey in a movie sometimes." Had he seen the original production on Broadway? "Yes, that's why we did it, because I saw Eddie Dowling play Joe, and my God, did *he* project the charm! That is what he was loaded with. Charm. It fooled me into thinking the play was better than it was."

Financially *The Time of Your Life* was a disaster for Cagney Productions. Jim and Bill were bitter about the actions of the film's cameraman, James Wong Howe, and director, H. C. Potter. "We lost half a million dollars because of those boyos," said Jim. "Their dilatory tactics soaked us for fair. They insisted on two weeks' rehearsal before a crank was turned. In order to (so they said) block it all out to know where they were going, shot for shot. Two weeks of that. Then when we started to shoot, they decided we were going to do something else. Blocking completely changed. It was maddening."

The change in photography and direction after two weeks is in part explained by Richard Erdman, who played the film's delightfully chuckle-headed pinball machine player:

We rehearsed for those two weeks on that single set. Then the cameraman and director realized a little bit too late that the whole one side of the bar was a mirror. You can imagine the problems of the mirror picking up lights and the crew at work facing that mirrored bar, and we had only one camera. Then too there was the problem of our director, H. C. Potter, who didn't have what you'd call an agreeable personality. I played Willie, the pinball machine nut who keeps trying to win, *doesn't* all the way through the picture, then just before the end of the picture, *does,* and all hell breaks loose on the machine in terms of special effects—flags waving and all that. I had to play that machine for ten weeks, waiting for my big moment, my big scene, when I finally win and the machine goes happily berserk. What follows will give you an idea of what kind of human being Jim Cagney is.

My moment finally arrived. There I was, terribly nervous, playing my big scene after the extended wait. I finally did my scene and director Potter said to me coldly, "That's it?"

I said, "What do you mean, Mr. Potter?"

He said, "That's all you are going to do?"

I was stunned. "Yes," I said, "that's all I've got."

He looked at me even more coldly and said, "We'd better break for lunch; then we'll try it again."

I was destroyed. He said these things right in front of the entire company. Jim came up to me, took me to lunch, and said, "Let's talk about other things. Baseball." So we talked about other things and baseball.

We went back to do my scene again, and again, and again. This time *eleven* takes. Potter was becoming more and more disagreeable.

Then Jim had had enough. He stopped us at the end of a take and walked over to Potter in front of the company and said to him, "Hank, the kid is right," and let me off the hook. I guess I *was* right, because two months later *Life* magazine did a two-page layout on *The Time of Your Life* and called mine the funniest scene of the year. I got a note from Jim that said, "Kid, you're still right." Any wonder that he is my hero, both as an actor and as a human being?

What did Saroyan think of the film? Even with the altered ending, he loved it. He wrote the Cagneys to say that he thought they had "made one of the most original and entertaining movies I have seen . . . you and your associates have expertly edited and translated into the medium of the motion picture a most difficult and almost unmanageable body of material. I send you congratulations, profound thanks and all good wishes."

Critical response to *The Time of Your Life* was mostly good, with a thread running through it of "Why did they try this kind of material?" One of Jim's favorite critics, John McCarten of *The New Yorker,* found the film reasonably diverting. "Saroyan," said McCarten, "is pretty blurred in his thinking, but his strivings to resolve his misty notions result fairly frequently in very funny stuff. . . . It is no fault of James Cagney who heads the cast that he isn't quite as satisfactory as the rest. There probably isn't an actor alive who'd make much of a champagne drinking barfly given to talking a kind of highflown gibberish and playing God in the lives of many of the people around him."

The public did not warm to *The Time of Your Life,* and this was a serious blow to the Cagneys. United Artists was now nipping at their heels about the money they had spent developing properties, and the banks were waiting to be paid as well. (The Cagneys ultimately did pay the banks every cent due them.) More seriously, movie audiences were diminishing at this time. The millions of women who in wartime went to the movies two or three times a week were staying home with their husbands back from the service. Moreover, the studios, under a court ruling becoming final in 1948, were forbidden to own their own movie theaters. Finally—and ominously— the specter of television was beginning to haunt the studios.

These were all things that were worrying Jim and Bill as well. Banks were not going to be kind to them in view of their record. United Artists was in trouble because of declining movie attendance and rising costs everywhere. Bill allowed *The Time of Your Life* to be released by UA, but he was searching for a new, secure base while retaining Cagney Productions as an independent unit. Instead of a new, secure base he found an old, secure base. Jim was going back to the factory.

# 19 · Back to the Factory

Jim said of Cagney Productions' move early in 1949:

I sure as hell never expected in the order of things that we'd ever go back to Warners. Our basic reason was a five-letter word beginning with $m$ and ending in $y$. But it just wasn't the dough. It's easier to make pictures when you have the factory setup. And I'd never have to face The Shvontz. Brother Bill was there to face the old bastard, and those two money-oriented businessmen could talk on the same level and be perfectly happy together. Also, Hal Wallis was gone off to be an independent producer, and I never much cared for him. To clinch the Warners deal, one little item came up in discussions, and that was income from the reissue rights to my old pictures. Brother Bill had that on the agenda for the future.

Bill Cagney had indeed struck a very rewarding deal with Warners. The contract his brother signed on May 6, 1949, was liberal. Jim need make only one film a year for Warners, he could buy stories and supervise their writing, Cagney Productions would be an active unit on the Warners lot, and Jim could make films for it. For each Warners picture he would receive $250,000. Few stars in Hollywood had that kind of power at that time.

His first film for Warners under the new contract was *White Heat*, a turbulent masterpiece that was to reinforce his old gangster image, and not only a gangster but a violent, psychotic one clawing his way from and to hell. There has been much speculation about why Cagney, who had for so long been agitating for a change in screen personality, should—after triumphs in other genres like *Yankee Doodle Dandy*—take on the persona of Cody Jarrett, the rottenest character he would ever play. The answer is uncomplicated: the Cagneys badly needed, badly wanted a success. They both recognized *White Heat* as it.

The unadorned fact was that Cagney Productions had done well financially with two of its independent productions, *Johnny Come Lately* and *Blood on the Sun,* then gone deeply into the red with *The Time of Your Life.* The Cagneys not only needed a financial revival but sought respect from the Hollywood creative community. There was a pragmatic basis for this. The saw "You're only as good as your last picture" extended itself more and more into the process of bank loans. The banks were looking not only into the books but into the reviews. Hollywood money was beginning to dry up because the big studios were dying, television was aborning, and the financial success of individual films was proof that you knew your business. The Cagneys had to establish this reputation.

*White Heat* was Cagney territory. No Hollywood actor could have played Cody Jarrett as he did. Warner Brothers knew this, and its publicity machine went into overtime, sending out a four-page release celebrating Jim's return to his "home" studio, a fact-filled life-and-career biography saying that his "return to the Warner fold is further marked by the fact that his first picture will be a return to the type of bing-bang melodrama that made him a top star in his earliest years. He will have a ruthless, mob-leading gunster's [*sic*] role in *White Heat,* his first gangster picture since *Angels with Dirty Faces* made eleven years ago." Thus far correct. Then the publicity hack who wrote this minibiography veered directly into fiction: "Cagney says, 'For ten years I've been reading gangster scripts, hoping for a good one. They were all the old stereotyped formula until this one came along. I'm excited about it. It will give me just the right change of pace.' "

In fact for ten years he had refused to read gangster scripts on the firm ground that whatever their quality they provided nothing in the way of pace changing. That *White Heat* was an exciting piece of work he did not at this time deny. To put forth his own ideas on why he had returned to gangster-dom, he wrote his own press release, four pages, which Warner Brothers sent out hard on the heels of the first, inaccurate one. In his own words Jim made the point that he had tried to humanize all his earlier gangsters by bringing in "some bits of humor by injecting different mannerisms, lines and pieces of business, as we say, that would elicit a laugh here and there. In this way I believed that I would make each of these outlaw characters human and therefore understandable and deserving of a modicum of sympathy." So why then choose this depraved psychotic, Cody? Because, he says, "*White Heat* points up dramatically and vividly the tremendous advances made in scientific detection over a period of recent years while the criminal remains essentially dumb. It is bound to have a beneficial effect when seen. . . . We are trying to make a gangster picture that will be a *good* gangster picture, a picture that will pay its way by helping deter crime, a good drama that all the world will see and enjoy. So, yes, I'm glad to be back in a hoodlum role. This particular one, I mean." If there is special pleading and self-justification in this—and there is—he certainly believed in the essence of what he was saying.

Shooting on *White Heat* began in mid-1949 under the taut control of Raoul Walsh. The writing is superb, and no one thought so more at the time than Jim Cagney. He came ultimately to dislike the film for other reasons as the months passed. He entered his work with thoroughness. This is a role he was born to play.

Ivan Goff and Ben Roberts wrote *White Heat*, and Jim came to see them early on in the writing. Roberts recalled:

When [Cagney] came into the project he just came to our office once. He lay down on the couch, like he always did, and said, "What are you going to do, fellas?"

After explaining it would be the study of an evil man, Roberts went on to say:

. . . but we want the audience to understand *why* he is evil. We see that behind his state of cruelty is a man who is driven, who is really sick, who is driving himself toward destruction. . . . Cagney said, "Well, it sounds interesting. Sounds like it will be fun to play. . . . Whatever you say, fellas!" Jimmy was marvelous that way. It was always like that with him on the pictures we did with him. He would say, "What are you going to do, fellas?" Then, "Whatever you say, fellas!"*

Goff and Roberts were to be associated with Jim in three more of his films.

*White Heat* is based on Ma Barker, a bank robber of the thirties who, Fagin-like, had trained her four sons in crime. Roberts said, "[We] synthesized Ma Barker down to having one son instead of four, and we put the evil of all four into one man." Ma Jarrett is played with loving, reptilian intensity by Margaret Wycherly, a former classical actress, who manages the almost impossible feat of bringing a sense of justified warmth and compassion to the love of her son, Cody. He, as played by Cagney, is mentally unbalanced and incisively shrewd, a cold and unfeeling killer, who needs his mother's love and thereby becomes to a small yet significant measure the object of

---

*For a searching analysis of *White Heat*'s genesis by Goff and Roberts, see *White Heat*, Wisconsin/Warner Bros. Screenplay Series, edited with an introduction by Pat McGilligan (University of Wisconsin Press, 1984).

our sympathy. It is time to recall Kenneth Tynan's observation about Cagney in *The Public Enemy* that "in one stroke Cagney abolished both the convention of the pure hero and that of approximate equipoise between vice and virtue."

Cody Jarrett is far over on the side of vice, yet can anyone seeing *White Heat* not experience a frisson of compassionate admiration, however fleeting, for Cody at the film's end, atop the Hortonsphere, pumping bullets into it and shouting ecstatically, "Made it, Ma! Top of the world!" before his world blows him up? That is the ultimate triumph of *White Heat*. True drama is conflict, true conflict in flux, and in this story of a near-demented killer we are given through superb writing and great acting a look into a ravaged psyche. Nothing quite like it existed in films before.

One of the little-noted but important aspects of the film is its humor. It occurs frequently in Cody's quiet, tight little smiles when he discusses his murderous plans as if he were setting up golf dates. The humor is at its most frightening when Cody exacts vengeance on Parker, the convict who tried to kill him. Parker, kidnapped from prison, has been put in the trunk of the limousine Cody and his pals escaped in.

The scene reads in the script:

EXT. FARMHOUSE                    NIGHT

. . . As the fugitives come outside Cody takes a chicken leg from the bag of food. A station wagon is parked by the psychiatrist's limousine. Cody raps on limousine trunk.

CODY: How ya doin', Parker? (Parker's voice is heard, muffled, unintelligible.) Stuffy, huh? (Fires three times into car's trunk; to others.) Air.

Still munching at his chicken leg, Cody gets into the station wagon with the others and drives away.

The macabre humor here is stinging as written, but it really comes to life only when Cagney, gnawing his chicken, gives his line not exactly as the authors wrote it, but—as he frequently did—with a freer, slightly more human variation on it. What Cagney says in the film, with jaunty solicitude is: "Oh, stuffy, huh? I'll give you a little air."

To underscore subtly the Oedipal connection between Cody and his mother, Jim suggested to Walsh that Cody at one point actually sit on his mother's lap for comfort. They got away with it because, in Jim's words, "What I tried to do there was to make it seem an action I had done many times before, when my epilepsy hit and Ma, as always, soothed me."

The emotional zenith of *White Heat* occurs in the prison mess hall

*White Heat,* with Virginia Mayo and Margaret Wycherly

when Cody, seeing Lefeld, a new arrival down the table, passes the word down through a number of other convicts: "Ask him how my mother is." (The script calls for "Ask him if he saw my mother," but Cagney changed the line to a more natural phrasing.) Talking at meals being forbidden, the convicts have to whisper, increasing the tension of the scene. Cody's question is passed down through four cons, each one in an individual frontal shot, which further raises the tension.

When the question reaches Lefeld, he confides a single word, which we can barely hear, and the word is then whispered from con to con until it reaches Cody as two words: "She's dead."

"Dead?" Cody says. He looks ahead, incredulous, trying to sort out this impossibility. He looks down to one side for a private second, again trying to assimilate this monstrous truth.

Then, face contorted in incredible pain, he picks up his tin cup and crashes it to the table, a bad child mercilessly deprived. The convicts look up, startled. A contorted sob begins to rack Cody, and here Cagney enacts writers Goff and Roberts's description of the moment when Cody's agony erupts: "From his throat issues an atavistic scream—primal, bestial, inhuman." He

*White Heat*

pulls himself up onto the table, but the terrible knowledge of his mother's death pursues him, and he must try to escape it and in some way reach her. He staggers along the table, falls off over a convict, who goes down with him, rises in time to knock down an advancing guard, then knocks down another, yet another, and finally a fourth, before a group of them carries him away as he croons savagely, "Let me out of here! Get me out of here!"

The three hundred men in the hall sit rigid in shocked silence, most of them actually so. Walsh did not explain to the extras the precise details of what would occur in the scene. One extra in the scene said to this writer, "I was seated just two tables away from Cagney when they did the scene, and it scared the bejesus out of us sitting there. You'd swear to God he'd gone insane. I've looked at that scene lots of times, and you'll note that we all looked shocked. We *were.*"

In *Cagney by Cagney* Jim offers as a source for this emotional tour de force a visit to a hospital for the insane on Ward's Island he once made. This is partly true. In preparing for the scene, he did recall that visit, but the heart of his wounded animal sobs derived from his father. Jimmy Steam in his charmer mood was graciousness itself. When the alcohol had begun rotting his brain and he went into what his family called the fits, he would moan in an agonized keening terrifying to hear. Cagney reproduced that sound in this scene.

He saw the scene only once and refused to look at *White Heat* ever again. "Seeing that bit again would be just too painful," he said. As the years went by, he tended to forget the many excellences of *White Heat* and could remember only the cheapness of his old antagonist, Jack Warner, whose penurious attitude to the budget irritated the writers. Warner, for example, disliked the idea of the three hundred extras needed for the mess hall scene and seriously asked Ben Roberts if the scene couldn't be shot in the prison chapel. Roberts asked him what Cody would be doing in the chapel—praying? Warner allowed the mess hall, but there was one economy he foolishly insisted on, and did not tell Cagney, since it directly affected one of his dearest friends.

Jim had asked that the small but potentially interesting role of Ryley, one of his cellmates, be given to Frank McHugh. Jim said:

What some of those cell scenes could have used very handily was good touches of humor. That has always been Frank's specialty— taking a straight role, building it up, adding those little touches that make the role and the scene memorable. In the script Ryley is a small part; Frank would have added to it, lines and bits of business, that would have made Ryley a real character instead of what it is now, a "feed" character. So I put in my request for Frank and was told he'd be forthcoming. Then they told me he was not available. They were goddamned liars.

A few weeks later Jim got Frank on the phone to find out what job he was on elsewhere and discovered he had never been approached. Jim said, "I sent my request for Frank right up to The Shvontz himself. Who got word back to me Frank was unavailable. So for Ryley they cast what was written, a straight part actor. So, it was old *Shtick-Dreck* [shithead] *Shtunk* [smelly] Shvontz Warner again. I never forgave him for that. And it was all the more galling that at brother Bill's suggestion, I'd written The Shvontz a week before thanking him for his congratulations on how the picture was doing."

Thereafter, for Cagney, *White Heat* always had unpleasant connotations.

In his autobiography he called it another "cheapjack job," saying that the studio "put everybody in it they could get for six bits." This point is amplified by Max Morath, who in an unpublished essay on *White Heat* makes interesting points about the film's casting:

> The power and prominence of today's casting directors may be occasionally overweening, but one does miss the more balanced casting ensembles, and the unusual players, that careful casting can put together. For instance, in Cody Jarrett's gang, as in so many vintage gangster pictures, it's hard to tell one hood from another. On one viewing they all look pretty much the same, like clones, in this case, of Steve Cochran, who plays "Big Ed." Similarly the T-Men . . . resemble one another so much in size and appearance that it seems almost a put-on. Viewing this film from the vantage point of almost fifty years later, we miss the rude mix of age, race and gender that would comprise [the T-Men] or Cody's gang of today.

One of the memorably vivid originals in *White Heat* was Virginia Mayo, who as Cody's mistress blended sluttishness and class into a superb characterization. Today she recalls the working days with Jim:

> We shot most of *White Heat* at the Warners ranch about a half hour drive from Burbank. On the first day of shooting Jim was a little waspish because (I believe) he was unhappy with playing a gangster again after making those philosophical pictures of his the public didn't buy. That first day he got a call on the set from Jack Warner, and that made Jim even more upset. They sure didn't like each other. Jim, as a fellow actor, was so helpful and suggested things to me, always asking me beforehand if it would be OK to suggest them. For instance, that scene where he knocks me off the chair onto the sofa. He and Raoul Walsh came over beforehand and asked if I thought I could do it. Well, I'm a dancer, so I said sure. I know how to take a fall, and we did it on one take. Jim was so powerful to work with. Such intensity! In the garage scene when I go out there to get the car to run away from him, he grabs me by the neck—well, if I had not memorized my lines thoroughly, I'd never have gotten through it. His hold on me was so strong that I could just blurt out my lines, which really helped the scene. One thing for sure: he always gave to you more than you gave to him.
>
> Funny, he never liked to kiss leading ladies. Not because of his age—he was still a good-looking, sexy man—no, but because he just didn't think that was his style. He'd grab you and kiss your forehead

but almost never on the lips. I was shocked and so disappointed that he didn't get the Best Actor for *White Heat*. Who was better? No one. But in those days they never, never gave Best Actor Oscars to the actors in gangster movies. I was so happy and proud working with him, and I know he liked me because he asked me to be in his next picture. Years later, when my husband and I were playing *No, No, Nanette* in Chicago, Jim was passing through town, and he asked us to lunch. We had wonderful memories to discuss. A lovely human being.

The critical acclaim for *White Heat* was heartening for both the Cagneys and Warner Brothers. Jim particularly treasured John McCarten's review in *The New Yorker*, which deplored the Cagney career move into the world typified by *Johnny Come Lately* and expressed its pleasure that Cagney was back among the bad guys: "Despite the scatterbrained nonsense of the script, Mr. Cagney, representing a homicidal maniac whose favorite girl is his dear old two-gun mother, comes up with a performance so full of menace that I hereby recommend him for whatever Oscar is given an artist for rising above the asininity of his producers." McCarten got a Cagney fan letter for that one, and a friendship developed between the two.

Then, as now, the most highly prized film review, or at least the one most quoted in studio ads, was a favorable one from *The New York Times* and its film critic, Bosley Crowther. He praised *White Heat*'s acting highly, comparing Cagney's "brilliantly graphic way" with his work in *The Public Enemy*. In the *Times* a week later Crowther, although not a bluenose, had some second thoughts, one of which remains current today: the example given the young seeing the film's thirteen murders presented so juicily, even buoyantly. Crowther spoke of "the unhealthy stimulation which such a film affords the weak and young. And the notions it spreads of moral values are dangerously volatile. For inevitably Mr. Cagney, bold and indomitable, appears a remarkable hero. . . . He loves his mother, he is scrupulously loyal to the best interests of his gang, he is brave, he detests a two-timer and he won't compromise with the law." What he also is of course is crazy, the essential point.

In his fascinating book *This Is Orson Welles*, Peter Bogdanovich, after showing *White Heat* to Orson Welles for his first viewing of the film, catechizes him:

OW: Cagney has just got to be called the number one screen-filler in film history.

PB: Screen-filler?

ow: A displacer of air. The real test of that awful term "star" quality—the French call *"présence."* And here's a paradox for you—no, I won't call it a paradox, it's just simply proof of what I've always claimed: that there simply is no such thing as "movie acting."

pb: As opposed, you mean, to acting in the theater?

ow: There's just acting—good, bad, adequate, and great. All this talk about the special technique required for playing to camera is sheer bollocks. Stage actors are supposed to be too big. Well, Cagney was a stage actor and nobody was ever bigger than that. He came on in the movies as though he were playing to the gallery in an opera house.

pb: Bigger than life?

ow: Well, not any bigger than *truth*. He played right at the top of his bent, but he was always *true*. Sure, acting *can* be too *broad*. Broad is wide—spread out. Cagney was *focused*. Christ, like a laser beam! . . . Cagney was one of the biggest actors in the whole history of the screen. Force, style, truth, and control—he had everything. He pulled no punches; God, how he projected! And yet nobody could call Cagney a ham. He didn't bother about reducing himself to fit the scale of the camera; he was much too busy doing his job.

In watching *White Heat*, Bogdanovich and Welles were caught up with Cagney's innately sympathetic character because the actor, according to Bogdanovich,

> could express ambiguities in a character even if they were not written into the script or featured by direction. He was also innately sympathetic, which is what gave his heavies such an intriguing tension. *White Heat*, particularly, has a decidedly subversive duality because of this—the advanced, somewhat inhuman technology and the undercover-informer cop (Edmond O'Brien) become morally reprehensible in the glare of Cagney's personality, though his character is in no way sentimentalized. (Nonetheless, Orson and I were hissing the law and rooting for Cagney like schoolboys.) He was that rarest of players—an actor who could transcend his vehicles. Like most of the other stars of the golden age of movies—which I would guess ended sometime in the early Fifties—he was one of a kind.

As countercheck to his reidentification as a gangster, Jim was determined to do a musical next. So dedicated was he to the idea that he startled Willie one afternoon after *White Heat* was finished with the suggestion that they might perform their old vaudeville act, *Lonesome Manor*, for their friends one night. Willie was so pleased at the idea that she got to her feet directly and challenged him to do it on the moment, without error. He failed to remember only one line.

In planning his musical—for it was to be "his," in that he would approve of script, cast, and director—he recalled that his idol George M. Cohan, in preparing for a scene in one of his musicals, had inveigled West Point's superintendent into allowing him to live as a cadet on the premises for a week. This concept was incorporated into the new musical, *The West Point Story*, with the difference that Cagney stayed for a month to direct the student show. How he was to dance in that same show was a problem easy enough to solve: one of the student actors had to become—in the old theatrical phrase—"indisposed." More accurately, disposed of.

Needing time to work on his dances, Jim started another picture, *Kiss Tomorrow Goodbye*, which he was inclined to only because it was a "William Cagney Production," one of the films Bill was allowed to make under the expansive Warners contract. "We had to do another programmer that would make money so we could finally pay off the bankers," said Jim. "So we did *Kiss Tomorrow Goodbye*, and guess what noble character I was called on to play? Another shtunk. I didn't want to do it, but it was from a well-known novel by a hell of a good writer, Horace McCoy." In the novel the Cagney character is complex, interesting. "He has a Phi Beta Kappa key, of all things, on top of which he was an ex-dancer. Not that you saw any of this in the picture. All the complex stuff was ironed out by the writer with the plea that there was no time for subtleties. He was probably right. Anyway, Bill said, 'Jim, we need the dough, and it's the last gangster I'll ever ask you to play.' He kept his word. I did play a few more rats after that, but no gangsters."

*Kiss Tomorrow Goodbye* is one of the rare Cagney films in which he has a rival in acting ability. Luther Adler, paragon of the Group Theatre and a scion of the great Yiddish Art Theatre acting family of Adlers, plays a crooked lawyer. In the scenes with Cagney one watches two master actors take a scruffy little scene and make brick out of straw. Jim was always happy to acknowledge actors who had influenced him. Of Luther Adler, he said: "An absolutely terrific actor, first-rate, and I wondered why he wasn't a star in Hollywood. I told him this once, and he pulled at his nose. Too Semitic. But I never thought so. I learned from him, and what's more, I learned from him in my own business. At which I was supposed to be an expert, and he something of a Johnny come lately." Cagney went on to describe a scene in which Adler was supposed to convey menace. He is seated at a desk when someone approaches and in effect becomes the camera looking down at

Adler. Jim said, "Luther looks up at the camera, and it was frightening because of the way he used his eyes. Now, the usual way to do that scene—and it's the way I'd have done it—would be to lift your head and look at the camera. What Luther did was raise his head but kept his eyes looking down, then, slowly, suspensefully lifted his eyelids to look up at the camera. Absolutely chilling."

Later Jim tried to get Adler in another film project, but nothing came of it, partly because brother Bill didn't relish competition for Jim. Bill also tried to soften the blow on Jim's psyche when the negative *Kiss Tomorrow Goodbye* reviews began to troop in. *Time* magazine set their tone with: "[It] sends Hollywood's aging [fifty-one] tough guy James Cagney off on another gay whirl of crime. . . . Cagney kills six men, breaks out of a chain gang, pulls off a daring heist, blackmails a bribe-taking cop and viciously swats a blonde doll (Barbara Payton) with a rolled-up towel. From a grapefruit to a towel in almost two decades is scant progress." Jim called it "a very well made bomb."

*Kiss Tomorrow Goodbye,* with Barton MacLane, Steve Brodie, and Ward Bond

*Kiss Tomorrow Goodbye*, with Barbara Payton

During the making of *Kiss Tomorrow Goodbye*—which was released after his next film—he began rehearsing the dance numbers for that film, *The West Point Story*, under Johnny Boyle's direction with the help of a choreographer-dancer with the surname Godfrey, a button-bright young lady. "Darling little gal, and little is the word. I can't imagine why she wasn't in the credits. By the time I saw this it was too late. One of the uncredited Hollywood crew people who made the pictures what they are."

Godfrey, with Johnny Boyle's help, choreographed the best number in the film, "B'KLYN" which is sung (in Cagney's case, mostly talked) "B, apostrophe, K no apostrophe, L, Y, N." Jim whirled ninety-seven-pound Godfrey around with ease, but when it came time for Virginia Mayo to take over in the number, there was a problem. She says, "A little problem, yes, that looked quite big at the time because I was a good head taller than the young lady choreographer and weighed a lot more. But we worked it out." Jim wore Cuban heels to compensate for the height difference, something Cohan did in all his dance numbers.

*The West Point Story* is very slight but very delightful stuff. Cagney is Elwin Bixby, a Broadway director of musicals, called in to stage West Point's

*The West Point Story*

traditional student show, *100 Nights,* always presented one hundred nights before graduation. He has been chosen by a no-goodnik New York producer who wants his cadet nephew, Tom (Gordon MacRae), to star on Broadway in that very show. This astounding set of circumstances also involves a beautiful Hollywood singing star, played with chilling authenticity by one Doris Day. Tom has all the talent of a, well, Gordon MacRae, and he turns out to be so plausibly MacRae-like that Doris gladly, even eagerly, gives up stardom to become his wee wifie as he faces life not as a Broadway star but as a second lieutenant. As for Cagney/Bixby, after endless travail that includes taking on the rigors of living a cadet's life (and wearing a uniform three sizes too small for him), having the show canceled for his breaking cadet rules, and having it reinstated by reluctantly showing the French ambassador the Medaille Militaire he won in World War II (the ambassador appeals to West Point's commandant), Bixby has just enough strength left to dance the vigorous number indisposed Gene Nelson was going to perform with Virginia Mayo.

This farrago of hokum spares one nothing in the way of plot tedium, including the tee-hee imbecility of a wrestler-type cadet (burly Alan Hale, Jr.) in drag as a blonde princess. The film is also breathtaking in its innocence and obstinately charming forthrightness. "It's one of my favorite pictures," said Jim. "Cornball as all hell, but don't let anyone tell me those songs by Jule Styne and Sammy Cahn aren't worth listening to. They were sure worth dancing to." To complete it all, Doris Day makes oversweetness a complete virtue, and when does Virginia Mayo not enchant?

One would think that by this, his forty-sixth picture, made in his twentieth year as a film actor, one would have seen everything there was to see of Cagney. Again he astonishes. He has a few temper tantrums in *The West Point Story* that are little gems of pantomimic disgust. When things don't go his way while he's directing a dance number, he turns a little kid's up-and-down hops of anger into aesthetically pleasing, well-orchestrated stomps of purest displeasure that look improvised. They are about as improvised as Salvador Dalí's mustache and are as richly comic.

Jim was pleased with the theme of his next film, *Come Fill the Cup,* a 1951 release. Alcoholism had been a part of his life from infancy, and his entire family had learned its lessons on the subject. He said, "The one thing we learned about booze from as early as we could remember was that for some people, like our old man, there was no such thing as social drinking. For people like him, you drank because you drank, and that made you drink more. The bottomless glass."

Things seemed totally propitious for the success of *Come Fill the Cup,* and there are many fine things in it. Cagney plays Lou Marsh, a recovering alcoholic who loses his job as city editor because of drink, regains it, and is given his toughest assignment, the recovery of another alcoholic, young Boyd (Gig Young), nephew to tycoon publisher John Ives (Raymond Massey).

"Troubles creatively began with *Cup* fairly early on," said Jim. "First, there was the casting of the publisher. Ray Massey is one of the finest actors in this or any other country, but Ray is a gentleman to his bones. I don't think he could play a flamboyant rogue to save his life, and that is an accurate description of the publisher, John Ives. We tried like hell to get Adolphe Menjou for the part, but he wasn't available." The result was a gentleman playing a nongentleman; it shows, and it doesn't work. Jim said, "But even worse, our important theme got lost about midpoint in the picture because of The Shvontz. Jack Warner had to stick his goddamned nose in the proceedings, and so, here in the midst of this important message we're conveying, we get a load of melodramatic crap—the insertion of a gangster subplot—that steers us right off course."

That turn is best described by screenwriter Ben Roberts, who, with his partner Ivan Goff, made *White Heat* the masterwork it is. Roberts recalls:

[The novel on which the film was based] has no gangster in it, and we wrote the story without a gangster. The bottle was the gangster. We were talking about a story like *The Lost Weekend.* Jack Warner said, "You can't tell a Cagney story without guns and gangsters."

We said, "Why not?"

He said, "Because that's what the audience expects."

We said, "We don't know how to put a gangster in this picture. It'll be bullshit. The story's going to switch tracks."

He said, "Well, that's what I want, and if you don't give it to me, I'll put someone else on it."

We tried to save the film. The first half was so wonderful. But we wrote this gangster character, he got Sheldon Leonard to play it, and the whole thing went right out the window. The last forty minutes of the film isn't watchable.

Nor is it. The Shvontz afflicted the story in another way. The novel *Come Fill the Cup* was written by a friend of Cagney's, Harlan Ware, who deepened the concept of alcoholism's universality by making one of the protagonists an African-American named Charley Dolan. Dolan helps Lou Marsh sober up, and they become close friends and finally room together. Cagney thought this was a particularly striking aspect of the novel; he had personally witnessed and resented ongoing prejudice against black vaudeville performers. When Roberts and Goff turned in a script that retained Dolan's blackness, Jack Warner was upset. He told Goff, "You think Cagney's gonna be under the same roof as a nigger?" The Shvontz insisted that Dolan's color be changed, and this was done, upsetting Jim and the writers again. The delightful actor James Gleason was cast as Dolan and played the role with his usual sensitivity and charm, but the chance to make a social statement of some significance was gone, and Jim's detestation of The Shvontz grew, if that was possible.

Warner also protested the casting of Gig Young as the publisher's nephew, but the writers fought him on this one and won. Young went on to win an Academy Award nomination in the role as Best Supporting Actor that year. "I liked Gig," said Jim. "Most amiable young man, lots of fun. I was concerned about him, though. Some typecasting there. I think he was a little too fond of booze himself." Cagney had reason to worry, but not about

*Come Fill the Cup*
With James Gleason

the booze. Young shot and killed himself and his fourth wife a few weeks after their marriage in 1978.

Memories of his father's insobriety inevitably dominated Cagney's playing of the drunk scenes. He had long observed that most alcoholics were sedentary, thus weakening their legs, forcing them to walk stiff-legged when under the influence. But Cagney also noticed something else common to most alcoholics:

God knows I've observed lots of drunk scenes in the movies, and too frequently the actors went about it the wrong way. I'm not speaking of comic drunks now, like that wonderful Jack Norton, a teetotaler in real life, who did essentially a balancing act. I'm speaking of actors who try to portray drunkenness convincingly and who so frequently fail because they're looking at it from the wrong end. By that I mean they portray the drunk as someone who is picturesque. He isn't. They try to portray the drunk as someone trying to get drunk, blotto, out, stupefied. Wrong. The drunk is trying to get sober, is trying desperately to appear sober, is trying to convince you as well as himself that he is sober.

Jim thought for a moment. "Here's an exact parallel. When Jack Barrymore had to limp as Richard III, he didn't adopt a grotesque walk because it was grotesque. He adopted the grotesque walk first, and thereafter he tried to walk as *well* as he could. The drunk does the same thing."

The Shvontz's insistence on a gangster angle in *Come Fill the Cup* provides a shoddy ending to a superior story. Jim said, "So, OK, here I am in a really beautifully written story on a most important subject, and they put comic tough guy, Damon Runyon–type Sheldon Leonard right at the climax of the picture, which should have had Jimmy Gleason in it somewhere. But no, we've got to get rid of him in the old sacrificial one-of-the-good-guys-gotta-die cliché, so we can have this hokey bit of melodrama with Gig and me facing Leonard." Leonard, holding a gun, orders the two men—both now reformed alcoholics—to take a big drink of whiskey each. "So how do we get out of this terrifying dilemma?" asked Jim. "Why, just as you would in the worst cowboy picture in the world—by my throwing the booze in Leonard's face." Thus fizzles to a wet end a film that could have been nominated for Best Picture of the Year.

To make 1951 just a bit worse, just before *Come Fill the Cup* began shooting, Jim volunteered to be in *Starlift,* a uniformly dreadful (well, Doris Day does sing Gershwin) film about various Warners stars who are ferried to an Air Force base near San Francisco to entertain troops prior to their departure for combat in the Korean War. *Starlift* is one of those thankless "all-star" films in which the actors talk in tones of forced cheerfulness. Cagney spends some moments as himself in a scene in which he faces an Army sergeant played by Dick Wesson, a putative mimic and comedian. Wesson, a good actor in other roles, is telling his story to a group of stars. One night the sound went off in the theater where he was the projectionist, and "I raced down to the screen, took over for Cagney, and nobody even knew the difference." Wesson assumes the Cagney stance from *Angels with Dirty Faces* and imitates him with a few lines from *White Heat.* Cagney enters shortly and completes the speech from the film.

Then, imitating himself, Cagney says, "Now look here, pal, I don't like people going around imitating me, understand? I don't like it."

Wesson, still using the Cagney voice, says, "I'm not imitating you. Since when is there a law against people talking like you?"

Cagney replies, "Well, you know, there ought to be. Between us, one of us is very bad." *Quod erat demonstrandum.*

A few inconsequential lines later Wesson says, "Just before you're going to hit a guy, you walk up and do something like this [*he hitches up his trousers in standard Cagney mimic fashion*]."

*Starlift,* with Dick Wesson, Ron Hagerthy, Doris Day, and Ruth Roman

Cagney says, repeating Wesson's action, "You mean like this?"
"Yeah, why do you do that?"
Cagney says, "That's simple," and opens his jacket. "No belt."
Laughter from the assembled stars. "Thanks, Mr. Cagney," says Wesson.
Forlorn sound of a kazoo.
A week later Jim received a letter from The Shvontz:
Dear Jim:

It is needless to tell you what [giving your time] means to
[*Starlift*]. Second, and even more important is your fine attitude in
making this appearance. I'm sure there were a number of other
things you could have done the day before you started your own
picture, but instead you worked all afternoon with the fellow who
played opposite you. I know *Come Fill the Cup* is going to be a
picture of which we can all be proud.

JACK WARNER

# 20 · Open-Field Running

John Ford was director, Irishman, and American military man in ascending order of importance to himself. His profound sense of the American experience he celebrated not only in his epochal westerns but in superb military documentaries. He made the latter as a lieutenant commander in World War II, and he remained in the Naval Reserve in peacetime, periodically returning to duty thereafter. His home base as director was 20th Century–Fox, where he was kingpin of the lot, virtually able to direct any films he liked.

Fox's head of production in 1952 was the volatile and competent Darryl Zanuck, who had been responsible for the successful cycle of gangster films and flamboyant musicals at Warner Brothers in the 1930s. He too had been a military man, having served underage in World War I and as a lieutenant colonel in World War II, also making documentaries.

Both men knew and admired the Maxwell Anderson play *What Price Glory?*, which had a spectacularly long run in 1924–25 and which is still generally regarded as the best American play about World War I. Its action revolves around two professional soldiers, Captain Flagg and First Sergeant Quirt, and their off-and-on relationship with a French village girl, Charmaine, who is in love with first one, then the other, in a cycle of never-ending changes. *What Price Glory?* was filmed in 1926 with Victor McLaglen, Edmund Lowe, and Dolores Del Rio with considerable success, offering special merriment to lip-readers, who could savor fully the salty curses exchanged by the two men.

Both Ford and Zanuck respected *What Price Glory?* for what it was: a roistering comedy underlaid by the tragic drama of war, partaking equally of the somber and the risible, being almost a definition of life in the armed services in time of war. Ford had a special affection for the play. To make money for his pet service charity, the Military Order of the Purple Heart, he staged it in 1949 in Los Angeles with an alternating all-star cast featuring John Wayne, Pat O'Brien, Gregory Peck, Maureen O'Hara, Ward Bond, Robert Montgomery, and Oliver Hardy. Ford felt an obligation to the play, yet he was disturbed by its antiwar theme at a time when the Korean War was calling for U.S. action against Communist Asia. Moreover, Fox was making plans for filming *What Price Glory?*, and Ford was the obvious one to direct it. While plans for it were going forward he went to Korea to make a documentary for the Navy on the new war.

A Ford biographer, Andrew Sinclair, says of Ford at that time:

His Korean experience, however, made him unhappy with the message of [*What Price Glory?*]. He was also out of temper because Cagney was given the lead role instead of John Wayne, who had played for him on stage. He quarreled with the screenwriters, Phoebe and Henry Ephron, because they did not know his values or understand his rough sense of humor. On the set of the French village on the Fox back lot Phoebe Ephron remarked that there were a lot of Catholic churches for one small French village. "Don't you think there are a lot of synagogues in a Jewish village?" Ford replied, sending off both screenwriters forever, deeply insulted. They were too green and thin-skinned to survive Ford's normal testing of a newcomer's responses, and they presumed bigotry when they were only enduring his trial by their error.

But these tribulations were as nothing compared with Ford's displeasure on learning that this version of *What Price Glory?* was to be a musical, the one circumstance that made Cagney accept the role of Captain Flagg.

Darryl Zanuck had assured producer Sol Siegel that a musicalization of the play would serve very well, though with special emphasis on the love and sex angles. In a memo to Siegel he wrote: "How the hell are we going to get [Corinne] Calvet's legs into this show? Her body was a big asset in *On the Riviera*. Is there any conceivable way we can think of to get her in shorts, or something of this sort? Perhaps we can design a sort of peasant costume with a split in the front."

Had John Ford been aware of this kind of planning it is extremely doubtful he would have directed the film, and certainly he would have had no truck with a film named *Charmaine*, as was also contemplated. Cagney, on the other hand, was entertaining high hopes of a doughboy musical. He could not imagine how it might be done, but then again that was not his job. After all, this musical was in the hands of Zanuck, the man who had made those kitschy and vastly entertaining Warners musicals of the 1930s, and

*What Price Glory?* with Dan Dailey, William Demarest, and Corinne Calvet

there was no better director anywhere than John Ford. Cagney felt confident of these auspices.

As soon as Ford was told of Zanuck's plans for a musical, he said in brief but effective terminology that Fox would have to get itself another boy. Zanuck knew better than to argue with the most determined man in Hollywood. The musical was out, except for two vapid songs that would allow audience treks for refreshments.

Cagney was nonplussed. No Shvontz to call down, no brother Bill to fight his battles. This was a one-picture contract, and Bill was already warming up his next picture, a Cagney production, on the Warners lot. Nothing for it but to press on and get this one out of the way. He had too much respect for Ford not to cooperate with him on every level, but he had heard stories of the old man's crotchets and furies.

Peter Bogdanovich told this writer of a luncheon he had with Cagney during which he gave an instance of Ford's very curious personality. Said Bogdanovich:

Cagney told this story, acting it out, and of course it was sidesplitting. Said Jim: "The crew was preparing the setup for the scene in which I get into the motorcycle sidecar so I can be driven by Bill

Demarest via the motorcycle to Paris on leave. I was confident about this because Bill was a veteran of the First World War and had actually driven motorcycles there during the war. The scene is all set to go, I'm ready to go, Bill's ready to go. Ford is standing on top of a small hill there, and he gestures to me to come up there. I go. He's smoking a dudeen, that little Irish pipe. Puff, puff, puff. He says to me, 'You gonna get on that bike with Bill?'

" 'Sure, Jack.'

"Puff, puff. 'Why?'

" 'Why? Because the script says so.'

"Ford stands there, doesn't look at me. Just puff, puff, puff. He stands there. 'OK.' I don't know what to make of it, go down, get in the sidecar. Bill takes off, and we go on the goddamnedest ride I ever had in my life, going down a steep-graded hill. The road at the bottom curved past a stone wall to our right; to our left was a brace of lights in charge of an electrician. As Bill started down the hill at forty miles an hour, he suddenly realized that the rubber had worn off the motorcycle's brake pedal, and his hobnailed boot slipped as he applied the brake.

"To stop us, Bill obviously couldn't slam into the wall, so he did the only thing left to do: he crashed into the lights, thereby efficiently breaking both legs of the electrician and in the process catching the handlebar in his groin. Bill and the electrician went right to the hospital, of course, and I trudged up the hill to Ford, who was still standing there with his pipe. Puff, puff, puff. 'Did I tell you?' he said. Puff, puff, puff. So now there is one word that sums up Jack Ford—and the Irish—and that word is 'malice'!"

Bogdanovich concluded: "Jim was telling us this in his marvelous style, acting it all out in high good humor, and that last word came out with every ounce of Cagney intensity, making it both a curse on and a tribute to his race."

As the making of *What Price Glory?* proceeded, Jim noticed that Ford did not seem to favor the enterprise. He was not much interested in what the writers did and, although faithful to his duties, was not ardent about them. It shows. *Time* magazine defined the picture as "a soft-boiled version of the hard-boiled Anderson-Stallings play of 1924. This adaptation adds Technicolor, songs and slapdash comedy routines to the original. It subtracts much of the play's bawdy vitality and grim view of war." The most accurate review of the Ford *What Price Glory?* was Philip Hartung's in *Commonweal:*

It is amazing that a director as good as John Ford should turn up with anything as mediocre as this remake. . . . It is interesting now only as a literary protest against war in the Twenties. . . . Cagney overplays Captain Flagg with a theatrical flair that somehow mixes up the role with his brilliant impersonation of George M. Cohan, and Dan Dailey, usually a good actor, hams up Quirt to follow the pace set by Flagg. . . . I'm sure this film doesn't set out to glamorize war but unfortunately its effect [is] that [the film] is now a comedy . . . and a lot of fun is mixed up with the mud and shooting and death. . . . Movies should go on and on declaiming against war and asking what price glory, but they should mean what they say.

In sum, this is, as Andrew Bergman calls it, "a strange and quirky film, the novel and wrong-headed work of a master director suffering from a total lapse in judgment."

Jim was glad to see the back of this one, and he always treasured the letter Ford sent him later which included this: "Seumas, my boy, you are still the greatest actor in the whole world . . . and the crack I made about doing a picture for you free still goes. Jack."

Jim rather liked the atmosphere of 20th Century–Fox, and he certainly enjoyed the company of *What Price Glory?*'s producer, Sol Siegel. He lunched with Siegel one day and casually mentioned an idea about a film that had been gestating in his mind for months. "You mean you would *write* it?" Siegel asked excitedly.

"No, no," said Jim. "I've just got a kind of general idea—several story ideas, that is. But it's a picture I'd like to develop. It would be too expensive for Cagney Productions to do all by itself. We'd need the support of a good studio, and I like what I see here."

Siegel eagerly asked him to put his thoughts on paper. Jim obliged a few days later and the following is all that remains of the project:

Sol Siegel,
Twentieth Century–Fox Corp.,                    May 29, 1952
10201 W. Pico Blvd.,
Los Angeles, Calif.


Dear Sol:

I said I would shoot an idea at you when I talked to on the phone last week. It might be worthy of consideration and development.

It struck me that there would be possibilities in the story of two hoofers, taking them back to the early 1900's, showing how they met—first at a cellar door dancing contest, each representing

a different faction, with the judges under the cellar door to deter-
mine the better man, and, of course, the inevitable riot when the
decision is given. Both Irish, both coming from virtually the same
backyard, they decide they can do well together.

At the first opening, both being quick of temper, they take
exception to the way the other executed a particular step in the
course of the routine at the finish of the act. One punches the
other in the nose and the blood streams out, and they take their
bows with one holding his nose. They exit, and the one first hit
punches the other in the nose, also drawing claret. They take their
remaining bows with their hands on their noses to hide the flow of
blood. Of course when they get backstage there is a hell of a brawl
and they are called up on the carpet at the booking office and told
they can't be used because of their hoodlum behavior backstage;
that they upset all the other actors with their noise and fighting in
their dressing rooms, etc. They promise that if they are allowed to
play, they would never do it again.

They open once more and after the first performance they go
to their dressing rooms, stand looking at each other, and one lets
fly, hits the other one in the puss with the right hand and grabs
him and says "Sh-h-h." They both exchange punches then and
continue to hush each other as they whack the hell out of each
other. Of course they inevitably find the little girl in the big act,
and one of them marries her and it becomes a three-act. The single one's nose out of joint, he might take to wandering about alone
and doing a little drinking, missing performances, and finally they
split.

Now this is just a general description of what would happen,
using all the wonderful stories about the two-man acts who made
show business history. I personally know of stories that could be
woven into incidents hilariously funny, and others tremendously
dramatic.

Their graduation from vaudeville to the revue stage, such as
the Winter Garden shows, the pitfalls of success, with money
rolling in and no sense to handle it, etc. I have a sequence hith-
erto untouched that can be, I think, exciting and amusing—with
the two fellows' pockets loaded with money, their show having
just closed, [they] hie themselves to Canada where booze is to be
had, taking over a small hotel in Quebec or Montreal, throwing
out all the guests, putting the keys in their pockets, going to all

the theatres inviting all performers to come and stay the week with them. Of course one of the acts in the vaudeville house has to be a girl band. The joint jumps for the week they are there, with everybody doing his stuff—the legits, acrobats, the magicians or whatever you may want to use, to be done in the lobby of the little hotel. This was an actual happening in the life of a very close friend of mine.

The love story can be one of many, but it must keep them in continuous hot water to retain the turbulent feeling that is ever present in show business, or have you ever known any turbulence. If you haven't, I can arrange it with [John] Ford. Just a rough sketch of what I had in mind. If you want to talk about it, I'll be in town for two weeks yet and we'll sit down. I have a writer friend who likes the idea and he knows how to put stuff together. So, if you think it's worth talking about, let me know.

I was glad to hear that the *Glory* job turned out well. That's always good news. All for now.

Best,

Jim

Sol Siegel was interested, but Bill Cagney was not, although he paid lip service to the idea. Jim kept thinking of this film for years, for as long as he was able to dance. He had been actively thinking of it since *Yankee Doodle Dandy* days but developed a curious kind of conflict about it. The absolutely ideal partner for him in this story was Gene Kelly, the free and easy scapegrace mick type. But Jim kept thinking longingly of Fred Astaire, the man he always wanted to be teamed with, the dancer he admired most in the world. At the same time he realized that his friend "Freddie," as he called him, although a supreme dancer, was perhaps too innately elegant and gentlemanly to be the sort of roughhouse character the Cagney story required. While Jim worked on *What Price Glory?* it occurred to him that Dan Dailey might do the part. But Jim yearned for Astaire. They were of an age, being born only ten weeks apart, and this musical would begin with them at their present age, in their fifties, going in flashback to their early days. "It is more convincing to get youthened up a bit than aged down a bit," Jim said. He never had the heart to ask "Freddie," whom he regarded as his master.

The next five years of Jim's acting life he described as open-field running. "Hit or miss" might be more accurate. He was led by his instincts and brother Bill's business savvy. Bill deferred to Jim's artistic sense although he did not hesitate to suggest literary properties that seemed filmable and bankable. The properties held by the Cagneys all had impeccable backgrounds in respect to popularity as novels. These were *Only the Valiant,* a western that in time starred Gregory Peck, and *Bugles in the Afternoon,* a Civil War epic that one day featured Ray Milland. Then there was *A Lion Is in the Streets,* the story of a Huey Long–type southern politician. The brothers decided that *Only the Valiant* and *Bugles in the Afternoon* were never going to be vehicles for Jim, so they sold them to Warner Brothers as William Cagney Productions in a profitable arrangement and concentrated on *A Lion Is in the Streets.*

The novel seemed particularly suited to their needs. It concerned a grass roots salesman with enough charismatic appeal to sell himself into the governor's mansion of Louisiana, followed by glory and destruction. Moreover, Cagney Productions was in fine fettle as a practical working extension of the family. Jim was star, Bill the producer, Jeanne a leading player, Dr. Ed was now story editor, and Dr. Harry was eminently available as medical adviser. But the Cagneys were all dressed up with no place to go. *A Lion Is in the Streets,* a product of their concentrated efforts, was not a disaster but was close enough to being one as made no difference. The novel, the film's source, is execrable. A reviewer for *The New Yorker,* June 26, 1995, in looking at the book again said in part:

> And so to the No. 1 best-seller of July 1, 1945, *A Lion Is in the Streets,* by someone named Adria Locke Langley. Dear me: "In Nature's own way, her inner being began its years of lying quiescent, encased—not sending out into the various spokes of her life that indefinable quality that makes for significant and meaningful living." Oh, *that* quality.
>
> The spokeswoman in question is named Verity. I would love to report that she is a lying bitch, but, sadly, she spends almost five hundred pages living up to her name. She is married to Hank Martin, who goes from being coarse, horny white trash to being the coarse, horny governor of the Magnolia State [*sic*]. The plot is a backwoods version of *Mr. Smith Goes to Washington*—the little guy made big—but the rubbery emotions bouncing around here are unique to Ms. Langley; she makes Frank Capra look like Mad Max. The book is a hymn to the power of justice, pummeling your ear and your conscience with such humorless zeal that poor old justice falls by the wayside, leaving power to stride on alone. The one diverting aspect of Hank's political strategy is that you can't tell

whether he's leading with his beliefs or with his pants . . . you know this guy is *hot*. The newly ravished Verity recalls the sound of her mattress under pressure: "the many cracklings of a while ago, cracklings that had grown rhythmical as if they were tapping a million drums—little, secret, earthly drums." Doom! Doom! Hank embarks on married life by running down his carnal menu: "Me, I like my kissin' with laughin' after lovin', 'r I like it with teasin' afore lovin', 'r I like it in earnest with lovin'." I reckon Hank Martin missed his vocation. Why go into government when you could be writing lyrics for Dolly Parton?

One cannot conceive of James Cagney being a lovable, old, gal-kissin', cracker slob. First his southern accent, insecure to begin with, on occasion veers off its unsteady course and heads directly for East Seventy-eighth Street and First Avenue although there is no diminution of the Cagney power at the moment he is speaking.

Bad though the novel is, it need not necessarily have made a bad movie. Within its own melodramatic structure *A Lion Is in the Streets* would have been sufficient as good entertainment with good acting (which it abundantly has) and content of some substance, which it did not. Hank Martin in the novel goes from swamp peddler to national figure, just as Huey Long did, and is assassinated, as Long was, at the height of his corrupt power in the state capital. The screenplay by Luther Davis included all this, but when director Raoul Walsh saw the script, he insisted that the final third be cut. It was overlong in any case. A substitute ending was provided, with Hank Martin being killed in his own hometown by a local lady, played by Jeanne Cagney. The sweep of a Huey Long, Caesar-like death degenerates into a neighborhood squabble.

Furthermore, Cagney ended up unable to empathize with Hank Martin, thereby violating one of his acting precepts: "People ask me how I can play rotten guys like Rocky Sullivan and Cody Jarrett, asking me if I feel any sympathy for them. No. No sympathy. But empathy, sympathy's cousin. I can understand how these guys got that way, I can put myself in their boots, and to that extent I am with them. I've got to look at these characters from their point of view."

This was not the case with Hank Martin. Bill Cagney said that with the exception of *A Lion Is in the Streets* Jim's audiences always liked him:

Even if they momentarily thought that what he did was abominable, when the picture closed, they liked this guy and they were glad they had spent that time with him because he was colorful. I

*A Lion Is in the Streets*

tried to get him—it always had to be done very subtly, you couldn't
act like you were telling him how to work—to go back to the original thing that he saw in the character [of Hank Martin] which was
this likable quality. But he was emphasizing a lousy quality, with the
result that he wasn't saving the scenes like he always did. Jim just
did not give. I think it was deliberate. I think he was so out of tune
with Huey Long, who he was playing—he hated him so—that he
did not get the audience to go along with him like he could when he
was playing the worst killer.

Surprisingly, critical appraisal of *A Lion Is in the Streets* was generally
favorable, Bosley Crowther going so far as to call it "a headlong and dynamic
drama" with "Cagney in one of his most colorful and meaningful roles." Several reviews pointed out correctly that *A Lion Is in the Streets* fared poorly
in comparison with Columbia Pictures' multi-Oscared film of Robert Penn
Warren's *All the King's Men* of four years earlier on the same theme.

Whatever else it was, *A Lion Is in the Streets* was the last film made by
Cagney Productions, which, except for a vague cosponsorship years later,
was thenceforth moribund. The family knew this, understood this, and was

*Run for Cover*

not bitter. "We did a good job," said Jeanne Cagney. "We were proud of what we had done, and we certainly had done yeoman's service on behalf of the concept of independent productions and producers."

The contract with Warners having come to an end, the Cagneys had an open field in which to run, with many options facing them. Bill by this time was tired of being a producer. He in effect dropped out of that business and again became his brother's manager. He dickered with Paramount for its upcoming western, *Run for Cover,* which had all the earmarks of a meaningful film. Its director was Nicholas Ray, an artist who gracefully illumined social rebellion in virtually all his films. Jim liked the script as well as its promised proximity to horses and great, unspoiled scenery.

The plot of *Run for Cover* is trite. Cagney is Matt Dow, unjustly imprisoned, who on release rides west, where he befriends Davey (John Derek), who is crippled after they are innocently caught up in a train robbery. Matt becomes the local sheriff and appoints Davey his deputy, who betrays Matt by running with local bad guys, who in turn shoot Matt, who in turn shoots Davey, who in turn shoots the bad guy who is about to shoot Matt again. Davey dies in Matt's arms.

Director Ray said of Cagney: "We've always seen Cagney as the tough little squirt throwing a grapefruit in a girl's face or taking on someone twice his size kicking hell out of him. But Jimmy has not only a great serenity, such as I've not seen in an actor, outside of Walter Huston at times, he has a great love of the earth, and of his fellow man, an understanding of loneliness. I wanted to try and use all that. The vehicle itself wasn't strong enough for it, and we didn't have the time to be as inventive as we would have liked."

"Old western plot stuff," said Jim. "But both Nick Ray and I had put in some ingenious touches. Offbeat stuff. But the assholes who cut the picture were unhappy with anything they hadn't seen before, and when the little things we put in would come up—because they were too new to the boys who were sitting in judgment on what should have been in the picture— anything that was novel was out. It became just another programmer."

Jim had had too much experience with programmers. He took off for a few months' rest on Martha's Vineyard. This proved fitting because it gave him the energy to effect and to enjoy one of the happiest years of his cinematic life.

# 21 · *Annus Mirabilis*

Jim looked back on 1955 as the most venturesome of his professional life, and one of the most rewarding. The five films released or completed that year—two were made in 1954—were not of equal merit, but he truly enjoyed making each one, for varying reasons.

*Run for Cover* was spoiled by the picture's timid producers at Paramount with their hypercautionary editing of what was at base an interesting western. "I will never be able, ever, to understand jerks like that," Jim said. "They spend good money on a cast and director fully able to handle the job of turning interesting material into watchable stuff; then they chop out the watchable stuff. In all my Hollywood days the people I despised the most were producers, people interested in producing nothing but money." Notwithstanding, the hard work involved in doing *Run for Cover* was in its way creative and worthy. He enjoyed the experience and learned from it.

Next came a film he loved doing and loved talking about. "You have to realize," he said, "that I always received a lot of scripts and had been getting them for years and years. It was always reading I enjoyed. One thing I may be vain about, and if it's self-praise, so be it: I know a good script when I see one, and I can always tell its worth by about page eight. When I got *Love Me or Leave Me*, I think I was about at page four when I said aloud, 'Oh, my God, yes. We do this one.' Beautifully written, an honest treatment of three difficult and interesting lives. And what songs! I had nothing to do with the music, but I could listen, and I did."

Jim had a particular admiration for Doris Day. During the making of *The West Point Story* he thought she was just another talented pretty girl, but as the shooting of *Love Me or Leave Me* began, he changed his mind. He liked her cute spunkiness, but he saw beyond that. She had beneath the cuteness all the apparatus of a good actress, and something more. He took her aside one day, a very rare thing for him to do with a fellow player, and said, "You know, girl, you have a quality that I've seen but twice before. There was a gal named Pauline Lord who created the title role in Eugene O'Neill's *Anna Christie,* and I'm also thinking of Laurette Taylor. Both these ladies could really get on there and do it with everything. They could take you apart playing a scene. Now you are the third one."

That deeply affecting quality, the thing that took one "apart," Jim defined as "unshrewdness," the feeling such a person projects of inherent, open niceness and a total lack of guile. When that is married to rich acting talent, one has a unique and fascinating personality to present, and all those qualities come through shiningly in the Doris Day of *Love Me or Leave Me.* It is one of those rare instances when the Cagney strength is fully matched by another performer. Day makes Ruth Etting unforgettable.

Ruth Etting was almost certainly the best of the popular singers in the 1920s. She could project winsomeness, seductiveness, hotcha, and sweetness, frequently all at once, in the same song. Personally she was—in a then current phrase—no angel. Doris Day, in her autobiography, refers to Etting as a "kept woman" who got her start through gangland connections. "There was a vulgarity about her that I didn't want to play," said Day, and that is why the film's producer, Joe Pasternak, wanted her: "to give Ruth Etting some dignity."

Etting was married to a minor underworld figure, Moe "The Gimp" Snyder. The Gimp, slang for "limp," was crippled, likely from birth, and had a stubborn mean streak, exacerbated by his continuous wrangling with Chicago nightclub operators who refused to subscribe to his laundry service. Gimp was a low-level hoodlum, certainly not a gangster, who yearned for status as a big shot. This he attained by becoming first Ruth's informal agent, then her protector-boyfriend, and ultimately her husband. In real life, as in the film, she uses him to get ahead, and to an extent this is a quid pro quo arrangement. But as in all good drama, there is a fundamental and genuine conflict: how can a marriage work that is based, as this one is, on the hopeless equation of love plus ingratitude minus love equaling happiness? Ruth, after marriage to the Gimp, finds she loves her faithful coach and accompanist, Johnny Alderman. She tries to stay away from him, cannot, and the Gimp shoots Johnny nearly fatally. True love comes through, and the Gimp goes away with bitter and wounded pride, still quite detestable but meriting pity.

*Love Me or Leave Me* is a dual triumph of acting in surprisingly equal balance. It is not Doris Day's picture (for the first time since 1931 Cagney is billed second), nor is it his, but a superb example of costarring. Jack Moffitt of the trade paper *Hollywood Reporter* puts it well: "Miss Day comes through as a subtle and sure emotional actress. . . . She makes every sullen glance, every cautious smile and every murmured commonplace phrase speak volumes. A great popular star has become a great actress." As for Cagney, there will "be those who will say that [he], as the crippled, obnoxious and pathetic Snyder, steals the picture. But they'll be selling him short. He makes the picture. Ridiculous, in his gaucheries and dynamic in ruthless determination, he makes his role a vivid and meticulous study of a small-souled man in the throes of an overwhelming infatuation. It's probably his greatest performance and it's certainly one of the screen's classic bits of realism."

Moffitt goes on to particularize a key aspect of Cagney's technique as a great actor, his ability to listen intently and fully to his fellow actors: "And while playing this exacting role, Cagney makes himself still greater in every scene by sustaining Miss Day and the other players by a certain vitality of his attention that can only be generated by the best of stars."

There was, said Jim, not a wasted frame in the picture. All the supporting players, especially Cameron Mitchell as Johnny Alderman, were impec-

*Love Me or Leave Me,* with Doris Day

cable. The high gloss of quality was everywhere apparent, the result (in Jim's opinion and likely unchallengeable) of the picture's provenance, Metro-Goldwyn-Mayer, for which both he and Day were working for the first time.

It was MGM that had had the foresight to go out and secure this naturally dramatic story by obtaining the well-paid consent of Miss Etting, Alderman, and the Gimp, all alive at the time. The Gimp was inevitably flattered to be portrayed by Cagney and was unable to understand how the star was able to reproduce his limp (albeit on the wrong foot) so exactly. "I went to my two doctor brothers," said Jim, "and told them that all I knew about the Gimp's lameness was that he was a victim of prenatal polio. Harry and Ed described to me just what that meant, so I went ahead, turning in my foot to the required distance and then following the old John Barrymore–Richard the Third principle of assuming a defect and then forgetting it, I tried to walk as well as I could with the handicap."

Jim, now fifty-six, was made to hide his graying hair here and there with blond dye, his natural red suppressed in the need for toning down the exuberance of his coloration in this Technicolor film. His limp is major at times, minor at others, depending in each instance on the emotional stresses of the

*Love Me or Leave Me*, with Doris Day

scene. He liked his director, Charles Vidor, whom he called "a nice version of Mike Curtiz." After Jim saw the movie again in 1980, his only comment was: "Just saw something I hadn't noticed before. There are no other women to speak of in the cast. Doris is so very much alone, which heightens the effect of the male world upon her. How many nice girls there are, and were, in this business who were just so afflicted—by the presence everywhere of intimidating males."

Then he recalled something else. "We had just done my opening shots, and after we finished them, I cussed myself out and said to Charlie Vidor, 'Sorry, Charlie, let's do them again.' 'What do you mean?' he said. 'The opening shots,' I said. 'I forgot to limp.' 'No, you didn't,' Charlie said. 'But I did,' I told him, and I was quite insistent. He asked me to hold off until after we'd seen the dailies, and what do you know, there they were, every limp in place. I didn't have the faintest idea I was doing them. Goes to prove something or other." It went to prove the Cagney power of concentration.

A fascinating side note to *Love Me or Leave Me* is Doris Day's marital situation at the time. Married to entrepreneur Marty Melcher, she had a long and ultimately catastrophic marriage. In her autobiography she cites "the parallel, in some respects, between [the Gimp] Snyder and Marty Melcher. . . . I hadn't realized at the time how much Ruth Etting and I had in common." Jim said: "It was as if the picture was a prediction of Doris's own life. Snyder lived vicariously through Etting, as Melcher did through Doris."

Jim was nominated for Best Actor for the third and final time and lost to Ernest Borgnine's *Marty.* The film won only a single Oscar—for Daniel Fuchs's Best Original Story—although one might have thought that more appropriately directed to include Ruth Etting, the Gimp, and Johnny Alderman. Incredibly Doris Day was not nominated.

Jim knew that roles like the Gimp were not only rare but at his age almost unattainable, and he occasionally thought of retirement. He was gratified that he had attained the highest honors professionally—the Oscar and especially the New York Film Critics Award—and it occurred to him that perhaps 1955 was the year when he should call it quits. Moreover, he had found a new love, sulky racing. He raced personally at Goshen, New York, and other tracks. Also occupying his time were a variety of conservation societies that he had joined and to which he contributed regularly. Conservation grew to be an obsession. On his auto trips across country he began to notice more and more the intrusion of concrete across the land, much of which he found excessive and the likely cause of a new kind of graft harnessed to "progress." He wrote of it:

> Lay down the ribbon of concrete, boys,
> And we'll divvy up lots of loot;
> We'll do it all quiet and neat, boys,
> At ten thousand dollars a foot.
> We'll certainly take care of our friends, boys,
> As we give the law the bend, boys.

He was increasingly saddened by the evidences of selfishness that he saw everywhere about him and how it seemed to be determining so much of our country's future. It made him, an inherent optimist, despair at times:

> What we are determines our basic needs,
> And the needs decree each course of action.
> No need, no action may be regarded as rule,
> With self-satisfaction, however minuscule,
> Calling the turn with utter finality,
> Obscuring for all of us each stern, stark reality.
> Seeing what we want to see, needing no other view,
> Until crisis arrives in the form of catastrophe,
> Functions then gone, will be lost to atrophy,
> Man's malignant stupidity collecting its due.

It was during one of those low moments that he received a call from John Ford that a film of the brilliant World War II comedy *Mister Roberts* was in the works, and wouldn't Jim take on the small but key role of the Captain? Moreover, Ford told him, he would have the joyful company of Jim's special buddy Spencer Tracy, set to play Doc. To sweeten the job even more, the movie would be made in Hawaii and on Midway Island, and Jim would hardly have anything to do but lie around on the white beaches with Tracy.

Jim had seen *Mister Roberts* during its long Broadway run and knew that the role of the Captain was superb. On the stage it was played by William Harrigan, son of the man of George M. Cohan's song "HARRI-GAN," which Jim had sung in *Yankee Doodle Dandy*. "Bill Harrigan saw the role somewhat different than I," said Jim. "Of course at the time I saw it I had no idea I'd be offered the part, and when the time came, I sat down, selected the Down East accent of a friend, and produced the character." It was not the character as played on the stage. Jim went on:

> The Captain was hated by the crew, and Mister Roberts, played by
> Henry Fonda, was the second officer, acting as a buffer between
> the Captain and the crew. The acting problem, as I saw it, was to be
> both a villain and a comic figure. This, after all, was a comedy with
> a very serious side to it. I set about characterizing the Captain that

way, and John Ford was all for it. I was not going to play the Captain as Bill Harrigan had on the stage, as purely a mean, villainous son of a bitch. That was my base, yes, but I was going to add humor.

This is exactly what he did, to the horror of Henry Fonda, who had played the role of Mister Roberts for years on Broadway, and of Josh Logan, coauthor and director of the play. Logan, who was not consulted about the screenplay, was angered by such profanation and by the rewriting of *Mister Roberts*'s dialogue by Frank Nugent, a Hollywood hack. Logan said, "[Nugent's] was the shopworn Hollywood trick of taking dialogue that was good to begin with and switching it around a bit, just enough to make it seem like his own—and Nugent's dialogue was bad, bad." Logan and Fonda were primarily outraged that the prisonlike atmosphere of the ship where no one ever received liberty—key to the play's entire meaning—had become under Ford's direction virtually a happy place with, said Logan, the so-called prisoners "swimming, diving, cavorting every afternoon like happy kids at a boys' camp.

"And in Christ's name," said Logan, "what has Ford made Cagney do [but] play the Captain like an old New England bumbler, without any hatred, without darkness, without threat? He's all Down East accent, and comic at that. Without a villain there's no threat; without threat there's no story."

Logan undervalues the amount of villainy Cagney invests in the Captain, but the rest of his criticism is accurate. For the first and only time in his career, Cagney succumbs to real overplaying. As the Captain he gives himself over at times to a barking rant that makes some of his words unintelligible. Moreover, he roars his anger too frequently in unmodulated bombast. Logan found it incredible that "one of the world's great actors, Cagney, had become persuaded to become a kind of Walt Disney character." Hardly persuaded; this was a Cagney creation, however ill conceived.

Within the context of the original *Mister Roberts*, this *is* Disney, but what of reaction to Cagney from the vast majority of filmgoers, those who had never seen *Mister Roberts* on the stage? It is likely that their reaction would echo critic Milton Luban of the *Hollywood Reporter*, who wrote of Cagney's "choleric rages almost literally convulsing the audience. It is hard to recall when there has been such laughter in a theatre as when Cagney chokes and collapses in blind fury, the ship's doctor hopefully bringing along a stretcher. The role is one of the high spots in Cagney's brilliant career, accomplishing the miraculous feat of out-villaining Captain Queeg and still being hilarious."

This film, then, is a *version* of *Mister Roberts*, one that its star of many

*Mister Roberts,* with Henry Fonda

years on the stage and its coauthor despised. Fonda, who loved John Ford (and vice versa) never got over it. He expressed his dissatisfaction to Ford during the shooting, whereupon Ford knocked him down, later apologized, and tried to defer to the spirit of the film's original by asking Fonda if he approved of certain shots. "Shoot it any way you like," said the dispirited Fonda, and shortly thereafter Ford began to drink during shooting. A notable toper after his films were completed, Ford started now to keep a case of beer next to his director's chair. At one point he was consuming two cases a day, and when he got fuzzy, his old friend and cast member Ward Bond would have to take over, always consulting Fonda.

Suddenly Ford developed severe gallbladder trouble, resulting in its rupture, and he was forced to leave the film. Jack Warner replaced him with Mervyn LeRoy, Cagney's pet bête noire, and the man who had wanted to direct *Mister Roberts* in the first place. This pleased Fonda because LeRoy decided to film the rest of the script in a fashion as close to the play as possible. The film emerged as a blend of Ford's outdoor approach and Mervyn LeRoy's talkiness. Cagney, given his long-standing aversion to LeRoy, had hardly a thing to do with him.

In any case, Jim had a marvelous time making *Mister Roberts.* Ford had been true to his word: there was plenty of time for beach lounging. Spencer Tracy did not play Doc after all, but his substitute, William Powell, was a most agreeable companion. "What a nice man," said Jim. "Hell of a good actor, just as urbane as he seemed on the screen and with a fund of theater stories that kept me hanging on his every word. We'd be out there in the sun for a goodly portion of our stay, then get a call to get before the camera. We'd go there, and I'd holler and jump up and down and then go straight back to the beach and the sun."

Jim also had the pleasure of meeting a young actor he had seen and admired on television, Jack Lemmon. Lemmon, in an interview with *Rolling Stone,* recalls:

> One of the keys to Cagney's superiority as an actor is that he's a master of observation. Every actor who's worked with him has a Cagney-on-acting story, but I think mine has got to be one of the best. Back in the early Fifties, when I was doing a lot of live television, I did a Kraft Theatre show where, as an exercise in discipline, I did everything left-handed. It took weeks of practice, but when I did the show, no one noticed it; not my wife, not even the director. I considered it a big achievement. About two years later, I meet James Cagney as we're beginning to start work on *Mister Roberts,* and he says to me, "I've seen kinescopes of some of your stuff with the Kraft Theatre. You were very good." I was completely thrilled with the compliment. Cagney turns to go, and then he looks back at me and says, "By the way, you're still not pretending you're left-handed, are you?" I almost shit. That marvelous son of a bitch was *that* observant.

Jim had been so impressed with the young man that he tried to get him under contract with Cagney Productions, but John Ford had seen Lemmon meanwhile and had cast him in *Mister Roberts.* It was a mutual pleasure for the two actors to meet in Hawaii. They have a hilarious scene in the film in which Lemmon, as Ensign Pulver, trying to duck the Captain, in fourteen months aboard ship as laundry and entertainment officer, meets him for the first time. Cagney and Lemmon rehearsed the scene endlessly because it was so funny they both would break up. Said Jim: "I used to collapse every time Jack said, 'Fourteen months, sir,' when I asked him how long he'd been aboard, but when we filmed it, I was able to hang on just *barely.*"

*Mister Roberts* was critically acclaimed, made a great deal of money, and won a Best Supporting Actor Oscar for Jack Lemmon. John Ford and

Mervyn LeRoy were credited as codirectors, and bitterly disappointed but resigned, Henry Fonda returned to the New York stage. After all, he said, "You can't tell an audience who saw only the movie, 'You should have seen the play.' "

*Mister Roberts* was important to Jim in yet another way. It was his last film for Warner Brothers. They had been together, off and on, for twenty-five years.

After this film came the inevitable return to Martha's Vineyard, but there he began to suffer a series of sea changes. He now felt a sense of strain in maintaining his acreage. Moreover, the island was beginning to become popular with tourists. His privacy was threatened by strangers making their way to the farm. He found it increasingly difficult to find farmhands. His land seemed to be getting sandier and more soil-exhausted. He had been trying energetically for nineteen years to reclaim it by using all kinds of soil conservation procedures.

He wrote at this time:

> If God is the ideal quite unattainable
> And Nature's fierce logic is most unassailable;
> If we observe with care the great human condition
> As we hurry in haste down the road to perdition,
> One phrase is large on mankind's scroll:
> All is ephemera—except soil and soul.

He still owned Louella Parsons's old San Fernando Valley ranch, Marsons Farm, where he bred his Morgan horses; it was his recreation place when he was working in California. In 1955 he bought a new dairy farm in Millbrook, New York. Here he hoped to settle down with his family and seventy Holstein-Friesian cows. He discovered the place with the help of Robert Montgomery, who lived nearby.

Willie, as always, was amenable to Jim's wishes, but she yearned for the comforts of Beverly Hills. Not only was it more comfortable, but it was a far easier place to raise children. She thought that Jim Junior and Casey were getting rather less than a square deal by being raised in various rustic atmospheres.

As always after a picture, Jim went to Martha's Vineyard with Willie and the kids, whom he was trying to raise much as his mother had raised him. This attempt failed for the basic reason that he was not in his children's company to the extent that Carrie had been with him and his siblings. When he was in a picture, it was work, home for dinner, into the library or bed to study lines for next day, and soon to sleep. His needs, Willie believed, were paramount. The Cagney children's psychological stresses were bound to grow under such conditions.

Shortly after returning from Hawaii with Willie, Jim was asked to accept an honorary degree, Doctor of Humane Letters, from Rollins College, Winter Park, Florida. This, the oldest and one of the smallest liberal arts colleges in that state, had a tradition of granting honorary degrees to showfolk, among them Mary Pickford, Jean Hersholt, Basil Rathbone, and Edward Everett Horton. The college asked only that each honoree give a little talk "on any subject of your choice." Jim's choice was a rare one in 1955: conservation.

His audience was startled. It was almost the last thing they expected to hear from an actor of his stripe. Jim swung vigorously into his topic. He spoke at length about the needs of the earth's growing population and the failure of us all to provide the earth with "living resources." He went on to recount ecological destruction throughout history, speaking of farmlands subverted, and suggested that one likely reason for the Confederacy's defeat was the depletion of its lands. He ranged widely in his instances of soil failure and the need for renewal, concluding, "Inasmuch as the future of all of us is dependent on the condition of our land, I think we all should have a try. Regardless of what we come up with, the problem will still be with us. For we must realize that without the land, man will cease to be. This history has shown us."

He sat down to polite applause, sensing that his audience, or most of it, had been expecting something closer to Hollywood gossip. "I noticed some of the younger people were listening attentively," he said to Willie. "They're the ones I'm trying to reach." The Florida trip was innovative for the Cagneys. In order to keep the time short away from their children, they flew. The trip down was heavenly; the journey back pure hell. It was an extremely bumpy flight, and a few passengers got nauseated. Jim said, "The final proof that flying is not good for you. Never again." He was not able to keep his word totally, but mostly he did.

Bob Hope had been Jim's close friend since the days of the Victory Caravan in 1942. The Hope career had been slipping in the mid-fifties, and his advisers were urging him to get more into the area of character comedy, the kind that called for genuine acting. He responded well to that need with *The Seven Little Foys,* a biographical account of Broadway's best-known parent, Eddie Foy, who dragooned his seven children into supporting him in vaudeville so that he could support them. *The Seven Little Foys* is an engaging movie, and its highlight is a seven-minute scene with Cagney reprising his George M. Cohan character by means of a dance shared with Foy. They are in their beloved Friars Club when Cohan gives an award from the members to Foy as Outstanding Father of the Year, followed by loving insults of the Hope-Crosby variety:

COHAN: Do you know what I'd give to have your seven kids?

FOY: Do you know what I'd give to have you take them?

COHAN: I met your kids. You couldn't afford it.

FOY: Well, at least you'd have an audience.

After more of this patter Cohan dances to "Yankee Doodle Dandy" on the banquet table, doing the stiff-legged Cohan walk and head waggle. After Foy does an expert rolling tap, Cohan calls for "a little 'Mary,' " and the pianist leads into the Cohan song as Foy and Cohan dance to it in gentle harmony. Bob Hope does excellent work, almost as expert on his feet as Cagney, but without the latter's delicate control of his arms, the unvarying sign of a good dancer. At the end the two men embrace; it's all highly affecting.

What the camera did not show of the dance was Cagney's agony while performing it. In jumping up on the table, he pulled a muscle, and the pain was electrifying, though there is no indication of it on his face as he dances blithely on. When he went back to the dressing room, part of his leg had swollen almost double, and Hope insisted he go to the hospital. "No, just have someone drive me home so I can put my foot up. It'll be OK in a few days."

When Jack Rose, *The Seven Little Foys* producer, first approached Jim about his salary for the job, he refused payment, not only as a favor to Hope but as a contribution to the memory of Eddie Foy: "When I was a starving actor, I could always get a free meal and a friendly welcome at the Foys. You don't forget things like that." Rose and Mel Shavelson, the film's director, expressed their gratitude by presenting Jim with a leather and inlaid silver horse trailer. It found ample use.

The year 1955 also brought to Jim a film that he prized almost as much as anything he did that busy year. *A Link in the Chain* is a little-known half hour film made for television by the Christophers, the Catholic-based television series that emphasized the efficacy of good works. Like all its participants, Jim did the job for union-scale pay.

"I really liked that little movie," Jim said. "I kept thinking of my mother all through the shooting. I know she would have loved it. She would have

Rehearsing
*The Seven
Little Foys*
with Bob
Hope

put it high on the list of things I ever did because of its theme, her favorite subject: education."

*A Link in the Chain* is principally a series of flashbacks. Cagney plays George Graham, a seventyish professor, attired in the opening scene in an ancient tux, going through his desk as he awaits his wife's call for them to attend his testimonial dinner. Much of the drama is monologue as he sifts through the items in his desk, each reminding him of a particularly bright and difficult student. He mimics the college dean rendering the Graham encomiums in high style: ". . . takes leave of us after a rich, full life of teaching, a life that has molded and changed thousands of other lives." The professor is repulsed by the idea of these words and announces that he won't attend the dinner, to hear lies of that sort told about him when he asks, "In truth, what lives have I changed?"

Since this is only a half hour film, it has to reveal quickly, and hardly in depth, the lives of three of the students he has changed, the implication being that they are representative of all his students. By flashback we visit the three at the time Graham knew them: Peter Fielding (James Lydon), a cripple embittered by his deformity and a young man skilled at caricature; Emily Peterson (Arlene Roberts), an angry campus revolutionary with a deep need to help people; and Thomas Gore (Sam Edwards), the college's most popular student, who has a brilliant and wealthy future as a professional football player. Thomas, however, has a most unusual obsession for one of his accomplishments: a deep desire to be a teacher and live Professor Graham's life.

During each encounter in the past Graham offers pragmatic advice for the student's future. Then, in a flash-forward to the present, we watch Graham's preparations for the testimonial dinner. Finally come voice-overs of his three students years later: Peter has won the Pulitzer Prize for political cartooning; Emily is now a world-traveling social worker; Thomas is deeply content, teaching the eighth grade in a North Dakota school. Graham sits at his desk as Emily's voice tells him of their changed lives and says that everything began with him. No, he says to himself, "I was but a link in the chain, a chain that was first forged with a word, some words that made me know I could be but one thing: a teacher. The words I'm referring to are the words of Daniel Webster, who too was but a link in the chain. I typed them up especially just in case I might be called upon to make a speech tonight. They're here somewhere."

He searches his desk, then finds them in the wastebasket. "Well, they're not the first kind words that should be remembered that have ended in the wastebasket. Here they are: the words of Webster. Listen."

Then Cagney, wearily—and looking surprisingly like the aged Franklin D. Roosevelt—drops the paper and slumps at his desk. We know he is dead, but his wife doesn't as she comes in, formally dressed, to tell him that the dean and two hundred people are waiting to honor him. She cannot rouse him and rushes out. Cagney's strong, calm voice is heard on the sound track, speaking Webster's words: "If we work upon marble, we will perish. If we work upon brass, time will efface it. If we rear temples, they will crumble to dust. But if we work upon man's immortal mind, if we imbue them with high principles, with the just fear of God and love of their fellow man, we engrave on those tablets something which no time can efface and which will brighten and brighten through all eternity."

*A Link in the Chain* mirrored not only Jim's mother's concern with education but his own. He said:

Looking back now, I can see that I have always had a pedagogic instinct, probably planted there by my mom. It's deep in me, and I can see that by just looking at the theme of much of the verse I write. I saw a television program once on CBS about young men from the mean streets of town who were seemingly not able to advance themselves. The program showed footage of the young men sitting on the stoops of old houses, doing nothing, just sitting there obviously ripe for mischief. And the commentator droned on, saying over and over again until it drove me absolutely nuts: "Where can they go? Where can they go? *Where* can these young men go?" Which just infuriated me to the point that I actually jumped out of my chair and shouted—after I had heard that god-damned "Where can they go?" just too many times. I got up and shouted, "To the *library*. That's where they can go. To the god-damned *library!*" I meant that, and I mean that, with every fiber of my being.

# 22 · Indian Summer

As his years grew, so too did Jim's feelings that he had been bountifully lucky in his lifetime, principally because of the influence of his mother and the continuing care of his wife.

He went to a party on Martha's Vineyard in the fifties, and among the guests met Dolly Haas, the actress wife of the great *New York Times* caricaturist Al Hirschfeld. Haas had been successful in her native Europe and on Broadway but had never attained great stardom. She walked up to Jim and said, "Oh, Mr. Cagney, you must be proud. *So* proud!"

Not knowing what she was talking about, he said, "Proud? Of what?"

She frowned a little and said, "Why, of your career. Of your Oscar. Of all you've done."

He shook his head with emphasis. "I had nothing to do with it."

"What?"

"Had nothing to do with it," he said. She shook her head. He went on: If you're talking about talent, and if there was talent there, where did it come from? I certainly had nothing to do with that. Some one of my ancestors provided some little thing in my genes that gave me something to work with. I'm grateful for that. But actually, taking a bow for that would be like taking a bow for having red hair or blue eyes. My feeling is: I never could take any bows for what I've done, could never feel proud of it. Too many elements of chance and luck. I have never kidded myself that I had anything to do with whatever talent I've been given.

Haas said, "Still, given that this talent of yours was in your genes, you had to develop that talent. You had to take care of it."

"True," Jim said. "But wouldn't anyone? It's just like combing your hair. A necessary duty."

He rarely went to parties like the one where he met Dolly Haas, usually attending only if some old pal asked him to show up. "I go to these frigging things," said Jim, "as a social obligation to neighbors and old friends, and I wouldn't stay long. After all, you can't be a hermit, although I must say I don't think that would be a bad life if you had enough to eat and books to read. So I try to be sociable when it's helpful. I am really not a member of the Edgartown cocktail circuit." His social activities were pretty much limited to his beloved club, The Players, when he was east.

In most men's clubs, which The Players was until very recently, there is always a hierarchy of the old, willingly or unwillingly pitted against—or at least in high contrast with—the new. Older members inevitably seek their peers, and one usually must age before being admitted to their inner circles. Not so with Jim at The Players. Through the years when he was in the East, he would turn up once a week with Frank McHugh, Jim coming down from his Dutchess County farm, Frank riding in from his home in Cos Cob, Connecticut. The two always chose "the long table" at the Players, the one that accommodates ten diners, in order to give the younger members the chance to meet them. One young member in the late fifties, Roger B. Hunting, said, "I, as well as other young Players, made it a habit to be at the club for lunch that day, which at first was Tuesday and then, when Frank's cleaning person changed his date, Wednesday. We would vie for seats at the table to listen to those two great old Players exchange memories, recollections, and dreams about their long careers in theater. One thing we noticed at once was that Mr. Cagney always preferred to be addressed as Jim rather than Jimmy. A marvelous man."

When Jim was in residence on the West Coast, he lived very quietly with Willie and the children at the Coldwater Canyon house, the children still in their separate building in the back. Brigid O'Brien, Pat's daughter, who knew the family well, says:

> The idea of the children, Jim Junior and Casey, living in quarters separate from their mom and dad was the strangest arrangement one could ever conceive. You really cannot have a happy family under such a setup, and they certainly didn't. Mom and Dad [Eloise and Pat O'Brien] said that years later every time the Cagneys got mad at their kids they changed their will. After we'd all grown up, once in a while I got together with Casey and with Ellen Jenkins, Allen's daughter, to talk over a project Ellen wanted to get going, a book to be coauthored by Ellen, Casey Cagney, Susan McHugh— Frank's daughter—and me. The book had an absolutely darling title, *Our Four Fathers*. But the idea fell through. Ellen and Casey

didn't have especially good memories of their childhood, and Susan wasn't enthusiastic, so it died. I don't think Willie Cagney had the *time* to be with her children much because she was so busy taking care of Jim.

In Beverly Hills the Cagneys' next-door neighbor, a Mrs. Sherwood, wanted to put up a swimming pool. In order to effect this, she needed the use of the Cagney driveway to move a truck to the site. It was left for Mrs. Sherwood's son, James, just graduated from college, to obtain permission from the Cagneys. James wrote the request, placed it in the Cagney mailbox, and in short order heard from Jim, who called James and suggested they have a chat while walking the brown hills of the neighborhood. During the walk Jim learned that young James was already a published poet; that pleased the older man considerably. They talked about literature, and James was thrilled to learn that Jim had actually met Bernard Shaw. " 'What did you think of him?' I asked Mr. Cagney," said James. "I don't remember his exact words but they were close to this: 'Shaw understood that politics is comedy, comedy is political, and that people are not seen as real until they are seen for real. But above all, never be clever—ever!' "

The Sherwoods soon had occasion to learn that Willie had a temper. After the swimming pool had been up for some weeks, Willie decided she did not like it. The Sherwoods had not yet put up a fence, as required by Beverly Hills statute, and rather than speak to them, Willie went down her driveway one afternoon through the shrubs surrounding the pool, carrying a bundle of weeds, which she tossed in the water, turned on her heels, and vanished. Mrs. Sherwood now needed a further permission from Jim so that the fence people could use the Cagney driveway to reach the pool. Young James wrote a note, placed it in the Cagney mailbox, and watched for Jim to return from work in his green war surplus jeep with its top down. When he did, he waved as usual when he saw the young man and invited him over.

Forty years after the event novelist James Sherwood recalls:

Mr. Cagney led me into his house. It seemed like no one was at home. The house was silent, and we went in together. I never once saw either of his kids and don't remember meeting Mrs. Cagney, though I had the feeling she was at home, perhaps napping upstairs. You could feel her there in the silence and the way he kept the silence, closing the door with care, walking almost on tiptoe. We went in the little den, somewhere near the front door. It was book-lined with facing leather chairs. He offered me a drink from a bar shelf, or stand, or something plain to my right. Not being a drinker—I had never with my own father had drinks—I chose what I saw on the stand, a scotch or something, and he chose the same thing. We sat about six feet apart, facing each other, my back to the door, he able to see past me, the light from the window coming in over his right shoulder. The chair wrapped him up, and he looked really comfortable, glass in hand.

Our conversation started with "What do you want to be?" When I told him an actor was part of my plan—specifically "A movie star just like you, Mr. Cagney"—he looked most disappointed and lowered his eyes as if I had misspoke and should change that idea pretty soon. We talked about my job at Paramount. I had been hired from a newspaper editing job by [Cecil B.] De Mille and was basically there to learn, with publicity and production department duties. Mr. Cagney mentioned his directing plans [at Paramount, upcoming], and I said, "Well, if you want me to drive you to work, I go every day." He smiled and said that was all right; he liked to drive himself.

We came to the pool. "How can I help you?" The law required a fence, height a minimum four feet or thereabouts. He said there was no problem, start anytime using his driveway. We finished our glass. He told me I was a good kid. I went home skipping in mind and heart. The next time we saw each other he waved as usual from the jeep to the pool. One day he stopped. "Nice fence." It was six feet, and my mother was pleased.

I said, "Sorry it's so high."

He shrugged, as if to say, "Understood." No mention was made of Mrs. Cagney or my stardom, an omission I felt was shared. We were men together in drink and women management.

Metro-Goldwyn-Mayer was so pleased with Cagney's work in *Love Me or Leave Me* that he seemed the logical substitute for his friend Spencer Tracy, who had been raising hell on location in Colorado for his newest picture, *Tribute to a Bad Man*. Tracy did not like the role and hated the script. When Cagney was approached about the job, he said no, but Tracy's friendship mattered, and taking over for him would be a gracious gesture. Moreover, as Nick Schenck of MGM told him over the phone, there were eighty-seven people, cast and crew, waiting out in the woods, leaderless. In addition, the rolling western hills in which the film was set, not the script, moved Jim.

His character, Jeremy Rodock, is a maverick horse breeder with a practical way of punishing horse thieves: hang them on the spot. Jeremy has a mistress, Jocasta, a liaison only gently hinted at in the film, robustly, intelligently played by the superb Greek tragedienne Irene Papas. Bad man though he is, Jeremy is on the side of sensible expediency, pragmatism, and as many horses as he can maintain. He fights both the horse rustlers and his turncoat chief wrangler, a rascal who has been involved with Jocasta years before. Jocasta has had enough of them both and is riding off with the film's goodhearted young leading man when she realizes she cannot fight the dictates of her heart, so buckety-buckety back to Jeremy, who proposes to her because censors of the time could hardly countenance anything less.

*Tribute to a Bad Man*'s reviews dwelt mainly, and with justice, on the beautiful scenery it captured on film as well as with Cagney's solid acting. There were now no wisecracks about the East Side tough guy unwisely consigned to horseback as with *The Oklahoma Kid*. It was now fully recognized that Cagney could ride authentically. *Time* magazine said, ". . . what a hoss-bustin', man-killin', skirt-rippin', jug-totin' buckaroo he can still believably pretend to be."

Jim was pleased with the fee he received from MGM, and after a three-week holiday he was told that an "emotionally rich" script was waiting for him at MGM. It was the story of a bachelor multimillionaire, Steve Bradford, who sets out to find the illegitimate son he sired more than twenty years before. The role of the woman in charge of the orphanage where he must go to unravel the past was to have been played by Helen Hayes. "I was really looking forward to that," said Jim, "but she had another commitment, and they replaced her with Barbara Stanwyck. That was fun, working with that lady." The film was called, for no discoverable reason, *These Wilder Years*.

Steve finds his boy, now securely happy in his own life, and they part in mutual regard, but Steve also encounters a sweet pregnant orphan at the home whom he adopts. The two of them wait cozily for the forthcoming birth while Stanwyck looks on approvingly. She also looks as if she would be more comfortable standing before a roulette wheel, but she makes even this soap opera palatable with Cagney's help. During setup waits he and Stanwyck discovered that they had many mutual friends in the New York theater of decades before. She had been a dancer in her youth, and, said Cagney, "she could shake a mean hip still. We got a phonograph going and did the Peabody, the Castle Walk, the Charleston, and the Black Bottom. Fun."

Bosley Crowther caught the mushy fragrance of *These Wilder Years* at once: "A slight scent of radio soap opera hovers over *These Wilder Years*. . . .

*Tribute to a Bad Man,* with Don Dubbins

And, of all people, hard-boiled James Cagney finds himself in the focal role that gives off the strongest aroma of sentimentality. . . . The picture is mawkish and dull." It was the general opinion.

By the mid-fifties Jim's closest friends were still Frank McHugh, Pat O'Brien, Spencer Tracy, and Robert Montgomery. His connection with Montgomery made for a matchlessly comfortable equation of friendship: the rich boy who wanted to be tough, the tough boy who wanted to be rich. More, it was the conflux of two basic American types: Cagney, the archetypal city boy who idolized America; Montgomery, also a great patriot, the blue-blood patrician type that first imagined, then led this country. Each man sought something from the other.

Although indirectly, this was expressed in their acting. Early on Cagney's hoodlum image had typecast him. For personal satisfaction he needed to show his innate gentleness and reveal his variety as an actor, and to this end he had played the college-educated agent in *G-Men.* But, as Cagney told Richard Schickel, all his roles then and later had something of the hoodlum in them. He could never escape the fighter image; it was too much him.

*These Wilder Years,* with Barbara Stanwyck and Betty Lou Keim

Montgomery had the opposite yet the same problem. He fairly reeked of good breeding—an American Noël Coward type. Like Cagney, Montgomery began to rebel at his image. He considered it undramatic, effete, and morally worthless. "I've always yearned to play gutty parts," he said. "That's why I did *Night Must Fall* and *The Earl of Chicago,* the former successfully, the latter not."* Indeed the latter was embarrassingly bad, his bone-bred suavity clashing noisily with the role of a dese-dose mobster. Like Cagney, in his acting he could not go fully against his heritage.

Politically the two also grew closer. Jim, first a quasi-socialist, then a registered Democrat, had by the late forties become unqualifiedly conservative. "Government more and more taking over things frightened me, and seeing these things, this control, being made permanent by some pretty inadequate bureaucrats scared me shitless," said Jim.

He had admired Montgomery from the very first days when they were helping the Screen Actors Guild come into existence. Said Jim: "Lots of

*Told me by Montgomery in 1980. I was going to ghostwrite his autobiography, a project aborted by his death a few months later.

screen actors may well not know how much they owe Bob. It's sometimes said that Republicans are antiunion. Malarkey. Our union, Screen Actors Guild, wouldn't have gained what it did as fast as it did without Bob. He became our leader in the fight against the producers, and Bob fought them no holds barred, knowing full well he was putting his career right on the line. It was Bob who bearded those all-powerful producers in their comfortable dens."

Jim especially admired Montgomery's attitude to the behemoths of the burgeoning television industry. Montgomery saw a clear parallel to the days in the film industry when the big studios dictated working conditions for all. He had begun his successful series, *Robert Montgomery Presents,* for NBC in 1950 and was very pleased by the results. But his future with the TV networks was seriously compromised by their establishing an unwritten law: in order to continue a series, one had to sell 50 percent of the show to the presenting network. He appealed to the FCC, appeared before Senate committees, and denounced the networks for their monopoly tactics. This did little good at the time, but it is generally agreed that his testimony before influential boards and committees provided an important stimulus toward freeing the television air.

*Robert Montgomery Presents* was going into its sixth year when he approached Jim and, in the latter's words, "told me the networks were trying to dump him, and if I did [a show called "Soldier from the War Returning"], it would get the Montgomery season off to a healthy start. Of course I was happy to oblige."

Jim had made two previous appearances on live television: the first, a Bob Hope show, doing something distinctly not up his alley, the presentation of a few beauty contest winners. He did the show because the Hollywood makeup men's union would get $10,000 if he did. His second live television appearance was a brief scene from *Mister Roberts* on *The Ed Sullivan Show,* plugging the film. Jim did not tell Montgomery, but like many actors, he was terrified of live television. There could be no comfort of another take, no starting all over again. As it turned out, his terror was justified, although little of this showed on the air. His third live television appearance was in "Soldier from the War Returning," presented on NBC, September 10, 1956.

Perry Lafferty, who directed the program, remembers it well:
This show had one of the shortest rehearsal schedules of any of the hourlong dramas on television anywhere, anytime. That is because Montgomery was so stingy. Rehearsals for his shows were Monday,

Tuesday, Wednesday, Thursday, and Friday. Saturday was off. Sunday the cameramen would come in, and you would explain the show and tell them in general terms what they were supposed to do. Then on Monday, which was show day, you went into the studio, and you were in the studio just that one day. Every single hour show that I ever knew of was in the studio at least two days. That extra day meant an awful lot in sharpening the show, honing it to perfection. And every single hour show that I ever knew of had at least one or two days longer to rehearse than the Robert Montgomery shows did. I'm making this point because here is James Cagney, who has no experience in television at all, doing one in a very abbreviated space of time. It was very brave of him, and he was so professional. He worked terribly hard. At one point he said to me, "Can I meet with you tomorrow and go through my hand business?" I had never heard such a request from an actor before. By "hand" business he meant handling the props in each scene, making sure the telephone is here, the pencil there, and the cup up here, and his hat is in the closet. I went through all that with him, and quietly and alone we did that for about an hour.

"Soldier from the War Returning" (the title derives from an A. E. Housman poem) was about an Army sergeant, George Bridgman (Cagney), on graves detail, returning a fellow soldier's body home from the Korean War. He is escorting the flag-draped coffin to the boy's hometown. *Time* magazine called it "a noble-minded but often pedestrian tone poem which confused patriotism with adulation of the anonymous dead. Cagney's usual clipped, staccato style was properly subdued—especially at the end when he tried to work out a salvation for his hero."

One of the smaller but vital roles was played by Heywood Hale Broun, actor-writer, who remembered that

Jim always got to rehearsals a half hour early to dance his way into warm-up and relaxation. He was not nervous; before beginning a scene, he would walk back and forth a bit to ease tension, referring to himself as a stall walker, a horse who through nervousness moves back and forth in his stall before release. When asked why he wasn't really nervous, this being a live show, Jim said, "Listen, after doing six-a-day in vaudeville, you'll never be nervous again. In a movie—and this is a kind of movie—it's one hour of tension, and then it's over. Easy." While doing the show, he wasn't used to the extreme restriction of cameras at that time, and this caused him some unease.

He was particularly fine in responding to me when I had my one big speech in the show. Jim, as the sergeant in charge of the body, asks me, "What was the kid like?" Whereupon the camera goes to me, stays on me during my vital speech. Now, when such a thing happens, most star actors, not being on camera, will relax and drop out of character and just wait until the camera swings back to them before resuming character. Not for Jim. Although he couldn't be seen, he looked me right in the eye, maintaining his role and reacting to every blessed thing I said. This is the sign of a *generous* actor.

At show time Jim unexpectedly fell prey to worry. Lafferty describes the climactic scene of the show:

Cagney, in this scene, was seated with the dead soldier's wife (played by Audra Lindley) in the backyard of her home in this small town, and Jim had this long monologue at least a page and a half long. He was very nervous. Halfway through it I suddenly saw that he had forgotten his lines. He didn't know what the next word is. We have a problem. Because it is a philosophical dissertation, *she* can't say anything. Nobody knew that he had gone up, but I did because I had the script. He just looked at her, and she looked at him. The silence was maybe ten seconds, but it felt like ten years. I cut to him, cut to her, cut to a two-shot. Finally he got the words back and finished it.

Next day Jack Gould wrote in *The New York Times:* "Mr. Cagney could so well teach some of these young actors the value of a pause." As for the play, Gould added: "[It] realized its exalted purpose in Mr. Cagney's movingly spoken definition of the hereafter. But, before that inspirational moment [and the pause], Mr. Wallace's play fell lamentably short of its ennobling theme. . . . In the closing scene, in which he had something to say, Mr. Cagney rose to his opportunity with convincing sincerity."

Jim never after underestimated the difficulties of live television. Never again, he said. There was nothing like its sheer terror—one performance that is both opening and closing night, just like a stage play except for the four cameras, two booms, twelve stagehands, and a cast of twenty-six.

One of the writers of *These Wilder Years*, Ralph Wheelwright, had written a story based on the life of Lon Chaney, and one day casually mentioned it to Jim, an old friend. Immediately interested, Jim asked for further details because he had been a Chaney fan from high school days and much admired the silent-film actor's ability to convey many nuances of emotion without speech. Jim thought of Chaney as a unique acting challenge: to portray Hollywood's foremost silent-screen actor without directly imitating him, as well as to convey the subtle, moving strength of Chaney's portrayals. Jim knew that Chaney was often mistakenly remembered as a horror picture star when in fact he had played a bewildering variety of parts in searching, memorable fashion. The trick of course would be in conveying this while at the same time honoring the subtleties of the well-known horror films Chaney *had* made, such as *The Phantom of the Opera* and *The Hunchback of Notre Dame.*

Since Chaney was an unqualified genius at makeup, that element loomed large in the new film, to be titled *Man of a Thousand Faces.* Michael F. Blake, the world's leading Chaney scholar and himself a professional makeup artist, explains the difficulties attendant on this process for the film:

> Cagney went through a variety of makeup tests in preparation for the re-creation of several famous character faces that would be used in the film. While making motion pictures had changed quite a lot since Chaney's time, makeup had yet to graduate to the technical levels of recent years. The days of cotton and collodion were passé, but foam rubber appliances had yet to advance from the full-face mask to individual pieces. In order to re-create Chaney's makeup for *The Hunchback of Notre Dame* and *Phantom of the Opera,* Bud Westmore . . . made foam rubber pieces that covered the entire face, save for the areas around the mouth and eyes. . . . Cagney's makeup as the Phantom was an entire mask glued onto his face. While it left the mouth area open, his speech nevertheless was limited in this makeup. . . . It took roughly an hour and a half to apply these two well-known makeups to Cagney's countenance. Even in scenes in which he appears "as is," Cagney wore a foam rubber piece on the tip of his nose to make it appear longer and more similar to Chaney's nose. The makeup budget for [*The Man of a Thousand Faces*] amounted to $28,500, which was extremely high for that time [1957], although by today's standards, this budget could conservatively be quadrupled.

Chaney's life was exceptionally dramatic. Born to deaf-mute parents, he learned the standard sign language of the deaf when young and thereafter communicated with his mother and father in this fashion. Because of his natural mimetic abilities, Lon entered show business as both actor and song and dance man, coming to Hollywood in its early days and making more than 150 films before he died of throat cancer at forty-seven.

He had a disastrous first marriage to a very young singer named Cleva,

*Man of a Thousand Faces,* with Robert Evans (left) as Irving Thalberg

but from it came their son, Creighton, who was to enter films under the name Lon Chaney, Jr., and, unlike his father, specialize in horror films. Cleva attempted suicide at a theater where Lon was working but was saved. He divorced her and was awarded custody of the child before marrying again, happily. Lon became world-famous and at the height of his career made his first and only sound film, just before death from the malady that forced him again to the use of sign language.

From these elements *The Man of a Thousand Faces* was effectively fashioned. Unfortunately at times Cagney's face did not suitably accommodate Chaney's original makeup. Jim's face was short and round; Chaney's was long and hollow-cheeked. One cannot create anything very frightening out of a cherubic countenance, which Cagney's basically was. In *The Man of a Thousand Faces* too much of the Chaney makeup seems gratuitous, padded onto Cagney's face, not becoming an integral part of it.

In *The Phantom of the Opera* the Phantom's greatest scene occurs while he is playing the organ masked and the heroine approaches him fearfully

*Man of a Thousand Faces*
ABOVE: As the Phantom
of the Opera
BELOW: As the Hunch-
back of Notre Dame

but determinedly and rips off the mask. Chaney at this moment rises, revealing his terrifying skeletal face, and the girl shrinks back in abject horror, as who does not, seeing that 1925 film. The Cagney duplication of the scene simply does not strike fire on two counts: when he is unmasked, he looks more cute than macabre, and the actress playing the heroine does not look very horrified, nor would she have much reason to be. Cagney's face here is rather pudgy with all the makeup added, and a very well fed Phantom is a contradiction in terms.

Fortunately this is the only misfire in the film. Cagney has never been better in his moments of tenderness, anger, love, and revulsion. He goes the gamut dramatically and, praise be, has two superb dance sequences, one as a clown on pointe, the other as a challenge dancer in a shadow act. The music for these two intriguing numbers is sprightly and charming. They were written by James Cagney and make one regret that he did not write others. There is also in the film a magnificent portrayal of Lon's mother by Celia Lovsky, one of those artless performances in which an actress does nothing more and nothing less than required.

Lon Chaney was given his first step to fame by Irving Thalberg, whose widow, Norma Shearer, insisted on casting young Robert Evans, in his preproducer days, as her husband because of the striking resemblance to Thalberg. Evans, an understated actor (to understate it), does indeed look like Thalberg. Jeanne Cagney appropriately plays Lon's sister in the film and not long after retired to do television and raise her family.

The critical acclaim for *The Man of a Thousand Faces* was universal, and it always remained one of Jim's favorites. He had now learned the new lesson that Hollywood stars had begun to assimilate: always get a piece of the action. He owned a good percentage of the picture.

# 23 · Not the Ending

A s the fifties marched along, Jim found it less and less a challenge to
seek out agreeable work. Brother Bill was no longer an active agent for
him, and it never occurred to Jim that he should employ one; he was
being sent scripts of all kinds. He was spending more and more time in the
East, giving occasional public talks, such as one at the White House Corre-
spondents' Dinner on May 24, 1956, which President Eisenhower attended.
He paid tribute to Cagney on that occasion: "No one in show business has a
warmer heart or has done more for the less privileged." This was one of the
few public acknowledgments ever made of Jim's continuous and abundant
contributions to charity.

He was unendingly generous to friends. In 1957 a producer friend at
Paramount, A. C. Lyles, badly needed a competent director for a screen-
play, *Short Cut to Hell,* based on the Graham Greene novel *This Gun for
Hire.* Jim said, "I knew A.C. was searching for someone, and I said to him,
'May I suggest someone?' *I'll* try it." Lyles was delighted and honored and
asked his salary requirements. Jim replied, " 'Would nothing be too much?'
So I did it in nineteen days. The young man who played the leading role did
not look like a leading man, which as far as I'm concerned is always a plus.
A boy named Ivers. Talented. Didn't stay in the business."

Robert Ivers plays a psychopathic killer who, after completing a job, is
paid off with marked money and spends the rest of the film searching for
the man who wronged him. There are murders, police chases, and some
shallow delving into killer psychology. In the end *Short Cut to Hell* simply
does not excite. Cagney appears in a prologue introducing the leading players, Ivers and Georgann Johnson, calling them "exciting." Exciting they are
not, competent they certainly are, but they toil in vain on behalf of a labori-
ous script. "Never again," Jim said. "I realized I have no interest in telling
other people their business."

At this time Jim happily found someone unusually skilled in telling him his business as a painter. From his early days of copying newspaper cartoons to his between-the-scenes habit of caricaturing fellow players, Jim felt comfortable with a pencil in his hand. One day while lunching at the Brown Derby with his sister Jeanne's boss, television host Jack Bailey, Jim saw in the next booth an unusual-looking youngster. Jim said:

He was a born cartoon. I couldn't resist sketching him on a napkin, strange ears and all. Jack asked me how long I'd been doing *that,* and I had to admit I'd been doing it now going on about fifty years. Jack was a pretty sharp cookie, a guy I had a lot of respect for. He used to introduce himself as "a past and present drunk," meaning he was with AA, and he surely knew how to paint. Jeannie had been working for him on the giveaway show *Queen for a Day,* as fashion hostess, and she knew what a kindly, talented man he was. So Jack insisted I go with him next day to Santa Monica and meet his teacher, Serge Bongart. What a break for me!

Bongart, born in Kiev in 1918, had been exhibited at the Metropolitan Museum of Art and other prominent museums and had founded his own school of art in 1949 in California. He did Jim the remarkable service of transforming him from a clever sketcher to an undoubted artist, talented in both watercolors and oils. The consolation this growing skill brought Jim as he grew older and more sedentary was incalculable. Willie encouraged him in this to the fullest. When his children grew out of adolescence, there was less and less communication among the four Cagneys, and family life grew to be, in the words of one family friend, "rather tattered and scattered." Painting, reading, and versifying now became Jim's principal occupations between pictures.

After his rewarding work for Universal in *The Man of a Thousand Faces,* close friends were constantly seeking out properties for him, and were finally convinced they had found something markedly different and very much worth his time. It was different, all right: a musical about a labor racketeer. The script was not quite Jimmy Hoffa doing a buck and wing, but it was not all that far from it. Certainly the antecedents of *Never Steal Anything Small* were impeccable: an unproduced play, *The Devil's Hornpipe,* by Maxwell Anderson and Rouben Mamoulian, top-level American playwright and superb theater and film director respectively. On the stage Mamoulian had directed two of the greatest musicals of all time, *Oklahoma!* and *Carousel.* Anderson, among his many triumphs, had written both book and lyrics for *Knickerbocker Holiday,* which included the words of the immortal "September Song."

*Never Steal Anything Small*, with Shirley Jones

As credits go, these could hardly be bettered, but the Anderson-Mamoulian material got swallowed up in a mélange of pseudo–Damon Runyon fiction intercut with pseudo–Kurt Weill. The original script not being available for study, there is no way of knowing what indirect influence Kurt Weill had on the material except to note that before his untimely death, he had successfully collaborated with Anderson a number of times. If *Never Steal Anything Small* was an attempt to do a music drama akin to *The Threepenny Opera*, it aborted early on. But its ultimate fault, as *Commonweal* said, was "its indecision to be taken seriously or not."

Cagney is Jack MacIllaney, who is running for head of Local 26 New York of the stevedores' union. He befriends a young lawyer, Dan (John Smith), and falls in love with Dan's wife, Linda (Shirley Jones). More than half the film consists of Jack's trying to put a wedge between the two and win her; the other half, of Jack's chicanery in stealing the labor election and, in the process, committing grand larceny. Jack's trying to win Linda is not as illogical as it seems despite his tummy and his years—in real life Jim was fifty-nine, Shirley twenty-four—because, as he candidly admits, the relationship is all one-sided in regard to affection, declaring it in one of the few good lines in the film: "I'm offering you the greatest luxury there is, a relationship where you can be the dishonest one." This, added to the Cagney personableness, makes him a not unlikely suitor, for all his years.

Jim's by now marked political conservatism was remarked on briefly by a friend of his who, upon seeing *Never Steal Anything Small*, said, "Boy, you really gave the unions hell in that one, didn't you?"

Jim replied that he had not, would indeed never, appear in a film that gave hell to the unions. He said to his friend, "I am a devout union man. I belong to two of them, Screen Actors Guild and AFTRA [American Federation of Television and Radio Artists], and I'd sure as hell never belong to anything I was against. Charlie Lederer [screenwriter and director of the film] was perfectly aware of my feelings on the subject of unions and labor, and he didn't put in my mouth any words I didn't want to say."

In answer to Linda's sincere but gentle criticisms of him, Jack tells her not to look down on unions because without them, "the jungle [the world] would be a whole lot crueler." He is surprised that "a well-read girl like you [hasn't] heard of such outstanding men as Samuel Gompers, John L. Lewis, Dubinsky, Meany, Reuther [which Cagney pronounces in the German way, ROYther]." She says he surely doesn't compare himself with them. He agrees: they are 100 percent; he is 15 percent. "But someday I may be like them." Ultimately Jack pleads guilty to the larceny he has committed in order to win his election, the fruits of which he will gain after only two years in prison.

The musical aspect of what had originally been called a "music-drama" dwindled severely during preproduction planning and in production. Jim had expected to sing five songs (lyrics by Anderson, music by Allie Wrubel). This dwindled to one and part of another. He sings the title song, but only over the opening and closing credits. Shirley Jones has two sweet songs befitting her personality. Cagney dances only once, his usual stiff-legged walk, and this with Cara Williams, playing his mistress, who belts out, "I'm Sorry, I Want a Ferrari," a number the two of them execute on a treadmill surrounding a vivid red model of the car. Maxwell Anderson's lyrics (if they are all his; no one else is credited) lapse into the hypermundane—e.g., Cagney singing "Please get me off the hook, / You're making me feel like a schnook."

*Time* magazine said that "not even the pleasure of catching Cagney at close to his best can entirely appease the sense that this really is an amoral little movie. Not even the greediest hands in labor's till have ever publicly demanded what this picture demands: the right to steal."

Shirley Jones today recalls:

I hadn't met Jim Cagney before this, but I certainly had been one of his biggest fans, so you can imagine the thrill I got in actually working with him. That working couldn't have been better. In the old days directors tended to be mechanical, and *so* in the end proved to be their product, as happened here. The joy of working with Cagney was that in the acting, he always *gave* to you. Totally unselfish. You never had any sense of your being alone in a scene, as you do with actors who are mainly concerned with themselves. Jim was always *with* you, listening to you carefully, truthfully, even when playing this part, which, after all, was a caricature. He sort of held court on the set, telling lots of wonderful stories about the days at Warners. We became good friends, and when the picture was finished, we had a big party at my house. I had hired a pianist to play all night long. When Jim came, he said turn up the rug, and we did, and he danced "Yankee Doodle Dandy" to our great delight. He liked me because I was also a singer, and he asked me to sing that night, which I was most happy to do. You know that *Never Steal Anything Small* was originally a musical, but it became increasingly apparent that this was not a musical story. It became neither fish nor fowl.

"A plum part and a trip to Ireland—unbeatable!" Jim said of *Shake Hands with the Devil*, his next effort, a 1959 film based on the 1934 novel of that name by Reardon Connor. Produced by an independent unit for United Artists release, the film was shot at Ardmore Studios, Bray, Ireland, and nearby. It has peculiarly modern resonances today when Ireland's IRA troubles seem to be looming larger than ever before. Cagney's favorite writers those days, Ivan Goff and Ben Roberts, visited him at Martha's Vineyard before leaving for Dublin to get the lay of the land and write the script. Roberts explained to Jim the cultural and psychological determinants of Sean Lenihan, the man he was to play:

We said, "Jimmy, this is a tough part. American audiences are going to find it hard to understand your character—that he is a revolutionary who is dedicated to the revolution. There is no *give*, none. The research we have done indicates to us that Ireland is full of these men and will be, forever. So it's not a very crowd-pleasing portrayal, to wind up killing a woman because you have vowed to have no compassion, but that is what this man will do.

[Cagney] said, "I understand the problem. I'm going to play it straight down the line. I'm not going to soften it any, and maybe if people see that, they will understand someone has to *give*, someone has to soften, eventually there has to be a meeting of the minds."

Cagney does indeed play Sean Lenihan with carefully controlled, merciless emotion given over entirely to the fight for freedom from England. Writers Goff and Roberts altered the novel's period from 1934 to 1921, the time of the Troubles, and changed virtually the whole of the novel to suit this framework. The title derives from the old Irish saying "Shake hands with the devil and you'll never get it back." In the Goff-Roberts version, Sean Lenihan, a great surgeon and medical professor, is secretly a leader of the revolutionary underground, obsessed with the idea that Ireland "must be free, sea to sea." Anything that contravenes that life rule of his must be ruthlessly eliminated. One of his students, Kerry O'Shea (Don Murray), an Irish-American, is led by British brutality to join Sean's underground, and he becomes aware of the curious conflict dominating Sean's existence: "Saving life on one hand, having to kill on the other."

Sean's unit of the IRA takes as hostage a prominent and lovely Englishwoman, Jennifer Curtis, who is also a member of the British aristocracy. Invariably, as the forces of liberation and oppression intensify their clash, she and Kerry become involved romantically. Finally a truce is signed, but Sean, not approving of it, takes Jennifer out to be killed. Kerry accuses him of killing for the sake of killing, declaring that he will not fight Sean's personal war, and as Sean aims his gun at Jennifer, Kerry kills him.

The details of the plot are many and convoluted and given much immediacy and depth by the supporting players, all from the Abbey Theatre. Cagney is quietly savage as the IRA commandant, and, said the *Irish Times*, since the drama had to be heightened, "that was achieved by making the Commandant a good deal larger than life. Cagney, however, brought such superb artistry to it that even in the final scene you could cast him as your emotions dictated—for his was the face, according to your choice, of a fanatic or of the implacable Irish dead."

Don Murray, who played Kerry with vivid intelligence, today recalls Cagney's acting style:

> As to preparing his scenes, Jim came from a day when they did not take things as seriously as later generations of film actors. He was a strikingly good actor but also what one would call a personality actor. He was always Cagney, and truly wonderful, but he was playing his own personality. I wouldn't say he "listened" in the modern sense much because he had so completely prepared everything he was going to do, and I don't think he was much affected by what the other actors were doing. Maybe that was a sign of age.

*Shake Hands with the Devil*

What Murray reveals here was that Cagney, no doubt due to age, was not "listening" to fellow actors with the intensity he did in his youth. Murray hits on a salient aspect of Cagney's acting in *Shake Hands with the Devil*. He plays the role almost with detachment, with the reserve that such a man— so intellectually committed to freedom at any price—would employ, shunning the emotional and letting only his mind dominate his actions.

Murray was asked if the actors made up what is usually described "a happy company," when all is in harmony:

It was indeed. A very happy company. But that always has to do with the star. If the star is relaxed and friendly and likable, then everybody becomes relaxed. That's just the way Jim was. I can't imagine anybody, male or female, pulling any kind of star crap when he was around. I think he just would have made fun of them because he was such a no-nonsense, unpretentious guy. He was very gregarious on the set, but off the set he stayed pretty much to himself. A number of the other actors like Richard Harris, Donal Donnelly, and I would go out to the pubs after, looking for the good

Guinness, and Jim would go home. He was of course a great raconteur, what with his stories of early Hollywood.

Another thing I liked about him: he was, as you know, quite a
short man, and totally unconscious about it. When we were out on
the turf somewhere, they would dig holes for me so I could stand in
them and be at his height level. This was done not to make him
taller than he was, but to make the frame better for us both. One
had to frame this two-shot properly. He would joke about it and
absolutely not care. One thing he said, kiddingly: "I'm used to playing with actors taller than I, but I soon cut them down to size."

Don Murray is struck by the modernity of *Shake Hands with the Devil*:
A picture almost forty years old treating of matters that were current forty years before *that*, and so apropos today. Cagney playing
the man who wanted to continue the violence and I playing the one
who wanted to make peace. The parallels are incredibly close to
what exists today. Jim and I became good friends. He then had two
farms, one in the East, the other in California, and he always
seemed to be having inadequate managers for his farms. Too many
people hired to work for a movie star slack off after a bit, feeling
they don't have to have the farm make a profit, given the star's good
means. I got Jim a manager for his Millbrook, New York, farm, finding him in a group I was associated with, connected to the Peace
Corps. The man I got Jim did so well Jim asked me to get another
for his California place.

Jim was reluctant to leave Ireland. He had hoped to do a little ancestor
hunting and to see the whole country, but a project he and Bob Montgomery had been discussing for years was suddenly shaping up. Bob, from
his World War II experience, had come to appreciate the complexities of
leadership. He saw that on the highly select level of highest naval operations
there was a mystique at once remote, intellectual, and highly pragmatic. He
dreamed, or as Jim said of his friend, "dared to dream," of filming this, of
making a naval movie without booming guns, one devoted to the lonely
reaches of high command.

The man Montgomery chose to epitomize this concept was Fleet Admiral William F. "Bull" Halsey, who commanded the U.S. naval forces at the
Battle of Guadalcanal in 1942, one of the epic conflicts of World War II.
Montgomery knew Halsey well and, after obtaining his permission to do the
film, held long talks with him about the problems of command. Montgomery also set a team of writers to interview Halsey's subordinate officers
to obtain deeper soundings of the seventy-seven-year-old hero. Jim met

Halsey twice before making the picture, once in his office for a preliminary talk and the second time at luncheon.

"I quickly learned," said Jim, "that Halsey was not a man of mannerisms. The power of the man did not come from exterior traits but from the human qualities which lay within. I was impressed by two characteristics: his kindhearted consideration for others and his fine sense of humor." While the script was being written, Jim spent time checking his livestock at both farms before returning to Beverly Hills and the work of playing Halsey, which he called the most difficult role of his career.

There was one pleasant social event at the time. The Screen Directors' Guild of America gave a party in Jim's honor at its theater to celebrate his thirty years in the industry. Fittingly, the master of ceremonies was Bob Montgomery, who came to the lectern looking grave. He said, "Ladies and gentlemen, thirty years ago a man came to Hollywood destined to have a great career." The crowd settled back to hear the rest of Cagney's praises. "I," said Montgomery, "am that man." The laughter from then on was constant, and Jim enjoyed it all immensely. Montgomery went on: "Jim and I made a pact once our friendship was formed. We agreed never to watch each other's films so our friendship would never deteriorate to the level of shoptalk. My part of that bargain, however, was based on dishonesty. Because I must confess now that I saw every one of his pictures and liked them."

Film clips from Jim's career were shown to the three hundred guests, who comprised not only many of his directors but several score fellow actors, including the two inevitables, Pat O'Brien and Frank McHugh. The film moments all revealed some typical aspect of Jim's screen persona, the two most appreciated being Mae Clarke with the grapefruit and his dancing "Yankee Doodle Dandy." Later he posed for press photographs with Mae, and as might be expected, someone stuck half a grapefruit in his hand. He gamely followed through with several menacing approaches to Mae and later said to her, "My God, they'll never let us alone on that one, will they?"

"Darling," she said, "I know how you hate it—and I hated it at the *time*—but I can't tell you how grateful I am for it now. What it means is that I can always get work. Talking to these casting directors today, all new to the business, and none of them knowing me from Adam—all I have to do is identify myself as the gal Cagney socked with the grapefruit, and I automatically get a *lot* of attention and frequently a job!" Jim was delighted for her.

Bob Montgomery, with his almost unlimited access to top Navy brass, together with Admiral Halsey's cooperation, made logistics for the film, *The*

*Gallant Hours*, comparatively easy. This was to be a combined Robert Montgomery–Cagney Productions effort although the latter organization existed only on paper. Bill Cagney had no interest in producing, but he did check out the details of his brother's contract. Montgomery insisted that the new ad hoc producing company be called A Cagney-Montgomery Production, and he took on the heavy task of directing.

In structuring his interpretation of Halsey, Jim said:

I knew I had one difficulty immediately. I had certain mannerisms, acting mannerisms that I'd built up through the years playing all those rough characters. So I had to lose those, and I told Bob whenever he even saw the hint of one to stop me and we'd shoot all over again. Naturally I watched Halsey very carefully when we were together, and I noticed something that I think is characteristic of great military leaders: they tend to make hardly any extraneous gestures at all. They are inevitably very self-contained men, so much depending on their demeanor and body language. They hold it in yet are consummately natural and honest in temperament. I'm talking of the *great* ones now. And that was my key to Bull Halsey.

*The Gallant Hours* is an overlong (115 minutes) treatment of how Admiral Halsey outguessed his superb tactician of an opponent, Admiral Yamamoto and thereby saved the newly liberated Guadalcanal from counterassault by the Japanese. The film would be utterly boring without Cagney's thoughtful performance. Nowhere in his career had he been called on to do so much by doing so little.

*The Gallant Hours,* after a while, seems to be an unending succession of dispatches brought to Halsey, all to be read, considered, pondered, acted upon, and it is a tribute to Cagney's skill that this reportorial format, which would defeat the average actor, works for him. There are very few actors who can make nonvocal thought meaningful and interesting. Cagney does so by the great actor's technique of actually thinking the necessary thoughts and letting them register naturally and unaffectedly on his features, opening himself up to these thoughts and these alone. Toward the end of *The Gallant Hours,* when he is increasingly alone in his command center, his acting becomes almost pure thought.

Cagney and Montgomery defeat the film's inherent static quality, the former by his acting, the latter by using voice-over commentary, shared by Art Gilmore and Montgomery himself. To further the narrative process emotionally, Montgomery employs the Roger Wagner Chorale throughout, but this becomes self-defeating when the music builds up minor moments

*The Gallant Hours*

that go nowhere, a typical example being when Halsey's orderly brings him a second cup of coffee. The *Times* of London chided Montgomery for allowing "a male voice chorus to moon incessantly over the sound track ludicrously opposed to the factual atmosphere."

The oddity of *The Gallant Hours* is that perhaps Cagney's finest acting job had to take place in a spiritless movie about a great armed force, in which the highlights are not the belching of great guns but the quiet ruminations of one man forced to consider grave matters of life and death that would affect thousands.

The critical reception for *The Gallant Hours* was almost universally positive, typical being Bosley Crowther's comment that the film "may very well irritate the patron who is looking for more explosive things [but] it comes out in [Montgomery's] direction as drama of intense restraint and power. But it is Mr. Cagney's performance, controlled to the last detail, that gives life and strong heroic stature to the principal figure in the film."

A quiet side note to the film, allowing a look at Cagney the man, comes from the film publicist and writer Burt Solomon:

In 1959 I was hired as a publicity apprentice by United Artists and, as lowest-ranking member of the department, drew most of the airport pickups and departures. In 1960 James Cagney did a publicity tour for *The Gallant Hours,* and I was sent to pick him up at the airport and bring him to The Players in Gramercy Park. I was very intimidated and nervous. He came walking down a ramp toward me with a bouncy step I recalled from his films. After introducing myself and retrieving his luggage, I accompanied him to the limousine. He knew the driver and greeted him warmly. At Mr. Cagney's invitation, I sat beside him in the back of the vehicle. With nothing to say, I felt like a kid from the Bronx, very awkward and unworldly. After several minutes he turned toward me, tapped me on the knee, and said something like "Sugar Ray is fighting tonight. What do you say we listen to it?" It was almost as though he sought permission. I knew boxing and readily agreed. The driver tuned in the fight. After each round Mr. Cagney engaged me in a discussion of what we had heard. Before many rounds elapsed, I was relaxed and we talked about the fight and boxing all the way to Gramercy Park. There was none of the gulf that exists between star and publicist. We said good-bye at The Players and that was the last time I saw him offscreen. He spoiled me. I naively expected everyone in the film industry to meet his standards of warmth and courtesy. I spent over twenty-two years in the business and worked with many "names" of the past and present. Few, if any, were as warm and courteous.

In 1960 the offer to do a Billy Wilder film in postwar divided Berlin excited Jim. He still had fond memories of his German professor at Columbia, Herr Mankiewicz, and felt a strong kinship with the language. "Near us in Yorkville was a German butcher," said Jim, "and that's where the Cagneys bought their meat. I frequently did that little job and I frankly delighted in pronouncing words like *Wurst.* So when *One, Two, Three* was suggested to me by Billy Wilder in a phone call, I felt a kinship because I liked not only the sound of *Wurst* but wurst itself, and all German food. I looked forward to the whole occasion."

This attitude did not last. *One, Two, Three* proved to be an ordeal, reminding him of the trouble he had had with Hal Wallis in the making of *Boy Meets Girl* twenty-three years before. At that time Wallis, in looking at the dailies, demanded that several scenes, already quick in tempo, be even more quickly paced. Cagney protested then, and did so again when Wilder insisted on more speed of delivery. But Wilder, not only director but coauthor of *One, Two, Three,* would brook no opposition. One scene, in which Cagney had to spiel off several pages of intricate dialogue while picking out shirts, ties, hat, and clothing for a young man to wear at his wedding, came a cropper. He had been given the dialogue the night before and was not secure with it and with one line in particular, "Where is the morning coat and striped trousers?" He would either bollix it up or not remember it. The complicating factor was that Wilder wanted the difficult little scene shot in one take.

Jim said in explanation of his difficulty, "The mechanics of learning. One line can bug you. I did a play once with Mary Boland. One night she blew a line. The next night, worrying about her line, I blew my own following line. After that I had trouble with that line every night. It's the rhythm." This scene in *One, Two, Three* had a rhythm Jim was unable to master, and Wilder was insistent on what he had specified. He was satisfied on the fifty-seventh take, and Jim was annoyed that even minuscule paraphrasing of Wilder's words had been verboten.

The plot of *One, Two, Three* is engaging for all its improbabilities. Cagney plays C. P. MacNamara, Coca-Cola's West Berlin representative, who is called on by the company president to take care of the boss's dithery daughter. She falls in love with a young Communist from East Berlin, marries him secretly, and becomes pregnant, all this before her parents arrive on a visit. Wanting a prestigious Coca-Cola post in England, MacNamara must regularize the situation before the boss arrives, and he does so by getting the boy expelled from East Berlin and into capitalist garb and employment just in time.

There are several Cagney "in" gags inserted by Wilder. MacNamara's office has a cuckoo clock with an Uncle Sam figurine that, when the hour strikes, comes out to wave the American flag to the tune of "Yankee Doodle Dandy," the tune MacNamara hums as he walks into his palatial home. At one point he threatens the young Communist with half a grapefruit, saying, "How would you like a little fruit for dessert?" Finally, an American soldier, played by Red Buttons, at one point does the Cagney shoulder shrug from *Angels with Dirty Faces.*

There is witty and sharp satire in *One, Two, Three* ("The race that produced the Taj Mahal, William Shakespeare, and striped toothpaste can't be all bad"), and some sight gags are funny (anti-American propaganda balloons, typical of which is one saying "Was Ist Los in Little Rock"). But Cagney, under Wilder's direction, keeps shouting his lines. The bellowing is endless. The pace is an unremitting gallop, and it wearies. Perhaps Wilder

*One, Two, Three*, with Pamela Tiffin and Horst Buchholz

maintained the pace because the material was so evanescent and fluffy that this seemed the only way to keep it afloat.

The role of the young Communist is played by Horst Buchholz, who has the unique distinction of being the only actor James Cagney actively disliked in all of his professional career. Said Cagney: "I got riled at S. Z. Sakall in *Yankee Doodle Dandy* for trying to steal a scene, but he was an incorrigible old ham who was quietly and respectfully put in his place by Mike Curtiz. No harm in the old boy. But this Horst Buchholz character I truly loathed. Had he kept on with his little scene-stealing didoes, I would have been forced to knock him on his ass, which I would have very much enjoyed doing."

Buchholz's selfishness as a player comes through in *One, Two, Three*. He is a sterling example of the actor who doesn't listen to fellow actors, who is clearly hearing only cues, waiting impatiently for his own lines to begin. "Seeing him again was one of the two or three reasons why I chose never to see *One, Two, Three* ever," said Jim. "I mean ever." He never did.

It was during the making of *One, Two, Three* that Jim decided to pack it in and never worry again about picking the wrong script and the wrong director as he had just done. He was finishing some interior shots on the film and, while waiting for a setup, walked out into the sunshine and saw that it was gorgeous. He walked back into the building and saw that it was not. That morning he had received a photograph of some friends standing on the deck of his boat, which he had lent them. Suddenly he felt a sweeping nostalgia for the boat and all the freedom it promised. He was through with acting. He meant it. At the time.

*One, Two, Three* got good reviews in the main. Stanley Kauffmann, despite some reservations about the force-fed farce, found it possessing "an over-all intelligent energy," and *Time* magazine said it was a "sometimes bewildered, often wonderfully funny exercise in nonstop nuttiness." The naysayers were led by Pauline Kael, who called the film "overwrought, tasteless and offensive—a comedy that pulls laughs the way a catheter draws urine. . . . Wilder hits his effects hard and sure; he's a clever, lively director whose work lacks feeling or passion or grace or beauty or elegance. His eye is on the dollar, or rather on success, on the entertainment values that bring in dollars. But he has never before, except perhaps in a different way in *Ace in the Hole,* exhibited such a brazen contempt for people."

Among whom, Cagney thought, he could count himself. "I did the best I could for Wilder," he said, "although I thought his tempo for my part of the picture was wrong, wrong, wrong. But he was overwhelmingly the dictator-director. Every little jot and tittle had to be done in his way. I don't think that's the way to get the best out of your actors, at least out of the ones who've been around the block a time or two. But maybe that's just his style with people he didn't like, and I got to know he didn't like me."

Jim returned to the States with only one ambition for the rest of his days: to paint. "People. Flowers. Barn doors. Anything."

# 24 · Memories

Shortly after returning to Beverly Hills in 1961 after making *One, Two, Three,* Jim was interviewed by Hedda Hopper and, as always with any reporter's questions, answered fully and with candor. He had no respect for or interest in Hopper as a gossip columnist. But he liked her:

She sort of reminded me of what Jack Barrymore called her great rival Louella Parsons: "a quaint old udder." But Hedda was kind of cute, even when along in years, and I respected her as an old pro in the business. She was a former chorus girl and made her way up the ladder to the movies, doing supporting leads until she quit and became a newspaperwoman. My principal interest in her was that she had been George M. Cohan's leading lady in the 1917 film that was made of one of his best plays, *Seven Keys to Baldpate.* Also, she asked questions directly, expected an honest answer, and, if she didn't get it, would hound you until she did.

Cagney was direct in this 1961 interview:

H. H.: Who is the world's greatest man?

CAGNEY: Ever? Christ.

H. H.: Greatest *living* man?

CAGNEY: (*Pauses*) Albert Schweitzer. He's kind of a stand-in for The Fella.

H. H.: In a town where names come and go like lightning, how have you managed to stay on top for thirty-one years?

CAGNEY: Who says I'm on top?

H. H.: I say you are. You're as big today as you ever were. And you were pretty big in the era when you played gangster roles at Warners. How have you managed to stay up there?

CAGNEY: I don't think there's any definite answer. Lots of luck, and not doing too many pictures.

H. H.: And hard work. You never stopped working.

CAGNEY: That's right. I tried to vary the fare as much as possible.

H. H.: So many big name stars complain about losing their privacy. You've managed to keep your private life quiet. How did you manage to do it?

CAGNEY: Probably by staying at home.

H. H.: You don't go to night clubs?

CAGNEY: No.

H. H.: And I know you don't go to many parties. What do you think about the publicity seekers? And they howl about their names in print after they've started a brawl. They are furious the next day.

CAGNEY: I think it's just damned poor judgment. They can solve it all by staying out of such places. If you must fight, do it at home.

Hopper said that there was a rumor floating around that he had been offered the lead in a planned Broadway musical based on *The Front Page,* and was it true? Yes, he said, it was true, and he would no more take the job than fly. She asked him where he got the "tenacity" to keep on doing his job. The answer to that one was easy: "Vaudeville. You had ten or fifteen minutes to do your act. When you got on, you did it. You performed or you didn't eat, and you were always ready." She asked him why the Irish made the best actors, and he said he didn't know they were. Why, she persisted, did the English actors like Olivier and Guinness make such fine actors? "Hard work. No one works harder." She asked him what he thought of people like Liz Taylor and Marlon Brando getting two million dollars for one picture.

H. H.: Holding up the companies, getting [to work] when they feel like it. Answer that, I dare you.

CAGNEY: (*Laughing*) I don't dare. (*Shrugging*) It's their way of doing it.

H. H.: I don't think Marlon Brando's that good. Do you?

CAGNEY: I don't know. I've never seen him. [*He did, years later, and liked him.*]

Within a month after returning to California, Jim had been offered six scripts, but he explained to the agents involved that he needed a long rest. He was going to announce his retirement gradually. Now he had ample time for family matters, mostly to do with his siblings. Casey, his daughter, had been at college for some time, but left to marry a writer, Jack Thomas. Jim Junior had difficulty finding a role in life and decided to try the U.S. Marines.

Jeanne Cagney, following the failure of her first marriage, married Professor Jack Morrison, a distinguished teacher of theater at the University of California, Los Angeles. The Morrisons had two girls, and Jeanne became the official fashion commentator on NBC-TV's *Queen for a Day.* She told the Hearst columnist Jack O'Brian: "With time so limited, we have to decide where to place our values. In our family it's family first, and our jobs and friends who are so precious to us. It leaves no time for midnight champagne parties." The Morrisons lived in Benedict Canyon in convenient commuting distance from NBC-TV and UCLA. Jim was close to them in familial fashion.

In speaking of Jim at this time, Jeanne said: "He's shy only in large groups. Our idea of fun is to get together at home with close friends like Frank McHugh, Pat O'Brien, Eddie Foy, Jr., or old pals from the Warner Brother days. Then the show biz stories, singing, dancing, jokes, reminiscences and warmly wonderful family and friendly memories are hard to top—or stop."

The family gatherings—Jim, his brothers and sister, and offspring—were usually held on Thursday nights. Drs. Harry and Ed both had retired, and Bill was in the real estate business. The Thursday evenings were mainly musical—Jim on the guitar, and all doing the old songs their mother had encouraged them to learn as children. The Cagneys were purely home folk. "That was Mama's doing," said Jeanne. "She'd say, 'Just who do you think you are?' in just the right way to keep any of us from taking it big. God bless her for that and for everything."

When he was east, Jim began to spend more and more time at The Players. He stayed at the club on his visits, then found an apartment almost next door, at 34 Gramercy Park East. Being in New York seemed to stimulate his writing of verse, and he had vague thoughts of returning to Ireland and staying awhile to research the O'Caignes. Certainly Ireland's troubles disturbed him more and more, after his experience with *Shake Hands with the Devil.* He wrote:

> The men of Tyrone and all the six counties
> (Intransigent seems to describe them)
> Supply all the bounties from all of those counties
> So England continues to bribe them.

> Elizabeth I, the queen called virgin,
> Set up the haves and have-nots
> By usurping the lands of the old Irish clans
> And gave them to Anglos and Scots.

> Essex and Raleigh and Cromwell,
> All Englishmen of distinction,
> Had an overall plan for the old Irish clans
> And the overall plan was extinction.

So you want us to take them to our hearts
And treat them as brother to brother.
A poor foolish dream and futile, my friend,
For they're not Irish, they're "other."

It was at this time that he bought a new farm and dispossessed himself of another. "I'm farm crazy!" he told a friend. The farm at Millbrook, New York, while satisfactory in itself, had begun to gather (for him) too many neighbors. A number of developers were beginning to cluster in the neighborhood. Jim had a particular hatred of developers. He said, "The only thing these bastards develop is the size of their pocketbooks." He drove around Dutchess County and finally found the farm of his dreams near Stanfordville, New York—at first 120 acres, eventually 711. He named it Verney Farm, from Willie's surname and his. They moved into an attractive little white house near the road, but as Cagney fans began to track him down, he built a new house on a nearby hill, just above a 6-acre lake. He designed the house himself, a very simple and small one with seven small rooms, filled with memorabilia.

He made it into a working farm, bred Scottish Highland cattle as well as Morgan horses, put up a barn and horse show ring, grew hay and sold the surplus to neighbors. It was at this tranquil time that his brother Harry died. Jim was not surprised: "I sensed years before that Harry would not live to be an old man. Gone at sixty-seven, and all because he overworked as a youth putting himself through college. Brother Ed died too at about the same age, and for the same reason. A real heartache with both of them gone. It made me realize that I owed it to Willie to take care of myself, so I had a thorough physical, and I was OK—dancing keeps one fit—but there was my old enemy, overweight. I fought that bastard unendingly."

His verse became more and more important to him. He found spiritual comfort in it. As he told Hedda Hopper, he had come to realize that for him Christ's life and words were ever meaningful as guides for his life and that a man neglected spirituality at serious risk to his completeness as a human. He never forgot the afternoon in 1924 when he was cutting down a tree to make a clearing for a house the single tax colony was building in New Jersey:

I had been using an ax and later a handsaw to fell the tree. When I was done, I sat on the stump and looked at another one nearby. On that stump was a little spider reaching up to catch something far too small for me to see. He accomplished that and sat there contentedly munching. And there I sat, thinking of his tiny world, when it occurred to me that there are great powers way far above *me*, looking at infinitesimally little me, sitting on my little stump, thinking of me just the way I was thinking of that spider, and all of us living in the great God-designed pattern of many universes, all different, yet all the same, and all of us needing to understand that and to live in harmony with that. I put those thoughts into a little verse:

All space is filled with wondrous things,
Unseen by human eye.
Before us hover kings and queens,
With realms that float and fly.
It was wise of them to make a choice,
And decide to remain invisible,
For early in the game they found,
To be seen is to be divisible.
Finding the world is full of hate,
Afflicting alike the small, the great,
Knowing no bounds, or social stations,
Enveloping towns, destroying nations,
Refusing all manner of Christian teaching,
Laughing aloud at the earnest beseeching
Of thoughtful men in thankless jobs;
Cynically calling them deluded slobs,
For presuming to hold that The Christ is living,
And all that's good is of God's own giving.

One of the things distinctly not of God's own giving was the threat in 1969 to Martha's Vineyard's beauty and rewarding insularity. Jim, and people of his psychological bent, had been coming to the island for their very good reasons. In his words:

Anybody who chooses to live on an island is seeking isolation. This single facet of the personality is a common thread; it is a thing that holds them together because they *choose* to be there. They are essentially of the same kidney. At the time I came, 1936, I was the only actor. There were quite a few artists, and the thing we all shared was: to get there again. And soon and for as long as possible. So the Vineyard grew to be very popular, and that's when I started, quite involuntarily, to pull away from it. . . . In 1969 I got a wire from a Mrs. Jones on the south shore saying, "They're going to tear down sixty-five acres of trees to put in a jet port." So then we went to work. I wired Senator Kennedy. I wired everybody. You know, I belittle the influence of actors in these matters, but now and then it works.

He sent a wire to the Ways and Means Committee of the Massachusetts Senate and everyone else he could think of with influence, pointing out that there was this upcoming "destruction of all that is natural and worthwhile." The airport was stopped. Jim said: "Then, not long after, I went to a dinner gathering, and here was this big six-foot asshole, who said to me gruffly, 'What's this I hear about you objecting to the jet airstrip?' I said, 'You got it right.'

I knew this guy flew. I asked him how often he used airplanes to get to the island.

'Twice a year,' he said, adding angrily, 'You can't stop progress.'

I said, 'Knocking down sixty-five acres of trees is progress?' "

The man seemed on the verge of apoplexy, and Jim walked away. He learned later that the man had a bad heart. It was a good thing Jim had not started a real argument: "If I'd pushed him any further, he might have died on the spot, giving us some very bad publicity." To a small degree Jim was experiencing disenchantment with the Vineyard.

In 1967 Jim suffered the tremendous loss of Spencer Tracy. The Boys Club was no more, with Jim and Frank McHugh in the East, and Tracy had been in the throes of illness under the very good care of Katharine Hepburn. Ralph Bellamy came East frequently for theater and television duties, and Pat O'Brien was touring his one-man show cross-country. Jim called Tracy periodically but found him hard to reach. He was grateful to Hepburn for her continuing care of his old friend, who Jim considered was the victim of a severe form of perpetual tension as the result of a bad thyroid problem. When Tracy's death was announced, Jim wept.

In 1971 Garson Kanin's book *Tracy and Hepburn* was published, and Jim was appalled at the idea of such a book appearing during the lifetime of Louise Tracy, Spencer's wife. They had been separated for years, but Tracy, a devout Catholic, had never contemplated divorce. But what upset Jim most profoundly about the book was Kanin's dwelling on the gradual loosening of the once-close ties between Cagney and Tracy. "On many issues," said Kanin, "Tracy and Cagney found themselves seriously at odds. The phone calls grew shorter, the time between visits longer, and eventually they saw little or nothing of each other. Spencer never gave up on Jimmy, and kept alive the memory of their great days. And each time I met Cagney anywhere his first question would be, 'How's old Spence?' "

These words angered Jim deeply. He said to this writer:

What would he know about what went on between me and Spence?

What Kanin is saying is that I gave up on Spence after a while, that

I stopped calling him, and so we lost touch. Bullshit. I had hardly ever called him because he was almost never at the number I was given, and so it became a kind of ritual between us that he would call *me*. At any hour of day or night. I knew this. I understood this, just as he did too. I welcomed those calls for as long as they came, and sometimes they would come at two in the morning. Never any salutation, never any "Hello, Jim," or "Hi" or anything similar. He'd just begin to talk as if it were a continuation of last time, which it frequently was. He'd start out with something like "Ever hear that story about John Drew and the green porcelain piss pot?" or "Just been thinking about that beanery on Eighth Avenue and their corned beef. So tender, so expressively inexpensive." And so on.

As for my calling him less and less, again bullshit. *He* started to call *me* less and less, I always assumed, for reasons of health. Pat [O'Brien] said he began to get fewer calls too, and there was no one closer to Spence than Pat. And as to Kanin's implying that Spence and I were at loggerheads because Spence was liberal and I became a Republican, *triple* bullshit. Spence always respected other people's moral and political commitments even if they were a hundred eighty degrees different from his—as long as those commitments were honestly held, as mine certainly were. Spence was not only a great actor, he was also a great *heart*, and a great heart does not turn away from old friends because they are different from you. The reverse is true. Speaking plainly, I loved the man. And still do.

One matter less distressing, but irritating nonetheless, arose periodically in Jim's retirement: sham Cagneys. There was one persistent phony who surfaced in the early 1970s and cut a wide swath among people in high places, people one would have thought easily capable of recognizing this fraud. James Bacon reported that in 1972 one of the screen's most imitated actors was being imitated too well by a slickster in the South. "I have always loved Sammy Davis doing 'You dirty rat!' " Jim said to Bacon, "but someone sent me a copy of the *Miami Herald* in which the character who looks like me and calls himself Jimmy Cagney was given the keys of the city by the mayor of Hollywood, Florida. What is worse, it showed him with a group of young girls. Did he do me credit or discredit there? It's worrisome."

In 1973 began the first of many Cagney retrospective film showings across the land, principally in universities and film societies. That year the New York Cultural Center showed a wide variety of the films, winning from *The*

*New Yorker*'s Penelope Gilliatt a memorable declaration of Cagney's essential sour-sweet film personality. She spoke of the star whose "packed body and the curious sweetness around the mouth, contradicted by eyes that have a satanic slant to them, introduced an anomaly that made his rival, Humphrey Bogart, look like a Claudius overwhelmed by conscience. Without a worried crease in his forehead, Cagney initiated in gangster films the notion of the villain with virtuous instincts."

The ultimate professional tribute to Cagney came on Wednesday, March 13, 1974, when he received the American Film Institute's Life Achievement Award at the Century Plaza Hotel in Los Angeles. George Stevens, Jr., head of the AFI, and members of the governing board had selected Jim to be the designate a year after honoring John Ford. The tribute to Ford was warranted, but he was not a man beloved as Cagney was. More than 1,360 people paid $125 a ticket to attend. Most of them were people in the industry, but there also were a number of hard-core film fans who went about seeking autographs among celebrities. For the money you got not only the chance to gawk at dozens of stars but a pretty decent plate of prime rib, asparagus, and cake topped by a Yankee Doodle top hat.

There were ample celebrities: Loretta Young, Mae West, Doris Day, Clint Eastwood, Paul Newman, Joanne Woodward, Gene Kelly, Howard Hawks, Danny Kaye, Frank Capra, Johnny Carson, Allen Jenkins, Mervyn LeRoy, Rosalind Russell, Desi Arnaz, Debbie Reynolds, Cesar Romero, Mick Jagger, Hal Wallis, John Lennon, George Burns, Jonathan Winters, Steve McQueen, William Wellman, Groucho Marx, and many others, including former Cagney leading ladies Ruby Keeler, Mae Clarke, Jane Bryan, Joan Leslie, Rosemary De Camp, Brenda Marshall, Barbara Stanwyck, and Joan Blondell. It was, said one observer, "the most star-studded gathering in Hollywood history. If a bomb had been dropped on the assemblage, Hollywood would have been wiped out."

The entire affair lasted five hours, what with intermittent delays caused by the technical needs of CBS-TV personnel who were taping everything for a ninety-minute version to be broadcast nationally five evenings later. The Paul Keyes Production Company staged the event with A. C. Lyles as coordinator. At 7:00 p.m. in the hotel's Presidential Suite there was a leadoff cocktail party, part of which Jim attended to chat with his old buddy Ronald Reagan, then governor of California. Reagan ordered a scotch, and Jim kidded him: "You will never get to the White House like that, bub."

The guests sifted down to the ballroom to be at their tables by 8:00 p.m. Jim arrived as scheduled at 8:15, to be greeted by a standing ovation and

Nelson Riddle's orchestra pulsing out "Yankee Doodle Dandy," everyone clapping in time. He and Willie walked to his table, at which sat Ronald and Nancy Reagan, Mr. and Mrs. Ralph Bellamy, Los Angeles Mayor Tom Bradley and wife, Eloise O'Brien (Pat was ill), Frank and Dorothy McHugh, Casey Cagney Thomas and husband, Jack, and Mr. and Mrs. James Cagney, Jr. Brother Bill Cagney was ill and could not be present.

An AFI board member introduced Charlton Heston to the assembly, and he promptly read from a photocopy of a 1921 *Variety* review: "A new act, Parker, Rand and Cagney. Two boys and a girl with a skit idea that gets nowhere have a turn without the semblance of a punch. There are no laughs and the songs mean little. One of the boys, James Cagney, can dance a bit. Small time is its only chance." After the laugh died down, Heston went on to state the purpose of the evening and to announce proudly that all sixty-five Cagney films were now accounted for in the AFI Collection at the Library of Congress. He then introduced the evening's host, Frank Sinatra, who described Jim as "part poet, painter, conservationist, humanitarian . . . and he's also got a pretty good sense of humor. Once in a Beverly Hills restaurant I walked up behind him and said to the back of his head, 'Ma's dead, you dirty rat.' He never turned around but simply and quietly said, 'Francis, that's the worst imitation I ever heard in my life.' "

Sinatra went on to say that in 1938 he was working as a singing waiter at a New Jersey roadhouse, probably making more money in tips than Cagney was getting at Warners. Jim smiled at this, and Sinatra said, "I should know. I later worked for Warner." This was the cue to speak of the one notable absence of the evening, Jack Warner, not present because of "ill health," another dubious assertion. Sinatra said he once asked Jim how his villain could still be so attractive to audiences. Jim's reply was: "Francis, always sprinkle the goodies along the way. Be as tough as you want, but sprinkle the goodies for laughs here and there. 'Cause anything they can laugh at, they can't hate."

This was followed by the houselights dimming and the showing of clips of two highly contrasted films, *The Strawberry Blonde* and *White Heat.* Lights up, and next on the program was George C. Scott, who spoke of "the kind of man" Jim was, quoting a description of General Lee as being entirely appropriate to Jim: "What he seemed he was: the wholly human gentleman, the essential elements of whose positive character were two and only two: simplicity and spirituality." This was followed by more movie clips, one of which was the Cohan-Foy table dance scene from *The Seven Little Foys,* the proper cue for Bob Hope to appear. Typical of his gags were "A love scene to Cagney was when he let the other guy live; he always played tough guys—you know, the parts now played by Tatum O'Neal," and "I wonder how Jimmy would do today. I can't see him making a film like *Last Tango in Paris.* Pat O'Brien would never give him absolution."

Sinatra then introduced for at-table bows Joan Blondell, George Raft, Frank McHugh, Ralph Bellamy, Allen Jenkins, Governor Reagan, and Jim's children, explaining that Bill Cagney could not be present but paying him ample tribute. Sinatra then introduced Willie as Jim's former vaudeville partner, "and they have been starring together as husband and wife. Will everybody who believes in love clap for Mrs. James Cagney!" Willie, exuding shyness, rose to tremendous applause. She said years later, "I'm glad I went through it for Jim's sake, but never again."

Next introduced was Doris Day, who praised Jim for the happiness their work together had brought her, adding, "And anyone who ever worked with you knows you're more than just an actor. You don't play a character, you live the character. You breathe life into your own performance and make the rest of us look really good." Tears glistened in her eyes. Lights dimmed, and the film clip of her singing "You Made Me Love You" followed.

The evening could hardly go by without the grapefruit scene from *The Public Enemy* being shown, followed by Mae Clarke speaking from her table: "It was forty-three years ago that Jimmy pushed that grapefruit in my face. And although I don't think he'd try it again, I made sure my table wasn't too close to his tonight. But seriously, Jim, everyone who ever worked with you loved you, baby. We did two films together besides *Public Enemy*—*Lady Killer* and *Great Guy.* And Jimmy, you're both!"

This was followed by an acutely embarrassing episode. Shirley MacLaine and Jack Lemmon came onstage to present their mutual tribute, Lemmon apologizing for the fact that he seemed to have lost a button from his dinner jacket. MacLaine pulled his coat together while giving her tribute, and Lemmon, ignoring his prepared speech, began to ramble on about his early days in television. He seemed to be (in the words of a *New York Daily News* reporter present) "feeling no pain." This discoursing went on for some time, and its relevance to Cagney was moot. Suddenly a heckler, wearing a green bandanna on his head, rose and shouted, "Lemmon! Come on. Get to the goddamned point, and get the hell off the stage—and shut up!" This was the director Sam Peckinpah, also far past feeling any pain. MacLaine grabbed the microphone and began to speak of Cagney's art. Lemmon tried to get the mike back, but she finally contrived to get him off-stage with her. Lemmon later said he was suffering from overmedication for hernia. Sam Peckinpah went downstairs for another drink at the hotel's public bar, argued with the bartender, got in a fight with him, and spent the night in jail.

There were more film clips. Frank Gorshin did his "you dirty rat" Cagney imitation, to be joined by Kirk Douglas and George Segal singing "Give My Regards to Broadway." Mayor Tom Bradley spoke, Governor Reagan spoke, Cicely Tyson spoke (to introduce the three young recipients of AFI's newly established James Cagney Fellowships), and Sinatra sang an amusing parody of "All the Way" as a Cagney tribute.

George Stevens, Jr., presented Jim with the Lifetime Achievement Award, and as Jim came to the stage to accept it, he did a few dance steps. Reaching the lectern, emotion showing, he said, "I'm a wreck," then gave his speech, every word of which was his, every word of which he had written out in large letters (obviating the need for glasses) on his own laundry shirt cardboards. He said:

When my friend A. C. Lyles told me of the plans that the AFI had for this evening, it gave me pause. I said to him. "You know, this is not the kind of thing I do every day. What will they expect of me?" And he said, "Oh, well, all you have to do is uh, uhhm, huhm," and I said, "What's that?" He said, "All you have to do is . . . hmm, uh, hmm." So I'm saying to you right now, all of you, with a little bit of necessary emphasis, hmm, uh, hmmm.

About the award, I'm very grateful for it. But why don't we just say for now that I'm merely the custodian, holding it for all those wonderful guys and gals who worked over the years to bring about this night for me. I'm thanking you for them and for me. Now, George—that's George Stevens—told me in a letter early on that one of the fundamental aims of the AFI was to establish motion pictures as an art form. Art. I'm a little bit hipped on the thing myself, and have been for a long time. And this brought to mind a work written by John Masefield, the English poet laureate. He wrote it with his pen dipped in a bit of vitriol, and I'm going to read it to you now.

What is the hardest task of art?
To clear the ground and make a start.
Midst wooden head and iron heart.

To sing, to the stopped adder's ear.
To tell the tale with none to hear
And paint what none else reckons dear.

To dance, or carve, or build or strive
Among the dead and half-alive
Whom greeds impel and terrors drive.

Now you, my English dancers, you
Began our English joy anew
In sand, with neither rain nor dew.

Oh, may you prosper, till the race
Is all one rapture at your grace
And England, Beauty's dwelling place.

Then you will knew what Shakespeare knew:
That when the millions want the few
Those can make heaven here, and do.

I like that. [*Applause.*] Art has many definitions. The one I like best is: "Art is life plus. Life plus caprice. Where the simple declarative sentence becomes a line of Shakespearean poetry. Where a number of musical notes strung together become a Beethoven sonata. Where a walk, done in cadence by a Fred Astaire or Edward Villella or Suzanne Farrell, becomes an exciting dance. That's art." That definition is given in a chapter on art by William Ernest Hocking in a book called *Strength of Men and Nations*. It's worth reading. I recommend it, because of the way art affects our everyday lives. Every time we walk out of the house in the morning, we are looking at architecture. We are looking at people doing things that are essentially themselves. What they're doing should be of great interest to everybody from an artistic point of view. Because if you look at it that way, you are holding the wonder we were born with.

Now I have a great many thanks to spread about this evening. We all know an event like this doesn't get itself on. It is the result of a lot of dedicated people working at peak pitch for a great many days. So Frankie—Frank Sinatra, one of the neighbors' children—thanks for the song. How many copies will it sell? Mmmmmm. And Ted Ashley, George Stevens, Sue Taurog, Chuck Heston, Mr. Scott, dear Doris Day, Bob Hope, Shirley MacLaine, Miss Tyson, Frank Gorshin—oh, Frankie, just in passing. I never said: "Mmmm, you dirty rat!" What I actually did say was "Judy, Judy, Judy!" And thank you, Mr. Segal, big Duke Wayne, bless him, and Kirk Douglas. And one more thing, Frankie Gorshin, that hitching of the trousers. I got that from a fella who hung out on the corner of Seventy-eighth

Street and First Avenue. I was about twelve years old, and he was most interesting to me. Because that's all he did [*doing the pants hitch-up movement*] all day. When somebody would greet him, he wouldn't deign to say hello; he just stood back and did this [*repeats the hitch-up*]. Now let's face it, we are all indebted to that fella. He was a type. And we had them—oh, how we did have them!

I must express my gratitude to that group from my early days at Warners—Joanie Blondell, at the risk of repetition. I think you'll bear with me. Bette Davis, Olivia De Havilland, and little Mae Clarke, who got the citrus massage. [*He looks at Mae Clarke.*] Mae, I'm glad we did not use the omelet which was called for in one of the early scripts. I'll bet you're glad too! At any rate, *that* would have been messy.

The other friends and coworkers of the early times: my old friend Frankie McHugh; Pat O'Brien, who isn't here tonight, but Eloise, bless her, and she's here with her son, Terry; and Ralph Bellamy, Allen Jenkins, George Tobias, Alan Hale, Billy Wellman, Lloyd Bacon, Bob Montgomery, Raoul Walsh, the unforgettable Mike Curtiz. [*Laughter from the Warner Brothers contingent.*] Howard Hawks, Bill Keighley, and Harvey Perry, a stuntman who hung a cauliflower on my ear, in the first fight I had in pictures. I remember him well. Also Jack. Jack Warner, who gave me a name I shall always cherish—affectionately, mind you—"The Professional Againster."

But we're old now and full of understanding, and that's all water over the dam. Am I right, Bill? My brother Bill. My sister, Jeanne. [*Jim chokes up.*] Gotta hold on, boy. And all those Cagneys who over the years pulled their share of the burden—through those long and troubled years. There were many.

And the names, the names, the names of my youth. Lagerhead Quinlavan, Artie Klein, Pete Leyden, Jake Bodkin, Specks Torporcer, Brother O'Mara, Picky Houlihan! They were all part of a very stimulating early environment which produced that unmistakable touch of the gutter without which this evening might never have happened at all. I bless them. I bless Paul Keyes and A. C. Lyles for their labor. And bless you!

# 25 · *Cagney by Cagney*

There is now the need for first-person singular. Before 1973 I knew Jim Cagney only through stories told of him by my old friends Pat O'Brien and Frank McHugh, and they were as one in this: Cagney was essentially a shy, retiring, although hardly reclusive man, kindly, generous, and very bright. All this I found deeply true, and more.

For a number of years Doubleday and Company, the country's largest publisher, had been after Cagney to write his autobiography, his reply invariably being "I can't write, and who cares about my life?" In time Sam Vaughan, Doubleday's editorial head, and Ken McCormick, the company's famous chief editor, who had brought many show business biographies to life, convinced Cagney that a responsible ghostwriter would do the writing as he wanted to see it done and that his life was more than worthy of record. Jim then asked that his then son-in-law, a writer, be assigned the job. This was done, but eventually the son-in-law, chiefly a writer of fiction, withdrew, and I was chosen for the job. The only stipulation I made was that I was not to revise anyone else's work. I must start from scratch, and this meant meeting Cagney as soon as was practicable.

On September 11, 1974, my phone rang. "Hello, this is Jim Cagney." It sounded just like Jim Cagney; the voice was also soft, what one usually calls "well spoken."

I grew very nervous. This was the actor I most admired. Revered. I blurted out, "I feel like I'm talking to Molière."

He laughed. "Yeah. Molière Paskudnik," the first of his many uses of Yiddish to me. A *paskudnik* is a no-good punk. I relaxed. That was what one did in his company, relaxed. It was his way of living offscreen.

We arranged for me to visit him at Verney Farm later that month, and I drove there from Michigan with my fifteen-year-old son, Linny, who (sorry, it must be said) was already at that age a marvel with intricate tape recorders, rich in understanding of things mechanical early denied me. Jim was only momentarily surprised to see me showing up with a boy but watched with admiring amazement while Linny set up the machine, adjusted the microphone, and left us to talk as he went outside to play with Lady, the Cagneys' dog.

In retrospect I could hardly have expected anything from Jim but the utter naturalness of his demeanor. Yet for the first hour of our talk I asked questions warily, not wanting to intrude on matters in his personal life he might not want to discuss. I soon saw he was willing to discuss almost anything, and when off-the-record subjects came up, he would point to the tape recorder and I would switch off. We soon developed a clear understanding: he saw at once the need for giving me full background information on every personal and professional subject we covered. I explained that I would ask him questions that might seem to be excessive but that biographical inquiry of any value had to be done in just this way. Communication between us was at once made easier in one area, show business vocabulary. I had been an actor since childhood, and he had no need to explain theater and film terminology.

Jim answered all my questions incisively and was highly voluble, going into peripheral matters that always were fascinating even if not directly germane to the immediate subject. He used the usual male profanity and did not stint in his use of colorful vulgarisms to describe people and events. Yet his syntax was efficient, sturdy, and accurate. His vocabulary was large ("prolix" and "fatuity" were used in the first minutes), and I soon learned he loved words. He had a passion for poetry. He was not a compulsive dictionary searcher like Charlie Chaplin, who scanned the pages just to pick up esoteric words he could use to impress people, most of all himself. With Jim, it was a matter of bringing to meaningful life what his best teacher in grade school had dinned into her students: "Words give you the strength and the means to live well and in harmony with the world."

Jim always had a well-thumbed dictionary at his side. Once we were talking of early memories, and I inadvertently used the word "eidetic," for which I apologized, not being, I hoped, a Chaplin word dropper. Jim would have none of the apology and pounced upon the word, telling me not to define it so he could have the pleasure of looking it up. He did so at once. "Eidetic" is a biographer's word, one I learned from a patron saint of our brotherhood, the witty and learned Alden Whitman, chief obituarist of *The*

*New York Times* for decades. "Eidetic" refers to vividly experienced and well-remembered images, usually from childhood.

Jim looked at me after having found the word and said, "Christ, if ever there was a word, and adjective, applicable to my memories, this is it." This in turn flowed into his speaking of his earliest memories, speaking not just of those he wanted to use or that had a specific point, but all of them sharply drawn and amply eidetic. Some of them were immensely saddening, like the little blond boy, a Botticelli figure, who would go out almost every day in the Cagney neighborhood and forage through the neighbors' garbage pails for food. Then there was the haunted-face boy Jim knew, who ran screaming down the block with a knife sticking in his back. Jim did not want those images in his autobiography. "Bad enough that I still think of them at times," he said. But there were the many and warmly remembered compensatory memories, most triggered by word association.

He said:

Whenever I hear someone called a horse's ass, I don't think that guy is being ill used at all, for a very particular reason. As a special treat when I was a little one, I'd be allowed to sit next to the driver of our local butcher shop's wagon as he delivered his wares. He and I sat high up there behind the biggest, fattest horse's rump you ever saw in your life, and for many years I don't think I saw a prettier sight. I've got an instinct to love horses, and here was this gigantic pair of buttocks, moving left-right, right-left, as Joe—the horse's name— plop-plopped down the street. It was to me, a fascinating sight, and as I analyze it now, I think what I found so attractive about it was that all that tremendous strength, moving along so briskly, was gentle and controlled. A gentle giant, Joe. I've always found that idea of the gentle giant very moving—someone with great strength who is quiet and controlled. How's that for an eidetic experience!

Jim began his working day with me at 10:00 in the morning, and we taped until about 12:30 p.m., when we broke for lunch, a meal he always prepared. He was a superb cook and could take the simplest meats and vegetables and turn them into very tasty dishes. Linny and I watched him with close attention, trying to remember the sequence of putting a dish together. He would take something elementary like a pork butt, cut it up, slather it over with brown mustard, then add currant jelly or some such, broil it, bring it out of the oven, then place the slices on his favorite bread, *Kommissbrot*—commissary bread of German origin—which he bought in nearby Stanfordville.

After lunch we would walk down to his little lake while he talked knowledgeably about the wildflowers growing there or about the local varieties of birds. Our afternoon talk session lasted for three hours, and although Jim was clearly not an old man in appearance or manner—he was seventy-five—I knew he was tired, and my son and I returned to our motel for my sorting out of notes and for dinner. I wanted the Cagneys to feel no obligations to us in respect to dinner or beyond, so I always emphasized my need to go over the day's work in the evening.

We saw little of Willie. She naturally respected our working hours and lunches, she was proud of Jim's cooking abilities, saying he was a much better cook than she was or ever would be. A tiny woman, barely five feet, she had lost the blond prettiness of her early and middle years. But she was as bright as her husband, possibly brighter, and it was clear that she considered her chief task in life the care and maintenance of James Cagney, to make the way smooth for him. This was also the way he felt about her.

One afternoon as she prepared to go shopping, she walked past us at the kitchen table, where we invariably worked, and asked him what he wanted at the store. He told her, "Oh, red pop, I guess." As she walked out to the car, he looked after her with what I can properly call *interest*. One knew he not only loved this woman but was beguiled by her, in this, the fifty-second year of their marriage. I saw this look on his face scores of times.

After many hours of taping, I knew I had enough material to begin work on the book. In view of all the books about him then in work or in print, he wanted his to be called *Cagney by Cagney*. He said, "Pat [O'Brien] insists I call it *The Faraway Fella,* which he says describes me perfectly, but my title is a little more practical and to the point."

Linny and I packed our bags one Sunday morning and prepared to drive back to Michigan, stopping by the farm to say good-bye.

"Do me a favor, son," Jim said to Linny. "Will you do that?"

"Yes, sure, Mr. Cagney."

"I want you to tell your mother that she raised a mighty fine young man. Don't forget."

He has never forgotten.

After typing out all our conversations on the tapes and sorting out the sequence of his life, I found an essential pattern for *Cagney by Cagney*, and for some months we communicated by letter, tapes, and phone. He and Willie made their seasonal journey to Beverly Hills, and he called to say that if I had any kind of question to telephone or write. "I'll get on to it right away," he said.

I sent him my outline, which he approved, then a few weeks later a couple of chapters. He liked them, but he was disturbed about one thing. "Aren't there an awful lot of *I*'s in it?" he said.

"Pretty hard to get rid of them in an autobiography," I said.

"Well, yes."

He was still dubious. I thought, how utterly typical.

Then trouble in paradise. A British writer named Michael Freedland, through his publisher, Stein and Day, announced to the world that his book, *Cagney: A Biography*, was to be published shortly. "That goddamned *pisher* [Yiddish for "squirt"]," Jim roared over the phone. I had never heard him truly angry, and it was impressive. "I gave this guy Freedland an hour's interview after the AFI dinner on the clear understanding that this was not to be for a biography but was to be used for a BBC broadcast. I'm getting my lawyer on it right now." His lawyer immediately filed an affidavit in State Supreme Court, Manhattan, arguing that Jim "was very upset with the prospect of the bunk in the book moving toward publication as a purported factual review of my life. [It is] full of inaccuracies, falsities and invented dialogue." He had read the galleys of Freedland's book.

Justice Thomas C. Chimera thereupon granted a restraining order on Stein and Day, ordering the publisher to appear in court to show why an injunction barring publication should not be issued. The Cagney argument had been that Freedland gave the book "the ring of truth" by "reference to the interview . . . thereby leading the reader to believe I cooperated in the preparation of the book."

Stein and Day duly appeared, and a week later Justice S. A. Fine of the New York State Supreme Court lifted the temporary order barring the company from publishing the Freedland book but ordering the publisher to revise the biography's acknowledgments so as to inform the reader that the book was not done with Cagney's approval. In the event, *Cagney: A Biography* turned out to be weak tea, inconsequential in scope and detail, containing almost nothing of value biographically. The book was little more than an expanded magazine article, printed with very ample margins, large type, and wide space between lines. "So, it turned out to be *dreck*," said Jim, "but it bugs me just the same. If this man would have had the manners to tell me what he was going to use the interview for, I'd have had some kind of respect for him. As it is—ah, hell. It's just best to forget people like that."

When Jim returned to Verney Farm in the spring, I visited him again for two weeks to get supplemental information, but at this juncture we had much more time to shmooze, his pet Yiddish word for gossip. As a child actor I had worked with some long-vanished actors he had worked with or knew. We had a large fund of shared memories of these people: Vaughan Glaser, Berton Churchill, Walter Catlett, Frank Fay, Walter Hampden, and others, including the frightfully memorable Corse Payton of Brooklyn, who used to bill himself as "The World's Best Bad Actor." I had lived for a number of years at The Lambs Club, and Jim had a wide acquaintanceship among its members.

Inevitably Jim wanted to know all he could about George M. Cohan, whose authorized biographer I was. Jim was fascinated by Cohan and wanted to know every detail of his idol's idiosyncrasies and habits. He was pleased to learn that he and Cohan shared a number of traits, chief of which was their surprising shyness—the tendency to be reclusive yet at the same time remain eminently clubbable, to be introverted yet fit the very picture of cocky wise guy.

Inevitably our talk turned to the elements of acting as he conceived them, and I made a point of presenting them in *Cagney by Cagney.* I had no way of knowing then that I would be visiting him annually after the book was published and that my understanding of his attitudes and opinions on acting would continue to grow.

*Cagney by Cagney* was published in 1976, advance copies having gone to the trade press. Ken McCormick was especially eager for the review from *Publishers Weekly*, the publication bible. It was an unqualified rave, which said in part, "The incomparable Jimmy Cagney puts as much verve and entertainment into his autobiography as he has into his remarkable screen performances. . . . The 'faraway fella,' as friend Pat O'Brien calls him, is truly a private man but he speaks candidly in these pages in a book which is swift-paced and wholly engaging."

Mel Gussow of *The New York Times* enjoyed the book thoroughly despite Cagney's Tory views on art and politics. These views, said Gussow, "are stubborn and uncharitable but we get to like him so much in the course of this wonderfully good-natured book that we even allow him his conservative crotchets."

Jim loved the review by John C. Mahoney in one of the "trades," the *Hollywood Reporter*, which led off: "Painter, poet, philosopher, ecologist, Irish actor with a rare command of Yiddish, street kid who never lost his roots though his branches reached the ethers of Olympus, chorus kid who probably would not have written his autobiography if so many had not insisted upon trying to do that job so badly. Characteristically, in showing how it can be done, Cagney elevates the form and shames the pretenders." Jim loved—and roared at—the "ethers of Olympus" business, and thereafter it became a password between us. In phone calls he would identify himself as Chief Ether Inspector in response to "Who is calling, please?," and I would announce myself as "Merely an Olympian myrmidon." The solemn fun of triviality.

After the book was published, we talked frequently by phone, and I visited him at the farm once a year. One of the last times we met, I went up to the farm for lunch. Principally we discussed friends in The Players—he had sponsored me for membership in 1975—and The Lambs, what had happened to whom, and we seriously addressed some supernal soup he had made. We had long passed the need for constant conversation. It was a case of Louis MacNeice's words about a confidant: "Than whom I do not expect ever again / To find a more accordant friend, with whom / I could be silent knowledgeably."

Our silences were now natural, and he was always a man to honor good food. ("I've got a fat man in me demanding to be let out," he once said. "The fat man won.") During one of the silences I saw his eyes stray from the table into abstraction. It was a look of recollection, one I had seen many times. It was, if I may say so, an eidetic look. I waited, ate. Then from him, a sigh. Not a quiet one. One that even he noticed.

"Did that come out of me?"

I smiled. We ate. He knew I wondered.

"My old man. After all this time you'd think I'd forget. But the image just gets sharper with the years. Larry Olivier told me that the older you get, the more you think of your father. It's true. I keep thinking of the cute way he'd talk to us, or hold us, or pretend to clip us on the chin. Then the drunken fits when he turned into someone else—an actual, a living Mr. Hyde. The booze made him a gentle monster. A lovable monster we truly loved."

"That still saddens you so deeply?"

"Oh, Christ, yes." He thought a moment. "But the deepest sadness is thinking: what fun we'd have had if that damned flu epidemic hadn't taken him. He was a *great* entertainer. He made us laugh like crazy. Any talent I've got, I got from him. The way I speak. The way I carry myself. I think of the *waste* of that man. That gets me more than anything. I keep thinking, if he had lived long enough, what with modern medicine, as the years rolled by, the alcoholism might be beaten. I keep having these endless speculations that go right up a blind alley."

"But outside of those thoughts, you're a happy man." He took my statement as the question it really was.

"A *contented* man." He frowned slightly. "No complaints. No. Just the sadness—the shadow of my old man, and of course the shadow of the Big Thirty. The Big Thirty—and I'm here to tell you this, the older you get even if you're ready—and I'm ready—the bigger the Big Thirty becomes."

"The Big Thirty" was a phrase he commonly used for death. It is written "-30-" and is the journalist's symbol for end of story. It was to have been employed in a film about Bat Masterson's last days, spent as sports editor of a New York newspaper, the role Cagney wanted to cap his career.

After lunch we went out on the patio to watch the ducks on his little lake. His earlier mood continued. "As I said, no complaints. Outside of a few *shlumps* I met in passing, what the hell would I have to complain about? With the career I had, the mom I had, the wife I've had?"

"If you could go back to any *one* year of your life and stay there, which would it be?"

"Funny. Willie and I were talking about that not too long ago. She would like it about 1939, when we were putting our house together in Beverly Hills. Me, about 1923, 1924, doing three-a-day or even five-a-day in vaudeville, with my wife. Life couldn't get sweeter than that."

"That was hard work."

"Was it not! The best work in the world for me. Remember what George M. said: once a song and dance man, always a song and dance man. That was his motto, and it's mine twice over. That's my real epitaph, and I can't think of a happier one."

# 26 · Marge

In my early years visiting the Cagneys, I occasionally noticed a middle-aged woman in their kitchen cooking our lunch the rare times when Jim did not. She was introduced to me as a family friend, Marge Zimmermann, owner of a restaurant nearby who would "help out," as Jim put it. I remarked to him that Marge bore a striking resemblance to doughty Ruth Donnelly, a George M. Cohan protégée, who went from Broadway to Hollywood, where through the years she played a long line of comedy characters, her best role being Lil in Jim's 1933 picture *Hard to Handle*. Jim allowed the resemblance. And the temperament. "Marge has got Ruth's spunkiness too."

As the years went by, I could see that Marge was becoming more and more an integral part of the Cagneys' existence, and I observed their obvious need of her. I asked Jim, over a lunch he made one day, how he and Willie had found their new friend. He said:

Found is right. She just fell into our laps. Willie and I used to eat out from time to time when we first got to this neighborhood. We were alone, the kids gone, and what's the percentage in cooking for two all the time? We got in the habit of going to a nice place with great food called the Silver Horn in Millbrook near Bob Montgomery's. We liked it because of the good food, and especially did I like it because no one made a fuss over us the way they do sometimes with this goddamned celebrity thing that I hate so much. Years ago, when I was making *The Fighting 69th*, an actor in the picture, a spunky little vaudevillian and good actor, Tommy Dugan, whom I'd known in vaudeville, said something very observant about me. He said, "Jim, you really haven't received much consolation or pleasure from this fame you've got, have you?" I admitted that I'd gotten *no* consolation or comfort from it. Particularly in restaurants, where lots of times they have the mistaken idea that we want a conspicuous table and special fussing over us. At the Silver Horn we were treated like everyone else, which we appreciated. There we asked for no favors except a corner table out of the way. Naturally in the course of all this we met Marge, who was the owner. She was always polite and helpful but didn't shower us with the unneeded attention we didn't care for that we'd get in other places. We learned later that she'd told her staff that when the Cagneys came in, we were to be treated exactly the way the other patrons were, and that is precisely what happened. The more we got to know Marge, the more we liked her for her openness and candor and feistiness—and her sense of humor. She was so much like Willie. She is still so much like Willie.

Here was the ultimate bonding between the Cagneys and Marge Zimmermann. Willie, always so busy taking care of her husband through the years and trying to do what she could for her children, never had time for a close woman friend except Eloise O'Brien and Dorothy McHugh, both of whom had their own heavy family responsibilities. So when in their leisure years Willie and Jim came to make friends in their Dutchess County neighborhood, it was mostly with people they encountered in daily living activities. Jim, raising his Morgan horses, found the perfect supervisor for his stable, Tom Fitzpatrick, with whom he formed a close Celtic-bound friendship. They sang together on their buggy trips around Verney Farm—Tom had a truer, more melodic voice than Jim, who would urge him to sing for friends doing the buggy rounds with them. Willie found Marge.

The friendship between the two women was initiated by their mutual hobby. "One day we were having dinner at the Silver Horn," said Willie, "and I casually asked Marge where she got all the interesting wall ornaments and other items she decorated the Silver Horn with. You could have knocked me over with the proverbial feather when she said, 'To get them, I go looking for junk. I don't go to antique shops, I go to junk shops. I go to these secondhand places for their cheap stuff, always knowing I'll sooner or later pick up a gem.' Now that has been my hobby for as long as I can remember. I said to Marge, 'Next time you go, could I come along?' She said, 'You betcha,' and that's how we started going all around the county looking for classy junk, and we had a great time doing just that."

Marge became the girlfriend Willie needed in the East when the Cagneys moved into isolation on Verney Farm. The children both were gone, both now married. Casey lived in California with her husband, Jack

Thomas, for a number of years before their divorce. James Junior's career in the U.S. Marines did not work out for him. He was musically inclined, played the guitar and wrote songs, one of which (according to Brigid O'Brien) was about the unhappy task of being the son of a famous man.

Willie, with her preference for Beverly Hills life, did not nag Jim on the matter. She knew her man. He found in Verney Farm the ultimate haven. "It's my place east of the sun and west of the moon," he said. This farm was Jim's destiny, and he knew that one did not fool around with destiny. This was the home he had always yearned for. This is what he had found in his aunt's Flatbush farm as a boy.

The only difficulty with their lives was that the older the Cagneys got, the more dependent they became on the care of others, mostly on the ministrations of professionals—nurse, cook, secretary. They hired these people from time to time until—for them, providentially—they found Marge, who became all these things and more. For Willie, it was blessed relief. Here in Marge was a woman much like herself: humorous, a lover of junky antiques ("or antique junk," as Willie described it), hardworking, and candid to the point of bluntness.

Willie began gradually to make Marge a part of their household. She would ask Marge occasionally to come over and cook a meal for them when special guests like the Bob Montgomerys or the Frank McHughs visited. At times Willie was tempted to offer paying Marge something, but she soon found out that this would have offended her new friend. For her part, Marge, knowing that cooking was becoming more and more a chore for Willie and Jim, started to bring over casseroles for their dinners.

Marge also knew that area of Dutchess County very well—the doctors, plumbers, farmhands, and utility workers, whose services the Cagneys needed. All these things were done for the Cagneys in the spirit and in the experience of friendship, and money was not involved. The three became such close friends that when the Cagneys made their annual trek to Beverly Hills one year, Willie asked Marge along as a houseguest, and she went.

A superlative cook, Marge quite won Jim's heart that way, and as lagniappe he enjoyed her feisty spirit of independence, a key characteristic of his wife. Then Marge's restaurant, the Silver Horn, closed, but fortunately she had no financial worries because she owned another quite profitable local restaurant, the Dutch Cabin, which she was teaching her daughter to manage. Jim's health at this time began to worsen.

Feeling considerably under the weather one day, he asked Marge to drive him to his doctor in New York. She assured him there were ample good doctors at nearby St. Francis Hospital and drove him there. Jim had been having throat problems, and the otolaryngologist he saw at the hospital asked Jim if he was diabetic. "I've been told that," he said. The doctor suggested a tolerance test, and Jim refused to take it. He went home.

Marge, who by now realized that the best way to deal with Jim was to be totally, vigorously candid, said, "To hell with you, Cagney, if you don't do it." Resignedly Jim asked what he would have to do. Marge said she didn't know, but they had better get to the hospital and have it done at once. He was given a treadmill test, and it was found after a thorough physical that his triglycerides were so high that had they gone untreated another few days, he would have suffered a massive stroke. Willie was horrified at the close call and insisted that Jim follow the medical and diet regimen that was prescribed for him.

"Thank God for Marge," Willie told me. "If she hadn't insisted on shaming Jim into taking that test, he would have been dead. This was a great turning point in our lives because now he'd have to have complete care of his medical and dietary needs. We had two alternatives: hire a permanent nurse-dietitian, or—what I hoped for—ask Marge to learn what he needed medically and take over. She was then free from the Silver Horn, so I asked her as a personal favor to take care of Jim." Marge became salaried.

This satisfied Jim completely. He did not want to be bothered with strangers about continually in the house. When Marge took over, his triglycerides were at 350, and in short order after learning the medical regimen he needed, Marge saw them come down to just over 100. She worked prodigiously to maintain his health by cooking all his meals, watching his in-between snacks (to which he was addicted), and calculating all that he ingested into his diabetic profile. Her great enemy was his habit of cheating with snacks.

Marge had no training for such work, but she set about learning what was required. She took instruction from the hospital dietitian and other medical personnel on diabetic care, and this became a major occupation. But there were other things that had to be done in the Cagney household. Willie was of an age when she felt her capabilities diminishing. "Chief cook and bottle washer" became more than a cliché description of Marge's duties. The Cagneys were intensely private people, tending to be slightly paranoid about strangers, and the movie star aura intensified their apprehensions. The older Jim got, the more iconic he became in the eyes of his fans, and the more they sought him out.

In 1977 Jim, getting careless with his diet when Marge was not around, overdid things and suffered a small stroke. Thinking the air at Martha's Vineyard would be more conducive to recuperation, the Cagneys went there with Marge, together with Casey and her husband, Jack. One day the Cagneys planned to go out in their boat, and Willie asked Marge to drive over to where the Thomases were staying and bring them over. Marge said, "Then, because he thought I had not intended to pick them up, Jack called me something highly inappropriate. I said to Jamesie later I wanted to go home, that I did not have to put up with anything like this." Willie was infuriated by this episode, and thereafter the Thomases were largely persona non grata with her.

For the rest of Jim's life there were varying degrees of estrangement between the Cagneys and their children. Willie tended to quarrel with Casey. "There always seemed to be tension between those two," said Brigid O'Brien. "One time Casey came over to visit our family, and she was astonished to hear that her mother was always regarded by us as being a lot of fun. Casey could scarcely believe it when my mom told her stories about the jolly times we used to have with Willie."

By 1978 the Cagneys and Marge had in effect become a family of their own, and this was compounded shortly by Jim's asking Marge's husband, Don, a civil engineer, to take early retirement and assume control of the Cagney farm and livestock. The more than seven hundred acres of Verney Farm were a going concern, producing hay and supporting a dozen or more Scottish Highland cattle. Jim also had a goodly brace of Morgan horses with a full-time man to supervise their breeding. In addition to a standard barn, there was a large horse barn with a show ring and a huge room devoted to display of the many show ribbons Jim's horses had won over the years. The show barn also housed a number of antique carriages, all kept in working order, which Jim would order up with a team to take guests on a tour of the farm.

These tours were a particular delight of his, and you went on them with heightened pleasure when you saw what joy the host showed in traversing his acreage and displaying its amenities. He dearly loved this farm.

There was no vanity in showing off the farm; there was only a whole-hearted delight. This is what he as a little boy had dreamed of having, and now that it was his, the dream was worth sharing. More, it was for him a deep affirmation of his country's worth.

"No place on earth," he said with quiet emphasis, "would or could afford the opportunities for a little East Side brat like me to make it except the United States. I guess that is the most vital connection between Cohan and me. I'm not ashamed to wave that flag. By Christ, I'm not."

Jim and Willie lived a life of deep contentment on the farm. When, however, they returned each year to Los Angeles, there was a shadow between them: the Thursday-night family gatherings at brother Bill's house in Newport Beach. "The family musical frolics for Carrie's children," Jim called them. Willie never attended.

Marge saw this and asked Jim about it. Now close to the Cagneys, she could speak her mind freely. "Why doesn't Willie go to these evenings? Isn't she invited?" she asked Jim.

"She wouldn't go even if she was asked," said Jim.

Marge expressed shocked incredulity, and Jim showed his discomfort. This division between his wife and his siblings was the one truly unhappy part of his life, and it was a wound never to heal. It could only have been devastating for him, his overwhelming love of Willie set against his deep family loyalty.

"It truly hurt him," said Pat O'Brien. "The ones he loved most—his wife, his family—forever at odds."

# 27 · On Acting

An entr'acte to let Cagney speak of his profession.

Inevitably we spoke much of acting, but usually not during work sessions. After the afternoon's taping we would go out on his patio and idly watch the grazing cows he loved so much slowly cross his north hill meadow. We relaxed over a drink, his always strawberry soda. The cattle were there for a purpose. He had long ago given up breeding and selling them; the red-and-white-haired Highlands, declared a close Cagney buddy, Roland Winters, looked too much like Jim's relatives for him to slaughter. So the Highlands became a point of rest for him. He spent several minutes each day just watching them, envying (he said) their placidity and wondering if thoughts ever came to them.

These times became periods of reflection for him, times when, as he told me, he thought about the concept and processes of thought itself, of philosophy. Of "why am I here?" Of the profession of acting as a human function. It was during these "cow watches," as he called them, that I, a journeyman actor who also taught acting at a variety of universities, took the unparalleled opportunity to question one of the great masters of the acting craft. I didn't begin by asking for his theories of acting. I hoped to assimilate his views by bringing up actors we both had seen and learning what Jim thought of them and why.

As for his general view of acting, that was fairly common knowledge. He had been interviewed on the subject a number of times. Forty years ago Len Boyd, a reporter, asked him: "How do you become an actor?" Cagney: "Just become one. Don't sit around thinking about it. Do anything that will let you stick around [a theater] so you can soak it up." He was not against youngsters' taking acting classes, but he cautioned: "Only so much can be learned from books. The rest must be learned from practice. It's as if one were instructed in the fundamentals of carpentry and let it go at that. He may know 'how' to build, but he won't be any good at it unless he does build, again and again, to achieve the type of perfection that comes only from continual performance."

Nothing earthshaking in that commonsense declaration, the basis for the belief of almost every actor that acting can never be taught but must simply be done, experienced, consummated.

What was it about Lowell Sherman, whom he so much admired, that enthralled Jim so much?* The answer:

A strange and fascinating mix. He could convey the most menacing kind of evil and yet, and still, be attractive. Without ever saying a word at times. Just look at him in that great silent picture of D. W. Griffith's *Way Down East.* Lowell is about as nasty a swine in that picture as you can imagine: arranging a fake marriage so he can sleep with sweet Lillian Gish, then running off, leaving her pregnant. You hate him, yet you can understand why she'd go for him because he had that strange thing called charm. Don't ask me how you can get *that.* Rotten though he was as a human being in these roles, Lowell scattered the goodies for the audience, and by goodies I mean something more than just an enchanting smile. By goodies I mean he played that character *from that character's point of view.* He wasn't acting the role of a villain. He just knew that real villains sincerely believe that what they are doing is the best for them and that somehow this is the *right* thing.

In other words, the seducer didn't set out to seduce this innocent girl by saying to himself, "Aha, now—rotten guy that I am— I'm going to be a really rotten, worse than rotten guy and seduce this perfectly sweet, innocent thing and besmirch her all I can!" No. What he did was to get on the side of the guy he was playing. He doesn't think of himself as a bad guy. Quite the contrary. He thinks of himself as a *good* guy, and we know he is not. But he doesn't know that. Hasn't the faintest idea he is. As an actor you always have to get solidly on the side of the guy you are playing.

Was that what Cagney always did? His answer:

Always. Cody Jarrett. Now there was about the rottenest guy in the world, and I had to play him according to his lights, according to his evaluation of himself, to *his* background. He was no dummy; he was

---

*I urge the seeing of *Mammy* (1930), *The Royal Bed* (1931), and *What Price Hollywood?* (1932), Lowell Sherman films of the early thirties available on video.

bright. He was all the other terrible things too, but to himself he was doing absolutely the right, the—for him—honest thing. Sounds funny, using that adjective "honest" for him. But it's so.

Through the years I think what I've learned is that in a very real sense, you have to love the character you play. A one-dimensional actor playing a villain can only see the man's villainy, so the actor projects to the audience only that quality. Real villains have depth, and that means good plus the bad.

In our discussions of acting, Jim grew curious about the way I taught the craft. I explained my processes, saying that I always, unvaryingly made the point to young actors that the only way to learn acting was by acting and that I was especially proud of our Educational Theatre Department at New York University in the fifties and sixties, when I was there, because not only students but faculty acted constantly, mostly in a laboratory series of plays week after week.

"Did you teach the Method?" he asked. "And let me say at once that I don't know what in the hell the Method is, except that it has something to do with the actor believing totally what he is acting. Or some goddamned thing."

No, I said, I had not taught the Method. Our department concentrated on giving the student as many roles as possible, mostly in the lab situation, so we could see and evaluate our work, but with the prime emphasis placed on acting experience and evaluation by instructors who were actors themselves. He approved of that. As for the Method, I said, I knew Lee Strasberg. Only slightly, but I had talked with him once at great length.

"Fill me in on the Method," Jim said. I sensed that he was impatient with all acting theories but was also determined to be fair in any such evaluation. Fortunately, in preparing for my work at NYU, I had asked the three leading teachers in New York City—Lee Strasberg, Stella Adler, and Sanford Meisner—for a chance to talk with them on their teaching methods and lab acting work. They kindly agreed, and I was able to tell Jim what their teaching processes were, or at least what I understood them to be. I had also talked at length with Strasberg, Adler, and Meisner students.

Jim listened with great patience as I spent about forty minutes outlining what I had learned from each of these outstanding teachers, summarizing them roughly and briefly here:

LEE STRASBERG. Strasberg taught affective memory, or sense memory—i.e., the actor reexperiencing an emotional event of his or her past in order to vivify his or her similar moment in a play or film. If, for instance, in the playing of Hamlet, Strasberg would expect the actor actually to feel and reexperience the death of his own father (or someone of comparable close-ness) in order to authenticate Hamlet's deep sense of grief at the loss of King Hamlet.

SANFORD "SANDY" MEISNER. Meisner disliked Strasberg's approach, calling it selfish and self-centered. Meisner asserted that what you do as an actor does not depend on you. Rather, it depends on what the *other* actor in the scene does, on your relationship with that other actor, on your ability to listen and react to him or her. Acting, said Meisner, lies in the doing, not just in the feeling.

STELLA ADLER. Strasberg's polar opposite in most ways. Her most quoted statement: "To think of your own mother's death each time you want to cry onstage is schizophrenic and sick. Use your creative imagination to create a part that belongs to your character, not to you. I don't want the actor to be stuck with his own life."

Jim said, "God save me from Strasberg. I admire Meisner, and I think Stella Adler must be a great teacher. The Strasberg stuff is dreary bullshit. Sure you have to believe the character you're playing, but you've got always to keep a very objective eye on yourself and what you're doing."

He spent some time talking about the very dangerous vanity quotient in the Strasberg approach. Jim thought that actors tended to be vain enough from the situational aspect of their profession:

Actors are reputed to be vain. A certain amount of truth in that. All you have to sell as product is yourself. You don't have Fuller brushes in hand; you have only yourself. So it is hard not to be wrapped up in yourself. But the actors who follow Strasberg make the great mistake of looking into *themselves* when for God's sake they should be looking into the *characters they're playing*. These actors' specific psychological selves should not be the determinants of the inner truth of the characters they are called on to play. The actors are not those characters. You should, in consequence, never play yourself or your inner self. The very nature of acting is that you are playing someone else. You can call on personal memory, sure, the way I remembered my father when I did the mess hall scene in *White Heat,* but that's a referral, not a living out.

When asked about actors who play nothing but themselves, people like Clark Gable, for instance—*personality* actors—Jim cut me short:

That's it. That's the word, the definition of them. Personality. They *should* play nothing but themselves. I never admired an actor more than I did Clark Gable even though I never saw him play any other role than himself. He was entitled to do that because his personality was so honestly masculine, forthright and rock-solid American, so rock solid his decent self. There are two kinds of actors: the ones who play other people and those who play nothing but themselves. Clark was the best of the latter, and he truly deserved the title King.

He went on to say, "Of course we always play a bit of ourselves in every part we do. In everything I've ever done, there is always a touch of the Yorkville streets. You can't as an actor leave all of yourself behind."

I then showed him a list I had made up of all the parts he had played in the movies. I here reproduce them, including his last two roles, which at that time he had not yet played. He had never seen his roles set out and so displayed, and it pleased him. "Hey, that's all right—the variety, I mean."

1. Wastrel
2. Hoodlum
3. Railroad worker
4. Insurance salesman
5. Hoodlum
6. Barber
7. Bellhop/ con man
8. Cabdriver
9. Racetrack driver
10. Boxer
11. Promoter
12. Ex-racketeer/ photographer
13. Reformed hoodlum
14. Showman
15. Con man/ movie star
16. Ex-racketeer
17. Gangster
18. Sailor
19. Truck driver
20. Marine flier
21. G-man
22. Fight manager
23. "Bottom"
24. Seaman
25. Pilot
26. Public official
27. Dancer
28. Screenwriter
29. Gangster
30. Western hero
31. Journalist
32. Bootlegger
33. Soldier
34. Foreman
35. Boxer
36. Dentist
37. Aviator
38. RCAF pilot
39. George M. Cohan
40. Journalist
41. Journalist
42. Spy
43. Barroom philosopher
44. Gangster
45. Stage director
46. Gangster
47. Journalist
48. Self
49. Marine captain
50. Politician
51. Sheriff
52. Racketeer
53. Navy captain
54. College professor
55. George M. Cohan
56. Horse rancher
57. Millionaire
58. Lon Chaney
59. Labor leader
60. Doctor/rebel
61. Admiral Halsey
62. Businessman
63. Police commissioner
64. Aged boxer

The distinctions between "hoodlum," "racketeer," and "gangster" are admittedly slight. I place the three in what I guess are rising order of social unworthiness. Counting these and a few other social undesirables, one realizes that in Cagney's career he really played only fifteen tough characters, or about a fourth of his roles. After examining this listing, Jim said, "Not bad for a tough East Side kid. I'm more genteel than they give me credit for."

Jim and I also talked at length about why people become actors. He thought it was for a very simple reason: almost all good actors, he said, are essentially shy people. Introverts. He could think of only one exception, his buddy Pat O'Brien. Jim believed shy people have to speak up if they want to be heard in this world, and that is why so many shy people become actors; the shyness goes when you become someone else. That, he believed, is why acting is so essentially a shy man's profession.

From Frank Fay and Lowell Sherman he learned ease and control, which he tried to maintain all his life. "I needed it," he said, "in my own life. A loving childhood, but strains there all the time, and a kid after a while lives in fear of upsets; you yearn for peace, for quiet, for control. That's why I made as a rule of my life four big words: no strain, no stress. What do kids call it now? Be *cool*. For me, no stress, no strain."

This was another reason why he loved the country and the quiet life, seasoned by his love of nature and the beauty and integrity of animals.

Inevitably he preferred actors noted for their reserve: George M. Cohan and Cohan's prize pupil, Spencer Tracy. He loved watching Tracy. "I'm easy to imitate," Jim said, "but you never saw anyone imitate Spence Tracy. You can't mimic reserve and control very well."

Bill Cagney understood Jim's shyness as a motivating force in his becoming an actor, but he found an even greater explanation in his brother's life: "All the unhappiness of his childhood was inside him."

The screenwriter Ben Roberts agreed, saying that Cagney acted that unhappiness on the screen instead of in real life: "He was a natural actor, and he didn't have to learn to do anything. He instinctively knew where to go, and how to squeeze a scene until it was absolutely dry. He was daring. It took a lot of guts sometimes to do the thing he did—because he exposed himself to the world every time he did. But he had no fear about that. He never said, 'I can't do it.' He always said, 'I'll take a crack at it, fellas.' He wasn't afraid to take a chance as an actor."

The Cagneys almost never went out to the movies, but he managed to see quite a few films on television and in that fashion more or less kept up with the rising talents of the age. He admired Marlon Brando but saw only one of his roles, *The Godfather,* which he liked. Jim also saw James Dean and judged him competent but was put off by the young actor's narcissism. He said of Dean, "What he does with his little side grins and eye crinkles is to say to the viewer, 'Look at me. Aren't I cute?' The problem is, the boy *is* cute, which somehow makes it worse. Obvious vanity in an actor's playing is pure hambone, however you slice it or disguise it. It means you aren't thinking of the role. It's self-congratulation—which is absolutely the worst thing an actor can do."

What did he think in general of modern film acting? In general he liked current young actors but thought some had an unfortunate tendency to revel in the very process of acting. This, he said, was not hamminess, which was self-congratulation. What made him uncomfortable was their knowledge—which he could see in their eyes—of how well they were doing. He saw that they were enjoying their own acting, "especially in the deep-sorrow bits."

"What they're saying," said Jim, "is 'I'm doing this beautifully.' And they *are*. But that's not acting. That's technique. Well, as long as the public buys it. But it's phony baloney."

Jim had a natural admiration for actors in his own genre, the skillfully rough-textured "close-to-nature boys," as he called them: Steve McQueen, George C. Scott, and John Wayne. Yet he also deeply admired sophisticated actors like Robert Montgomery, Cary Grant, Laurence Olivier, Rex Harrison, and Michael Redgrave. He loved the techniqueless technique of Alec Guinness. He loved comedians and comics (the former say funny things; the latter say things funny) of all persuasions, especially Joe Besser and Jonathan Winters. He did superb imitations of Stan Laurel and of a long-forgotten Jewish comic, Lou Holtz.

We had, I think, over a period of some weeks in random conversation covered most of what he thought of acting. So now to the vital question: what was his theory of acting?

In *Cagney by Cagney* he had already expressed his fundamental technique of acting which was: walk in, plant yourself squarely on both feet, look the other actor in the eyes, say what you have to say—truthfully. But was there any definable theory underlying that? What was the Cagney theory of acting?

"I can tell you in *three* words," he said. "I can tell you in *two*, if you'd prefer."

"No. Give me the entire spectrum."

"In three words, *just do it*. Don't *think* of doing it, or worry about doing it, or hold a postmortem on doing it, or stand in front of a mirror, or get out a slide rule to do it. Just, for Christ's sake, *do it*. There. That's my two-word theory."

"All right," I said. "Sure. Do it. Just do it. But what would you say to the young, untried beginning actor, all set to go out and get the necessary experience? Would you have anything to say to him and to her about *just* doing it?"

"I'd say to them, 'Just take a look at the best actors in the world, better than I'll ever be: the three-year-olds, the four-year-olds. They don't think about how they're holding their little tea party. They don't do anything but *pretend*. They just do it. The closer you look at those kids and do just what they're doing, the better actor you become.' "

# 28 · Next to Closing

On my annual visit to Verney Farm in 1978, I suggested something rather casually to Jim as a natural extension of his life and career: a musical based on both. I fully expected him to say no. He did not.

The idea intrigued him. There was no touch of vanity in this. He had during our *Cagney by Cagney* days reflected so much on his past life, its vagaries and its texture, that in sorting them out, he recognized that the most difficult yet most satisfying days of his existence were the ones spent in vaudeville. He had from time to time idly speculated that there had never really been a satisfactory musical about the "real" vaudeville, the one where he and Willie had spent their apprenticeship in show business. His letter to Sol Siegel of 20th Century–Fox was his only exploration of that. Consequently he was uniquely receptive to my idea, embryonic as it was, and it had an additional chance of gaining his interest because it would include, indeed costar, the actress playing Willie. The idea of the heroine of his own life sharing the spotlight excited him.

We talked it over. "Two problems," he said. "The casting. The writing." He felt totally unqualified at both, yet he knew he would have to be the linch-pin of the entire enterprise. "Let's think about it for several months," he said. I certainly felt unqualified to do any of the writing, but as a beginning Jim said I should write at least an outline of the show, and after Jim approved, it would be given over to a specialist in musicals. He and I were on the phone constantly for weeks, going over details of his life.

As for the actor to play Cagney, Jim reflected that the only dancer-actor capable of doing the Cagney steps in the Cagney way was Donald O'Connor. Would Donald be interested? He was. My outline, under the influence of Jim's wonderful yarn spinning of his vaudeville days, grew into a two-act play mostly utilizing vignettes from the Cagneys' years on the road in the early twenties. I looked on what I had written as germination for the musical, to be called simply *Cagney,* as raw material that librettist, lyricist, and composer would subsume into something worthily dramatic. But Jim unexpectedly liked the script the way it was because (I think) there were a number of scenes so intensely evocative of his early days that they seemed like diary pages. For good reason: he had almost dictated them.

The script was then read by a number of professionals, who said it needed rewrite, something I thought obvious from the beginning. But to get a firm focus on this, I sought out a close and knowledgeable friend, one of Broadway's leading producers, who would give me the straight stuff in a practical appraisal. This was the late Larry Kasha, who won a Tony in 1970 for producing Lauren Bacall's hit show *Applause.* Larry knew musicals up, down, sideways, inside out. I sent him my script, adding that I had never written a musical in my life and doubted very much that I could.

While Larry was reading the manuscript, excitement came to the Cagneys in the form of the Kennedy Center Honors. The trustees of the John F. Kennedy Center for the Performing Arts invited Jim to be one of the recipients of the Third Annual Kennedy Center Honors, along with Leonard Bernstein, Lynn Fontanne, Agnes de Mille, and Leontyne Price. The event was held on December 8, 1980, and the Cagneys loved every minute of it. Each honoree was allowed five couples as members of their personal party. The Cagneys brought along the Frank McHughs, the Pat O'Briens, the Bob Montgomerys, Marge and Don Zimmermann, and my wife, Vija, and me. I was invited principally to be company for Frank and Pat. The three of us, having no part in the proceedings except to hang around, chose mainly to sit in various White House corners to gawk at high governmental nobility and reminisce about old days at The Lambs Club.

It was nonetheless an exciting evening. Each of the five honors recipients was assigned a separate White House parlor to have his or her own reception line to greet the several hundred guests. The Cagneys occupied the Rose Room, and Pat and Frank, who had been White House guests twice before, took Vija and me on a tour of the place. Meanwhile Jim, although enjoying it all, was getting weary of the heavy handshaking and the unending "Mr. Cagney, I have been a fan of yours since I was—" Jim would shake, nod, smile warmly, and murmur thanks. I watched at a discreet distance, fascinated by the famous people, moving slowly in line, paying him homage—politicians, movie stars, tycoons, all kinds of makers and shakers, all of whom in that lovely room had become only one thing: fans of James Cagney. He was unfailingly courteous and genuinely grateful for the homage, but fatigue as well as a small measure of boredom was gaining on him. At one point a prominent Supreme Court justice stood before him, going enthusiastically into "Mr. Cagney, I have been a fan of yours since I was a little boy." Since this distinguished gentleman looked at least a decade older than Jim, this moment had its own piquancy. As the man stepped along, Jim saw me looking at him, winked, and made a face that said, "Can you *believe* this? Yorkville Jim meets the Supreme Court!"

I returned home to find Larry Kasha's letter assessing my Cagney libretto (if that's what it was). In typical, gentle honesty, Larry said, "Your métier, kid, is show business biography. Stick to it." He phoned later to say that my script reminded him of those gaudy, warmhearted George Jessel–produced movie musicals of the forties whose leading roles went appropriately to John Payne rather than James Cagney. Besides, Larry said, a Cagney musical without the movies was unthinkable. For me, the musical died right there. Others have since tried to put Jim's life to music. It deserves no less tribute.

One of the Cagney neighborhood friends was the brilliant Czech film director Milos Forman, who bought a lovely farm in Connecticut not far from the Cagneys. Forman was a man of charm who endeared himself to the Cagneys. He had optioned E. L. Doctorow's best-selling novel *Ragtime* for a film, and at a Cagney dinner he was discussing the plot and characters. As he did so, Jim, because of growing sciatica, was sitting with his head slightly lowered, listening, and whenever especially interested, he raised his leonine head and looked intently at the speaker. Forman saw him do this several times and said to himself, "My God, if I could get him interested in the film," but put the thought out of his mind, knowing Jim's determination not to act again. The idea was even less likely in view of the Cagney health—problems of diabetes, sciatica, and several small strokes. After dinner Willie took Forman aside and told him that she had seen the way he had looked at Jim, and yes, she wanted Jim to play a part, to become active again.

Forman was overwhelmed. "Don't tell *her* now," Willie said to him, indicating Marge.

"Tell me what?" asked Marge.

Willie said, "Milos wants Jim to play a part in *Ragtime,* and I want him to do it."

"*What? You* want him to do it?"

"Yes," said Willie, "I do."

Fiercely protective of Jim's health and his love of retirement, Willie had come to realize that he was in a serious state of vegetation. Worsening eyesight had taken away much of his pleasure in his beloved painting, and the same affliction was making inroads on his other hobby, reading. Willie decided that under proper conditions a return to acting would give Jim a better psychological hold on life. She had detected some slippage of spirit, a form of ennui that was threatening his usually equable temperament. Their family doctor confirmed this to her, saying that in his view, acting would effectively recharge Jim's batteries.

Both Willie and Marge were present when the idea of acting again was suggested to him. "No," he said. "I'm retired." Two-second pause. "What kind of part?" The women howled with laughter. *Ragtime* was already in the Cagney library, and Jim had read the book. He had bought it because he had once known a prominent character in this mix of documentary and fiction, Evelyn Nesbit.

*Ragtime* centers on a fictional young African-American piano player, Coalhouse Walker, who, denied justice by a bigoted captain of a volunteer fire brigade, takes the law into his own hands by seizing the J. P. Morgan Library to publicize his situation. The library is under siege from the police squad headed by a real-life character, New York Police Commissioner Rhinelander Waldo, the role Forman asked Jim to play. Jim read the script and agreed. It was not a big role. He didn't feel up to one.

In order to give Jim the feeling that he was among friends, Marge asked Forman to cast a few Cagney cronies in supporting roles. This was done at once. Although they had no scenes together, Pat O'Brien, cast as Harry K. Thaw's attorney, was able to join Jim on the set, and they reveled in the zeitgeist of the thirties again. Forman thoughtfully cast Eloise O'Brien, who hadn't acted in years, as Thaw's mother. She and Willie renewed the intimacy of the old days as well. Also cast was Donald O'Connor as Nesbit's dance instructor.

First filming was done in the Park Slope section of Brooklyn, and Jim's reappearance on location drew substantial, applauding crowds. The bulk of *Ragtime*'s filming was to be done in England, and following custom, there would be no travel by air. Jim, Willie, Marge, and the O'Briens went over in style on the *QE2*. They had an exhilarating time until the day before debarkation. With appalling suddenness, Jim told Willie he could not go through with the job; he would have to cancel out. He had no explanations except "I just can't go through with it." The consequences of this, Willie knew, would be severe. Not (she reasoned) for the film; Forman could easily cast a dependable Commissioner Waldo in England. The real injury done would be to Jim's *amour propre;* his self-respect would suffer a palpable injury, perhaps even propel him into depression. Respecting his wishes, his

*Ragtime*

wife asked no questions. He had suffered a few slight strokes in recent months, and she assumed he was concerned about his impaired memory. It would have been dreadfully embarrassing for him were he to forget his lines, he who had always been so prompt and thorough in learning them. She felt that by now he distrusted even his old skill at paraphrasing.

Willie and Marge were with him in his dressing room the first morning of rehearsal, the time for him to tell Forman he was quitting. The dresser came into the room to announce that things were ready on the set. Jim rose and prepared to go. Marge got up and asked where he was going. He replied simply, "I'm an actor," walked past her and over to the set. Not another word was said about his not playing the part. He said later, "The thought of acting again stirred my stumps."

Jim and Pat had a glorious time in England, seeing shows, seeing sights, seeing old friends. There was a special Hollywood Night at the London Palladium, and they were honored guests, later to be presented to the leading guest, the Queen Mother. Marge had been told that the Queen Mother especially wanted to meet Jim. When he was told this, with true Celtic bluntness he said, "To hell with her."

Marge, a bone-bred loyal Canadian, utterly shocked at these words, rose to her feet and began to sing fervidly, loudly, "God save our gracious queen—"

Jim broke down laughing. "OK, what the hell am I expected to do?" he said.

Marge explained that it was all very simple: all he had to do was to be backstage to meet Her Majesty. After the performance Jim was there, Willie and Marge remaining in their box while the Queen Mother went backstage to meet a lineup of Hollywood celebrities.

After Her Majesty had left the theater, Willie and Marge hurried backstage to ask Jim excitedly what she had said to him. He said, "How the hell do I know? I turned off my hearing aid." This left him deaf as a mahogany post. After the queen mother bestowed her attention on Jim, uttering who knows what, she progressed down the line of movie stars, and Jim's pants fell down. Peggy Lee, standing near him, helped him, all the while laughing herself to tears. "Christ, it's a good thing this happened now," said Jim. "I forgot my goddamned belt."

The Cagneys returned to the States invigorated. Jim felt a new strength of spirit. One of the reasons Willie had wanted to see him act again was that she had long thought he was getting out of touch with his own reality, that he was becoming the Too Faraway Fella.

In *Ragtime* he was particularly glad to have had his reunion with Pat O'Brien, and their meeting was marked not only by the feeling that they were back in the thirties but also with the sense that they had never been apart. Pat's career had not followed the arc that Jim's had because, as Pat said, "I couldn't act one half so well as the boyo," meaning Cagney. Jim would dispute that. Pat, in any case, always believed that his own fame was a matter of luck. Brigid O'Brien said, "Dad always thought he was terribly lucky: being at the right place at the right time." As the years went by and the Cagney fame exceeded that of his old Warner Brothers cohorts, the more tightly he retained their friendship. He called Pat and Frank McHugh at least three times a week. Ralph Bellamy was another he sought out continually, and Bob Montgomery, living in the neighborhood, became a constant visitor at Verney Farm.

Whenever Jim was in a restaurant with these old friends, he was especially solicitous of them when the inevitable "Mr. Cagney, I hate to trouble you, but would you mind autographing my menu?" came. He always did, but this was followed by his "I'm sure you want Mr. O'Brien's [McHugh's, Bellamy's, etc.] autograph too" even when the autograph seeker had no idea in the world who Mr. Bellamy was.

After *Ragtime*, the eastern sector of the United States began to pay him particular honor. The New York Press Club paid tribute to him, an attention he enjoyed because of his affection for writers. The National Board of Review gave him a special citation, and New York's mayor, Ed Koch, presented him with the key to the city. Harvard's Hasty Pudding Club made him their Man of the Year.

Deeply appreciative of these though he was, the honor that moved him the most occurred in 1981, when George Steinbrenner of the New York Yankees asked Jim to throw the first ball out for the opening game of the World Series. Jim said, "As I look back at it now, I'd rather have been a New York Yankee, a New York Giant, or a Brooklyn Dodger than win *three* Oscars. Mind you, I'm proud of the little guy, but to be a professional ballplayer? I think that's every American boy's dream, and I wasn't exempt from it. To think that I was in Yankee Stadium itself, throwing out a ball to start a game—a World Series game! Dreams don't come better than that."

The Cagneys' biggest celebration of the year was the Fourth of July, although they loved Christmas. The Fourth had long become a joyous ritual for Jim. He and Willie usually invited a few guests who came to see the American flag flying on the pole Jim had erected when he built his house. At its base he grew red, white, and blue petunias. Standard flag etiquette says one raises the flag at sunup and lowers it at sundown. Jim would have none of that. He flew his flag twenty-four hours a day, taking it down only when it needed repair or replacement. "I think too much of the flag not to see it constantly," he said.

When he was a child, all the kids on the Seventy-ninth Street block where he lived celebrated the Fourth by building on the street an impromptu bonfire of old crates and discarded furniture. Invariably a fire engine came and put the fire out, simply causing the kids to build another one a block away. "So the Fourth of July was initially just an exciting experience for us with no rhyme or reason," said Jim. "But my mother, as usual, made sense out of it for me. She said those bonfires we started meant the Fourth of July and that meant freedom, and when you said 'freedom,' you meant the Fourth of July. She didn't exactly condone the bonfires, but I notice she never advocated I stop going to them, even though some of them could have set a tenement going up."

By 1981 the Cagneys' Fourth of July celebrations were a pale shadow of their former selves. Pat lived in Los Angeles, and 1981 saw the deaths of Frank McHugh and Bob Montgomery. Jim said, "The death of those two guys left a hole in my life that can never be filled. Bob, the great American patriot and great showman. A hero. Frank, dear Frank. Of all our gang,

Frank was the funniest one, and the only people who saw him at his funniest were the boys down at The Players and The Lambs. He'd take those skinny little parts they gave him at Warners and make them little bits of comic genius. I saw him just a few days ago on television in the musical version of *State Fair,* a nothing part, and Frank made it bloom with his charm. An *actor."*

Notwithstanding the absence of old friends, Jim kept up the Fourth as valiantly as he knew how. He always attended the local neighborhood parades, staying from first to last, applauding every float and keeping time to the drumbeat with his hands. "And whenever the flag would go by," said Willie, "Jim would cry openly, not hiding his tears for an instant. No one will ever know what the flag meant to him and had meant to him from the time he was a boy. He always said Bob Montgomery was the best American he knew. Well, Jim Cagney was the best American I ever knew, and that is not just bragging about the man I loved. That's just fact."

One of the Cagneys' burdens in late life was the growing estrangement between them and their children. There was some movement by the children to get their inheritances before their parents' demise. This was not resented by either Jim or Willie. Casey was offered the Cagney property at Twentynine Palms, California, a valuable piece of acreage, but she didn't want it. "She felt it was inadequate," said Marge. "Jim then gave her a condominium, but this was gone after a while, and she asked for yet another. Casey got a divorce and remained on the West Coast, seeing her parents infrequently."

James Cagney, Jr., married and had several children, divorced, and remarried, all this after his stint in the Marine Corps. He worked for a while as an assistant to the builders of America's Cup–class sailing yachts in Newport, Rhode Island. During this time he told his dad that his heart was set on getting the Martha's Vineyard property, the 218-acre farm, Roaring Brook, which Jim deeded to him in 1976. In 1983 Jim Junior put it up for sale and was quoted in the *Los Angeles Times:*

> I haven't been able to use it. I view the Vineyard property as one of
> my father's monuments. The sale could total $1.1 million. The best
> way to describe life on the farm when we were kids was pure Huck
> Finn. It was running through the woods, building tree houses, slid-
> ing down the side of a hill on the cranberries. Dad spent the sum-
> mers winding down from the job, sailing, helping with the haying.
> When I told him I was selling Roaring Brook, he said, "I under-

stand." I don't think he'll come back to the Vineyard. He's like old wine now. He doesn't travel too well.

Jim understood, but when it was announced that Jim Junior had finally sold the property, there was a deep pang of regret that his last connection with Martha's Vineyard was gone. Jim Junior rarely came to visit his parents in any case, and after Roaring Brook was sold, his visits stopped altogether. He seemed to have little direction in life, and the Cagneys heard rumors that he had become alcohol- and drug-addicted. After entering a hospital in January 1984, he died of a heart attack at forty-two. Jim was reported as "greatly upset." Marge was his representative at the funeral.

In 1982 St. Martin's Press commissioned Doug Warren to write a Cagney biography. In writing to a number of Cagney friends, Warren learned that Jim had been sent one of the letters and was unhappy about (in Warren's words)

> past intrusions on his privacy and was not happy with the prospect of yet another biography. The author [Warren] pointed out that the book would definitely be written, because there was a signed contract, and that if Cagney placed obstacles in the way, it would be simply a dull book. Its publication could, however, give Cagney an opportunity to set the record straight, to correct errors made by previous biographers. The conversation took a positive turn, and before it ended, Mrs. Zimmermann said she would discuss the matter with Cagney and get back to the author.

Jim approved.

After a financial division of advance money and royalties was arranged, Warren met with Jim for fifteen hours of taped interviews. The result in 1983 was *James Cagney: The Authorized Biography by Doug Warren with James Cagney.*

It is a delicate matter for one biographer to assess another's work on the same subject, but I cannot ignore my responsibility in the matter. Quite simply, from my perspective, *James Cagney: The Authorized Biography* is just basic journalism and scant biography. In my view, it reads, as the *Detroit News* reviewer said, "like a press handout." All reviews I could find gave the book a hard time. *Publishers Weekly* scored "its turgid prose that adds very little to what Cagney fans already know about his career," and the *Hollywood Reporter*'s Robert Osborne condemned the book's "many inaccuracies," listing a number of them. The authoritative film journal *Films in Review* criticized the book's many factual errors and misspellings, citing such things as "Hal Wallace" for "Hal Wallis" and the identification in a picture caption of Frank McHugh as Jimmy McHugh, errors typical of the book's general sloppiness. If reproducing these comments seems ungracious of me, I can only plead that *Veritas* is something more than Harvard's motto.

In 1982 a singular event in Jim's life was misreported in a New York newspaper's subhead: CAGNEY LOST IN RADIO CITY. The truth was given in a 1987 *Reader's Digest* article by Ralph Bellamy, "Unforgettable Jimmy Cagney." Bellamy wrote about the event:

> He was an old man, and ill, and they had kept him waiting a long time in a room below the stage of New York City's Radio City Music Hall. Above, a "Night of 100 Stars" dragged on, and the audience was growing impatient. Then it was time. A trapdoor opened, and the old man was elevated to stage level, alone in the spotlight. No dancing, no routine; just an old man sitting in a chair. But it was Jimmy Cagney. The audience rose to its feet, applauding, cheering. Jim's eyes flickered in surprise, then filled with tears as the show-stopping ovation grew. He had largely been out of the public's eye for more than two decades, but it was clear that night in 1982 that he had never been out of the public's heart.

Several New York papers carried the story that Jim had been forgotten in a subbasement far under the stage while the many Broadway and Hollywood stars paraded in file down the runway on the big stage. What the producers had done was good showmanship. They saved the best for last.

After *Ragtime* Jim was of two minds about going back to work again. It would be so easy to relax and vegetate, but he knew that this would not be good for him. He had to do something to fight off the lethargy that threatened to overwhelm him. The one who was to benefit from this was producer Robert Halmi, who had in hand the script for a TV movie that had been fashioned for Katharine Hepburn, the story of a famous tennis player living out the problems of old age and retirement. Hepburn, set for the role, had injured herself in a fall and could not do it. Halmi thought that changing the story to that of an old boxer would make it suit Cagney, and he sent Jim the script.

Jim thought the story might be of interest, but he wondered if he was up to it. Should he do it? He asked three people: Ralph Bellamy, Pat O'Brien, and his doctor. Bellamy said no, citing television's spotty record with its made-for-TV movies. Pat O'Brien said, "Hell, yes. Do it, Jim. It's medicine." The Cagneys' doctor said close to the same thing: "Yes. It will charge your batteries." Willie agreed.

Three nights after he called Pat, a news story announced Pat's death from a heart attack while he was in the hospital, recuperating from a coronary condition. Jim was told later—and wept. He had always thought Pat, the one with the most life among all the lads, his best friend, might survive him. He would take Pat's advice. Jim would do the Halmi show, a story now called *Terrible Joe Moran*.

He was considerably pleased to hear that his costar would be Art Carney, an actor Jim had long admired. Rehearsals had barely begun when a distinctly jarring note intruded on the Cagneys' lives. A magazine writer, Anthony Cook, after an interview with Jim during the making of *Terrible Joe Moran*, wrote an article for the March 1984 issue of *Life* magazine titled "Cagney's Curious Comeback." It bore an ominous subhead: "Is the Ailing Star Being Helped or Used by the Mystery Woman Who Dominates His Life?"

The mystery woman was Marge, who in the Cook account appeared as a Svengali-like termagant who bossed Cagney about as if he were a little boy dependent on her every instruction. Cook found her a menacing influence on the Cagneys' lives, saying that she had "gained power of attorney" and was now executor of the Cagney will, an assignment once Jeanne Cagney's. But even yet more ominous, according to Cook, was Marge's building of an expensive new home on the Cagneys' property near the latter's "unpretentious cottage." Marge's daughter was also starting to build on the land there.

Cook was clearly unaware that in 1982 the Cagneys had made a new will and that after a talk with the Zimmermanns and to their considerable surprise, Jim had designated them his executors. All his estate went to Willie per the terms of the James and Frances Cagney Revocable Trust. As for Jeanne, she was at the time seriously ill from the lung cancer that killed her two years later. Jeanne, moreover, had already been given the bulk of Jim's estate in the form of millions of dollars' worth of real estate, which included the palatial house on Martha's Vineyard built originally for Carrie Cagney and the sumptuous Coldwater Canyon estate. James Junior had received property from his parents worth more than a million dollars. By that time Casey had received two condominiums and a very large amount of money in cash. The Cagneys intended to leave Marge and Don the farm after Willie's death in recognition of the considerable services rendered them through recent years.

When the *Life* magazine article reached the newsstands, the Cagneys exploded. The *New York Daily News* on February 24, 1984, printed Jim's reaction, given by phone to a *News* reporter. Jim said of the Cook piece: "It's a load of garbage. To me it's unimportant, but when somebody attacks persons I trust, then I have to answer back. They [the Zimmermanns] are first class. We wouldn't be here without them. We have complete trust in them. But my wife and I are in complete control of our lives. Anyone who would trust an article like that would have to be crazy."

Unprecedentedly Willie got on the phone. She, who admitted frankly through the years that she did not like to talk to reporters, made an exception here. She was asked by the *News* reporter if Marge was "a mystery woman," and her reply was emphatic: "Of course not! Marge is a truthful, honest woman. We have complete trust in her. She always consults Jim and me on matters that have to be attended to. I think it's a sad thing to do that to a gal who's been doing everything for us."

Ex-heavyweight boxing champion Floyd Patterson, a Cagney family friend, was so enraged by the article that he advised the Cagneys to sue Cook: "I would, if this had happened to me." Patterson called the Cook story "rubbish. I've been up there [Verney Farm] on many occasions, and all I know is, when I'm eighty-four, I hope to have somebody around me like Marge." This was the same sentiment expressed by Dorothy McHugh, Frank's widow: "When I am Jim and Willie's age, I would welcome having Marge's help and care." Milos Forman said that he was "outraged at this shabby journalism. I was with Cagney every day for months. Privately he told me how much they appreciate, love and value Don and Marge. The worst thing about the article is how offensive it is to Jim."

Willie, in her last words to the *Daily News* reporter, said: "We invited [Cook] up to the house to speak with us and he refused. Now this. To say that Jim and I have no control over our lives is nonsense. We have minds of our own."

From another perspective, the Zimmermann *casus belli* is revealingly discussed by Richard Schickel, who interviewed Jim at length on the *Ragtime* set in London and later wrote and produced an excellent television documentary, *Cagney: That Yankee Doodle Dandy.* In his Cagney book Schickel writes:

> As the years passed and his health weakened, Marge became a full-time aide. She was then a large, blunt, ferociously loyal woman in her late fifties, notable for a particularly short fuse on her temper, yet in her way quite likable. She and Cagney had a rather nice, humorously bantering relationship. Still, one could not help but notice that in their partnership she seemed to make all the decisions, both large and small, and that he was clearly the passive partner, constantly deferring to her. Considering the image we have all carried away from his movies, the force and energy of his public

personality, this relationship and his manner in it excited a certain amount of speculation that would later spill over into the press in a highly unpleasant fashion. Be that as it may, I felt Marge's influence was benign and essential, assuming (as I do) that the decision to return to the screen was not imposed on Cagney.

It was not. He had wanted *Ragtime* and had needed *Ragtime*. He needed to get back to work; he told me so directly, and in those words. From my personal viewpoint, as one who knew the Cagneys well and Marge less so, but amply, Schickel uses the two adjectives that best describe her relationship with the Cagneys: "benign" and "essential." Jim liked and needed her comic bullying about his health, and Willie appreciated it more than she could say. Marge's emotions were deep yet close to the surface when it came to the Cagneys. Her bark was quite as sharp as her bite. But her love for these two people was all-consuming, and to support them emotionally in their last years, she worked prodigiously. As for Cook's story, and beyond, there is no better summing up than Schickel's:

> And, it must be said, Cook's piece was a tissue of innuendos, deliberately placing the worst possible interpretations on ambiguous facts, quoting from sources who had their own interests to advance. In any event, one can testify, from personal observation, that Marge Zimmermann undertook the process of remobilizing Cagney with the best of intentions—that is, with a desire to prolong her beloved "Jamesie"'s life by giving him something to live for. She may later have found herself in waters unknown to her and tricky to anyone— namely, that of deal-making show business. Certainly one must judge *Terrible Joe Moran* a mistake, but one which anyone might honestly have made if, loving Cagney, it was difficult to acknowledge that his physical decline was now such that it rendered all but the simplest professional demands impossible for him to fulfill.

If ever I'd had any doubt about Marge's worth to the Cagneys, and I did not, it would have been wholly removed by something Willie told me: "Yeah, Marge doesn't suffer fools gladly, and she sure can raise a fuss, but she always does it for Jim. Without her—I'm here to tell you—Jim would have died years before he did."

# 29 · Last Bow

Early in 1984, when Robert Halmi began production on *Terrible Joe Moran*, he was justifiably apprehensive. He had invested three million dollars in the undertaking, and at times it looked as if Jim might not be able to make it. At any moment one of his standard ailments could—and frequently did—flare up. He had spinal spurs, bursitis, sciatica, after-effects of stroke and diabetes. The insurance company for *Terrible Joe Moran* required $200,000 for the Cagney appearance.

Marge was with him constantly, taking his blood pressure, measuring his diet for diabetes control, and seeing that he did not overeat, the one and only besetting sin of his maturity. A minor fault surely, but with him it could have had fatal consequences.

Willie and Marge well knew the truth of that statement. Just a year before, on what proved to be his last trip to Los Angeles, Jim was dining out in a fancy restaurant, and as usual, Marge was nearby to apportion his food. He had to check with her on everything he ordered, and by this time he had become educated to the process. On this occasion he wanted a rich soup and, rare with him, a glass of wine. Marge said:

I always had to watch what he ate, of course, but this time I also learned I had to watch *how* he ate. The soup and wine came. He took the wine down in about two seconds, and the soup went down like *that.* He went out like a light. Willie and I were frightened to death. We had to call an ambulance, and after a very brief hospital stay he came home, and then it became apparent to Willie and me that I'd have to watch over him constantly. Not get in his face but hover in the background. Had he taken his time eating, had I insisted on his having a little orange juice—his blood sugar was too low—he'd have been OK. So from then on I'd check his blood every week, and we fought the good Fight of the Triclycerides.

The *Terrible Joe Moran* rehearsals, despite Jim's health problems, were going along fairly well when yet another ailment obtruded, an odd horror called dyspraxia that diminished his control of speech. During rehearsal Jim's words began to run together, and the slurring seemed irreparable. He was mentally as sharp as ever, but for the first time in his life he could not put words together without their squashing one another. Cagney, of all actors in the world, the one who brought the Shakespearean phrase "trippingly on the tongue" to vivid life. The words no longer tripped; they lagged and slurred. Halmi hired a speech specialist, Dr. Fred Attanasio, who every day came on the set—an old, lovely Manhattan brownstone—to help Jim. The doctor discovered that Jim's speech muscles were healthy enough. The difficulty was in his inability to "sequence motor movements"—in plain language, to make those muscles work efficiently.

Slowing the rat-a-tat Cagney speed was the initial problem. He had to go syllable by syllable, especially with words even the average person would have difficulty with, like one that became his bête noire, "entrepreneur." The doctor gave Jim a rubber ball to hold in his hand, and he was instructed to squeeze it when a difficult cluster of consonants had to be mastered. "For each syllable of a difficult word, I'd ask him to squeeze the ball," Attanasio said. Despite this, too many syllables were coming out mushy. Time was passing, and the sound track was simply unusable. Director Joseph Sargent said, "I was ready to throw in the towel. The CBS people could not believe what they were hearing—or not hearing."

Just when it seemed that Jim's health could not possibly bear up under a setback, one presented itself: a large cyst on his shoulder that gave him great pain, especially when people embraced him, as happened all the time. "He'd never show it," said Sargent. "He'd be in sudden, shocking pain and never show it."

People went out of their way to help him. New York City policemen volunteered eagerly to carry Jim in his wheelchair up long flights of stairs. On the flat he would have trouble moving his chair over a rumpled rug or slight obstruction, and someone would be there to aid him, sometimes to the point when he did not want to be aided. But at times help was essential. The girl in charge of props would lie on the carpet out of camera range and pull the wheelchair along.

It was a joy and deep honor for Art Carney to play Cagney's sidekick in the picture, Troy, Joe's lifelong friend, devoted to the old prizefighter. Carney had worshiped Cagney from boyhood when he had used his mother's hair set gel to fashion his hair in what Carney fondly believed was Cagney fashion.

Carney deliberately did not go out of his way to help Jim physically, knowing that too much of that would make him uncomfortable and dissatisfied.

It was understood that Jim would work only four hours a day, but the time invariably stretched out to six hours because he would get interested in what he and others were doing. After work a car came to take him and party back to the hotel. One late afternoon Jim directed the driver to go up to Ninety-sixth Street, and Willie said, "Where are we going?" Jim guided the driver to an old building at 135 East Ninety-sixth. "See that?" he said. "That's St. Francis de Sales, where I made my first communion."

On Thanksgiving Day, a day of respite from filming, Jim got Willie and Marge into the car and went back to St. Francis again. Marge, who had previously met the pastor, Father Raich, went in to bring him out to meet the Cagneys. After he left, Willie, of formidable Scottish Presbyterian stock, said with great feeling, "If my mother ever knew I shook the hand of a Catholic priest, she'd kill me!" Jim choked with laughter.

The church was holding a parish party that day for the children, and Jim suggested they drop in and observe. He noticed that the refreshments were very skimpy and asked why. "That's all we can afford," said Father Raich. Jim told Marge to go out to the nearest bakery and order two hundred dollars' worth of cookies. The party was a great success.

*Terrible Joe Moran* is a story steeped in sentiment. Joe, a wealthy long-retired boxer, is living in great comfort in a Manhattan brownstone with Troy (Carney), himself a former fighter, who cooks and keeps house for Joe. Fifteen years after last seeing him, there appears Joe's granddaughter, Ronnie (Ellen Barkin), an aspiring writer, who needs money for her boyfriend, Nick, in heavy and life-threatening debt to the mob. Nick coerces Ronnie, who is loath to do so, into visiting her grandfather and ingratiating herself to the point where she can get money from him for Nick's needs. She finally agrees.

Ronnie doesn't like her grandfather because apparently he deserted her grandmother, but Joe says, "Look. I had a career, I was a champ. When you're a champ, there's nothing else. No room to be a husband, but I didn't know that, see? And your grandmother knocked me off my pins. She's a great dame, but she's poison." She also had a string of husbands and is currently "in Europe somewhere."

The mutuality of dislike once stated, the mutuality of growing affection between Joe and Ronnie must take its course in this well-acted and impeccably directed melodrama. And on it goes until Joe personally pays off Nick's debt to a head capo who, by an astounding coincidence that astounds no one, is a hood acquaintance of Joe's from the old days. The hood reveals to Joe that in a "fixed" bout he won in his youth Joe actually won the fight legitimately. But this is Joe's only solace. He has learned of Ronnie's connivance in winning his favor, considers her a gold digger, and cuts her out of his life, going into seclusion, heartbroken. Then, would you believe it, she turns against her boyfriend, demands to see Joe, and throws herself into his welcoming embrace, both weeping happily.

As the shooting of the film went on, the director was horrified. Said Joseph Sargent: "I was terrified. The thickness of Jim's lisping and slurring made his words valueless. We had to have everything he said dubbed by another actor. This man would then look at the footage, and because Jim was uttering the correct labials and plosives, the actor who dubbed was able to do a good job. He was at one time a Cagney mimic, but he also had the task of not only getting the Cagney voice down pat but also the added age."

Who was this actor? Sargent answers:

That's the secret that's been kept under wraps all these years. I don't remember the impersonator's name, in fact. I know he was a New York actor. He was sneaked into a studio because even CBS didn't know it wasn't Jim's voice. To explain the great improvement to them, the producer said we had found new technology that cleared up the Cagney voice. They bought it. In any case, not one word on that sound track is James Cagney's voice. Thank God he didn't have to learn his lines. He read them all off the TelePrompTer. But it is still the Cagney spirit in the way he used his face and gave us great touches of the old Cagney magic. The thing that pleased me the most was his enjoyment of being back in harness again. Just being on the set cheered him up; to be working again obviously thrilled him very much. Such a great pro, a marvelous person to work with. Did everything I asked him to do, cooperated at once. Only one little bit of trouble he had, and that was with the leading woman, Ellen Barkin. He found her a pain in the ass because he felt she was taking advantage of the Method approach to acting: what is my motivation here, et cetera? I understood her position because I was Lee Strasberg–trained myself, but with Jim, it was "Learn your lines and hit your marks." So I took Ellen aside and told her not to hold up Mr. Cagney. In the first place he doesn't have the sustaining power and the less we tax him, the better. She understood.

*Terrible Joe Moran* must be seen by Cagney admirers at least once, and that may be enough. The script contains some good belligerent lines for

Cagney, and despite the mush ("D'ye know how to put your arms around an old man?"), this is standard evening television, very well directed. It is not a James Cagney movie. How can it be without his voice? It is rather dispiriting to hear another man's voice coming from the Cagney mouth, but only if you know about it. The dubbing is done so well that it seems genuine, if aged, Cagney. In any case, bodily immobile though he is, Cagney still manages to impale an emotion with a side glance. This is a James Cagney silent movie.

The reviews of *Terrible Joe Moran* were, as might be expected, a very mixed bag, whose principal theme was "It's great to have him back, but . . ." Leading the naysayers was Howard Rosenberg of the *Los Angeles Times*, who adjured his readers to "beware a sucker punch to your heart strings" and who found Cagney's presence in this "routine and inoffensively humdrum TV movie . . . puzzling." Rosenberg could not find the rationale for a beloved actor, not needing the money, coming back to act in a "humdrum production that offered limited promise, and at a time of life when he was best served by resting on his past glories."

The rationale was simple. The rationale was self-esteem, to be able to function again.

John O'Connor of *The New York Times* had another slant on *Terrible Joe Moran*. After calling Cagney a beloved national institution, he said, "Unfortunately, as is evident from scattered interviews, his health, at the age of eighty-four, is also precarious. . . . Using him as a production centerpiece would seem to border on reckless insensitivity. . . . And yet the gamble pays off . . . the old Cagney magic comes through. It is more than simply detecting reverberations of the past in his performance. There is a special Cagney spirit that keeps coming through with inimitable verve."

As he now entered the final years, Jim displayed in interviews with a searching reporter like Richard Schickel what the latter called "a sadness as deep as it was inexplicable." It is explicable.

In the last few years of his life there was sadness but no melancholy. He was never the man to give way to self-pity. His sadness was inevitable, given its three causes, listed in ascending order of importance to him: his children, the loss of his creative powers, and the debility of age.

Jim was the nurturing one of Casey and Jim Junior's parents, says Brigid O'Brien, yet during most of his career he had had little time for them in his schedule. The children were not to blame for the emotional poverty of their childhoods. Casey told Brigid that she and her brother were not allowed to have children over to play because Willie did not want the attendant noise that would disturb Jim's line-learning periods. There was, moreover, the burden on children of their living in a home separate from their parents. Families do not grow and cohere in such circumstances.

Because he came from straitened circumstances, Jim expected that his children would rise from their considerably better backgrounds and seek out careers, principally through the education he was eager to provide them with. Neither child was inclined that way, and Jim was saddened at what seemed to him to be a lack of focus in their lives. He could not understand it.

The second cause of his sadness was the inability in old age to do the things he felt he had been born to do: write, paint, act, and dance. The latter he knew had to end, but the other three he thought would be his until death. He had been happy to give up the acting because it allowed him time needed for the writing and the painting. As for writing, he gradually found that his verse was a sometime thing, mostly the result of vagrant thought. Even acting became a struggle when age overtook him.

But painting, he believed, was something of a destiny, a lasting birthright. He was fond of recalling his very young childhood drawings, his copying Winsor McCay's *Little Nemo* and *Little Sammy Sneeze*. In his maturity Jim felt that his life was a sure reach into painting skill, inspired by a master, Serge Bongart. Jim had become a versatile painter, an artist no less in that sphere than in his acting. Painting, he believed, was his greatest victory in life. If he rather overdid the "acting is just a job" routine—he did love his profession—he mostly meant it. Painting became his prime joy.

When he reached his eighties, all his creative powers were imperiled by illness, and of them all, the one he came to love most, painting, was most threatened.

Diabetes had almost completely blinded one eye, and the other was giving him trouble. The happiest hours of his retirement had been spent in the rustic little studio Don Zimmermann built for him in a meadow a half mile from the house. By age eighty Jim could no longer make that journey with ease. Worse, he could not see well enough. That studio was his particular joy, the fulcrum of his creative powers at what he considered their best, and with those gone, there was ample reason for sadness. That is why, although at first reluctantly, yet with increasing certainty of its value for him, he returned to acting. He was functioning again.

The final, the third reason for his sadness was death's approach. It is something most eighty-plus-year-old men consider at length, though some more than others. Prospero in speaking of his retirement to Milan describes this consideration imperishably: "where every third thought shall be my grave." Alan Dent's obituary of the great drama critic James Agate said that "the halls of death never had a more unwilling visitant." Add Cagney. In his eighties, the whimsical couplet he had written in youth

Each man starts with his very first breath

To devise shrewd means for outwitting death.

now took on gently ironic meaning. He had just about run out of means, and he well knew it. There was no one more attuned to life, no one more entranced by and in harmony with its rhythms.

After *Terrible Joe Moran,* all ambition was spent. He knew he could do no more, and that brought a degree of contentment. He had outlived all his old pals except Ralph Bellamy, but Bellamy lived in California, and his visits east were rare.

In November 1984, when Marge was not around one afternoon, he went on what he called "a pasta binge" and paid for it severely. His lungs began to fill up with fluid, and he was taken by ambulance, protesting all the while, to Lenox Hill Hospital in New York City. The congestion was quickly relieved, and he wanted to leave the hospital at once. The doctors demurred, wanting him to remain under observation. "Under observation for what?" he asked a visitor, Roland Winters. "My problem is very basic. I'm too goddamned old, and there is no cure for that."

Later that month he was back in residence at Verney Farm and was reconciled to spending the winter there although he had been hoping to visit Jeanne in California. On December 7, 1984, she died of lung cancer at the age of sixty-five. The funeral mass at Our Lady Queen of Angels Church in Newport Beach was held three days later. Jim was unable to attend, and it is unlikely he wanted to. The occasion would have been heartrending for him. He had eminently fulfilled his mother's request to take care of his little sister. Financially she never had worries because of him, and she had done well professionally, with a thirty-five-year career in theater, radio, and film. After her divorce from Jack Morrison, in 1970, she spent much of her time working with the Catholic Church, the March of Dimes, and other charities. Now, of the Yorkville Cagneys, there were only two: Jim and Bill, who survived his older brother by two years.

"That was a uniquely close family," said Jack Morrison. "This dirt-poor Irish family was indeed so close, each to each, that it was impossible for an outsider to penetrate, at least on any lasting basis. A favorite family story was this one: Once when they were living on Seventy-eighth near First, someone from another part of the block kept dropping in on them, and in answer to the question asked, 'What's he hanging around for?,' family wit Eddie said, 'I think he wants to work himself down into our circle.' Willie Cagney could never join that circle. She was never invited."

Jim's last two years coincided with my wife's, and during her fatal illness I could not visit him. I kept in touch by phone, and although his words were slurred, their sense was not. The keen mental acuity was his to the end.

For diversion, there was only television. His favorite over the years was Jackie Gleason in almost every one of his comic incarnations, in both early days and reruns. "Incredible resemblance—my dad and Jackie," said Jim. "Same way they held themselves, the way they turned their heads, the way they walked. Funny in the same way. They both could roar, but it was funny roaring. You knew they could never hurt anyone but themselves." Pete McGovern, Gleason's chum and publicist, said Cagney wrote fan letters to Jackie all the time. Gleason would read them appreciatively, throw them in the wastebasket, and after he left, the Gleason staff would scramble for them. The Great One attended Jim's eighty-sixth birthday party on July 17, 1985, at the Hotel Carlyle, New York, where he loudly declared, "I don't think I can leave here until Cagney does a dance on the table."

In the second week of March 1986, Jim, after a serious heart attack the previous week, was taken again to Lenox Hill Hospital for further testing. The doctors now told Willie that her husband had about two weeks to live. They recommended that Jim stay with them, close to the best medical aid. Willie said, "Oh, no. He's going home where he wants to be."

Marge came into the room to see him, and he said, "You're going to take me home, aren't you, kid?," in a tone indicating that he knew he was dying. "Are you crazy, Cagney? You think I'm going to leave you here?" Willie had explained that he had only gone to the hospital for a change of medication, but he was not fooled. Marge said, "After I said to him, 'Are you crazy, Cagney?' he laughed, and Willie and I took him home to die in his own bed, and we were brokenhearted, never showing it. It was joking around as always. Wisecracking all the time, the way he liked to hear the two of us carrying on. 'Coupla dumb broads,' he'd say, laughing at us."

On Saturday, March 29, after a good meal, Jim went to bed and slept soundly. He was awakened the next day, Easter morning, by a nurse, and Don Zimmermann, who came to wheel him in to breakfast. Jim said something to the nurse in a mumble, and as she strained forward to hear what he said—which was obviously a joke—he winked, smiled, and died.

His head dropped suddenly to his chest. He left as he had lived, directly, gently, humorously. It was 7:30 a.m. Dr. David Kurish of Sharon, Connecticut, who was called, pronounced Jim dead, listing the cause of death as cardiac arrest. Dr. Kurish was asked not to release the news until Marge had seen to it that the body had been taken away. She told the undertaker not to bring a hearse but a station wagon, to fool the reporters. He did, and Jim was taken in that fashion to the funeral home.

The news announced, the area around Verney Farm became pandemonium, cars coming from everywhere, helicopters hovering. "A zoo," Marge described it. For his funeral Jim had told both Willie and Marge that he wanted the old parish church, St. Francis de Sales, he had so recently revisited. Cardinal John J. O'Connor offered St. Patrick's Cathedral for the funeral mass, but Willie stated Jim's wishes.

Tuesday, April 1, as Jim's casket was brought into the church by his pallbearers, who included Ralph Bellamy, Mikhail Baryshnikov, Floyd Patterson, A. C. Lyles, and Milos Forman, a big crowd gathered outside St. Francis de Sales. Inside the eight-hundred-seat church were comparatively few people, but they included New York's mayor, Edward I. Koch, and the governor of the state, Mario Cuomo, and his wife. Willie sat in a folding chair at the back of the church until the casket, borne by the pallbearers, was carried before the altar. Cardinal O'Connor participated in the service, and the eulogy was given by Father John Catoir, head of the Christophers, the Catholic media group for which Jim had made *A Link in the Chain.*

Catoir called Jim "good to the heart of his being" and cited the extraordinary amount of love he gave in life and received from so many. After Mass Cardinal O'Connor came over to Willie and offered an apology for the action of the priest who, in 1917, had failed to come as promised to hold the funeral service for Jim's dad. "If I had known of this a few days ago," said O'Connor, "I would have visited your husband and apologized to him. As it is, just having heard of it, I can only apologize to you now." He kissed her on the cheek.

In helping carry the casket out of the church, Ralph Bellamy stumbled on the unfamiliar steps, and for one or two moments things looked ominous. But recovery was quick, and the descent continued unmarred. In a tribute to Jim, the hundreds lining Ninety-sixth Street broke into hearty applause. Jim had taken his final bow. Scores of people carried American flags and waved them. The casket was then driven to its final resting place at Gate of Heaven Cemetery, Hawthorne, New York.

Marge, in arranging for the inscription on Jim's gravestone, asked Willie what she wanted.

"Simple as possible," she said. "Just 'James Cagney, 1899–1986. God bless America.' That says it all, in just the way he wanted it." He had indeed become an American icon. In Robert Sklar's words, "He had taken the spirit of city streets and made it national."

In 1940 Jim wrote a few lines of verse in dialogue form between an old man and a young woman. She says to him:

> Why do you weep, poor dear old man?
> It hurts me within when you weep.

He replies:

> I weep for the long lost wonderful years
> I once thought were mine to keep.

Her answer is:

> Why would you keep them, poor dear old man?
> That's too much to ask. Just living those so-called
> Wonderful years is life's most onerous task.
> For time passes and life passes, and all
> Things end in the sadness,
> Except for those sometimes fortunate ones
> Who find peace in a benevolent madness.

This prefiguring of Alzheimer's or its equivalent is striking, but here again is the sadness that Jim clearly foresaw for himself, speaking from his most bountiful and vital years.

When Jack Warner died, Jim said, "Jack made it to eighty-six. I'll be happy with that." Jim made eighty-six with eight months to spare. At the end there was no fear, only the sadness he knew was life's last measure. He also knew that, in Hamlet's phrase, the readiness is all, and was glad he did not have to leave betimes. He was ready when the time came.

The Cagney will, dated September 13, 1982, gave everything to Willie as her natural entitlement as copossessor of the James and Frances Cagney Revocable Trust. Because he had been so liberal to both his children before his death Jim felt he had done well by them. To explain this and to prevent misunderstandings (or so he hoped), Jim added Article VI to his will:

VI. *INTENTIONAL OMISSION*

> I have, except as otherwise specified in this Will, intentionally and with full knowledge omitted to provide for my heirs, expressly including, but not limited to, any person now living or hereafter born who is, or claims to be, my spouse, my child or the issue of a deceased child of mine.

I have intentionally made no provision for any grandchild of mine because I believe it is the obligation of each parent to adequately provide for his own children during the parent's lifetime just as I have done, and just as I believe my children should do for their children.

Notwithstanding, as executor Marge saw to it that the grandchildren—Casey's two children and Jim Junior's two—received a substantial amount of money.

Willie's only close relative was a very old sister in Iowa, a place Willie was determined never to visit again except in passing. With the Coldwater Canyon estate now owned by Jeanne's children, there was nothing in California for Willie. She was thankful that Marge was available to share her life as before, and by now the two women had grown extremely close. Marge cooked for Willie every day, and they pursued their old hobby of seeking out antique junkyards.

As the years went by after Jim's death, Willie was faced with a continuing problem. What was she to do with all his memorabilia? Verney Farm was choked with the things he had kept over the long years. She had no one to leave them to on her side, and she had long been estranged from Jim's relatives. A recent lacerating argument with Casey had mostly severed their connection, and Jim Junior was dead. In any case, Willie had never planned to give the Cagney collections of a lifetime to either Jim Junior or Casey. They had become mostly strangers to her in their maturity.

Jim had a tremendously valuable and extensive collection of memorabilia, ranging from the boots and spats he wore in *Yankee Doodle Dandy* to original scripts of his films, as well as his own paintings and the first pair of tap shoes he had worn in vaudeville. There were also the saddle he had used in *The Oklahoma Kid*, an autographed picture sent to him by Mae Clarke showing him grinding the grapefruit in her face, mint-condition posters of his films, and—most precious of all to Willie—scores of scrapbooks and photo albums documenting the Cagney career, which she had faithfully put together over a fifty-year period. She had contemplated giving them to a university film library, but after giving it much thought, she decided to put all the material up for auction.

In that way, she explained to the vendor, William Doyle Galleries of New York, the average Cagney fan would have the chance to buy a piece of Jim's heritage. Whether this was a wise decision or not is moot. In any case, Willie very badly wanted to empty the farm of these hundreds of items.

Every piece was a tangible reminder of her loss, and she did not want the material to be disposed of by anyone but herself.

In the event, it was on the whole, the average Cagney fan who was able to participate meaningfully in sale of the collection. A majority of the items sold for only a few hundred dollars apiece, and as restaurateur Peter Ballante of Fort Lee, New Jersey, said, "For just a couple of hundred bucks I got an original Cagney scrapbook, a real piece of him. A genuine bargain for me, a guy who loved Cagney from the time I first went to the movies." Doyle Galleries, on East Eighty-seventh Street held the auction at the nearby St. Ignatius Loyola School in three sessions on September 30, 1992. Admission was through purchase of a tastefully illustrated catalog costing twenty dollars. Everything offered was sold, including furniture and decorations from the Beverly Hills and Martha's Vineyard houses, a collection of exquisite antique firearms, Jim's own guitar and organ, many of his suits, hats, and costumes, all dated, marked by studio labels. Of particular sentimental value were his baseball uniform and catcher's mask from Yorkville days.

Also included in the auction were 16 mm copies of exactly half the sixty-four films he made. Only three of them (*The Gallant Hours, The Time of Your Life,* and *Johnny Come Lately,* all Cagney productions) were made after 1943. So much of his heart had been in the thirties.

To sum up the character and personality of James Cagney, there stands only one expert, his wife. Of all the people on earth, she knew him by far the best. They were together sixty-five years. Let her view of him stand as definition.

In 1984 Cleveland Amory interviewed Willie, pointing out that she had spent a lifetime avoiding interviews. She made an exception for Amory only on condition that he not write anything "mushy." "I agreed," said Amory, "under duress." Willie went on to say that she got into the habit of avoiding interviews "because years ago I couldn't stand to read those silly little woman-at-home things with all those cutesy, sweetie-pie 'he's just wonderful' stories." Amory nodded and asked her what her husband was like. "He's just wonderful," she said, stopped and laughed, then went on:

> Well, he really is. He is the most decent, honest man anybody could imagine. He hasn't an envious bone in his body. And he's the most amazingly unconceited man, let alone actor, I ever met in my life. You know, I really didn't have a sense of humor until I got the example from him. Even now, on his worst days, he can laugh. He always says that you can laugh at almost anything if you try. Most actors

aren't very good at being alone—and they are particularly not good at being alone with just one other person for any length of time. Jim was always different. He's always saying that whatever he did was just a job. Even today, it's a terrible struggle to get him to watch any of his old pictures. When I watch one, he'll say something like, "Why did I walk like that? God. I look like I'm hitting the walls on both sides of the hall!" I like to tell him that he's just looking at one scene and not getting the whole picture. One thing I could do without is his incredible memory. Maybe it's just because mine is so bad. One day not long ago, we were getting into the car in New York, and he saw a man across the street. "You see that fellow over there?" Jim said to me. "He sat next to me in school. His name is Nathan Sidelsky." "Prove it," I told him. "Go say hello." So he did. And you know what? It *was* Nathan Sidelsky. The only problem was, he didn't remember who Jimmy Cagney was. Jim loved it. He laughed all day about that.

I had occasion in 1981 to ask Willie to sum up her view of her husband for me. She said:

It's all there in what he paints and writes. His honesty, his being the same to everyone. His love of beauty. His artistry. No vanity. His generosity. You can see a lot of him in his handwriting. I don't believe in fortune tellers or palm reading, but I've always been a fan of handwriting analysis, in which I fully believe. In (I think it was) 1950 Muriel Stafford, who had a syndicated column analyzing handwriting, examined Jim's after I bullied him into giving her a sample.

The first thing she noticed of course was the most distinctive thing about his handwriting: the big loops he makes under the line with his j's, g's, y's, and p's especially. Those long, very full lower loops. Stafford explained that in handwriting analysis these loops are sometimes called moneybags, revealing a money consciousness, which Jim certainly had, from boyhood, stimulated by his brother Bill and by the desperately poor Cagney family's need to feed Kitty year in, year out. Stafford went on to say Jim's handwriting was of a person independent and honest to an extreme, that he was very warmhearted with a strong feeling for the opposite sex, aggressive yet charming.

She said his writing also showed he was a restless person—always had to be busy—and just plain liked people. All these things she said about him are perfectly true. But there's one thing about him no handwriting or any other kind of analysis can show, and that is the word I'd have to use if someone ever asked me to sum up Jim in a single word. The word is *goodness*. Just plain goodness. That's the heart of Jim Cagney.

Willie died on October 10, 1994, at Sharon Hospital, Sharon, Connecticut. She was ninety-five.

The bulk of her estate went to her sister and several nieces. Verney Farm was given to Marge as reward for her work as cook, manager, nurse, confidante, and friend. The will was contested by James Junior's children, who seem to believe that the specific and intentional exclusion of them in his will by James Cagney, reaffirmed by his widow in her will, is invalid. In consequence Willie's will is presently in litigation, and the high likelihood is that legal fees will consume what remains of the Cagney estate. In the interim Verney Farm has had to be sold by the Zimmermanns to meet all the taxes due on it. The buyer, Edgar Smith, a man with an agricultural background, will keep it as a functioning farm and—what would delight Jim immeasurably—has begun planting trees on the property.

As an actor in the thirties and forties James Cagney had only two peers in Hollywood: Spencer Tracy and Edward G. Robinson, both of whom closely rivaled him in their quiet intensity and concision of playing. Encountered today, the eye-bulging overacting of Paul Muni, their only other rival back then, shows too much the melodramatic theater he came from.

The only film actors today who come near Cagney in his particular abilities are two virtual spin-offs of him, Al Pacino and Robert De Niro, and their elder, Marlon Brando, another master of tightness and well-controlled fierceness. Four of these seven actors came from the meaner streets of New York, a peculiar advantage, it would seem. Cagney was always grateful that he was given, in his words, "a touch of the gutter" to season his art.

For art it was, however wrought or developed. He was fond of saying that if ever art was practiced in his part of Hollywood, he never saw it. But if art is both the conscious and unconscious development of one's deep creative instincts in the service of lasting truth, Cagney was not only an artist but a very great one.

He had no superior as a film actor and very few peers: Brando, Robert Donat, Alec Guinness, Charles Laughton, Laurence Olivier, Ralph Richardson, Edward G. Robinson, and Spencer Tracy. Possibly Fredric March. But none of these had his all-reaching dynamism, and none so well represented to Americans the qualities they consider uniquely their own: dispatch, engaging openness, and feisty independence. Cagney became for many Americans the person they think they are.

The last time I was at the farm, Jim was watching his Morgan horses gallop around their field. He said, "Wonderful, aren't they? And the most wonderful thing about them is that they don't know they are. They are just so supremely, unselfishly themselves. The best anyone can be."

# Appendixes

STAGE APPEARANCES
CAGNEY ON RADIO
FEATURE FILMS
SHORT FILMS
CAGNEY ON TELEVISION

# Select Bibliography

# Index

# Stage Appearances

**Pitter Patter**   Book by Will M. Hough. Lyrics and music by William B. Friedlander. From Willie Collier's farce, *Caught in the Rain*. Dances and ensembles staged by David Bennett. Longacre Theatre, September 29, 1920.
*Cast:* Bob Livingston (John Price Jones); Bryce Forrester (George Edward Reed); Violet Mason (Mildred Keats); Mrs. George Meriden (Virginia Cleary); James Maxwell (Frederic Hall); Muriel Mason (Jabe Richardson); "Dick Crawford" (William Kent, replaced by Ernest Truex); George Thompson (Charles LeRoy); Howard Mason (Hugh Chilvers); Prop. of Candy Shop (George Spelvin); Butler (Arthur Greeter). *The girls:* Dawn Renard, Anne Foose, Billie Vernon, Rae Fields, Hazel Rix, Aileen Grenier, Florence David, Mabel Benelisha, Katharine Powers, Sunny Harrison, Estelle Callen, Mildred Morgan, Florence Carroll, Pearl Crossman, Violet Hazel, Grace Lee, Agnes Walsh and Marie Boerl. *The boys:* Messrs. Fields, Cagney, Le Voy, Grager, Maclyn, Smith, Jackson, Jenkins, and Mayo.
*Songs:* "Somebody's Waiting for Me," "Pitter Patter," "I Saved a Waltz for You," "Wedding Blues," "Bagdad on the Subway," "Send for Me," and "True Love."

**Outside Looking In**   By Maxwell Anderson. From Jim Tully's auto-biography, *Beggars of Life*. Directed by Augustin Duncan. Greenwich Village Playhouse, September 7, 1925. Moved to Thirty-ninth Street Theatre in December 1925. 113 performances.
*Cast:* Shelly (Wallace House); Bill (Raphael Byrnes); Rubin (Slim Martin); Mose (Harry Blakemore); Little Red (James Cagney); Edna (Blyth Daly); Baldy (Reginald Barlow); Hopper (Barry McCollum); Arkansas Snake (David A. Leonard); Oklahoma Red (Charles Bickford); Deputy (G. O. Taylor); Chief of Police (Walter Downing); Railroad Detective (Morris Armor); Ukie (Sydney Machat); Blind Sims (Richard Sullivan); Brakeman (George Westlake); Another Deputy (Frederick C. Packard, Jr.); Sheriff (John C. Hickey).

**Broadway**   By Philip Dunning and George Abbott. Staged by the authors. Produced by Jed Harris (assisted by Crosby Gaige). Broadhurst Theatre, September 16, 1926. 603 performances.
*Cast:* Nick Verdis (Paul Porcasi); Roy Lane (Lee Tracy, understudied by James Cagney); Lil Rice (Claire Woodbury); Katie (Elizabeth North); Joe (Joseph Spurin-Calleia); Mazie Smith (Mildred Wall); Ruby (Edith Van Cleve); Pearl (Eloise Stream); Grace (Molly Richardel); Ann (Constance Brown); Billie Moore (Elizabeth Allen); Steve Crandall (Robert Gleckler);

Dolph (Henry Sherwood); Porky Thomson (William Foran); Scar Edwards (Arthur Vees, replaced by John Wray, who engineered Cagney's loss of the London company's lead); Dan McCorn (Thomas Jackson); Benny (Frank Verigun); Larry (Millard Mitchell); Mike (Roy R. Lloyd, replaced Cagney as lead in the London company, Cagney taking his role in the New York production).

**Women Go On Forever**   By Daniel N. Rubin. Staged by John Cromwell. Produced by William A. Brady, Jr., and Dwight Deere Wiman. Forrest Theatre, September 7, 1927. 117 performances.
*Cast:* Minnie (Elizabeth Taylor); Mary (Edna Thrower); Billy (Sam Wren); Pearl (Constance McKay); Mrs. Daisy Bowman (Mary Boland); Mr. Givner (Francis Pierlot); Dr. Bevin (Willard Foster); Jake (Morgan Wallace); Pete (Osgood Perkins); Harry (Douglass Montgomery); Louie (Edwain Kasper); Daly (David Landau); Hulbert (Myron Paulson); Mabel (Mary Law); Eddie (James Cagney); Sven (Hans Sandquist).

**The Grand Street Follies of 1928 (A Topical Revue of the Season)**   Book and lyrics by Agnes Morgan, Marc Loebell, and Max Ewing. Music by Max Ewing, Lily Hyland, and Serge Walter. Entire production directed by Agnes Morgan. Dances by James Cagney and Michel Fokine. Music directed by Fred Fleming. Produced by The Actors-Managers, Inc. Booth Theatre, May 29, 1928. 114 performances.
*Cast:* Dorothy Sands, Albert Carroll, Marc Loebell, Paula Trueman, George Bratt, James Cagney, Hal Brogan, Vera Allen, Otto Hulett, Lily Lubell, Ruth McConkle, Mae Noble, Frances Cowles, Jean Crittenden, Robert White, Dela Frankau, Michael McCor-

mack, Robert Gorham, Blake Scott, Sophia Delza, Harold Minjur, Richard Ford, Mary Williams, George Elias Hoag, Laura Edmond, Joanna Roos, George Hoag, George Heller, Milton LeRoy, Harold Hecht, and John Rynne.

Cagney appeared in seven sketches, his highlight feature being a musical burlesque of Max Reinhardt's *Romeo and Juliet* production, Cagney playing Tybalt as danced by Harland Dixon.

**The Grand Street Follies of 1929**
Book and lyrics by Agnes Morgan. Music by Arthur Schwartz and Max Ewing. Additional numbers by William Irwin and Serge Walter. Produced by The Actor-Managers, Inc. Staged by Agnes Morgan. Dances by Dave Gould. Booth Theatre, May 1, 1929. 53 performances.
*Cast:* Albert Carroll, Otto Hulett, Marc Loebell, Dorothy Sands, Paula Trueman, Dela Frankau, James Cagney, Junius Matthews, Hal Brogan, Blaine Cordner, George Heller, Mary Williams, Mae Noble, Kathleen Kidd, and Katharine Gauthier.

Cagney appeared in eight sketches, his highlight sketch as a dancer in "Caesar's Invasion of Britain," as set to music by Noël Coward.

**Maggie the Magnificent**   By George Kelly. Staged by the author. Produced by Lauren and Rivers, Inc. Cort Theatre, October 21, 1929. 32 performances.
*Cast:* Katie Giles (Mary Frey); Etta (Joan Blondell); Margaret (Shirley Warde); Mrs. Reed (Marian S. Barney); Mrs. Buchanan (Mary Cecil); Ward (Frank Rowan); Elwood (James Cagney); Mrs. Groves (Doris Dagmar); House Boy (Rankin Mansfield); Burnley (J. P. Wilson); Stella (Frances Woodbury); Mrs. Winters (Ellen Mortimer).

**Penny Arcade** By Marie Baumer. Directed by William Keighley. Produced by Mr. Keighley and W. P. Tanner. Fulton Theatre, March 11, 1930. 24 performances.
*Cast:* Bum Rogers (Ackland Powell); George (Don Beddoe); Mrs. Delano (Valerie Bergere); Angel (Eric Dressler); Happy (Millard Mitchell); Joe Delano (Paul Guilfoyle); Mitch McKane (Frank Rowan); Sikes (George Barbier); Myrtle (Joan Blondell); Harry Delano (James Cagney); Jenny Delano (Lenita Lane); Nolan (Martin Malloy); Dugan (Ben Probst); Dick (Harry Gresham); Mabel (Desiree Harris); Fred (Jules Cern); Vivian (Annie-Laurie Jacques); Mr. James (Edmund Norris); Rose (Lucille Gillespie); Jim (John J. Cameron); Anna (Eleanor Andrus); Bob (Marshall Hale); Jack (William Whithead); Johnson (Harry Balcom).

# Cagney on Radio

The Cagney radio career, although not substantial, stretched out over three decades. He appeared on the radio informally via interview on a number of unrecorded (in both senses) occasions. The following incomplete listing gives his principal programs. More than half his broadcasts were made in behalf of his beloved Franklin D. Roosevelt, the armed forces during World War II, and charity, the last mostly for the Motion Picture Country Home and Hospital, to which the hefty Cagney fee was always donated. The following shows have almost all been recorded, most of them available through Radio Yesteryear, Sandy Hook, Connecticut.

1933 **Footlight Parade** The Warner Brothers film. Musical highlights. Half hour.

1936 **Is Zat So?** James Gleason's 1925 Broadway play. Cagney starring with Robert Armstrong. (Lux Radio Theatre.) Hour.

1938 **America Calling** Reaffirming the Bill of Rights. Hour.

1939 **Ceiling Zero** The Warner Brothers film. With Pat O'Brien. (Lux Radio Theatre.) Hour.

**The Hand of Providence** "The story of two crooks and a lady." (Gulf Screen Guild Theatre.) Hour.

**Angels with Dirty Faces** The Warner Brothers film. With Pat O'Brien. (Lux Radio Theatre.) Hour.

**Federal Theatre broadcast** Screen stars united on behalf of the Federal Theatre Project, then under fire from Congress. Half hour.

**Sheela** The remarkable only appearance of Gracie Allen as a serious actress, in this half-hour radio play by Sidney Cook and Hartman Reynaud. Cagney was co-starred in this tragic drama about the Irish uprising of 1916. (Gulf Screen Guild Theatre.) CBS. (No known recording exists.) October 22. The October 25, 1939, issue of *Variety* reviewed *Sheela*:

"Gracie Allen took a highdive into heavy dramatic emoting on the Gulf Screen Guild show over CBS last Sunday (22), teaming with James Cagney and J. M. Kerrigan in a brief but potent yarn of the Black and Tan rebellion in Dublin. As the Irish girl whose brother has been killed by the English and who betrays her sweetheart in revenge, the comedienne had trouble with the brogue and her voice was a trifle high-pitched, but she brought expressive intensity to the reading.

"As the sweetheart, Cagney was eloquently low-keyed, and both he and Kerrigan handled the Irish brogue with apparent ease. Principal fault with the opus was that its brevity prevented proper definition of character and situation.

"Miss Allen, Cagney and Kerrigan later joined George Burns in a fairly amusing session of patter, then all four offered an intentionally hokey song-and-dance routine, punctuated with very corny gags. It was very funny and must have been uproarious to the studio audience."

**1940   Next Time We Live** Cagney as newspaperman in love story. (Gulf Screen Guild Theatre.) Half hour.

**Revlon Revue**  Cagney as guest on Gertrude Lawrence's variety show. Half hour.

**Johnny Get Your Gun**  Cagney in leading role of Dalton Trumbo's harrowing 1939 novel. Dramatization by Arch Oboler. Half hour.

**Torrid Zone**  The Warner Brothers film. Brian Donlevy in the Pat O'Brien role. (Gulf Screen Guild Theatre.) Half hour.

**1941   The Strawberry Blonde** The Warner Brothers film. With Olivia De Havilland. (Gulf Screen Guild Theatre.) Half hour.

**1942   The Church of the Penitent Thief**  Cagney as convict at Dannemora who spearheads effort to establish there the chapel of St. Dismas, the thief who died next to Christ. (Radio Reader's Digest.) Half hour.

**The Hollywood March of Dimes of the Air**  Screen stars in solicitation on behalf of FDR's Birthday Polio Fund. Cagney and Maureen O'Sullivan

doing interior monologues as bride and groom during the ceremony. Hour.

**Captains of the Clouds**  The Warner Brothers film. Half hour.

**Yankee Doodle Dandy**  The Warner Brothers film. Musical highlights. Half hour.

**Your Favorite Stories as Told by Your Favorite Stars**  Cagney reading for servicemen James Thurber's short story "You Could Look It Up." (Yarns for Yanks.) Half hour.

**1943   Command Performance** Cagney with Jack Benny, Ginger Rogers, and Deanna Durbin. (Armed Forces Network.) Half hour.

**Bombs Away**  Cagney as pilot fighting the Japanese, a story pointing up the need for all Americans to save scrap metal for the war effort. (Armed Forces Network.) Half hour.

**1944   Night Must Fall**  The Emlyn Williams play with Dame May Whitty and Cagney playing Danny with an Irish accent. (Lady Esther Screen Guild Theatre.) Half hour.

**Democratic National Committee Program**  "Get out and vote for FDR," with a variety of stars.

**1945   Blood on the Sun** The Cagney Productions film. With Sylvia Sidney. (Lux Radio Theatre.) Hour.

**1948   Love's Lovely Counterfeit** "Suspense." An original story by J. M. Cain, with Cagney as a racketeer. Hour.

**Johnny Come Lately**  The Cagney Productions film. With Agnes Moorehead. (Camel Screen Guild Theatre.) Half hour.

**No Escape** "Suspense." Cagney as inadvertent hit-and-run driver. Half hour.

1950 **The West Point Story**
The Warner Brothers film. Musical highlights. Half hour.

# Feature Films

*(By year of release)*

## 1930

**Sinner's Holiday** (Warner Brothers)
*Writers:* Harvey Thew and George
Rosener, from the play *Penny Arcade*
by Marie Baumer
*Director:* John G. Adolfi
*Camera:* Ira Morgan
*Running time:* 55 minutes
*Cast:* Angel Harrison (Grant Withers);
Jennie Delano (Evalyn Knapp); Harry
Delano (James Cagney); Myrtle (Joan
Blondell); Mr Delano (Lucille La
Vern); Buck (Noel Madison); George
(Otto Hoffman); Mitch McKane (War-
ren Hymer); Sikes (Purnell B. Pratt);
Joe Delano (Ray Gallagher); Happy
(Hank Mann)

**Doorway to Hell** (Warner Brothers)
*Writer:* George Rosener, from the story
"A Handful of Clouds" by Rowland
Brown
*Director:* Archie Mayo
*Camera:* Barney "Chick" McGill
*Running time:* 78 minutes
*Cast:* Louis Ricarno (Lewis [Lew]
Ayres); Sam Marconi (Charles Judels);
Doris (Dorothy Mathews); Jackie
Lamar (Leon Janney); Captain O'Grady
(Robert Elliott); Steve Mileway (James
Cagney); Captain of Military Academy
(Kenneth Thomson); Joe (Jerry
Mandy); Rocco (Noel Madison); Bit
(Bernard "Bunny" Granville); Machine

Gunner (Fred Argus); Girl (Ruth Hall);
Gangsters (Dwight Frye, Tom Wilson,
Al Hill)

## 1931

**Other Men's Women** (Warner
Brothers)
*Writer:* William K. Wells, from a story
by Maude Fulton
*Director:* William A. Wellman
*Camera:* Barney "Chick" McGill
*Running time:* 70 minutes
*Cast:* Bill (Grant Withers); Lily (Mary
Aston); Jack (Regis Toomey); Ed
(James Cagney); Marie (Joan Blondell);
Haley (Fred Kohler); Pegleg (J. Farrell
MacDonald); Waitress (Lillian Worth);
Bixby (Walter Long); Railroad Workers
(Bob Perry, Lee Morgan, Kewpie Mor-
gan, Pat Hartigan)

**The Millionaire** (Warner Brothers)
*Writers:* Julian Josephson and Maude
Powell, with dialogue by Booth Tark-
ington, from *Idle Hands* by Earl Derr
Biggers
*Director:* John G. Adolfi
*Camera:* James Van Trees
*Running time:* 82 minutes
*Cast:* James Alden (George Arliss); Bar-
bara Alden (Evalyn Knapp); Bill Mer-
rick (James Cagney); Carter Andrews
(Branwell Fletcher); Mrs. Alden (Flo-
rence Arliss); Peterson (Noah Beery);
Dr. Harvey (Ivan Simpson); McCoy

(Sam Hardy); Dan Lewis (J. Farrell MacDonald); Briggs (Tully Marshall); Doctor (J. C. Nugent)

**The Public Enemy** (Warner Brothers)
*Writers:* Kubec Glasmon and John Bright; adaptation and dialogue by Harvey Thew, from *Beer and Blood* by John Bright
*Director:* William A. Wellman
*Camera:* Dev Jennings
*Running time:* 84 minutes
*Cast:* Tom Powers (James Cagney); Gwen Allen (Jean Harlow); Matt Doyle (Edward Woods); Mamie (Joan Blondell); Ma Powers (Beryl Mercer); Mike Powers (Donald Cook); Kitty (Mae Clarke); Jane (Mia Marvin); Nails Nathan (Leslie Fenton); Paddy Ryan (Robert Emmett O'Connor); Putty Nose (Murray Kinnell); Bugs Moran (Ben Hendricks, Jr.); Molly Doyle (Rita Flynn); Dutch (Clark Burroughs); Hack (Snitz Edwards); Mrs. Doyle (Adele Watson); Tommy as a Boy (Frank Coghlan, Jr.); Matt as a Boy (Frankie Darro); Officer Pat Burke (Robert E. Homans); Nails' Girl (Dorothy Gee); Officer Powers (Purnell Pratt); Steve the Bartender (Lee Phelps); Little Girls (Helen Parrish, Dorothy Gray, Nanci Price); Bugs as a Boy (Ben Hendricks III); Machine Gunner (George Daly); Joe the Headwaiter (Sam McDaniel); Pawnbroker (William H. Strauss)

**Smart Money** (Warner Brothers)
*Writers:* Kubec Glasmon and John Bright, with additional dialogue by Lucien Hubbard and Joseph Jackson
*Director:* Alfred E. Green
*Camera:* Robert Kurrie
*Running time:* 90 minutes
*Cast:* Nick Venizelos (Edward G. Robinson); Irene Graham (Evalyn Knapp); Jack (James Cagney); Marie (Noel Francis); District Attorney (Morgan Wallace); Mr. Amenoppopolus (Paul Porcasi); Greek Barber (Maurice Black); D.A.'s Girl (Margaret Livingston); Schultz

(Clark Burroughs); Salesman (Billy House); Two-Time Phil (Edwin Argus); Sleepy Sam (Ralf Harolde); Sport Williams (Boris Karloff); Small Town Girl (Mae Madison); Dealer Barnes (Walter Percival); Snake Eyes (John Larkin); Lola (Polly Walters); Hickory Short (Ben Taggart); Cigar Stand Clerk (Gladys Lloyd); Matron (Eulalie Jensen); Desk Clerk (Charles Lane); Reporter (Edward Hearn); Tom, a Customer (Eddie Kane); George, the Porter (Clinton Rosemond); Machine Gunner (Charles O'Malley); Joe, Barber Customer (Gus Leonard); Cigar Stand Clerk (Wallace MacDonald); Dwarf on Train (John George); Gambler (Harry Semels); Girl at Gaming Table (Charlotte Merriam); with Larry McGrath, Spencer Bell, Allan Lane

**Blonde Crazy** (Warner Brothers)
*Writers:* Kubec Glasmon and John Bright
*Director:* Roy Del Ruth
*Camera:* Sid Hickox
*Running time:* 73 minutes
*Cast:* Bert Harris (James Cagney); Ann Roberts (Joan Blondell); Dapper Dan Barker (Louis Calhern); Helen Wilson (Noel Francis); A. Rupert Johnson, Jr. (Guy Kibbee); Joe Reynolds (Raymond Milland); Peggy (Polly Walters); Four-Eyes, Desk Clerk (Charles [Levinson] Lane); Colonel Bellock (William Burress); Dutch (Peter Erkelenz); Mrs. Snyder (Maude Eburne); Lee (Walter Percival); Hank (Nat Pendleton); Jerry (Russell Hopton); Cabbie (Dick Cramer); Detective (Wade Boteler); Bellhops (Ray Cooke, Edward Morgan); Conman (Phil Sleman)

## 1932

**Taxi!** (Warner Brothers)
*Writers:* Kubec Glasmon and John Bright, from the play *The Blind Spot* by Kenyon Nicholson
*Director:* Roy Del Ruth

*Camera:* James Van Trees
*Running time:* 70 minutes
*Cast:* Matt Nolan (James Cagney); Sue Reilly (Loretta Young); Skeets (George E. Stone); Pop Reilly (Guy Kibbee); Buck Gerard (David Landau); Danny Nolan (Ray Cooke); Ruby (Leila Bennett); Marie Costa (Dorothy Burgess); Joe Silva (Matt McHugh); Father Nulty (George MacFarlane); Polly (Polly Walters); Truckdriver (Nat Pendleton); Mr. West (Berton Churchill); William Kenny (George Raft); Monument Salesman (Hector V. Sarno); Cleaning Lady (Aggie Herring); Onlooker (Lee Phelps); Cabbie (Harry Tenbrook); Cop with Jewish Man (Robert Emmett O'Connor); Dance Judges (Eddie Fetherstone, Russ Powell); Cop (Ben Taggart); The Cotton Club Orchestra

**The Crowd Roars** (Warner Brothers)
*Writers:* Kubec Glasmon, John Bright, and Niven Busch, from a story by Howard Hawks and Seton Miller
*Director:* Howard Hawks
*Camera:* Sid Hickox and John Stumar
*Running time:* 85 minutes
*Cast:* Joe Greer (James Cagney); Anne (Joan Blondell); Lee (Ann Dvorak); Eddie Greer (Eric Linden); Dad Greer (Guy Kibbee); Spud Connors (Frank McHugh); Bill Arnold (William Arnold); Jim (Leo Nomis); Mrs. Spud Connors (Charlotte Merriam); Dick Willshaw (Regis Toomey); Auto Drivers (Harry Hartz, Ralph Hepburn, Fred Guisso, Fred Frame, Phil Pardee, Spider Matlock, Jack Brisko, Lou Schneider, Bryan Salspaugh, Stubby Stubblefield, Shorty Cantlon, Mel Keneally, Wilbur Shaw); Mechanic (James Burtis); Ascot Announcer (Sam Hayes); Tom, Counterman (Robert McWade); Official (Ralph Dunn); Announcer (John Conte); Red, Eddie's Pitman (John Harron)

**Winner Take All** (Warner Brothers)
*Writers:* Wilson Mizner and Robert Lord, from the magazine story *133 At 3* by Gerald Beaumont
*Director:* Roy Del Ruth
*Camera:* Robert Kurrle
*Running time:* 68 minutes
*Cast:* Jim Lane (James Cagney); Peggy Harmon (Marian Nixon); Joan Gibson (Virginia Bruce); Pop Slavin (Guy Kibbee); Rosebud, the Trainer (Clarence Muse); Dickie Harmon (Dickie Moore); Monty (Allan Lane); Roger Elliott (John Roche); Legs Davis (Ralf Harolde); Forbes (Alan Mowbray); Ben Isaacs (Clarence Wilson); Butler (Charles Coleman); Ann (Esther Howard); Lois (Renee Whitney); Al West (Harvey Perry); Pice (Julian Rivero); Ring Announcer (Selmer Jackson); Manager (Chris Pin Martin); Intern (George Hayes); Tijuana Referee (Bob Perry); Second (Billy West); Reporter (Phil Tead); Waiter (Rolfe Sedan); Boxing Spectator (John Kelly); Ring Announcer, Championship (Lee Phelps); Society Man (Jay Eaton); Blonde (Charlotte Merriam)

## 1933

**Hard to Handle** (Warner Brothers)
*Writers:* Wilson Mizner and Robert Lord, from a story by Houston Branch
*Director:* Mervyn LeRoy
*Camera:* Barney "Chick" McGill
*Running time:* 81 minutes
*Cast:* Lefty Merrill (James Cagney); Ruth Waters (Mary Brian); Lil Waters (Ruth Donnelly); Radio Announcer (Allen Jenkins); Marlene Reeves (Claire Dodd); John Hayden (Gavin Gordon); Mrs. Hawks, Landlady (Emma Dunn); Charles Reeves (Robert McWade); Ed McGrath (John Sheehan); Joe Goetz (Matt McHugh); Mrs. Weston Parks (Louise Mackintosh); Antique Dealer (William H. Strauss); Merrill's Secretary (Bess Flowers); Hash-slinger (Lew Kelly); Colonel Wells (Berton Churchill); Colonel's Associate (Harry Holman); Fat Lady with Vanishing

Cream (Grace Hayle); Dance Judge (George Pat Collins); District Attorney (Douglass Dumbrille); Andy (Sterling Holloway); Jailer (Charles Wilson); with Jack Crawford, Stanley Smith, Walter Walker, Mary Doran

**Picture Snatcher** (Warner Brothers)
*Writers:* Allen Rivkin and P. J. Wolfson, from a story by Danny Ahern
*Director:* Lloyd Bacon
*Camera:* Sol Polito
*Running time:* 77 minutes
*Cast:* Danny Kean (James Cagney); McLean (Ralph Bellamy); Patricia Nolan (Patricia Ellis); Allison (Alice White); Jerry (Ralf Harolde); Casey Nolan (Robert Emmett O'Connor); Grover (Robert Barrat); Hennessy, the Fireman (George Pat Collins); Leo (Tom Wilson); Olive (Barbara Rogers); Connie (Renee Whitney); Colleen (Alice Jans); Speakeasy Girl (Jill Dennett); Reporter (Billy West); Machine Gunner (George Daly); Head Keeper (Arthur Vinton); Prison Guard (Stanley Blystone); Hood (Don Brodie); Reporter (George Chandler); Journalism Teacher (Sterling Holloway); Mike, Colleen's Boyfriend (Donald Kerr); Pete, a Drunken Reporter (Hobart Cavanaugh); Reporter Strange (Phil Tead); Sick Reporter (Charles King); Reporter outside Prison (Milton Kibbee); Editors (Dick Elliott, Vaughn Taylor); Bartender (Bob Perry); Barber (Gino Corrado); Speakeasy Proprietor (Maurice Black); Record Editor (Selmer Jackson); Police Officer (Jack Grey); Captain (John Ince); Little Girl (Cora Sue Collins)

**The Mayor of Hell** (Warner Brothers)
*Writer:* Edward Chodorov, from a story by Islin Auster
*Director:* Archie Mayo
*Camera:* Barney "Chick" McGill
*Running time:* 90 minutes
*Cast:* Patsy Gargan (James Cagney); Dorothy Griffith (Madge Evans); Mike (Allen Jenkins); Mr. Thompson (Dudley Digges); Jimmy Smith (Frankie Darro); Smoke (Farina); Mrs. Smith (Dorothy Peterson); Hopkins (John Marston); Guard (Charles Wilson); Tommy's Father (Hobart Cavanaugh); Johnny Stone (Raymond Borzage); Mr. Smith (Robert Barrat); Brandon (George Pat Collins); Butch Kilgore (Mickey Bennett); Judge Gilbert (Arthur Byron); the Girl (Sheila Terry); Joe (Harold Huber); Louis Johnston (Edwin Maxwell); Walters (William V. Mong); Izzy Horowitz (Sidney Miller); Tony's Father (George Humbert); Charlie Burns (George Offerman, Jr.); Tommy Gorman (Charles Cane); Johnston's Assistant (Wallace MacDonald); Car Owner (Adrian Morris); Hemingway (Snowflake); Guard (Wilfred Lucas); Collectors (Bob Perry, Charles Sullivan); Sheriff (Ben Taggart)

**Footlight Parade** (Warner Brothers)
*Writers:* Manuel Seff and James Seymour
*Directors:* Lloyd Bacon and Busby Berkeley
*Camera:* George Barnes
*Running time:* 104 minutes
*Cast:* Chester Kent (James Cagney); Nan Prescott (Joan Blondell); Bea Thorn (Ruby Keeler); Scotty Blair (Dick Powell); Silas Gould (Guy Kibbee); Harriet Bowers Gould (Ruth Donelly); Vivian Rich (Claire Dodd); Charlie Bowers (Hugh Herbert); Francis (Frank McHugh); Al Frazer (Arthur Hohl); Harry Thompson (Gordon Westcott); Cynthia Kent (Renee Whitney); Joe Farrington (Philip Faversham); Miss Smythe (Juliet Ware); Fralick, the Music Director (Herman Bing); George Appolinaris (Paul Porcasi); Doorman (William Granger); Cop (Charles C. Wilson); Gracie (Barbara Rogers); Specialty Dancer (Billy Taft); Chorus Girls (Marjean Rogers, Pat

Wing, Donna Mae Roberts); Chorus Boy (David O'Brien); Drugstore Attendant (George Chandler); Title-Thinker-Upper (Hobart Cavanaugh); Auditor (William V. Mong); Mac, the Dance Director (Lee Moran); Mouse in "Sittin' on a Backyard Fence" Number (Billy Barty); Desk Clerk in "Honeymoon Hotel" Number (Harry Seymour); Porter (Sam McDaniel); Little Boy (Billy Barty); House Detective (Fred Kelsey); Uncle (Jimmy Conlin); Sailor-Pal in "Shanghai Lil" Number (Roger Gray); Sailor Behind Table (John Garfield); Sailor on Table (Duke York); Joe, the Assistant Dance Director (Harry Seymour); Chorus Girls (Donna La Barr, Marlo Dwyer)

**Lady Killer** (Warner Brothers)
*Writer:* Ben Markson, from *The Finger Man* by Rosalind Keating Shaffer
*Director:* Roy Del Ruth
*Camera:* Tony Gaudio
*Running time:* 76 minutes
*Cast:* Dan Quigley (James Cagney); Myra Gale (Mae Clarke); Duke (Leslie Fenton); Lois Underwood (Margaret Lindsay); Ramick (Henry O'Neill); Conroy (Willard Robertson); Jones (Douglas Cosgrove); Pete (Raymond Hatton); Smiley (Russell Hopton); Williams (William Davidson); Mrs. Wilbur Marley (Marjorie Gateson); Brannigan (Robert Elliott); Kendall (John Marston); Spade Maddock (Douglass Dumbrille); Thompson (George Chandler); The Escort (George Blackwood); Oriental (Jack Don Wong); Los Angeles Police Chief (Frank Sheridan); Jeffries, Theater Manager (Edwin Maxwell); Usher Sergeant Seymour (Phil Tead); Movie Fan (Dewey Robinson); Man with Purse (H. C. Bradley); J. B. Roland (Harry Holman); Dr. Crane (Harry Beresford); Butler (Olaf Hytten); Ambulance Attendant (Harry Strong); Casino Cashier (Al Hill); Man in Casino (Bud Flanagan [Dennis

O'Keefe]); Hand-out (James Burke); Jailer (Robert Homans); Lawyer (Clarence Wilson); Porter (Sam McDaniel); Los Angeles Cop (Spencer Charters); Western Director (Herman Bing); Letter-Handler (Harold Waldridge); Director (Luis Alberni); Property Man (Ray Cooke); Hood (Sam Ash)

1934

**Jimmy the Gent** (Warner Brothers)
*Writer:* Bertram Milhouser, from a story by Laird Doyle and Ray Nazarro
*Director:* Michael Curtiz
*Camera:* Ira Morgan
*Running time:* 67 minutes
*Cast:* Jimmy Corrigan (James Cagney); Joan Martin (Bette Davis); Mabel (Alice White); Louie (Allen Jenkins); Joe Rector [Monty Barton] (Arthur Hohl); James J. Wallingham (Alan Dinehart); Ronnie Gatston (Philip Reed); the Imposter (Hobart Cavanaugh); Gladys Farrell (Mayo Methot); Hendrickson (Ralf Harolde); Mike (Joseph Sawyer); Blair (Philip Faversham); Posy Barton (Nora Lane); Judge (Joseph Crehan); Civil Judge (Robert Warwick); Jitters (Merna Kennedy); Bessie (Renee Whitney); Tea Assistant (Monica Bannister); Man Drinking Tea (Don Douglas); Chester Coote (Bud Flanagan [Dennis O'Keefe]); Man in Flower Shop (Leonard Mudie); Justice of the Peace (Harry Holman); File Clerk (Camille Rovelle); Pete (Stanley Mack); Grant (Tom Costello); Ferris (Ben Hendricks); Halley (Billy West); Tim (Eddie Shubert); Stew (Lee Moran); Eddie (Harry Wallace); Irish Cop (Robert Homans); Ambulance Driver (Milton Kibbee); Doctor (Howard Hickman); Nurse (Eula Guy); Viola (Juliet Ware); Blonde (Rickey Newell); Brunette (Lorena Layson); Second Young Man (Dick French); Third Young Man (Jay

Eaton); Reverend Amiel Bottsford (Harold Entwistle); Bailiff (Charles Hickman); Ticket Clerk, Steamship (Leonard Mudie); Steward (Olaf Hytten); Second Steward (Vesey O'Davoren); Chalmers (Lester Dorr); Secretary (Pat Wing)

**He Was Her Man** (Warner Brothers)
*Writers:* Tom Buckingham and Niven Busch, from a story by Robert Lord
*Director:* Lloyd Bacon
*Camera:* George Barnes
*Running time:* 70 minutes
*Cast:* Flicker Hayes (James Cagney); Rose Lawrence (Joan Blondell); Nick Gardella (Victor Jory); Pop Sims (Frank Craven); J. C. Ward (Harold Huber); Monk (Russell Hopton); Red Deering (Ralf Harolde); Mrs. Gardella (Sarah Padden); Dutch (J. M. [John] Qualen); Dan Curly (Bradley Page); Gassy (Samuel S. Hinds); Waiter (George Chandler); Whitey (James Eagles); Fisherman (Gino Corrado)

**Here Comes the Navy**
(Warner Brothers)
*Writers:* Ben Markson and Earl Baldwin, from a story by Ben Markson
*Director:* Lloyd Bacon
*Camera:* Arthur Edeson
*Running time:* 86 minutes
*Cast:* Chesty O'Connor (James Cagney); Biff Martin (Pat O'Brien); Dorothy Martin (Gloria Stuart); Droopy (Frank McHugh); Gladys (Dorothy Tree); Commander Denny (Robert Barrat); Lieutenant Commander (Willard Robertson); Floor Manager (Guinn Williams); Droopy's Ma (Maude Eburne); First Girl (Martha Merrill); Second Girl (Lorena Layson); Aunt (Ida Darling); Riveter (Henry Otho); Hat Check Girl (Pauline True); Porter (Sam McDaniel); Foreman (Frank La Rue); Recruiting Officer (Joseph Crehan); CPO (James Burtis); Supply Sergeant (Edward Chandler);

Professor (Leo White); Officer (Niles Welch); Sailor (Fred "Snowflake" Toone); Skipper (Eddie Shubert); Admiral (George Irving); Captain (Howard Hickman); Navy Chaplain (Edward Earle); Lieutenant (Emmett); Bit (Gordon [Bill] Elliott); Workman (Nick Copeland); Attendant (John Swor); Marine Orderly (Eddie Cuff); Hood at Dance (Chuck Hamilton); Sailor (Eddie Fetherstone)

**The St. Louis Kid** (Warner Brothers)
*Writers:* Warren Duffy and Seton Miller, from a story by Frederick Hazlitt Brennan
*Director:* Ray Enright
*Camera:* Sid Hickox
*Running time:* 67 minutes
*Cast:* Eddie Kennedy (James Cagney); Ann Reid (Patricia Ellis); Buck Willetts (Allen Jenkins); Farmer Benson (Robert Barrat); Richardson (Hobart Cavanaugh); Merseldopp (Spencer Charters); Brown (Addison Richards); Gracie (Dorothy Dare); Judge Jones (Arthur Aylesworth); Harris (Charles Wilson); Joe Hunter (William Davidson); Louie (Harry Woods); The Girlfriend (Gertrude Short); Pete (Eddie Shubert); Gorman (Russell Hicks); Sergeant (Guy Usher); Cops (Cliff Saum, Bruce Mitchell); Policeman (Wilfred Lucas); Girl (Rosalie Roy); Office Girl (Mary Russell); Motor Cop (Ben Hendricks); Mike (Harry Tyler); Paymaster (Milton Kibbee); Cook (Tom Wilson); Secretaries (Alice Marr, Victoria Vinton); Farmer (Lee Phelps); Girl in Car (Louise Seidel); Giddy Girl (Mary Treen); First Girl (Nan Grey); Second Girl (Virginia Grey); Third Girl (Martha Merrill); Sheriff (Charles B. Middleton); Prosecutor (Douglas Cosgrove); First Deputy (Monte Vandergrift); Second Deputy (Jack Cheatham); Driver (Stanley Mack); Attendant (Grover Liffen); Broadcast Officer (Frank Bull); Sergeant (Wade Boteler);

Policeman (Frank Fanning); Second Policeman (Gene Strong); Flora (Edna Bennett); Man (Clay Clement); Detective (James Burtis) and Eddie Featherstone, Joan Barclay

## 1935

**Devil Dogs of the Air**
(Warner Brothers)
*Writers:* Malcolm Stuart Boyland and Earl Baldwin, from the story "Air Devils" by John Monk Saunders
*Director:* Lloyd Bacon
*Camera:* Arthur Edeson
*Running time:* 86 minutes
*Cast:* Tommy O'Toole (James Cagney); Lieutenant William Brannigan (Pat O'Brien); Betty Roberts (Margaret Lindsay); Crash Kelly (Frank McHugh); Ma Roberts (Helen Lowell); Mac (John Arledge); Commandant (Robert Barrat); Captain (Russell Hicks); Adjutant (William B. Davidson); Senior Instructor (Ward Bond); Fleet Commander (Samuel S. Hinds); Officer (Harry Seymour); Second Officer (Bill Beggs); Mate (Bob Spencer); Officers (Newton House, Ralph Nye); Medical Officer (Selmer Jackson); Student (Bud Flanagan [Dennis O'Keefe]); Instructor (Gordon [Bill] Elliott); First Student (Don Turner); Second Student (Dick French); Third Student (Charles Sherlock); Messenger (Carlyle Blackwell, Jr.); Girl (Martha Merrill); Lieutenant Brown (David Newell); Mrs. Brown (Olive Jones); Mrs. Johnson (Helen Flint); Communications Officer (Joseph Crehan)

**G-Men** (Warner Brothers)
*Writer:* Seton I. Miller, from *Public Enemy No. 1* by Gregory Rogers
*Director:* William Keighley
*Camera:* Sol Polito
*Running time:* 85 minutes
*Cast:* James "Brick" Davis (James Cagney); Jean Morgan (Ann Dvorak);

Kay McCord (Margaret Lindsay); Jeff McCord (Robert Armstrong); Brad Collins (Barton MacLane); Hugh Farrell (Lloyd Nolan); McKay (William Harrigan); Danny Leggett (Edward Pawley); Gerard (Russell Hopton); Durfee (Noel Madison); Eddie Buchanan (Regis Toomey); Bruce J. Gregory (Addison Richards); Venke (Harold Huber); The Man (Raymond Hatton); Analyst (Monte Blue); Gregory's Secretary (Mary Treen); Accomplice (Adrian Morris); Joseph Kratz (Edwin Maxwell); Bill, the Ballistics Expert (Emmett Vogan); Agent (James Flavin); Cops (Stanley Blystone, Pat Flaherty); Agent (James T. Mack); Congressman (Jonathan Hale); Bank Cashier (Ed Keane); Short Man (Charles Sherlock); Henchman at Lodge (Wheeler Oakman); Police Broadcaster (Eddie Dunn); Intern (Gordon [Bill] Elliott); Doctor at Store (Perry Ivins); Hood Shot at Lodge (Frank Marlowe); Collins's Moll (Gertrude Short); Gerard's Moll (Marie Astaire); Durfee's Moll (Florence Dudley); Moll (Frances Morris); Hood (Al Hill); Gangster (Huey White); Headwaiter (Glen Cavender); Tony (John Impolito); Sergeant (Bruce Mitchell); Deputy Sheriff (Monte Vandergrift); Chief (Frank Shannon); Announcer (Frank Bull); Nurse (Martha Merrill); Lounger (Gene Morgan); J. E. Glattner, the Florist (Joseph De Stefani); Machine Gunners (George Daly, Ward Bond); Prison Guard (Tom Wilson); Police Driver (Henry Hall); McCord's Aide (Lee Phelps); Hood at Lodge (Marc Lawrence); Man (Brooks Benedict)

**The Irish in Us** (Warner Brothers)
*Writer:* Earl Baldwin, from a story by Frank Orsatti
*Director:* Lloyd Bacon
*Camera:* George Barnes
*Running time:* 84 minutes

Cast: Danny O'Hara (James Cagney);
Pat O'Hara (Pat O'Brien); Lucille Jackson (Olivia De Havilland); Mike
O'Hara (Frank McHugh); Car-Barn
Hammerschlog (Allen Jenkins); Ma
O'Hara (Mary Gordon); Captain Jackson (J. Farrell MacDonald); Doc
Mullins (Thomas Jackson); Joe Delancy
(Harvey Perry); Lady in Ring (Bess
Flowers); Neighbor (Mabel Colcord);
Doctor (Edward Keane); Cook (Herb
Haywood); Girl (Lucille Collins);
Announcer (Harry Seymour); Chick
(Sailor Vincent); Referee (Mushy Callahan); Messenger Boy (Jack McHugh);
Men (Edward Gargan, Huntly Gordon,
Emmett Vogan, Will Stanton)

**A Midsummer Night's Dream**
(Warner Brothers)
Writer: William Shakespeare (scenario by
Charles Kenyon and Mary McCall, Jr.)
Directors: Max Reinhardt and William
Dieterle
Camera: Hal Mohr
Running time: 132 minutes
Cast: Bottom (James Cagney); Lysander
(Dick Powell); Flute (Joe E. Brown);
Helena (Jean Muir); Snout (Hugh Herbert); Theseus (Ian Hunter); Quince
(Frank McHugh); Oberon (Victor Jory);
Hermia (Olivia De Havilland);
Demetrius (Ross Alexander); Egeus
(Grant Mitchell); First Fairy [Prima
Ballerina] (Nina Theilade); Hippolyta,
Queen of the Amazons (Verree Teasdale); Titania (Anita Louise); Puck
(Mickey Rooney); Snug (Dewey Robinson); Philostrate (Hobart Cavanaugh);
Starveling (Otis Harlan); Ninny's Tomb
(Arthur Treacher); Fairies: Pease-Blossom (Katherine Frey); Cobweb
(Helen Westcott); Moth (Fred Sale);
Mustard-Seed (Billy Barty)

**Frisco Kid** (Warner Brothers)
Writers: Warren Duff and Seton I.
Miller, from a story by Warren Duff
Director: Lloyd Bacon
Camera: Sol Polito

Running time: 77 minutes
Cast: Bat Morgan (James Cagney); Jean
Barrat (Margaret Lindsay); Paul Morra
(Ricardo Cortez); Bella Morra (Lily
Damita); Charles Ford (Donald
Woods); Spider Burke (Barton
MacLane); Solly (George E. Stone);
William T. Coleman (Addison
Richards); James Daley (Joseph King);
Judge Crawford (Robert McWade);
McClanahan (Joseph Crehan); Graber
(Robert Strange); Slugs Crippen
(Joseph Sawyer); Shanghai Duck (Fred
Kohler); Tupper (Edward McWade);
Jumping Whale (Claudia Coleman);
The Weasel (John Wray); First Lookout
(Ivar McFadden); Second Lookout (Lee
Phelps); Evangelist (William Wagner);
Drunk (Don Barclay); Captain (Jack
Curtis); Miner (Walter Long); Man
(James Farley); Shop Man (Milton
Kibbee); Salesman (Harry Seymour);
Madame (Claire Sinclair); Young Drunk
(Alan Davis); Dealer (Karl Hackett);
First Policeman (Wilfred Lucas); Second Policeman (John T. [Jack] Dillon);
First Man (Edward Mortimer); Second
Man (William Holmes); Usher (Don
Downen); Mrs. Crawford (Mrs. Willfred North); Speaker (Charles Middleton); Man (Joe Smith Marba); Doctor
(Landers Stevens); Mulligan (Frank
Sheridan); Men (J. C. Morton, Harry
Tenbrook); Dealer (Lew Harvey); Rat
Face (Eddie Sturgis); Captain [Vigilante] (William Desmond); Maid (Jessie
Perry); Contractors (Edward Keane,
Edward Le Saint); Vigilante Leaders
(Robert Dudley, Dick Rush); Doctor
(John Elliott) and Helene Chadwick,
Bill Dale, Dick Kerr, Alice Lake, Vera
Steadman, Jane Tallent

**Ceiling Zero** (Cosmopolitan
Productions/Warner Brothers)
Writer: Frank Wead, from his play *Ceiling Zero*
Director: Howard Hawks
Camera: Arthur Edeson
Running time: 95 minutes

*Cast:* Dizzy Davis (James Cagney); Jake Lee (Pat O'Brien); Tommy Thomas (June Travis); Texas Clark (Stuart Erwin); Tay Lawson (Henry Wadsworth); Lou Clark (Isabel Jewell); Al Stone (Barton MacLane); Mary Lee (Martha Tibbetts); Joe Allen (Craig Reynolds); Buzz Gordon (James H. Bush); Les Bogan (Robert Light); Fred Adams (Addison Richards); Eddie Payson (Carlyle Morre, Jr.); Smiley Johnson (Richard Purcell); Transportation Agent (Gordon [Bill] Elliott); Baldy Wright (Pat West); Doc Wilson (Edward Gargan); Mike Owens (Garry Owen); Mama Gini (Mathilde Comont); Birdie (Carol Hughes); Stunt Fliers (Frank Tomick, Paul Mantz); Pilots (Jimmy Aye, Howard Allen, Mike Lally, Harold Miller); Mechanic (Jerry Jerome); Hostesses (Helene McAdoo, Gay Sheridan, Mary Lou Dix, Louise Seidel, Helen Erickson); Office Workers (Don Wayson, Dick Cherney, Jimmie Barnes, Frank McDonald); Teletype Operator (J. K. Kane); Tall Girl (Jayne Manners); Girls (Maryon Curtiz, Margaret Perry)

## 1936

**Great Guy** (Grand National)
*Writers:* Henry McCarthy, Henry Johnson, James E. Grant, and Harry Rusking, from the "Johnny Cave" stories by James Edward Grant
*Director:* John G. Blystone
*Camera:* Jack McKenzie
*Running time:* 75 minutes
*Cast:* Johnny Cave (James Cagney); Janet Henry (Mae Clarke); Pat Haley (James Burke); Pete Reilly (Edward Brophy); Conning (Henry Kolker); Hazel Scott (Bernadene Hayes); Captain Pat Hanlon (Edward J. McNamara); Cavanaugh (Robert Gleckler); Joe Burton (Joe Sawyer); Al (Ed Gargan); Tim (Matty Fain); Mrs. Ogilvie (Mary Gordon); Joel Green (Wallis Clark); The Mayor (Douglas Wood);

Clerk (Jeffrey Sayre); Meat Clerk (Eddy Chandler); Store Manager (Henry Roquemore); Client (Murdock MacQuarrie); Woman at Accident (Kate Price); Detective (Frank O'Connor); Furniture Salesman (Arthur Hoyt); Truck Driver (Jack Pennick); Reporter (Lynton Brent); City Editor (John Dilson); Guests (Bud Geary, Dennis O'Keefe); Parker (Robert Lowery); Grocery Clerk (Bobby Barber); Nurse (Gertrude Green); Burton's Girl Friend (Ethelreda Leopold); Cop at Accident (Bruce Mitchell); Party Guests (James Ford, Frank Mills, Ben Hendricks, Jr.); Deputy (Kernan Cripps); Second Meat Clerk (Bill O'Brien); Chauffeur (Lester Dorr); Receiving Clerk (Harry Tenbrook); Mike the Cop (Lee Shumway) and Gertrude Aston, Vera Steadman, Mildred Harris, Bert Kalmar, Jr., Walter D. Clarke, Jr.

## 1937

**Something to Sing About**
(Grand National)
*Writer:* Austin Parker, from a story by Victor Schertzinger
*Director:* Victor Schertzinger
*Camera:* John Stumar
*Running time:* 80 minutes
*Cast:* Terry Rooney (James Cagney); Rita Wyatt (Evelyn Daw); Hank Meyers (William Frawley); Stephanie Hajos (Mona Barrie); Bennett O'Regan (Gene Lockhart); Orchestra Soloist (James Newhill); Pinky (Harris Barris); Candy (Candy Candido); Soloist (Cully Richards); Café Manager (William B. Davidson); Blaine (Richard Tucker); Farney (Marek Windheim); Easton (Dwight Frye); Daviani (John Arthur); Ito (Philip Ahn); Miss Robbins (Kathleen Lockhart); Transportation Manager (Kenneth Harlan); Studio Attorney (Herbert Rawlinson); Edward Burns (Ernest Wood); Man Terry Fights (Chick Collins); Dancers

(Harland Dixon, Johnny Boyle, Johnny "Skins" Miller, Pat Moran, Joe Bennett, Buck Mack, Eddie Allen); Singer (Bill Carey); Specialty (The Vagabonds); Girls (Elinore Welz, Eleanor Prentiss); Arthur Nelson's Fighting Cats (Pinkie and Pal); Cabbie (Frank Mills); Stuntman (Duke Green); Studio Official (Larry Steers); Sailor in Drag (John "Skins" Miller); SF Theatre Manager (Eddie Kane); Studio Guard (Edward Hearn); Three Shades of Blue (Dottie Messmer, Virginia Lee Irwin, Dolly Waldorf); Ship's Captain (Robert McKenzie); Head Waiter (Alphonse Martel)

1938

**Boy Meets Girl** (Warner Brothers)
*Writers:* Bella and Sam Spewack
*Director:* Lloyd Bacon
*Camera:* Sol Polito
*Running time:* 80 minutes
*Cast:* Robert Law (James Cagney); J. C. Benson (Pat O'Brien); Susie (Marie Wilson); C. Elliott Friday (Ralph Bellamy); Rossetti (Frank McHugh); Larry Toms (Dick Foran); Rodney Bevan (Bruce Lester); Announcer (Ronald Reagan); Happy (Paul Clark); Peggy (Penny Singleton); Miss Crews (Dennie Moore); Songwriters (Harry Seymour, Bert Hanlon); Major Thompson (James Stephenson); B. K. (Pierre Watkin); Cutter (John Ridgely); Office Boy (George Hickman); Smitty (Cliff Saum); Commissary Cashier (Carole Landis); Dance Director (Curt Bois); Olaf (Otto Fries); Extra (John Harron); Wardrobe Attendant (Hal K. Dawson); Nurse (Dorothy Vaughan); Director (Bert Howard); Young Man (James Nolan); Bruiser (Bill Telaak); Cleaning Woman (Vera Lewis); Nurses (Jan Holm, Rosella Towne, Loi Cheaney); LA Operator (Janet Shaw); Paris Operator (Nanette Lafayette); N.Y. Operator (Peggy Moran); Jascha (Eddy Conrad);

and Sidney Bracy, William Haade, Clem Bevans

**Angels with Dirty Faces**
(Warner Brothers)
*Writers:* John Wexley and Warren Duff, from a story by Rowland Brown
*Director:* Michael Curtiz
*Camera:* Sol Polito
*Running time:* 97 minutes
*Cast:* Rocky Sullivan (James Cagney); Jerry Connelly (Pat O'Brien); James Frazier (Humphrey Bogart); Laury Martin (Ann Sheridan); MacKeefer (George Bancroft); Soapy (Billy Halop); Swing (Bobby Jordan); Bim (Leo Gorcey); Hunky (Bernard Punsley); Pasty (Gabriel Dell); Crab (Huntz Hall); Rocky [as a Boy] (Frankie Burke); Jerry [as a Boy] (William Tracy); Laury [as a Girl] (Marilyn Knowlden); Steve (Joe Downing); Blackie (Adrian Morris); Guard Kennedy (Oscar O'Shea); Guard Edwards (Edward Pawley); Bugs, the Gunman (William Pawley); Police Captain (John Hamilton); Priest (Earl Dwire); Death Row Guard (Jack Perrin); Mrs. Patrick (Mary Gordon); Soapy's Mother (Vera Lewis); Warden (William Worthington); RR Yard Watchman (James Farley); Red (Chuck Stubbs); Maggione Boy (Eddie Syracuse); Policeman (Robert Homans); Basketball Captain (Harris Berger); Pharmacist (Harry Hayden); Gangsters (Dick Rich, Steven Darrell, Joe A. Delvin); Italian Storekeeper (William Edmunds); Buckley (Charles Wilson); Boys in Poolroom (Frank Coghlan, Jr., David Durand); Church Basketball Team (Bill Cohee, Lavel Lund, Norman Wallace, Gary Carthew, Bibby Mayer); Mrs. Maggione (Belle Mitchell); Newsboy (Eddie Brian); Janitor (Bill McLain); Croupier (Wilber Mack); Girl at Gaming Table (Poppy Wilde); Adult Boy (George Offerman, Jr.); Norton J. White (Charles Trow-

bridge); City Editor, Press (Ralph Sanford); Police Officer (Wilfred Lucas); Guard (Lane Chandler); Cop (Elliott Sullivan) and Lottie Williams, George Mori, Dick Wessel, John Harron, Vince Lombardi, Al Hill, Thomas Jackson, Jeffrey Sayre

## 1939

### The Oklahoma Kid

(Warner Brothers)
*Writers:* Warren Duff and Robert Buckner, with Edward Paramore, from a story by Edward Paramore
*Director:* Lloyd Bacon
*Camera:* James Wong Howe
*Running time:* 85 minutes
*Cast:* Jim Kincaid (James Cagney); Whip McCord (Humphrey Bogart); Jane Hardwick (Rosemary Lane); Hudge Hardwick (Donald Crisp); Ned Kincaid (Harvey Stephens); John Kincaid (Hugh Sothern); Alec Martin (Charles Middleton); Doolin (Edward Pawley); Wes Handley (Ward Bond); Curley (Lew Harvey); Indian Jack Pasco (Trevor Bardette); Ringo (John Miljan); Judge Morgan (Arthur Aylesworth); Hotel Clerk (Irving Bacon); Keely (Joe Delvin); Sheriff Abe Collins (Wade Boteler); Kincaid's Horse (Whizzer); Professor (Ray Mayer); Deputy (Dan Wolheim); Juryman (Bob Kortman); Old Man in Bar (Tex Cooper); Secretary (John Harron); President Cleveland (Stuart Holmes); Times Reporter (Jeffrey Sayre); Land Agent (Frank Mayo); Mail Clerk (Jack Mower); Settler (Al Bridge); Drunk (Don Barclay); Bartenders (Horace Murphy, Robert Homans, George Lloyd); Manuelita (Rosina Galli); Pedro (George Regas); Post Man (Clem Bevans); Indian Woman (Soledad Jiminez); Foreman (Ed Brady); Homesteader (Tom Chatterton); Henchman (Elliott Sullivan) and Joe Kirkson, William Worthington, Spencer Charters

### Each Dawn I Die (Warner Brothers)
*Writers:* Norman Reilly Rainer, Warren Duff, and Charles Perry, from the novel by Jerome Odlum
*Director:* William Keighley
*Camera:* Arthur Edeson
*Running time:* 92 minutes
*Cast:* Frank Ross (James Cagney); Hood Stacey (George Raft); Joyce Conover (Jane Bryan); Warden John Armstrong (George Bancroft); Fargo Red (Maxie Rosenbloom); Mueller (Stanley Ridges); Pole Cat Carlisle (Alan Baxter); W. J. Grayce (Victor Jory); Pete Kassock (John Wray); Dale (Edward Pawley); Lang (Willard Robertson); Mrs. Ross (Emma Dunn); Garsky (Paul Hurst); Joe Lassiter (Louis Jean Heydt); Limpy Julien (Joe Downing); D.A. Jesse Hanley (Thurston Hall); Bill Mason (William Davidson); Stacey's Attorney (Clay Clement); Judge (Charles Trowbridge); Temple (Harry Cording); Lew Keller (John Harron); Jerry Poague (John Ridgeley); Patterson (Selmer Jackson); Mac (Robert Homans); Snake Edwards (Abner Biberman); Mose (Napoleon Simpson); Accident Witness (Stuart Holmes); Girl in Car (Maris Wrixon); Men in Car (Garland Smith, Arthur Gardner); Policeman (James Flavin); Gate Guard (Max Hoffman, Jr.); Turnkey (Walter Miller); Guard in Cell (Fred Graham); Bailiff (Wilfred Lucas); Jury Woman (Vera Lewis); Prosecutor (Emmett Vogan); Judge Crowder (Earl Dwire); Bud (Bob Perry); Johnny, a Hood (Al Hill); Convict (Elliot Sullivan); Court Officer (Chuck Hamilton) and Nat Carr, Wedgewood Nowell, Frank Mayo, Dick Rich, Lee Phelps, Jack Wise, Granville Bates

### The Roaring Twenties
(Warner Brothers)
*Writers:* Jerry Wald, Richard Macaulay, and Robert Rossen, from a story by Mark Hellinger

*Director:* Raoul Walsh
*Camera:* Ernie Haller
*Running time:* 104 minutes
*Cast:* Eddie Barlett (James Cagney); Jean Sherman (Priscilla Lane); George Hally (Humphrey Bogart); Lloyd Hart (Jeffrey Lynn); Panama Smith (Gladys George); Danny Green (Frank McHugh); Nick Brown (Paul Kelly); Mrs. Sherman (Elisabeth Risdon); Pete Henderson (Ed Keane); Sergeant Pete Jones (Joseph Sawyer); Lefty (Abner Biberman); Luigi, the Proprieter (George Humbert); Bramfield, the Broker (Clay Clement); Bobby Hart (Don Thaddeus Kerr); Orderly (Ray Cooke); Mrs. Gray (Vera Lewis); First Mechanic (Murray Alper); Second Mechanic (Dick Wessel); Fletcher, the Foreman (Joseph Crehan); Bootlegger (Norman Willis); First Officer (Robert Elliott); Second Officer (Eddy Chandler); Judge (John Hamilton); Man in Jail (Elliott Sullivan); Jailer (Pat O'Malley); Proprietor of Still (Arthur Loft); Ex Cons (Al Hill, Raymond Bailey, Lew Harvey); Order-takers (Joe Devlin, Jeffrey Sayre); Mike (Paul Phillips); Masters (George Meeker); Piano Player (Bert Hanlon); Drunk (Jack Norton); Captain (Alan Bridge); Henchman (Fred Graham); Doorman (James Blaine); Couple in Restaurant (Henry C. Bradley, Lottie Williams); Commentator (John Deering); Soldier (John Harron); Bailiff (Lee Phelps); Waiter (Nat Carr); Policeman (Wade Boteler); Customer (Creighton Hale); Saleswoman (Ann Codee); Cab Drivers (Eddie Acuff, Milton Kibbee, John Ridgely) and James Flavin, Oscar O'Shea, Frank Wilcox, the Jane Jones Trio, Harry Hollingsworth, Frank Mayo, Emory Parnell, Billy Wayne, Philip Morris, Maurice Costello, John St. Clair

## 1940

**The Fighting 69th** (Warner Brothers)
*Writers:* Norman Reilly Raine, Fred

Noblo, Jr., and Dean Franklin
*Director:* William Keighley
*Camera:* Tony Gaudio
*Running time:* 90 minutes
*Cast:* Jerry Plunkett (James Cagney); Father Duffy (Pat O'Brien); Wild Bill Donovan (George Brent); Joyce Kilmer (Jeffrey Lynn); Sergeant "Big Mike" Wynn (Alan Hale); "Crepe Hanger" Burke (Frank McHugh); Lieutenant Ames (Dennis Morgan); Lieutenant "Long John" Wynn (Dick Foran); Timmy Wynn (William Lundigan); Paddy Dolan (Guinn "Big Boy" Williams); the Colonel (Henry O'Neill); Captain Mangan (John Litel); Mike Murphy (Sammy Cohen); Major Anderson (Harvey Stephens); Private Turner (De Wolfe [William] Hopper); Private McManus (Tom Dugan); Jack O'Keefe (George Reeves); Moran (John Ridgely); Chaplain Holmes (Charles Trowbridge); Lieutenant Norman (Frank Wilcox); Casey (Herbert Anderson); Healey (J. Anthony Hughes); Captain Bootz (Frank Mayo); Carroll (John Harron); Ryan (George Kilgen); Tierney (Richard Clayton); Regan (Edward Dew); Doctors (Wilfred Lucas, Emmett Vogan); Sergeant (Frank Sully); Doctor (Joseph Crehan); Supply Sergeant (James Flavin); Jimmy (Frank Goghlan, Jr.); Eddie (George O'Hanlon); Major (Jack Perrin); Alabama Men (Trevor Bardette, John Arledge, Frank Melton, Edmund Glover); Engineer Officer (Edgar Edwards); Medical Captain (Ralph Dunn); German Officers (Arno Frey, Roland Varno); Hefferman (Robert Layne Ireland); O'Brien (Elmo Murray); Waiter (Jacques Lory); Chuck (Jack Boyle, Jr.) and Creighton Hale, Benny Rubin, Eddie Acuff, Jack Mower, Nat Carr, Jack Wise

**Torrid Zone** (Warner Brothers)
*Writers:* Richard Macaulay and Jerry Wald

*Director:* William Keighley
*Camera:* James Wong Howe
*Running time:* 88 minutes
*Cast:* Nick Butler (James Cagney);
Steve Case (Pat O'Brien); Lee Donley
(Ann Sheridan); Wally Davis (Andy
Devine); Gloria Anderson (Helen Vinson); Bob Anderson (Jerome Cowan);
Rosario (George Tobias); Sancho
(George Reeves); Carlos (Victor Kilian); Rodriguez (Frank Puglia); Gardner (John Ridgely); Sam (Grady
Sutton); Garcia Sancho (Paul Porcasi);
Lopez (Frank Yaconelli); Hernandez
(Dick Boteler); Shaffer (Frank Mayo);
McNamara (Jack Mower); Daniels
(Paul Hurst); Sergeant of Police
(George Regas); Rita (Elvira Sanchez);
Hotel Manager (George Humbert);
First Policeman (Trevor Bardette); Second Policeman (Ernesto Piedra); Chico
(Manuel Lopez); Charley (Tony Paton)
and Max Blum, Betty Sanko, Don
Orlando, Victor Sabuni, Paul Renay,
Joe Molina

**City for Conquest** (Warner Brothers)
*Writer:* John Wexley, from the novel
*City for Conquest* by Aben Kandel
*Director:* Anatole Litvak
*Camera:* James Wong Howe
*Running time:* 101 minutes
*Cast:* Danny Kenny (James Cagney);
Peggy Nash (Ann Sheridan); Old Timer
(Frank Craven); Scotty McPherson
(Donald Crisp); Eddie Kenny (Arthur
Kennedy); Googi (Elia Kazan); Mutt
(Frank McHugh); Pinky (George
Tobias); Dutch (Jerome Cowan); Murray Burns (Anthony Quinn); Gladys
(Lee Patrick); Mrs. Nash (Blanche
Yurka); Goldie (George Lloyd); Lilly
(Joyce Compton); Max Leonard
(Thurston Hall); Cobb (Ben Welden);
Salesman (John Arledge); Gaul (Ed
Keane); Doctors (Selmer Jackson,
Joseph Crehan); Callahan (Bob Steele);
Henchman (Billy Wayne); Floor Guard
(Pat Flaherty); MC (Sidney Miller);

Dressing Room Blonde (Ethelreda
Leopold) and Lee Phelps, Charles Wilson, Ed Gargan, Howard Hickman,
Murray Almer, Dick Wessell, Bernice
Pilot, Charles Lane, Dana Dale [Margaret Hayes], Ed Pawley, William
Newell, Lucia Carroll

1941

**The Strawberry Blonde**
(Warner Brothers)
*Writers:* Julius J. and Philip C. Epstein,
from the play *One Sunday Afternoon*
by James Hagan
*Director:* Raoul Walsh
*Camera:* James Wong Howe
*Running time:* 97 minutes
*Cast:* Biff Grimes (James Cagney); Amy
Lind (Olivia De Havilland); Virginia
Brush (Rita Hayworth); Old Man
Grimes (Alan Hale); Nick Pappalas
(George Tobias); Hugo Barnstead (Jack
Carson); Mrs. Mulcahey (Una O'Connor); Harold (George Reeves); Harold's
Girl Friend (Lucile Fairbanks); Big Joe
(Edward McNamara); Toby (Herbert
Heywood); Josephine (Helen Lynd);
Bank President (Roy Gordon); Street
Cleaner Foreman (Tim Ryan); Official
(Addison Richards); Policeman (Frank
Mayo); Bartender (Jack Daley); Girl
(Suzanne Carnahan [Susan Peters]);
Boy (Herbert Anderson); Baxter (Frank
Orth); Inspector (James Flavin); Sailor
(George Campeau); Singer (Abe
Dinovitch); Guiseppi (George Humbert); Secretary (Creighton Hale);
Treadway (Russell Hicks); Warden
(Wade Boteler); Young Man (Peter Ashley); Bank President (Roy Gordon);
Policemen (Max Hoffman, Jr., Pat Flaherty); Girl (Peggy Diggins); Hanger-on
(Bob Perry); Woman (Dorothy
Vaughan); Dandy (Richard Clayton);
Girl (Ann Edmonds); Nurse (Lucia Carroll) and Harrison Green, Eddie Chandler, Carl Harbaugh, Frank Melton, Dick
Wessell, Paul Barrett, Nora Gale

## The Bride Came C.O.D.
(Warner Brothers)
*Writers:* Julius J. and Philip G. Epstein, from a story by Kenneth Earl and A. A. Musselman
*Director:* William Keighley
*Camera:* Ernest Haller
*Running time:* 92 minutes
*Cast:* Steve Collins (James Cagney); Joan Winfield (Bette Davis); Tommy Keenan (Stuart Erwin); Allen Brice (Jack Carson); Peewee (George Tobias); Lucius K. Winfield (Eugene Pallette); Pop Tolliver (Harry Davenport); Sheriff McGee (William Frawley); Hinkle (Edward Brophy); Judge Sobler (Harry Holman); Reporters (Chick Chandler, Keith Douglas [later Douglas Kennedy], Herbert Anderson); Keenan's Pilot (De Wolfe [William] Hopper); McGee's Pilot (William Newell); Ambulance Driver (Charles Sullivan); Policeman (Eddy Chandler, Tony Hughes, Lee Phelps); Mabel (Jean Ames); Headwaiter (Alphonse Martell); Dance Trio (The Rogers Dancers); First Operator (Peggy Diggins); Second Operator (Mary Brodel); Valet (Olaf Hytten); Detective (James Flavin); Announcer (Sam Hayes); Airline Dispatcher (William Justice [later Richard Travis]); Newsboys (Lester Towne, Richard Clayton, Garland Smith, Claude Wisberg) and Lucia Carroll, Peter Ashley, John Ridgely, Saul Gorss, Jack Mower, Creighton Hale, Garrett Craig

## 1942

### Captains of the Clouds
(Warner Brothers)
*Writers:* Arthur T. Horman, Richard Macaulay, and Norman Reilly Raine, from a story by Horman and Roland Gillett
*Director:* Michael Curtiz
*Camera:* Sol Polito and Wilfred M. Cline; aerial photography by Elmer

Dyer, Charles Marshall, and Winton C. Hoch
*Running time:* 113 minutes
*Cast:* Brian MacLean (James Cagney); Johnny Dutton (Dennis Morgan); Emily Foster (Brenda Marshall); Tiny Murphy (Alan Hale); Blimp Lebec (George Tobias); Scrounger Harris (Reginald Gardiner); Air Marshal W. A. Bishop (Himself); Commanding Officer (Reginald Denny); Prentiss (Russell Arms); Group Captain (Paul Cavanagh); Store-Teeth Morrison (Clem Bevans); Foster (J. M. Kerrigan); Doctor Neville (J. Farrell MacDonald); Fyffo (Patrick O'Moore); Carmichael (Morton Lowry); Chief Instructor (Frederic Worlock); Officer (Roland Drew); Blonde (Lucia Carroll); Playboy (George Meeker); Popcorn Kearns (Benny Baker); Kingsley (Hardie Albright); Mason (Roy Walker); Nolan (Charles H. Alton); Provost Marshall (Louis Jean Heydt); Student Pilots (Byron Barr [Gig Young], Michael Ames [Tod Andrews]); Willie (Willie Fung); Blake (Carl Harbord); Indians (James Stevens, Bill Wilkerson, Frank Lackteen); Dog Man (Edward McNamara); Bellboy (Charles Smith); Clerk (Emmett Vogan); Woman (Winifred Harris); Churchill's Voice (Miles Mander); Drill Sergeant (Pat Flaherty); Bartender (Tom Dugan); Mechanic (George Offerman, Jr.); Orderly (Gavin Muir); Duty Officer (Larry Williams) and John Hartley, John Kellogg, Charles Irwin, Billy Wayne, Rafael Storm, John Gallaudet, Barry Bernard, George Ovey, Walter Brooks, Ray Montgomery, Herbert Gunn, Donald Dillaway, James Bush

### Yankee Doodle Dandy
(Warner Brothers)
*Writers:* Robert Buckner with Edmund Joseph and Julius J. and Philip G. Epstein
*Director:* Michael Curtiz

*Camera:* James Wong Howe
*Running time:* 126 minutes
*Cast:* George M. Cohan (James Cagney); Mary (Joan Leslie); Jerry Cohan (Walter Huston); Sam Harris (Richard Whorf); Dietz (George Tobias); Fay Templeton (Irene Manning); Nellie Cohan (Rosemary De Camp); Josie Cohan (Jeanne Cagney); Schwab (S. Z. Sakall); Erlanger (George Barbier); Manager (Walter Catlett); Nora Bayes (Frances Langford); Ed Albee (Minor Watson); Eddie Foy (Eddie Foy, Jr.); Harold Goff (Chester Clute); George M. Cohan [age 13] (Douglas Croft); Josie [age 12] (Patsy Lee Parsons); Franklin D. Roosevelt (Captain Jack Young); Receptionist (Audrey Long); Madame Bartholdi (Odette Myrtil); White House Butler (Clinton Rosemond); Stage Manager in Providence (Spencer Charters); Sister Act (Dorothy Kelly, Marijo James); George M. Cohan [age 7] (Henry Blair); Josie Cohan [age 6] (Jo Ann Marlow); Stage Manager (Thomas Jackson); Fanny (Phyllis Kennedy); White House Guard (Pat Flaherty); Magician (Leon Belasco); Star Boarder (Syd Saylor); N.Y. Stage Manager (William B. Davidson); Dr. Lewellyn (Harry Hayden); Dr. Anderson (Francis Pierlot); Teenagers (Charles Smith, Joyce Reynolds, Dick Chandlee, Joyce Horne); Sergeant (Frank Faylen); Theodore Roosevelt (Wallis Clark); Betsy Ross (Georgia Carroll); Sally (Joan Winfield); Union Army Veterans (Dick Wessel, James Flavin); Schultz in *Peck's Bad Boy* (Sailor Vincent); Irish Cop in *Peck's Bad Boy* (Fred Kelsey); Hotel Clerks (George Meeker, Frank Mayo); Actor, Railroad Station (Tom Dugan); Telegraph Operator (Creighton Hale); Wise Guy (Murray Alper); Army Clerk (Garry Owen); Nurse (Ruth Robinson); Reporters (Eddie Acuff, Walter Brooke, Bill Edwards, William Hopper); First Critic (William Forrest); Second Critic (Ed Keane); Girl (Dolores Moran); Chorus Girls, "Little Johnny Jones" (Poppy Wilde, Lorraine Gettman [Leslie Brooks])

## 1943

**Johnny Come Lately**
(Cagney Productions)
*Writer:* John Van Druten, from the novel *McLeod's Folly* by Louis Bromfield
*Director:* William K. Howard
*Camera:* Theodore Sparkhuhl
*Running time:* 97 minutes
*Cast:* Tom Richards (James Cagney); Vinnie McLeod (Grace George); Gashouse Mary (Marjorie Main); Jane (Marjorie Lord); Aida (Hattie McDaniel); W. W. Dougherty (Edward McNamara); Pete Dougherty (Bill Henry); Bill Swain (Robert Barrat); Willie Ferguson (George Cleveland); Myrtle Ferguson (Margaret Hamilton); Dudley Hirsh (Norman Willis); Blaker (Lucien Littlefield); Winterbottom (Edwin Stanley); Chief of Police (Irving Bacon); First Cop (Tom Dugan); Second Cop (Charles Irwin); Third Cop (John Sheehan); Butler (Clarence Muse); First Tramp (John Miller); Second Tramp (Arthur Hunnicutt); Tramp in Box Car (Victor Kilian); Bouncer (Wee Willie Davis); Old Timer (Henry Hall)

## 1945

**Blood on the Sun**
(Cagney Productions)
*Writer:* Lester Cole, with additional scenes by Nathaniel Curtis, from a story by Garrett Fort
*Director:* Frank Lloyd
*Camera:* Theodore Sparkhuhl
*Running time:* 98 minutes
*Cast:* Nick Condon (James Cagney); Iris Hilliard (Sylvia Sidney); Ollie Miller

(Wallace Ford); Edith Miller (Rosemary De Camp); Colonel Tojo (Robert Armstrong); Premiere Tanaka (John Emery); Hijikata (Leonard Strong); Prince Tatsugi (Frank Puglia); Captain Oshima (Jack Holloran); Kajioka (Hugh Ho); Yamamoto (Philip Ahn); Hayoshi (Joseph Kim); Yamada (Marvin Miller); Joseph Cassell (Rhys Williams); Arthur Bickett (Porter Hall); Charley Sprague (James Bell); Amah (Grace Lem); Chinese Servant (Oy Chan); Hotel Manager (George Paris); Johnny Clarke (Hugh Beaumont); American Newspapermen in Tokyo (Gregory Gay, Arthur Loft, Emmett Vogan, Charlie Wayne)

## 1946

### 13 Rue Madeleine

(Twentieth Century–Fox)
*Writers:* John Monks Jr. and Sy Bartlett
*Director:* Henry Hathaway
*Camera:* Norbert Brodine
*Running time:* 95 minutes
*Cast:* Bob Sharkey (James Cagney); Suzanne De Bouchard (Annabella); Bill O'Connell (Richard Conte); Jeff Lassiter (Frank Latimore); Charles Gibson (Walter Abel); Pappy Simpson (Melville Cooper); Mayor Galimard (Sam Jaffe); Duclois (Marcel Rousseau); Psychiatrist (Richard Gordon); Emile (Everett G. Marshall); Madame Thillot (Blanche Yurka); Karl (Peter Von Zerneck); Hans Feinkl (Alfred Linder); Hotel Clerk (Ben Low); RAF Officer (James Craven); Joseph (Roland Belanger); Burglary Instructor (Horace MacMahon); Briefing Officer (Alexander Kirkland); La Roche (Donald Randolph); Peasant Lady (Judith Lowry); Dispatcher (Red Buttons); German Staff Officer (Otto Simanek); Psychiatrist (Walter Greaza); Van Duyval (Roland Winters); Tailor (Harold Young); Chief Operator (Sally McMarrow); Flyers (Coby Neal, Karl Malden); French Peasant (Jean Del Val); Narrator (Reed Hadley)

## 1948

### The Time of Your Life

(Cagney Productions)
*Writers:* Scenario by Nathaniel Curtis, from the play by William Saroyan
*Director:* H. C. Potter
*Camera:* James Wong Howe
*Running time:* 109 minutes
*Cast:* Joe (James Cagney); Nick (William Bendix); Tom (Wayne Morris); Kitty Duval (Jeanne Cagney); Policeman (Broderick Crawford); McCarthy (Ward Bond); Kit Carson (James Barton); Harry (Paul Draper); Mary L. (Gale Page); Dudley (James Lydon); Willie (Richard Erdman); Arab (Pedro De Cordoba); Wesley (Reginald Beane); Blick (Tom Powers); a Drunk (John "Skins" Miller); Society Lady (Natalie Schafer); Society Gentleman (Howard Freeman); Blind Date (Renie Riano); Newsboy (Lanny Rees); Girl in Love (Nanette Parks); Nick's Mother (Grazia Marciso); "Killer" (Claire Carleton); Sidekick (Gladys Blake); Nick's Daughter (Marlene Aames); Cook (Moy Ming); Bookie (Donald Kerr); B Girl (Ann Cameron); Sailor (Floyd Walters); Salvation Army Man (Eddie Borden); Salvation Army Woman (Rena Case)

## 1949

### White Heat (Warner Brothers)

*Writers:* Ivan Goff and Ben Roberts, from a story by Virginia Kellogg
*Director:* Raoul Walsh
*Camera:* Sid Hickox
*Running time:* 114 minutes
*Cast:* Cody Jarrett (James Cagney); Verna Jarrett (Virginia Mayo); Hank Fallon (Edmond O'Brien); Ma Jarrett (Margaret Wycherly); "Big Ed" Somers (Steve Cochran); Philip Evans (John Archer); Cotton Valetti (Wally Cassell); Het Kohler (Mickey Knox); The Trader (Fred Clark); The Reader (G. Pat Collins); Roy Parker (Paul Guilfoyle);

Happy Taylor (Fred Coby); Zuckie Hommell (Ford Rainey); Tommy Ryley (Robert Osterloh); Bo Creel (Ian Mac-Donald); Chief of Police (Marshall Bradford); Ernie Trent (Ray Montgomery); Police Surgeon (George Taylor); Willie Rolf (Milton Parsons); Cashier (Claudia Barrett); Popcorn Vendor (Buddy Gorman); Jim Donovan (De Forrest Lawrence); Ted Clark (Garrett Craig); Judge (George Spaulding); Clerk (Sherry Hall); Guards (Harry Strang, Jack Worth); Russell Hughes (Sid Melton); Margaret Baxter (Fern Eggen); Nat Lefeld (Eddie Foster); Tower Guard (Lee Phelps)

### 1950

### The West Point Story
(Warner Brothers)
*Writers:* John Monks, Jr., Charles Hoffman, and Irving Wallace, from a story by Irving Wallace
*Director:* Roy Del Ruth
*Camera:* Sid Hickox
*Running time:* 107 minutes
*Cast:* Elwin Bixby (James Cagney); Eve Dillon (Virginia Mayo); Jan Wilson (Doris Day); Tom Fletcher (Gordon MacRae); Hal Courtland (Gene Nelson); Bull Gilbert (Alan Hale, Jr.); Harry Eberhart (Roland Winters); Bixby's "Wife" (Raymond Roe); Lieutenant Colonel Martin (Wilton Graff); Jocelyn (Jerome Cowan); Commandant (Frank Ferguson); Acrobat (Russ Saunders); Officer-in-Charge (Jack Kelly); Hoofer (Glen Turnbull); Piano Player (Walter Ruick); Senator (Lute Crockett); Cadets (James Dobson, Joel Marston, Bob Hayden, De Witt Bishop)

### Kiss Tomorrow Goodbye
(Cagney Productions / Warner Brothers)
*Writer:* Harry Brown, from the novel by Horace McCoy
*Director:* Gordon Douglas

*Camera:* Peverell Marley
*Running time:* 102 minutes
*Cast:* Ralph Cotter (James Cagney); Holiday (Barbara Payton); Inspector Weber (Ward Bond); Mandon (Luther Adler); Margaret Dobson (Helena Carter); Jinx (Steve Brodie); Vic Mason (Rhys Williams); Reece (Barton MacLane); Ezra Dobson (Herbert Heyes); Doc Green (Frank Reicher); Tolgate (John Litel); District Attorney (Dan Riss); Cobbett (John Halloran); Byers (William Frawley); Detective Gray (Robert Karnes); Detective Fowler (Kenneth Tobey); Carleton (Neville Brand); Ralph's Brother (William Cagney); Judge (George Spaulding); Bailiff (Mark Strong); Satterfield (Matt McHugh); Julia (Georgia Caine); Driver (King Donovan); Doctor (Frank Wilcox); Butler (Gordon Richards)

### 1951

### Come Fill the Cup (Warner Brothers)
*Writers:* Ivan Goff and Ben Roberts, from the novel by Harlan Ware
*Director:* Gordon Douglas
*Camera:* Robert Burks
*Running time:* 113 minutes
*Cast:* Lew Marsh (James Cagney); Paula Copeland (Phyllis Thaxter); John Ives (Raymond Massey); Charley Dolan (James Gleason); Boyd Copeland (Gig Young); Dolly Copeland (Selena Royle); Julian Cuscaden (Larry Keating); Maria Diego (Charlita); Lennie Carr (Sheldon Leonard); Ike Bashaw (Douglas Spencer); Don Bell (John Kellogg); Hal Ortman (William Bakewell); Travis Asbourne II (John Alvin); Kip Zunches (King Donovan); Homicide Captain (James Flavin); Welder (Torben Meyer); Ora (Norma Jean Macias); Lila (Elizabeth Flournoy); Bobby (Henry Blair)

### Starlift (Warner Brothers)
*Writers:* John Klorer and Karl Klamb,

from a story by John Klorer
*Director:* Roy Del Ruth
*Camera:* Ted McCord
*Running time:* 103 minutes
*Cast:* Themselves (Doris Day, Gordon MacRae, Virginia Mayo, Gene Nelson, Ruth Roman); Nell Wayne (Janice Rule); Sergeant Mike Nolan (Dick Wesson); Corporal Rick Williams (Ron Hagerthy); Colonel Callan (Richard Webb); Chaplain (Hayden Rorke); Steve Rogers (Howard St. John); Mrs. Callan (Ann Doran); Turner (Tommy Farrell); George Norris (John Maxwell); Bob Wayne (Don Beddoe); Sue Wayne (Mary Adams); Dr. Williams (Bigelowe Sayre); Mrs. Williams (Eleanor Audley); Theater Manager (Pat Henry); Chief Usher (Gordon Polk); Piano Player (Robert Hammack); Captain Nelson (Ray Montgomery); Copilot (Bill Neff); Ground Officer (Stan Holbrook); Flight Nurse (Jill Richards); Litter Case (Joe Turkel); Virginia Boy (Rush Williams); Pete (Brian McKay); Will (Jack Larson); Nebraska Boy (Lyle Clark); Nurses (Dorothy Kennedy, Jean Dean, Dolores Castle); Boy with Cane (William Hunt); Army Nurse (Elizabeth Flournoy); Driver (Walter Brennan, Jr.); Lieutenants (Robert Karnes, John Hedloe); Boy with Camera (Steve Gregory); Morgan (Richard Monohan); Soldiers in Bed (Joe Recht, Herb Latimer); Doctor (Dick Ryan); Crew Chief (Bill Hudson); Miss Parson's Assistant (Sarah Spencer); Noncom (James Brown); Waitress (Ezelle Poule); and the following guest stars: James Cagney, Gary Cooper, Virginia Gibson, Phil Harris, Frank Lovejoy, Lucille Norman, Louella Parsons, Randolph Scott, Jane Wyman, Patrice Wymore

## 1952

**What Price Glory?**
(Twentieth Century–Fox)
*Writers:* Phoebe and Henry Ephron, from the play by Maxwell Anderson and Lawrence Stallings
*Director:* John Ford
*Camera:* Joseph MacDonald
*Running time:* 111 minutes
*Cast:* Captain Flagg (James Cagney); Charmaine (Corinne Calvet); Sergeant Quirt (Dan Dailey); Corporal Kiper (William Demarest); Lieutenant Aldrich (Craig Hill); Lewisohn (Robert Wagner); Nicole Bouchard (Marisa Pavan); Lieutenant Moore (Casey Adams); General Cokely (James Gleason); Lipinsky (Wally Vernon); Cognac Pete (Henry Letondal); Lieutenant Schmidt (Fred Libby); Mulcahy (Ray Hyke); Gowdy (Paul Fix); Young Soldier (James Lilburn); Morgan (Henry Morgan); Gilbert (Dan Borzage); Holsen (Bill Henry); Company Cook (Henry "Bomber" Kulkovich); Ferguson (Jack Pennick); Nun (Ann Codee); Lieutenant Cunningham (Stanley Johnson); Captain Davis (Tom Tyler); Sister Clotilde (Olga Andre); Priest (Barry Norton); The Great Uncle (Luis Alberni); Mayor (Torben Meyer); English Colonel (Alfred Zeisler); English Lieutenant (George Bruggeman); Lieutenant Bennett (Scott Forbes); Lieutenant Austin (Sean McClory); Captain Wickham (Charles Fitzsimmons); Bouchard (Louis Mercier); MP (Mickey Simpson)

## 1953

**A Lion Is in the Streets**
(Cagney Productions)
*Writer:* Luther Davies, from the novel by Adria Locke Langley
*Director:* Raoul Walsh
*Camera:* Harry Stradling
*Running time:* 88 minutes
*Cast:* Hank Martin (James Cagney); Verity Wade (Barbara Hale); Flamingo (Anne Francis); Jules Bolduc (Warner Anderson); Jeb Brown (John McIntyre); Jennie Brown (Jeanne Cagney); Spurge (Lon Chaney, Jr.); Rector (Frank McHugh); Robert J. Castelberry

(Larry Keating); Guy Polli (Onslow Stevens); Mr. Beach (James Millican); Tim Beck (Mickey Simpson); Lula May (Sara Haden); Singing Woman (Ellen Corby); Prosecutor (Roland Winters); Smith (Burt Mustin); Sophy (Irene Tedrow); Townswoman (Sarah Selby)

### 1955

**Run for Cover**
(Pine-Thomas/Paramount)
*Writer:* William C. Thomas, from a story by Harriet Frank and Irving Ravetch
*Director:* Nicholas Ray
*Camera:* Daniel Fapp
*Running time:* 92 minutes
*Cast:* Matt Dow (James Cagney); Helga Swenson (Viveca Lindfors); Davey Bishop (John Derek); Mr. Swenson (Jean Hersholt); Gentry (Grant Withers); Larsen (Jack Lambert); Morgan (Ernest Borgnine); Sheriff (Ray Teal); Scotty (Irving Bacon); Paulsen (Trevor Bardette); Mayor Walsh (John Miljan); Doc Ridgeway (Guy Schilling); Bank Manager (Emerson Treacy); Harvey (Denver Pyle); Townsman (Henry Wills)

**Love Me or Leave Me**
(Metro-Goldwyn-Mayer)
*Writers:* Daniel Fuchs and Elizabeth Lennart, from a story by Daniel Fuchs
*Director:* Charles Vidor
*Camera:* Arthur E. Arling
*Running time:* 122 minutes
*Cast:* Ruth Etting (Doris Day); Martin "The Gimp" Snyder (James Cagney); Johnny Alderman (Cameron Mitchell); Bernard V. Loomis (Robert Keith); Frobisher (Tom Tully); Georgie (Harry Bellaver); Paul Hunter (Richard Gaines); Fred Taylor (Peter Leeds); Eddie Fulton (Claude Stroud); Jingle Girl (Audrey Young); Greg Trent (John Harding); Dancer (Dorothy Abbott); Bouncer (Phil Schumacher); Second Bouncer (Otto Teichow); Bouncer

(Henry Kulky); Orry (Jay Adler); Irate Customer (Mauritz Hugo); Hostess (Veda Ann Borg); Claire (Claire Carleton); Stage Manager (Benny Burt); Mr. Brelston, Radio Station Manager (Robert B. Carson); Assistant Director (James Drury); Dance Director (Richard Simmons); Assistant Director (Michael Kostrick); First Reporter (Roy Engel); Second Reporter (John Damler); Woman (Genevieve Aumont); Propman (Roy Engel); Stagehands (Dale Van Sickel, Johnny Day); Chorus Girls (Larri Thomas, Patti Nestor, Winona Smith, Shirley Wilson); Doorman (Robert Malcolm); Waiter (Robert Stephenson); Drapery Man (Paul McGuire); Guard (Barry Regan); Photographers (Jimmy Cross, Henry Randolph); Chauffeur (Chet Brandenberg)

**Mister Roberts**
(Orange Productions/Warner Brothers)
*Writers:* Frank Nugent and Josh Logan, from the play by Josh Logan and Thomas Heggen
*Directors:* John Ford and Mervyn LeRoy
*Camera:* Winton C. Hoch
*Running time:* 123 minutes
*Cast:* Lieutenant (J. G.) Roberts (Henry Fonda); Captain (James Cagney); Ensign Frank Thurlowe Pulver (Jack Lemmon); Doc (William Powell); CPO Dowdy (Ward Bond); Lieutenant Ann Girard (Betsy Palmer); Mannion (Phil Carey); Reber (Nick Adams); Stefanowski (Harry Carey, Jr.); Dolan (Ken Curtis); Gerhart (Frank Aletter); Lidstrom (Fritz Ford); Mason (Buck Kartalian); Lieutenant Billings (William Henry); Olson (William Hudson); Schlemmer (Stubby Kruger); Cookie (Harry Tenbrook); Rodrigues (Perry Lopez); Insignia (Robert Roark); Bookser (Pat Wayne); Wiley (Tige Andrews); Kennedy (Jim Moloney); Gilbert (Denny Niles); Johnson (Francis Conner); Cochran (Shug Fisher); Jonesy (Danny Borzage); Taylor (Jim

Murphy); Nurses (Kathleen O'Malley, Maura Murphy, Mimi Doyle, Jeanne Murray-Vanderbilt, Lonnie Pierce); Shore Patrol Officer (Martin Milner); Shore Patrolman (Gregory Walcott); MP (James Flavin); Marine Sergeant (Jack Pennick); Native Chief (Duke Kahanamoko); Chinese Girl Who Kisses Bookser (Carolyn Tong); French Colonial Officer (George Brangier); Naval Officer (Clarence E. Frank)

**The Seven Little Foys**
(Paramount Pictures)
*Writers:* Melville Shavelson and Jack Rose
*Director:* Melville Shavelson
*Camera:* John F. Warren
*Running time:* 93 minutes
*Cast:* Eddie Foy (Bob Hope); Madeleine Morando (Milly Vitale); Barney Green (George Tobias); Clara (Angela Clarke); Judge (Herbert Heyes); Stage Manager (Richard Shannon); Brynie (Billy Gray); Charley (Lee Erickson); Richard Foy (Paul De Rolf); Mary Foy (Lydia Reed); Madeleine Foy (Linda Bennett); Eddie Jr (Jimmy Baird); George M. Cohan (James Cagney); Irving (Tommy Duran); Father O'Casey (Lester Matthews); Elephant Act (Joe Evans, George Boyce); Santa Claus (Oliver Blake); Driscoll (Milton Frome); Harrison (King Donovan); Stage Doorman (Jimmy Conlin); Soubrette (Marian Carr); Stage Doorman at Iroquois (Harry Cheshire); Italian Ballerina Mistress (Renata Vanni); Dance Specialty Double (Betty Uitti); Priest (Noel Drayton); Theater Manager (Jack Pepper); Tutor (Dabbs Greer); Customs Inspector (Billy Nelson); Second Priest (Joe Flynn); Brynie [age 5] (Jerry Mathers); Presbyterian Minister (Lewis Martin)

1956

**Tribute to a Bad Man**
(Metro-Goldwyn-Mayer)

*Writer:* Michael Blankfort, from a story by Jack Schaefer
*Director:* Robert Wise
*Camera:* Robert Surtees
*Running time:* 95 minutes
*Cast:* Jeremy Rodock (James Cagney); Steve Miller (Don Dubbins); McNulty (Stephen McNally); Jocasta Constantine (Irene Papas); Lars Peterson (Vic Morrow); Barjak (James Griffith); Hearn (Onslow Stevens); L. A. Peterson (James Bell); Mrs. L. A. Peterson (Jeanette Nolan); Baldy (Chubby Johnson); Abe (Royal Dano); Fat Jones (Lee Van Cleef); Cooky (Peter Chong); Shorty (James McCallion); Red (Clint Sharp); Tom (Carl Pitti); First Buyer (Tony Hughes); Second Buyer (Roy Engel); Cowboys (Bud Osborne, John Halloran, Tom London, Dennis Moore, Buddy Roosevelt, Billy Dix)

**These Wilder Years**
(Metro-Goldwyn-Mayer)
*Writer:* Frank Fenton, from a story by Ralph Wheelwright
*Director:* Roy Rowland
*Camera:* George J. Folsey
*Running time:* 91 minutes
*Cast:* Steve Bradford (James Cagney); Ann Dempster (Barbara Stanwyck); James Rayburn (Walter Pidgeon); Suzie Keller (Betty Lou Keim); Mark (Don Dubbins); Mr. Spottsford (Edward Andrews); Judge (Basil Ruysdael); Roy Oliphant (Grandon Rhodes); Old Cab Driver (Will Wright); Dr. Miller (Lewis Martin); Aunt Martha (Dorothy Adams); Hardware Clerk (Dean Jones); Traffic Cop (Herb Vigran); Miss Finch (Ruth Lee); Gateman (Matt Moore); Chauffeur (Jack Kenny); Doorman (Harry Tyler); Stenographer (Luana Lee); Board of Directors (William Forrest, John Maxwell, Emmett Vogan, Charles Evans); Football Player (Tom Laughlin); Bellhop (Bob Alden); Boy in Pool Room (Michael Landon); Ad Lib Boy (Jimmy Ogg); Spottsford's Secretary (Elizabeth Flournoy); Farmer

(Russell Simpson); Prim Lady (Kathleen Mulqueen); Hotel Clerk (Russ Whitney); Proprietress (Lillian Powell)

## 1957

### Man of a Thousand Faces
(Universal International)
*Writers:* R. Wright Campbell, Ivan Goff, and Ben Roberts, from a story by Ralph Wheelwright
*Director:* Joseph Pevney
*Camera:* Russell Metty
*Running time:* 87 minutes
*Cast:* Lon Chaney (James Cagney); Cleva Creighton Chaney (Dorothy Malone); Hazel Bennett (Jane Greer); Gert (Marjorie Rambeau); Clarence Locan (Jim Backus); Irving Thalberg (Robert J. Evans); Mrs. Chaney (Celia Lovsky); Carrie Chaney (Jeanne Cagney); Dr. J. Wilson Shields (Jack Albertson); Pa Chaney (Nolan Leary); Creighton Chaney [age 21] (Roger Smith); Creighton Chaney [age 13] (Robert Lyden); Creighton Chaney [age 8] (Rickie Sorenson); Creighton Chaney [age 4] (Dennis Rush); Carl Hastings (Simon Scott); Clarence Kolb (Himself); Max Dill (Danny Beck); George Loane Tucker (Phil Van Zandt); Comedy Waiters (Hank Mann, Snub Pollard)

### Short Cut to Hell
(Paramount Pictures)
*Writers:* Ted Berkman and Raphael Blau, from the novel *This Gun for Hire* by Graham Greene
*Director:* James Cagney
*Camera:* Haskell Boggs
*Running time:* 87 minutes
*Cast:* Kyle (Robert Ivers); Glory Hamilton (Georgann Johnson); Stan (William Bishop); Bahrwell (Jacques Aubuchon); Adams (Peter Baldwin); Daisy (Yvette Vickers); Nichols (Murvyn Vye); Los Angeles Police Captain (Milton Frome); Waitress (Jacqueline Beer); Girl (Gail Land); Los Angeles Police-

man (Dennis McMullen); Hotel Manager (William Newell); Adams's Secretary (Sarah Selby); Inspector Ross (Mike Ross); Conductor (Douglas Spencer); Piano Player (Danny Lewis); A. T. (Richard Hale); Mr. Henry (Douglas Evans); Patrolman (Hugh Lawrence); Patrolman (Joe Bassett); Used-Car-Lot Manager (William Pullen); Trainman (Russell Trent); Ticket Seller (Joe Forte); Ext Road Driver (Roscoe Ates); Guard (John Halloran); James Cagney appears in a brief prologue to the film

## 1959

### Never Steal Anything Small
(Universal International)
*Writer:* Charles Lederer, from the play *Devil's Hornpipe* by Maxwell Anderson and Rouben Mamoulian
*Director:* Charles Lederer
*Camera:* Harold Lipstein
*Running time:* 94 minutes
*Cast:* Jack MacIllaney (James Cagney); Linda Cabot (Shirley Jones); Dan Cabot (Roger Smith); Winnipeg (Cara Williams); Pinelli (Nehemiah Persoff); Words Cannon (Royal Dano); Lieutenant Tevis (Anthony Caruso); O. K. Merritt (Horace MacMahon); Ginger (Virginia Vincent); Sleep-Out Charlie (Jack Albertson); Lennie (Robert J. Wilke); Hymie (Herbie Faye); Ed (Billy M. Greene); Ward (John Duke); Osborne (Jack Orrison); Doctor (Roland Winters); Model (Ingrid Goude); Fats Ranney (Sanford Seegar); Thomas (Ed [Skipper] McNally); Deputy Warden (Greg Barton); Policeman (Edwin Parker); Judge (Jay Jostyn); First Detective (John Halloran); Second Detective (Harvey Perry); Waitress (Phyllis Kennedy); Coffee Vendor (Rebecca Sand)

### Shake Hands with the Devil
(Pennebaker Productions/United Artists)

*Writers:* Ivan Goff and Ben Roberts, from Reardon Conner's novel adapted by Marian Thompson
*Director:* Michael Anderson
*Camera:* Erwin Hillier
*Running time:* 110 minutes
*Cast:* Sean Lenihan (James Cagney); Kerry O'Shea (Don Murray); Jennifer Curtis (Dana Wynter); Kitty (Glynis Johns); General (Michael Redgrave); Lady Fitzhugh (Sybil Thorndike); Chris (Cyril Cusack); McGrath (John Breslin); Cassidy (Harry Brogan); Sergeant (Robert Brown); Mary Madigan (Marianne Benet); The Judge (Lewis Carson); Mike O'Callaghan (John Cairney); Clancy (Harry Corbett); Mrs. Madigan (Eileen Crowe); Captain [Black & Tans] (Alan Cuthbertson); Willie Cafferty (Donal Donnelly); Tommy Connor (Wilfred Dawning); Eileen O'Leary (Eithne Dunne); Doyle (Paul Farrell); Terence O'Brien (Richard Harris); Sergeant Jenkins (William Hartnell); British General (John Le Mesurier); Michael O'Leary (Niall MacGinnis); Donovan (Patrick McAlinney); Paddy Nolan (Ray McNally); Sir Arnold Fielding (Clive Morton); Liam O'Sullivan (Noel Purcell); Captain [Black & Tans] (Peter Reynolds); Colonel Smithson (Christopher Rhodes); Sergeant [Black & Tans] (Ronald Walsh); Captain Fleming (Alan White)

## 1960

**The Gallant Hours**
(Cagney-Montgomery Productions/United Artists)
*Writers:* Beirne Lay, Jr., and Frank Gilroy
*Director:* Robert Montgomery
*Camera:* Joe MacDonald
*Running time:* 115 minutes
*Cast:* Fleet Admiral William F. Halsey, Jr. (James Cagney); Lieutenant Commander Andy Lowe (Dennis Weaver); Captain Harry Black (Ward Costello); Lieutenant Commander Roy Webb (Richard Jaeckel); Captain Frank Enright (Les Tremayne); Major General Roy Geiger (Robert Burton); Major General Archie Vandergrift (Raymond Bailey); Vice Admiral Robert Ghormley (Carl Benton Reid); Captain Horace Keys (Walter Sande); Captain Bill Bailey (Karl Swenson); Commander Mike Pulaski (Vaughan Taylor); Captain Joe Foss (Harry Landers); Father Gehring (Richard Carlyle); Manuel (Leon Lontoc); Admiral Isoroku Hamamoto (James T. Goto); Rear Admiral Jiro Kobe (James Yagi); Lieutenant Harrison Ludlum (John McKee); Major General Harmon (John Zaremba); Colonel Evans Carlson (Carleton Young); Captain Tom Lamphier (William Schallert); Admiral Callaghan (Nelson Leigh); Admiral Scott (Sydney Smith); Admiral Murray (Herbert Lytton); Admiral Chester Nimitz (Selmer Jackson); Admiral Ernest J. King (Tyler McVey); Red Cross Girl (Maggie Magennio); with James Cagney, Jr., Robert Montgomery, Jr.

## 1961

**One, Two, Three** (Mirisch Company/Pyramid Productions/United Artists)
*Writers:* Billy Wilder and I. A. L. Diamond, from a one-act play by Ferenc Molnar
*Director:* Billy Wilder
*Camera:* Daniel Fapp
*Running time:* 108 minutes
*Cast:* C. P. MacNamara (James Cagney); Otto Ludwig Piffl (Horst Buchholz); Scarlett (Pamela Tiffin); Mrs. MacNamara (Arlene Francis); Ingeborg (Lilo Pulver); Hazeltine (Howard St. John); Schlemmer (Hans Lothar); Peripetchikoff (Leon Askin); Mishkin (Peter Capell); Borodenko (Ralf Wolter); Fritz (Karl Lieffen); Dr. Bauer (Henning Schluter); Count Von

Droste-Schattenburg (Hubert Von Meyerinck); Mrs. Hazeltine (Lois Bolton); Newspaperman (Tile Kiwe); Zeidlitz (Karl Ludwig Lindt); Military Police Sergeant (Red Buttons); Tommy MacNamara (John Allen); Cindy Mac-Namara (Christine Allen); Bertha (Rose Renee Roth); Military Police Corporal (Ivan Arnold); East German Police Corporal (Helmud Schmid); East German Interrogator (Otto Friebel); East German Police Sergeant (Werner Buttler); Second Policeman (Klaus Becker); Third Policeman (Siegfried Dornbusch); Krause (Paul Bos); Tailor (Max Buschbaum); Haberdasher (Jaspar Von Oertzen); Stewardess (Inga De Toro); Pierre (Jacques Chevalier); Shoeman (Werner Hassenland)

## 1968

This year James Cagney narrated the opening of *Arizona Bushwackers,* a film produced by A. C. Lyles for Paramount Pictures. Cagney does not appear.

## 1981

**Ragtime**
*Writer:* Michael Weller, from the novel by E. L. Doctorow
*Director:* Milos Forman
*Camera:* Miroslav Ondricek
*Running time:* 155 minutes
*Cast:* Rheinlander Waldo (James Cagney); Younger Brother (Brad Dou-

rif); Booker T. Washington (Moses Gunn); Evelyn Nesbit (Elizabeth McGovern); Willie Conklin (Kenneth McMillan); Delmas (Pat O'Brien); Evelyn's Dance Instructor (Donald O'Connor); Father (James Olson); Tateh (Mandy Patinkin); Coalhouse Walker, Jr. (Howard E. Rollins); Mother (Mary Steenburgen); Sarah (Debbie Allen); Houdini (Jeff DeMunn); Harry K. Thaw (Robert Joy); Stanford White (Norman Mailer); Jerome (Bruce Boa)

## 1984

**Terrible Joe Moran** (Made for television by Robert Halmi Productions; telecast on CBS March 27, 1984)
*Writer:* Frank Cucci
*Director:* Joseph Sargent
*Camera:* Mike Fash
*Running time:* 102 minutes
*Cast:* Joe Moran (James Cagney); Troy (Art Carney); Ronnie (Ellen Barkin); Nick (Peter Gallagher); Capo (Joseph Sirola); Moe (Mayor Edward I. Koch); Himself (Floyd Patterson); Minty (Harris Laskawy); Pico (Lawrence Tierney); Young Hopeful (Terry Ellis); Young Boxer (Peter Deanello); Lady with Dog (Susan Lowden); Real Estate Agent (Anna Berger); Announcer (Andrew MacMillan); Benny the Wino (Maurice Shrog); First Thug (Mike Starr); Black Boxer (Joe Seneca); Meat Handler (David Wohl); Mrs. Hoskins (Marilyn Raphael); Marge (Shelly O'Neill)

# Short Films

## 1931

**Practice Shots**  No. 11 of Bobby Jones's *How I Play Golf* series. *Director:* George Marshall. *Cast:* James Cagney, Anthony Bushell, Donald Cook, Louise Fazenda

## 1933

**Hollywood on Parade #8**
*Cast:* James Cagney, Frankie Darro, Joe E. Brown

**Intimate Interview**
(Talking Picture Epics)
*Director:* Grace Elliott

## 1934

**Screen Snapshots #11**
(Columbia Pictures)
*Cast:* Boris Karloff, Bela Lugosi, Genevieve Tobin, Pat O'Brien, James Cagney, Maureen O'Sullivan, Eddie Cantor

**The Hollywood Gad-About**
(Louis Lewyn for Skibo Productions, Inc.)  Presented by E. W. Hammons and Educational Films Corporation of America Treasure Chest Short. *Cast:* Gary Cooper, Eddie Cantor, Mary Astor, Shirley Temple, Alice White, James Cagney, Chester Morris

## 1935

**A Trip Through a Hollywood Studio**
(Warner Brothers)
*Cast:* Dolores Del Rio, Ann Dvorak, Hugh Herbert, Wini Shaw, Rudy Vallee, Pat O'Brien, Busby Berkeley, James Cagney

**Hollywood Star Hobbies**
(Metro-Goldwyn-Mayer)
*Cast:* James Cagney and all-star baseball team

## 1938

**For Auld Lang Syne**
(Warner Brothers)  Sponsored by the motion picture industry for the Will Rogers Memorial Commission *Director:* George Bilson *Cast:* Paul Muni, James Cagney, Dick Powell and His Cowboy Octette, Benny Goodman and His Band, Rudy Vallee, Bonita Granville, Pat O'Brien, Johnny "Scat" Davis, Allen Jenkins, Marie Wilson, Mabel Todd, Hugh Herbert, and Frank McHugh and the Schnickelfritz Band

## 1943

**Show Business at War #10** (Vol. IX of *The March of Time*) (Twentieth Century–Fox)

*Cast:* Bette Davis, Humphrey Bogart, Ginger Rogers, James Cagney, Myrna Loy, Rita Hayworth, Kay Francis, Frank Sinatra, Alexis Smith, Gertrude Lawrence, The Mills Brothers, Jack Benny, Bob Hope, Fred MacMurray, Ginny Simms

**You, John Jones**
(Metro-Goldwyn-Mayer)
*Director:* Mervyn LeRoy
*Cast:* James Cagney, Ann Sothern, Margaret O'Brien

### 1944

**Battle Stations**
(Twentieth Century–Fox) Narrated by James Cagney and Ginger Rogers

### 1962

**Road to the Wall** (CBS for the U.S. Department of Defense) Narrated by James Cagney

### 1966

**The Ballad of Smokey the Bear**
(General Electric Theatre in cooperation with the U.S. Department of Agriculture) Cagney as the voice of Big Brother

# Cagney on Television

In the early years of television, Cagney made an informal guest appearance on a local Los Angeles Bob Hope program, and later was a guest of Jack Paar on his network evening program, *The Tonight Show*. His other appearances:

## 1955

**The Ed Sullivan Show** June 20. A scene with Henry Fonda from *Mister Roberts* to plug the forthcoming Warner Brothers film. Sullivan presented Cagney with a new Thunderbird sedan in gratitude.

**This Is Your Life** Honoring William A. Wellman. After doing the show, Cagney was ill-disposed to appear on television again. He said, "I'm not dependable. There I was, waiting my turn and watching the show on a set in the next room, and Bill's eighty-five year old mother comes on. Now, I've already met her. I knew she and Bill were going to be hugging and kissing in front of twenty-five million people—yet all of a sudden I felt that familiar tugging right here [*pointing to his heart*]. And there I was, bawling out loud. Crying like a baby. Can't help it. I'm an Irishman. Enjoy nothing better than a good cry. What are you going to do with us?"

**A Link in the Chain**
(The Christophers)
*Writer:* Larry Marcus
*Director:* Arthur Ripley
*Running time:* 30 minutes
*Cast:* Professor George Graham (James Cagney); Peter Fielding (James Lydon); Tom Gore (Sam Edwards); Emily (Allene Roberts); Young Man (Charles Smith); Miss Wilson (Kathryn Card); Little girl (Nancy Gilbert); First Student (Rita Walsh); Second Student (Allene Coates)

## 1956

**Robert Montgomery Presents: Soldier from the War Returning**
(NBC) September 10
*Director:* Perry Lafferty
*Running time:* 1 hour

## 1984

**Terrible Joe Moran** (CBS) March 27. Film made for television.
*Director:* Joseph Sargent
(See Appendix: Feature Films.)

# Select Bibliography

Note the adjective. In recent years there has appeared a particularly noisome sub-genre among film books: overview books purportedly biographical in nature, featuring many photographs of the subject and his or her films, totally derivative as to sources and stating none of them, most of said books (in Alden Whitman's words) "written in Day-Glo English." None of these appear in this listing.

### BY CAGNEY

*Cagney by Cagney.* New York: Doubleday, 1976.
"How I Got This Way," as told to Pete Martin. *Saturday Evening Post,* January 7, 14, and 21, 1956.
"James Cagney Talking." *Films and Filming,* March 1959.
Oakes, Philip. "Interview with James Cagney." *Sight and Sound,* Winter 1958–59.

### ON CAGNEY

*Primary books:*
Bergman, Andrew. *Cagney.* New York: Pyramid, 1973.
Dickens, Homer. *The Films of James Cagney.* Secaucus, N.J.: Citadel Press, 1972.
Freedland, Michael. *James Cagney.* New York: Stein and Day, 1982.
McGilligan, Patrick. *Cagney: The Actor as Auteur.* New York: A. S. Barnes, 1975; rev. ed., San Diego, 1982.

Offen, Ron. *Cagney.* Chicago: Regnery, 1972.
Schickel, Richard. *James Cagney: A Celebration.* Boston: Little, Brown & Co., 1985.
Sklar, Robert. *City Boys: Cagney, Bogart, Garfield.* Princeton, N.J.: Princeton University Press, 1992.
Warren, Doug. *James Cagney: The Authorized Biography.* New York: St. Martin's Press, 1983; rev. ed., 1986.

*Secondary books:*
Arliss, George. *My Ten Years in the Studios.* Boston: Little, Brown & Co., 1940.
Behlmer, Rudy. *Inside Warner Brothers.* New York: Simon and Schuster, 1985.
Bellamy, Ralph. *When the Smoke Hit the Fan.* New York: Doubleday, 1979.
Berg, A. Scott. *Goldwyn.* New York: Alfred A. Knopf, 1989.
Bickford, Charles. *Bulls, Balls, Bicycles and Actors.* New York: Simon and Schuster, 1965.

Blake, Michael F. *Lon Chaney: The Man Behind the Thousand Faces.* Vestal, N.Y.: Vestal Press Ltd., 1990.

———. *A Thousand Faces: Lon Chaney's Unique Artistry.* Vestal, N.Y.: Vestal Press Ltd., 1995.

Broun, Heywood Hale. *Whose Little Boy Are You?* New York: St. Martin's/Marek, 1983.

Cohen, Henry, ed. *The Public Enemy.* Madison: University of Wisconsin Press, 1981.

Curtis, James. *Featured Player: An Oral Autobiography by Mae Clarke.* Matuchen, N.J.: Scarecrow Press, 1997.

Dick, Bernard F. *Billy Wilder.* Boston: Little, Brown & Co., 1980.

Evans, Robert. *The Kid Stays in the Picture.* New York: Hyperion Books, 1994.

Eyman, Scott. *Ernst Lubitsch: Laughter in Paradise.* New York: Simon and Schuster, 1993.

Fields, Armond, and L. Marx. *From the Bowery to Broadway: Lew Fields and the Roots of American Popular Theatre.* New York: Oxford University Press, 1993.

Fonda, Henry. *Fonda: My Life. As Told to Howard Teichmann.* New York: New American Library, 1981.

Garnett, Tay. *Light Your Torches and Pull Up Your Tights.* New Rochelle, N.Y.: Arlington House, 1973.

Gottfried, Martin. *Jed Harris: The Curse of Genius.* Boston: Little, Brown & Co., 1984.

Greene, Graham. *The Pleasure Dome.* Edited by John Russell Taylor. London: Oxford University Press, 1980.

Hamman, G. D., ed. *James Cagney in the Thirties.* Hollywood: Filming Today Press, 1994.

Haskin, Byron. *Byron Haskin Interviewed by Joe Adamson.* Metuchen, N.J.: Scarecrow Press, Inc., 1984.

Higham, Charles. *Warner Brothers.* New York: Scribners, 1975.

———. *Bette: The Life of Bette Davis.* New York: Macmillan Publishing Co., 1981.

Hirschhorn, Clivé. *The Warner Brothers Story.* New York: Crown Publishers, 1979.

Hoare, Philip. *Noël Coward.* London: Sinclair-Stevenson, 1995.

Kandel, Abel. "James Cagney: Man of Principle." *Close-Ups: The Movie Star Book.* Edited by Danny Peary. New York, 1978.

Kanin, Garson. *Tracy and Hepburn.* New York: Viking, 1970.

Kazan, Elia. *Elia Kazan: A Life.* New York: Alfred A. Knopf, 1988.

Kroll, Jack. "James Cagney." In Elizabeth Weis, ed., *The Movie Star.* New York, 1981.

Lahr, John. *Notes on a Cowardly Lion.* New York: Alfred A. Knopf, 1969.

LeRoy, Mervyn. *Mervyn LeRoy: Take One.* New York: Hawthorn, 1974.

Logan, Joshua. *Movie Stars, Real People and Me.* New York: Delacorte Press, 1978.

Madsen, Axel. *Billy Wilder.* Bloomington: Indiana University Press, 1969.

Marx, Arthur. *The Secret Life of Bob Hope.* London: Robson Books, 1993.

McBride, Joseph. *Frank Capra: The Catastrophe of Success.* New York: Simon and Schuster, 1992.

O'Brien, Pat. *The Wind at My Back.* New York: Doubleday, 1964.

Pechter, William S. "Cagney vs. Allen vs. Brooks." In Elizabeth Weis, ed., *The Movie Star.* New York, 1981.

Sennett, Ted. *Warner Brothers Presents.* New Rochelle, N.Y.: Arlington House, 1971.

Sinclair, Andrew. *John Ford.* New York: Dual Press/James Wade, 1979.

Sperling, Cass Warner, and Cork Miller, with Jack Warner, Jr. *Hollywood Be Thy Name: The Warner Brothers Story.* Rockin, Calif.: Prime Publishing, 1994.

Swindell, Larry. *Body and Soul: The Story of John Garfield.* New York: William Morrow & Co., 1975.

Thomas, Bob. *Astaire, the Man, the Dancer.* New York: St. Martin's Press, 1984.

———. *Clown Prince of Hollywood: The Antic Life and Times of Jack L. Warner.* New York: St. Martin's Press, 1990.

Tynan, Kenneth. *Curtains.* London: Atheneum, 1961.

Wallis, Hal, and Charles Higham. *Starmaker.* New York: Macmillan Publishing Co., 1980.

Walsh, Raoul. *One Man in His Time.* New York: Farrar, Straus and Giroux, 1974.

Warner, Jack L. *My First Hundred Years in Hollywood.* New York: Random House, 1965.

Welles, Orson, and Peter Bogdanovich. *This Is Orson Welles.* New York: HarperCollins, 1993.

Wilson, Robert, ed. *The Film Criticism of Otis Ferguson.* Philadelphia: Temple University Press, 1971.

Yablonsky, Lewis. *George Raft.* New York: McGraw-Hill Book Co., 1974.

Zolotow, Maurice. *Billy Wilder in Hollywood.* New York: G. P. Putnam, 1977.

### ARTICLES
### (IN CHRONOLOGICAL ORDER)

Kirstein, Lincoln. "Cagney and the American Hero." *Hound and Horn,* April 1932.

Cagney, James. "Am I a Tough Guy?" *Picturegoer Weekly,* July 2, 1932.

Potamkin, H. A. "The Personality of the Player: A Phase of Unity." *Close-Up,* March 1933.

Jones, Carlisle. "James Cagney Can Hit a Lady Without Hurting—Much." *Picturegoer Weekly,* July 22, 1933.

Cagney, James. "Sock!" *The New Movie Magazine,* August 1933.

Rankin, Ruth. "If One Cagney's Good, Two Should Be Better!" *Photoplay,* October 1933.

Mook, S. R. "Cagney—Thinker!" *Screenland,* November 1933.

Maddox, Ben. "Two 'Toughs' from the Chorus." *Photoplay,* February 1934.

Blondell, Joan. "What I Think of Jimmy." *Screenland Magazine,* March 1934.

Cagney, James. "What I Think of Joan." *Screenland Magazine,* March 1934.

Symes, Elizabeth. "A Woman Looks at James Cagney." *Film Weekly,* June 29, 1934.

Jory, Victor. "The Three Sides of Jimmy." *The New Movie Magazine,* April 1935.

Cagney, James. "Goodbye to Gangsters." *Film Weekly,* June 14, 1935.

"Making a Dream Come True." *Picturegoer Weekly,* October 5, 1935.

Baldwin, Lois. "Why Jimmy Took a Walk." *Photoplay,* November 1936.

Mooring, W. H. "Can Cagney Take It?" *Film Weekly,* June 5, 1937.

————. "Cagney's Home Again." *Film Weekly*, April 30, 1938.

Crouse, Russel. "An Angel with a Clean Face." *Stage*, December 1938.

Durant, John. "Tough On and Off." *Collier's*, August 31, 1940.

Smith, H. Allen. "The Cantankerous Cagneys." *Saturday Evening Post*, October 2, 1943.

Steele, Joseph. "Portrait of a Shy Guy." *Photoplay*, October 1943.

Cosby, Vivian. "Love Story—Cagney Twenty-Year-Old Variety." *Movieland*, March 1944.

Cole, Lester. "Unhappy Ending." *Hollywood Quarterly*, October 1945.

Cheatham, Maude. "The Ideal Realist." *Silver Screen*, November 1947.

Brown, John Mason. "Cagney Rides Again." *Saturday Review*, October 1, 1949.

Tynan, Kenneth. "Cagney and the Mob." *Sight and Sound*, May 1951.

Parsons, Louella. "Cagney's Year." *Cosmopolitan*, June 1955.

Bergquist, Laura. "The New Craze for Cagney." *Look*, September 20, 1955.

Shipp, Cameron. "Cagney." *Collier's*, October 28, 1955.

Benz, Hamilton. "The Gentle Tough of Martha's Vineyard." *Coronet*, November 1955.

Miller, Don. "James Cagney." *Films in Review*, August/September 1958.

"Yankee Doodle Dandy." *Newsweek*, April 22, 1968.

Haskell, Molly. "Partners in Crime and Conversation." *The Village Voice*, December 7, 1972.

McGilligan, Patrick. "Just a Dancer Gone Wrong: The Complication of James Cagney." *Take One*, September 1973.

Gardella, Kay. "The Real James Cagney Speaks Up." *New York Daily News*, February 10, 1974.

Lawrence, K. G. "Homage to James Cagney." *Films in Review*, May 1974.

Cagney, James. "The Guild." *Screen Actor*, Summer 1979.

Buckley, M. "James Cagney." *Films in Review*, March 1981.

Leslie, Joan. Interview, Southern Methodist University Oral History Collection, Los Angeles, August 13, 1981.

"The Conversation: Studs Terkel and James Cagney." *Esquire*, October 1981.

Kennedy, Eugene. "Cagney: The Little Giant's Back in Town." *Sunday News Magazine, New York Daily News*, November 22, 1981.

White, Timothy. "James Cagney's Armchair Tour." *Rolling Stone*, February 18, 1982.

De Camp, Rosemary, Interview, Southern Methodist University Oral History Collection, Los Angeles, July 13, 1982.

Clarke, Mae. "Making Movies with James Cagney." *American Classic Screen*, July/August 1983.

Cook, Anthony. "Cagney's Curious Comeback." *Life*, March 1984.

Tonley, Rod. "Nobody Ever Said Cagney Wasn't a Fighter." *TV Guide*, March 24, 1984.

Freeman, Don. "The Craft of Cagney." *Emmy Magazine*, July/August 1984.

Amory, Cleveland. "The Lifetime of James Cagney: The Gentle Force of a Strong Man." *Parade*, August 5, 1984.

Speck, Gregory. "James Cagney." *Interview*, December 1985.

"James Cagney Succumbs at 86: Quintessential Tough Guy." *Variety*, April 2, 1986.

Buckley, M. Obituary, *Films in Review.* June/July 1986.

McGilligan, Patrick. "Yankee Doodle Diary." *Film Comment,* July/August 1986.°

Hagopian, Kevin. "Declarations of Independence: A History of Cagney Productions." *Velvet Light Trap,* November 22, 1986.

Bellamy, Ralph. "Unforgettable Jimmy Cagney." *Reader's Digest,* May 1987.

°This article, by the otherwise dependable (on Cagney film matters) Mr. McGilligan, is largely an attack on Marge Zimmermann, based principally on the Cook article and the animadversions cast on Mrs. Zimmermann by William Cagney. As for Bill Cagney's dislike of her, there can be no doubt, but his dislikes might have been better directed against Mrs. James Cagney, who was the principal source of non-contact between the Cagney brothers in late years. The McGilligan article treats Mrs. Zimmermann as a figure somewhere between Delilah and the Wicked Witch of the West, an opinion he is entitled to, but as an eyewitness of the proceedings he covers, I find it quite inaccurate. McGilligan speaks of Cagney's being "held in thrall by Zimmermann." This quite simply is daffydom, as I view it. No one ever in his life held Jim Cagney "in thrall." Not even his wife.

As for Marge Zimmermann, the fact is that great thanks are due her from all who loved Cagney—for the deep solicitude and care of him she tendered with such love over his last years.

In his article McGilligan also speaks of a projected film biography of Cagney that would show him in 1975 (or thereabouts) as likely being "wheezy, croaking his recollections to a ghostwriter." Speaking as that ghostwriter, I can testify that there was no wheezing or croaking, literal or figurative. James Cagney—to repeat a point made in my text and to refute McGilligan's underlying implication—was mentally acute to the last day of his life.

# Index

*Cagney's films are listed by title. Italic page numbers indicate photographs in text.*

Abbott, George, 61
acting techniques, *see* Cagney, James
    acting style/techniques
Adler, Luther, 259–60
Adler, Stella, 354
Alperson, Edward L., 150
*American Cavalcade of Dance*, 224
American Film Institute, 331, 332
Anderson, Maxwell, 310
*Angels with Dirty Faces*, 162,163,
    164–5, *164*, 393, 406–7
Annabella (actress), *241*
Arliss, George, 78–80, *81*
Armstrong, Robert, *134*
Astaire, Fred, 147, 274
Ayres, Lew, 76

Bacon, Lloyd, 114, 138, 144, 160,
    166
Bailey, Jack, 310
Barkin, Ellen, 375
Barrat, Robert, 232
Barrymore, John, 159
baseball teams, 20–1
Bellamy, Ralph, *161*
Bennett, Constance, 126 and *n*
Bennett, Edna, *125*
Benny, Jack, 225–6
Berkeley, Busby, 110
Bickford, Charles, 55, *56*, 57
Bioff, Willie, 173–4
Bishop, William A. (Billy), 197–8
*Blonde Crazy*, 86, 87, 88, 398
Blondell, Joan, *94*, *111*, 125
    in *Blonde Crazy*, 86, 88
    in *He Was Her Man*, 121–2, *123*

Hollywood, view of, 78
    as a tootsie, 68–9
*Blood on the Sun*, 236–7, *238*, 239, 394,
    411
Bogart, Humphrey, 125–6, 167, 168,
    *178*
Bond, Ward, 260
Bongart, Serge, 310
Bootah (childhood friend), 20, 21
Boyer, Charles, 221
Boyle, Johnny, 155, *156*, 224
*Boy Meets Girl*, 160–2, *161*, 406
Boys Club
    Cohan's style, 204
    end of, 130, 329
    founding of, 127–128
    and Irish repertory company, 159,
        160
    political discussions within, 217
Brent, George, 183–4
Brian, Mary, *104*
*Bride Came C.O.D., The*, 195–6, *196*,
    410
Bright, John, 117
*Broadway* (play), 61–4, 389
Brodie, Steve, *260*
Bromfield, Louis, 229, *231*, 232–4
Brown, Chamberlain, 59
Brown, Joe E., 139, *143*
Buchholz, Horst, 322, *322*
Buckner, Robert, 180, 202 and *n*
Burke, James, *152*

*Cagney: A Biography*, 341
*Cagney by Cagney*, xiii, xv–xvi, 337,
    342

Cagney, Carolyn Elizabeth (Carrie)
(mother)
Cagney's relationship with, 208,
239–40
and Cagney's boxing career, 30
childhood of, 4
death of, 240
health of, 18, 239, 240
and *Life with Father,* 237
as mother, 7–8, 10, 18–19, 26, 32, 36
patriotism of, 217, 365
pregnancies of, later in life, 29–30,
35
and *The Strawberry Blonde,* 195
Willie Cagney, resentment of, 44, 49,
175
Cagney, Catharine (Casey) (daughter),
adoption of, 184
childhood living arrangements of,
184–5, 296–7, 376–7
and father, 185–6, 289–90
inheritance, 366
marriage of, 325, 346–7
mother, estrangement from, 349
Cagney, Edward (brother), 10, 36
Cagney, Frances Willard (Willie) (wife),
xi, 43, 340
career
acting career, end of, 68
as chorus girl, 41
in dancing school, 64–5, 68
in vaudeville, 44–8, 50–5, 59–60
character of, 297, 347
children of, 184, 297, 349, 366–7,
382
death of, 385
friendships, 346
with Marge Zimmermann, 370,
371
with O'Brien and McHugh, 114
marriage and courtship, 41, 43, 48,
184, 185, 290, 383–5
and Cagney family resentment, 44,
49, 175, 350
and Cagney's acting career, 46, 54,
361–2
Cagney, Harry (brother), 32, 36
Cagney, James Frances (father), 26–7,
343
as bar owner, 23, 24

as bartender, 4–5
death of, 35–6
drinking habit of, 4, 5–6, 13, 18,
26–7, 263
and keening (the fits), 3, 26–7, 255
Cagney, James (Jim), 335–6, 342
acting, 85, 92, 122, 135, 165, 173,
197, 316
grapefruit scene, 82, 83, 84–5, 333,
336
makeup for *Man of a Thousand
Faces,* 305, 306
*see also* Cagney, James: acting
career; Cagney, James: acting
style/techniques
acting career
*Broadway* casting disappointment,
62–4, 174
compared to other greats, 385–6
contract disputes with Warner
Brothers, 98–9, 102, 147–8,
151–2
contracts with Warner Brothers,
159, 249
discouragement, 46, 53–4
films, feature length, 397–419, *see
also individual titles*
films, short, 421–2
first film, 73–4
first legitimate theatre, 55–9
first play, 33
first theatre act, 38–40
memorabilia, 382–3
radio shows, 187–8, 393–5
in retirement, 362–3
stage career, 65–6, 68–71, 389–91,
*see also individual titles*
success, 86, 170, 212–13
television appearances, 302–4,
423
vaudeville, 40, 44–8, 50–5, 59–60,
344, 359
zenith of his career, 212–13
acting style/techniques
acting "lessons," 47, 51–2, 58–9,
99–100
adding "goodies," 85–6, 99–100,
332, 352
assuming a defect and then forgetting it, 283

comedy/humor added, 88, 158, 234, 252, 285–6
concentration, 284
control, 47, 51–2, 173, 356
dancing style, 7, 34, 38–9, 40–1, 92–3, 155–6, 291
drunks, portraying, 265–6
emotional depth, 74, 91, 172, 214, 253–5
hands, use of, 105–6, 107, 153
honoring the author's intention, 220
improvisation, 86, 176–7, 208
influence of Barry McCollum, 58–9
influence of Frank Fay, 51–2
influence of Lowell Sherman, 99–100, 352
listening intently, 58–9, 173, 244, 282, 304, 313, 315
love scenes, 203
observation, master of, 288
practice, learning from, 351–2
preparation, 193
registering thoughts naturally, 318
similarities to George Cohan, 199, 200
singing style, 203–4
song and dance man, 155–6, 205, 344
"star" quality, 257–8
temper tantrums, 263
villains, empathizing with, 276–7, 332, 352
villains with virtue, 82, 99–100, 252, 258, 331, 353
violence, 94–5
awards/honors, 46, 165, 205, 215–16, 284, 290, 317, 331–6, 360–1, 368
character/personality, xi, xv, 19–20, 22, 38, 90, 118, 150, 174, 315, 320, 332, 337, 338, 345–6, 356, 383–5, 386
generosity of, 256, 309, 374
loner, as an adult, 115, 296, 315, 328, 342
childhood
birth, 5
fights, 7–8, 16–17
gangs, 15, 336
influences acting, 356
revisits neighborhood, 170
education, 9–10, 24, 36–37, 47
early employment
aspirations, 36
bellhop, 32
bouncer, 28
boxing, 28–29, 30
choreographer, 66–67
copyboy, 25
dancing school, 64–65, 68
director, 309
library work, 26
ticket clerk, 29
Wall Street runner, 39
*see also* Cagney, James: acting career
family, 175, 296, 378–9
children, relationship with, 184, 185–6, 289–90, 349, 366–7, 376–7
family life, 6, 24, 326, 350
father, relationship with, 3, 93, 169, 214, 343
grandfather, bond with, 11–12
impostor "sons," 184$n$
motto, 13
O'Caigne name, 3–4, 17
*see also* Cagney, James: marriage; *specific family members*
friendships, 127–130, 300, 326, 364, *see also specific individuals*
health, 348, 361–2, 363, 368, 372–4, 375, 376, 377–8, 379–82, 429$n$
marriage, xiii, 43, 48, 50, 184, 340
adoration of wife affects films, 192
ashamed of adultery, 222
youthful romances, 33, 34
*see also* Cagney, Frances Willard (Willie)
politics
airstrip, objecting to, 328–9
Communist sympathies, accused of, 119, 189, 191
a conservative, 301, 312
cotton workers' strike, support of, 118–119
Franklin D. Roosevelt, support of, 234–5

Cagney, James (Jim), politics (*cont.*)
  Hollywood Victory Committee,
    218
  labor unions, support of 77–8,
    106–7, 123, 124, 312
  a liberal, 100, 115, 117, 118
  quasi-socialist, 65, 118
  Republican influences, 235
  Screen Actors Guild, service to,
    106, 123, 218
  Victory Caravan, 220–4
  wartime bond-selling films, 218
  wartime radio programs, 217–8,
    225–6
  wartime tour in England, 224–5
Cagney, James, Jr. (Jim Junior) (son),
    366–7
  adoption of, 184
  childhood living arrangements of,
    184, 296
  father, time with, 185–6, 289–90
  musical talent of, 185–6, 347
  and real estate gift, 366–7, 369
  as U.S. Marine, 325, 347
Cagney, Jeanne Carolyn (sister), 237
  as actress, 170, 205, 207, 210, 245,
    308
  birth of, 37
  death of, 378
  education of, 170
  marriage of, 325–6
  on *Queen for a Day*, 310, 325
  and real estate gift, 369
Cagney memorabilia, 382–3
Cagney-Montgomery Productions,
    318
Cagney Productions
  and book options, 242, 275
  and family's involvement, 227, 275
  films of, 228–34, 229–34, 236–7,
    242–8, 259–60, 275–8
  finances of, 250, 259
  formation of, 216 and *n*, 249
Cagney, Robert (brother), 29
Cagney, William (Bill) (brother), 36
  as actor, 147*n*
  as associate producer, 186
  as business manager for Cagney, 89,
    202, 249, 278

and Cagney Productions, 216, 229,
    236
  as childhood salesman, 9
Calvet, Corinne, 270
*Captains of the Clouds,* 197, 197–8,
    394, 410
Carney, Art, 373–4
Carney, Willie, 16–18
Caruso, Enrico, 148–9
*Ceiling Zero,* 145–7, *146,* 393, 404–5
Chaney, Lou, 304–6
Chaplin, Charlie, 154–5
*City for Conquest* (book), 191
*City for Conquest* (film), *190,* 191–4,
    409
Clarke, Mae, *83,* 84–5, 114–15, *116,*
    153, 317, 333
Cohan, Agnes, 214
Cohan, George M., 199–208, 212–16
  Cagney's admiration of, xiii, 59, 342
  rejects Cagney for part, 59
  as song and dance man, 155–6, 291
Coldwater Canyon, Cagney's property
    in, 171, 188–9
*Come Fill the Cup,* 263, 265, 413
*Command Performance,* 225–6, 394
Communist sympathizers, 119, 189,
    191
conservation, 19, 284–5, 289, 290, 340
Coward, Noël, 97–8
Crisp, Donald, *190*
*Crowd Roars, The,* 94, 95, 96, 399
Crowther, Bosley, 257
Curtiz, Michael (Mike), 119, 165, 205,
    209–11, 214

Dailey, Dan, 270
Daly, Blyth, 56
Davis, Bette, *120,* 120–1, 195–6, *196*
Daw, Evelyn, 157
Day, Doris, 267, 280–4, 282, 283, 333
Dead End Kids, *163*
Dean, James, 356–7
De Camp, Rosemary, 207, 210
De Havilland, Olivia, 138, 195
Delsarte, François, 106*n*
Delza, Sophia, 67
Demarest, William (Bill), 270, 270–1
de Rochemont, Louis, 241

*Devil Dogs of the Air,* 131, *132,* 403
Dies Committee, 189
Dieterle, William, 140
Dixon, Harland, 155, *156*
Dodd, Claire, *111*
Donnelly, Ruth, *104,* 105, 345
*Doorway to Hell,* 76, 77, 397
Dubbins, Don, *300*
Dunning, Philip, 61, 62
Durbin, Deanna, 226
Dvorak, Ann, *94, 95*

*Each Dawn I Die,* 171–4, *172,* 407
Ellis, Patricia, *108, 125*
Epstein, Julius (Julie) and Phil, 202–3, 213
Erdman, Richard, 246–7
Etting, Ruth, 281
Evans, Madge, *109*
Evans, Robert, *306*
*Every Sailor,* 38, *38*–40

Fair, Jim, 127
Fanchon and Marco, 110
farming, Cagney's interest in, 235, 347, 349
  and animals, 189, 327, 351
  applies to Farmington School, 31
  childhood inspiration for, 14–15
  finding managers for, 246, 316
  and Martha's Vineyard, 149–150, 238, 289
  Verney Farm, 327, 346, 347, 349, 385
  *see also* horses, Cagney's interest in
*Faun, The,* 33
Fay, Frank, 51–2, *52n*
Ferguson, Otis, 136, 158, 188
Fields, Lew, 47
Fighting Irish, 181
*Fighting 69th, The,* 181–3, *181, 182,* 408
Fitzpatrick, Tom, 346
Flatbush farm, 14–15, *see also* Verney Farm
Flynn, Harry, 149–50
Fonda, Henry, 286, 287, *287,* 289
*Footlight Parade,* 110, *111, 112,* 393, 400–1
Foran, Dick, *161*

Ford, John, 268–72, 287
Forman, Milos, 361
Four Cohans, 205
Foy, Eddie, 290–1
Francis, Noel, 87
Frank, George, 151
Free Acres (single tax colony), 65
Freedland, Michael, 341
*Frisco Kid,* 144–5, *145,* 404
Frou Frou (poodle), 50–1

Gable, Clark, 354–5
*Gallant Hours, The,* 316–17, 318–19, *319,* 418
Garson, Greer, 215
George, Gladys, *178, 179*
George, Grace, *231*
Gibson, Wynne, *42,* 50
Gleason, Jackie, 379
Gleason, James, 265
*G-Men,* 133, *134,* 135–6, 403
Gordon, Mary, 137, *137,* 153
Grand National Pictures, 152, 155, 158
  and *n,* 227–8
  and Cagney films, 152–4, 155–8
*Grand Street Follies, The,* 66–8, *67,* 390
grapefruit scene, 82, *83,* 84–5, 333, 336
*Great Guy,* 152, 152–4, 155, 405
Green, Abel, 216

Haas, Dolly, 295
Hagerthy, Ron, *267*
Halloran, Jack, *238*
Halsey, William F. (Bull), 316–17, 318
Hamilton, Margaret, 234
Hansen, Chuck, 135
*Hard to Handle,* 102, *103, 104,* 105, 399–400
Harlow, Jean, *83*
Harris, Jed, 61, 62, 63, 64
Haskin, Byron, 104
Hathaway, Henry, 242
Hawks, Howard, 146
Hayworth, Rita, *194, 195*
Hecht, Ben, 107
Hellinger, Mark, 176
Herbert, Hugh, 140
*Here Comes the Navy,* 122, *124,* 402

Hessling, Peter (Bootah), 20, 21
Heston, Charlton, 332
*He Was Her Man,* 121–2, *123,* 402
Holloway, Sterling, 107
Hollywood Victory Committee, 218, 220
Hope, Bob, 290–1, *292,* 332–3
Hopper, Hedda, 324–5
horses, Cagney's interest in
　childhood experiences with, 15, 339
　and Morgan horses, 186, 289, 327,
　　349, 386
　and Cagney's riding ability, 167,
　　299
Howard, Moe, 89
Hunchback of Notre Dame (Cagney),
　307
Huston, Walter, *207, 210,* 213

"I Don't Want to Play in Your Yard"
　(song), 169
impersonations of Cagney, 162, 266,
　321, 330, 332, 334, 335–6
　and the phrase "You dirty rat!" 93,
　　330, 334, 335
*Irish in Us, The,* 136–8, *137,* 403–4
Irish Mafia, *see* Boys Club

James, Burton and Florence, 32–3
*James Cagney: The Authorized Biogra-
　phy,* 367–8
*Jean-Christophe* (Rolland), 29
Jenkins, Allen, 44, 110, 123, *125,* 138,
　150
Jewell, Isabel, *146*
*Jimmy the Gent,* 119–21, *120, 121,*
　401–2
John Jays (baseball team), 20
*Johnny Come Lately,* 229–30, 231, *231,*
　232–4, 394, 411
Jones, Shirley, *311,* 312–13

Kasha, Larry, 360, 361
Kazan, Elia (Gadge), 192–3
Keeler, Ruby, *111, 112*
Keighley, William, 133
Kein, Betty Lou, *301*
Kelly, George, 68–9
Kennedy Center Honors, 360–1
Kibbee, Guy, 139

Kilian, Victor, 55, 232
*Kiss Tomorrow Goodbye,* 259–60, *260,*
　*261,* 413
Klein, Artie, 127
*Knute Rockne—All American,* 180
Kohler, Fred, 144, *145*

labor unions, Cagney's support of, 77–8,
　106–7, 123, 124, 312
*Lady Killer,* 114–15, *116,* 401
Lafferty, Jack (Dirty Neck), 82
Langner, Lawrence, 59
Lemmon, Jack, 288, 333
Lenox Hill Settlement House, 32
LeRoy, Mervyn, 102–4, 104n, 287
Leslie, Joan, *207,* 208, *210*
Levey, Ethel, 203
*Lew Fields' Ritz Girls of 19 and 22,*
　47–8
Life Achievement Award, 331–6
Linahan, Leo, 30
Lindsay, Margaret, 115, 131, *132,* 135,
　145
*Link in the Chain, A,* 291–3, 423
*Lion Is in the Streets, A* (novel),
　275–6
*Lion Is in the Streets, A* (film), 276–7,
　*277,* 414–15
*Little Sammy Sneeze,* 6–7
Litvak, Anatole (Tola), 191, 192, 193
Lloyd, Roy, 63, 64
Logan, Josh, 286
*Lonesome Manor,* 59–60, 258–9
Lord, Marjorie, *231*
Lord, Robert, 144
*Love Me or Leave Me,* 280–4, *282, 283,*
　415

MacLaine, Shirley, 333
MacLane, Barton, 133–5, *260*
*Maggie the Magnificent,* 68–9, 390
Mamoulian, Rouben, 310
*Man of a Thousand Faces,* 305–8, *306,*
　*307,* 417
Martha's Vineyard farm, 149–50, 238,
　289
*Martha, The,* 114
Massey, Ray, 263
*Mayor of Hell, The, 109,* 109–10, 400

Mayo, Virginia, 253, 256–7, 261
McAlliser, Neil, 119
McCarten, John, 257
McCarthy, Charlie, 187–8
McCollum, Barry, 58
McDaniel, Hattie, 231
McHugh, Dorothy, 114, 346
McHugh, Frank, 190, 365
    and Boys Club, founding of, 127–8
    and Cagney, xi, 66
    in *Devil Dogs of the Air*, 131
    in *Here Comes the Navy*, 122, 124
    in *The Irish in Us*, 138
    in *A Midsummer Night's Dream*, 139
    as supporting actor, 96–7, 255, 366
    and *The Fighting 69th*, 182
    and *The Roaring Twenties*, 176–7
McManus, John T., 233
McNamara, Edward, 148–9, 153, 201,
        230, 231
Meisner, Sanford (Sandy), 354
Melcher, Marty, 284
Method acting, 353–4, 375
Metro-Goldwyn-Mayer (MGM), 283
    and Cagney films, 280–4, 298–300
*Midsummer Night's Dream, A*, 138–41,
        144, 142, 143, 144, 404
*Millionaire, The*, 78–80, 81, 397–8
*Mister Roberts*, 285–9, 287, 415–16
Mitchell, George, 20
Mizner, Wilson, 97, 105
Montgomery, Robert (Bob)
    as actor, 301
    and Cagney, 63, 175–6, 300, 317
    and Cagney-Montgomery Produc-
        tions, 318
    death of, 365
    and *Robert Montgomery Presents*,
        302–3
    and Screen Actors Guild, 106, 301–2
Morgan, Frank, 127
Murray, Don, 314–16

Nelson, Carolyn Elizabeth, *see* Cagney,
        Carolyn Elizabeth (Carrie)
Nelson, Henry (father of Carrie), 4,
        10–12
*Never Steal Anything Small*, 310–13,
        311, 417

"Night of 100 Stars," 368
Nut Club (baseball team), 20–1

Oberon, Merle, 220, 222, 223–4
O'Brien, Eloise, 114, 346, 362
O'Brien, Pat, 146, 164, 187
    in *Boy Meets World*, 161, 161
    and Cagney, xi, 65–6, 115
    career of, 180, 364
    death of, 369
    in *Devil Dogs of the Air*, 131
    in *Here Comes the Navy*, 122, 124
    in *Ragtime*, 362
    on Victory Caravan, 223
O'Caigne family name, 3–4, 17
*Oklahoma Kid, The*, 167–70, 168, 407
Oliver, Nellie, 34
*One, Two, Three*, 320–3, 322, 418–19
Original Nut Club, *see* Nut Club
Ornitz, Samuel, 117
Oscars (Academy Awards), 46, 165,
        215–16, 284
*Other Men's Women*, 78, 79, 397
*Outside Looking In*, 55–9, 56, 389
Overman, Lynne, 128, 129

Paramount, 278–9, 280
    and Cagney films, 278–9
Pavlova, Anna, 34
Payton, Barbara, 261
Peabody (dance), 92–3, 93n
Peckinpah, Sam, 333–4
*Penny Arcade*, 69–71, 70, 391
Perry, Harvey, 138
*Picture Snatcher*, 107, 108, 109, 400
*Pitter Patter*, 40, 42, 389
*Playboy of the Western World, The*,
        159–60
The Players (club), 296, 326
Potter, H. C., 246–7
Powell, Dick, 140
Powell, William, 288
*Public Enemy, The*, 80–2, 83, 84, 84–6,
        166, 171, 398

Queen Mother, 363–4

radio programs with Cagney, 393–5
Raftery, Edward C., 214

Raft, George, 93, 171, *172*, 173
*Ragtime*, 362–3, *363*, 419
Reagan, Ronald, 331
Reinhardt, Max, 139
*Ritz Girls*, 47–8
*Roaring Twenties, The*, 176–7, *178*,
    *179*, 407–8
Robinson, Edward G., 87
Rockne, Knute, 170, 179, 180
Roman, Ruth, 267
Rooney, Mickey, 140
Roosevelt, Franklin D., 234, 235
Rowan, Frank, 70
*Run for Cover*, 278, 278–9, 280, 415

Sakall, S. Z. (Cuddles), 207, 211–12
Saroyan, William, 242, 243, 247
Schertzinger, Victor, 157
Screen Actors Guild, 106, 302
Screen Directors' Guild of America, 317
*Seven Little Foys, The*, 290–1, 292, 416
*Shake Hands with the Devil*, 313–16,
    *315*, 417–18
*Shame of the Cities, The*, 118
"Shanghai Lil," 110
*Sheela*, 393–4
Sheridan, Ann, *163*, *187*, *190*
Sherman, Lowell, 99–100, 352 and *n*
Sherwood, James, 297–8
*Short Cut to Hell*, 309, 417
Sidney, Sylvia, 236–7, *239*
Siegel, Sol, 272
*Sign on the Door, The*, 99–100
Sinatra, Frank, 332
*Sinner's Holiday*, 73–4, *74*, *75*, 397
Skolsky, Sidney, 200–1
*Smart Money*, 86, 87, 398
*Snapshots of 1923*, 52
Snyder, Moe (The Gimp), 281
"Soldier from the War Returning,"
    302–4, 423
Solomon, Burt, 319–20
*Something to Sing About*, 155, *156*,
    156–8, *157*, 405–6
song and dance men, 155–6, 205, 291,
    344
Stanwyck, Barbara, 299, *301*
*Starlift*, 266–7, *267*, 413–14
Steffens, Lincoln, 118, 119

Stevens, George, Jr., 334
*St. Louis Kid, The*, 122–4, *125*, 402–3
Strasberg, Lee, 353–4
*Strawberry Blonde, The*, *194*, 194–5,
    394, 409
*Stray Lamb, The*, 242

*Taxi!*, 90, 90–5, *91*, 398–9
*Terrible Joe Moran*, 369, 372, 373–6,
    419, 423
*These Wilder Years*, 299–300, *301*,
    416–17
*13 Rue Madeleine*, 241, 241–2, 412
*This Is Your Life*, 423
Thomas, Casey, *see* Cagney, Catharine
    (Casey)
Tiffin, Pamela, 322
*Time of Your Life, The*, 242–7, *244*, 412
Tobias, George, *190*
Torporcer, George (Specs), 127
*Torrid Zone*, 186–8, *187*, 394, 408–9
Tracy, Lee, 62
Tracy, Spencer (Spence), 128, 329–30,
    356
Travis, June, *146*
*Tribute to a Bad Man*, 298–9, *300*, 416
Truex, Ernest, 44
Twentieth Century–Fox
    and Cagney films, 241, 269–72

United Artists, 228, 248
USS *Arizona*, 122

vaudeville, Cagney career in, 40, 44–8,
    50–5, 59–60, 344, 359
Verney Farm, 327, 346, *347*, 379, 385,
    *see also* Flatbush farm
Vernon, Frances Willard, *see* Cagney,
    Frances Willard (Willie)
verse by Cagney, 102, 124–5, 126–7,
    285, 289, 326–7, 328, 377, 381
Victory Caravan, 220–4

Wallis, Hal, 139, 162, 202
    and *G-Men*, 133
    and *The Oklahoma Kid*, 169
    and *Torrid Zone*, 187
    and *Boy Meets Girl*, 160, 161
    and *Angels with Dirty Faces*, 165

Walsh, Raoul, 176, 177

Warner Brothers studio, 72–73, 159, 182–183, *see also specific individuals*

and Cagney films, 73–6, 78–88, 90–7, 102–15, 119–24, 131–47, 160–5, 167–70, 171–4, 181–3, 186–8, 191–8, 202–9, 212–16, 249–59, 261–7, 285–9, *see also individual titles*

Warner, Harry, 72

Warner, Jack L. (the Shvontz), 202

and absence from Cagney's award dinner, 332

and Cagney billing error, 147–8

caricature of, 157

and *Come Fill the Cup,* 263–4

and contract negotiations with Cagney, 89, 98, 99, 102

and relations with Cagney, 71, 102, 151, 175

and nicknames, 89, 102, 336

and Warner Brothers, 72

and *White Heat,* 255

Warner, Sam, 72

Wead, Frank, 146

Weill, Kurt, 311

Welles, Orson, 257–8

Wesson, Dick, 267

*West Point Story, The,* 259, 261–3, 262, 395, 413

Wexley, John, 191

*What Price Glory?,* 268–72, 270, 414

White, Alice, 121

*White Heat,* 249–58, 253, 254, 412–13

Whorf, Richard, 207

Wilder, Billy, 320–1, 323

William Cagney Productions, Inc., *see* Cagney Productions

Williams, Bert, 60–1

Wilson, Marie, *161*

*Winner Take All,* 96, 97, 399

Winsten, Archer, 162

Winters, Ella, 118, 119

Withers, Grant, 78

*Women Go On Forever,* 65, 66, 390

Woods, Edward, *84*

World Series, Cagney opens, 365

World War II

and bond-selling films, 218

and Cagney's tour of England, 224–5

and *Command Performance,* 225–6, 394

and Hollywood Victory Committee, 218, 220

and radio programs, 217–18, 225–6

and Victory Caravan, 220–4, 218–20, 422

and *You, John Jones,* 218–20, 422

Wray, John, 174

Wycherly, Margaret, 251, 253

*Yankee Doodle Dandy,* 202–9, 207, 209, 210, 211, 212–16, 394, 410–11

Yiddish, Cagney's interest in, 24–5, 89, 91–2, 158

*You John Jones,* 218–20, 422

Young, Gig, 264–5

Young, Loretta, 90

Zanuck, Darryl, 151, 241, 268, 269

Zimmermann, Marge, 345–50, 362–4, 369–71, 372, 429n

The illustrations reproduced within the text of this book were provided with the permission and courtesy of the following:

*Academy of Motion Picture Arts and Sciences:* 163, 231 (bottom), 282, 306; *The Cagney Estate:* 38, 56; *The George Eastman House:* 74, 75, 77, 79, 81, 83 (both), 84, 87 (both), 90, 94, 95, 96, 104, 105, 108 (both), 109, 111 (top), 112, 116 (top), 120, 123, 132 (top), 134, 137, 142 (both), 143 (both), 145, 164, 178 (top), 181, 182, 187, 190 (both), 196, 197, 231 (top), 241, 244, 260, 262, 265, 267, 277, 287, 292, 300, 307 (bottom), 311, 315, 322; *The Kobal Collection:* 90, 163, 172, 239, 253, 261, 301, 307 (top), 319; *The Museum of Modern Art, New York:* 168, 178 (bottom), 179, 194, 207 (both), 209, 210, 211, 238, 254, 270, 278, 283, 363

The insert illustrations were provided with the permission and courtesy of the following (page numbers refer to insert page):

*Archive Photos:* 8 (bottom), 11 (bottom); *Eve Arnold:* 12 and 13 (all); *The Cagney Estate:* 1, 2 and 3 (all); *Citadel Press:* 5 (bottom), 9 (bottom), 15 (middle); *The Kobal Collection:* 6 (bottom); *Moonstone Press:* 15, top; *The Museum of Modern Art:* 6 (top), 14; *Marge Zimmermann:* 7 (bottom; photo by Scotty Welbourne), 10 (bottom), 16

All other photos are from the author's collection.

A NOTE ABOUT THE AUTHOR

John McCabe was a professional actor from the age of seven, first appearing with various stock companies in his native Detroit. He blended the acting profession with his schooling for decades, finally receiving a doctorate from the Shakespeare Institute, Stratford-upon-Avon, England, in 1954. While at Stratford he met Stan Laurel and Oliver Hardy, then touring British music halls. From this encounter came a deep friendship with Laurel and the authorized biography Mr. Laurel and Mr. Hardy (1962), which established John McCabe as the world authority on this great comedy team. Other show business biographies followed, and in 1973 he was selected to ghostwrite James Cagney's autobiography, Cagney by Cagney.

In addition to his many years as a professional actor, John McCabe has taught acting at Detroit's Wayne State University, the City College of New York, Interlochen Arts Academy, and New York University, where, as professor of dramatic art, he headed the Educational Theater Department. Now retired from teaching, he divides his year between homes in Brooklyn, New York, and Mackinac Island, Michigan. At the latter he has returned to acting at Grand Hotel, where he lecture-performs a play by Shakespeare each summer.